GREECE,
THE DECADE
OF WAR

GREECE,
THE DECADE OF WAR
OF WAR
OCCUPATION, RESISTANCE AND CIVIL WAR

DAVID BREWER

BLOOMSBURY ACADEMIC
LONDON · NEW YORK · OXFORD · NEW DELHI · SYDNEY

BLOOMSBURY ACADEMIC
Bloomsbury Publishing Plc
50 Bedford Square, London, WC1B 3DP, UK
1385 Broadway, New York, NY 10018, USA
29 Earlsfort Terrace, Dublin 2, Ireland

BLOOMSBURY, BLOOMSBURY ACADEMIC and the Diana
logo are trademarks of Bloomsbury Publishing Plc

First published in Great Britain by I. B. Tauris & Co. Ltd in 2016
This edition published in Great Britain by Bloomsbury Academic in 2021
Reprinted in 2021, 2022

Cover image: Parachuters over Crete, 1941 (© akg-images/Alamy)
Cover design: Graham Robert Ward

A catalogue record for this book is available from the British Library.

A catalog record for this book is available from the Library of Congress.

ISBN: PB: 978-1-3501-6543-4
ePDF: 978-0-8577-2447-2
eBook: 978-0-8577-3703-8

Typeset by Jones Ltd, London

To find out more about our authors and books visit
www.bloomsbury.com and sign up for our newsletters.

For Emma, Sophie and Selena,
John, Alexandra and James

David Brewer is the author of *Greece, the Hidden Centuries* and *The Flame of Freedom: The Greek War of Independence, 1821–1833*. After studying Classics at Oxford University he divided his working life between teaching, journalism and business before devoting himself to the study of the history of Greece.

Praise for *Greece, the Hidden Centuries*:

'Thoroughly researched and very well written. Highly recommended.'
John Freely

'Will remain a classic study for many years to come.'   Alan Palmer

'A fine achievement.'   *Times Literary Supplement*

Praise for *The Flame of Freedom*:

'fascinating ... Brewer has done a splendid and useful job for which he is to be warmly congratulated.'
Adam Zamoyski, *The Sunday Times*

'fresh and compelling ... this account of the war unfolds with the narrative drive of an exciting historical novel.'
Nicholas Gage, *Wall Street Journal*

'rigorously researched, engagingly written and capturing perfectly the dramatic yet tragic course of Greek independence.'
Saul David, *Sunday Telegraph*

'remarkably detailed and highly readable.'
Dominick Coyle, *Financial Times*

'*The Flame of Freedom* makes terrific reading, as thrilling as a good novel.'   Roderick Beaton, *Times Literary Supplement*

Contents

Illustrations

Acknowledgements

I am very grateful to my agent Andrew Gordon of David Higham Associates for his help and advice, and to all at I.B.Tauris, especially to my editor Jo Godfrey for her contribution to the shape of this book. My thanks too to Jessica Cuthbert-Smith for her very detailed copy-editing, and to David Cox for bringing clarity to the maps.

Two libraries have been excellent sources of material: King's College, London, for its wide selection of books on Greece, and the London Library for books on the wider aspects of the period covered. My thanks to the unfailingly helpful staff at both libraries.

Diana Owen has been a meticulous reader of each chapter as it has been written, and her comments have been invaluable. Thank you, Diana.

My previous books have been dedicated, very deservedly, to my wife Elisabeth for all she has contributed to them. However, we both feel that this book should be dedicated to our children. I am happy to say, with gratitude and affection, that my daughters and my stepchildren, their spouses and partners, and their own children, have enriched my life beyond measure.

Abbreviations

AMAG	American Mission for Aid to Greece
AMFOGE	Allied Mission for Observing Greek Elections
AMM	Allied Military Mission (British and American)
BEM	British Economic Mission
£BMA	British Military Administration pounds
BMM	British Military Mission
Cominform	Communist Information Bureau
Comintern	Communist International
CEEC	Committee for European Economic Co-operation
CS	Counter Sabotage unit (Italian)
DSE	Dhimokratikós Stratós Elládhos, Democratic Army of Greece (Communist)
EAM	Ethnikón Apelevtherotikón Métopon, National Liberation Front (Communist political arm)
ECA	European Co-operation Administration
EDES	Ethnikós Dhimokratikós Ellinikós Síndhesmos, National Democratic Greek League (non-Communist resistance)
EKKA	Ethnikí kai Kinonikí Apelevthérosi, National and Social Liberation (smaller non-Communist resistance group)
ELAS	Ethnikós Laikós Apelevtherotikós Stratós, National People's Liberation Army (Communist resistance)
EOK	Ethnikí Orgánosi Kritón, National Organisation of Cretans
EP	Ethnikí Politophilakí, National Civil Guard
EPE	Enoméni Parátaxis Ethnikophrónon, United Patriotic Rally (Greek political party)
ERP	European Recovery Programme
ESPO	Ethnikí Sosialistikí Patriotikí Orgánosi, Ethnic Socialist Patriotic Organisation (German agency)
FYROM	Former Yugoslav Republic of Macedonia
IMRO	International Macedonian Revolutionary Organisation
ISLD	Inter Services Liaison Department

JRC	Joint Relief Commission
JUSMAPG	Joint United States Military Advisory and Planning Group
KKE	Kommounistikón Kómma Elládhos, Communist Party of Greece
KOSSA	Communist Organisation of the Army and Security Corps
LKE	Laikó Kómma Elládhos, Populist Party (Greek political party)
MCS	Mechanical Cultivation Services
OPLA	Omádhes Prostasías Laikoú Agónos, Units for the Protection of the People's Struggle (Communist)
PEEA	Politikí Epitropí Ethnikís Apelevtheróseos, Political Committee of National Liberation (proposed Communist government)
RAF	Royal Air Force (UK)
SKE	Sosialistikón Kómma Ellíadhos, Socialist Party of Greece (precursor of KKE)
SOE	Special Operations Executive
UNESCO	United Nations Educational Scientific and Cultural Organisation
UNRRA	United Nations Relief and Rehabilitation Administration
UNSCOB	United Nations Special Committee on the Balkans
USAGG	United States Army Group Greece

Notes on Pronunciation and Names

Pronunciation

Greek names can be an irritant or even a barrier to a reader who is not sure how to pronounce them. Stress often falls in unexpected places, so has been marked, but pronunciation of Greek is relatively straightforward because, unlike in English, each letter or combination of letters is always pronounced in the same way. In the transliteration of Greek used here, the vowel sounds are:

a	as in b*a*sket
e	as in b*e*d
i	as in the first i in bl*i*ni
o	as in b*o*x – even at the end of a word
ou	as in b*oo*t

The only unusual consonant sounds are:

ch	as in lo*ch*
dh	a soft th as in *th*en – but
th	a hard th as in *th*in

Names

Anglicised versions have been used for the better-known place names – Athens, Corinth – and for personal names of kings – Constantine, George. Other personal names are generally the Greek version except – a bit of a hybrid – Georgios rather than Yeóryios or George.

All translations are by the author unless otherwise indicated.

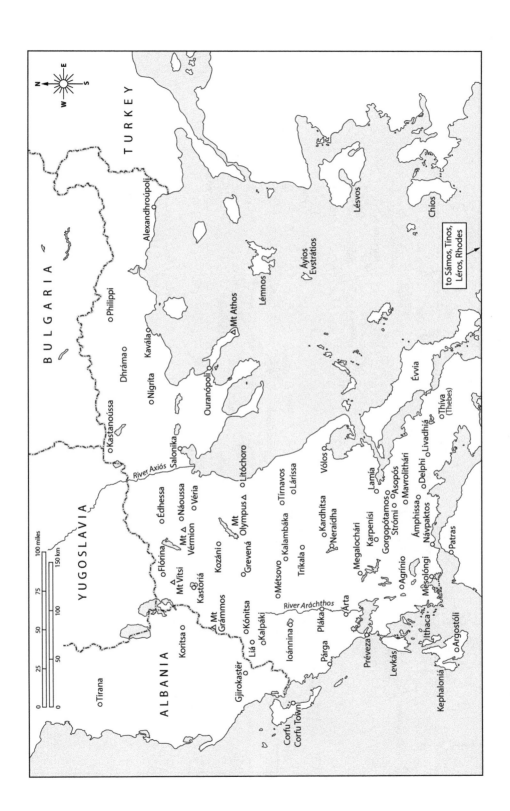

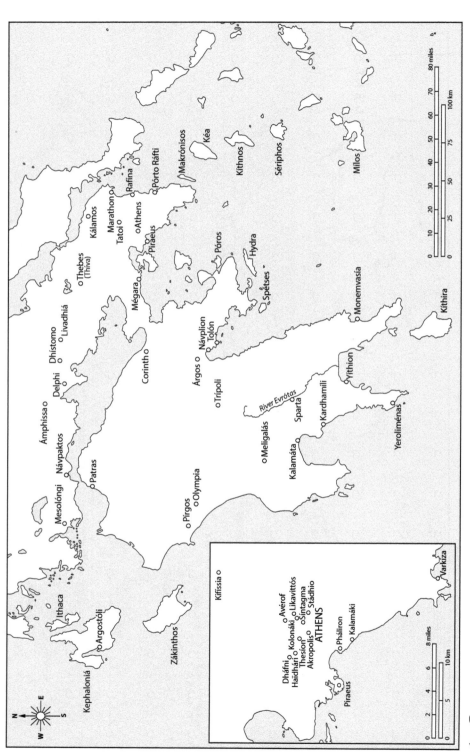

1 Greece

Decisions that influence the course of history arise out of the individual experience of thousands or millions of individuals.

Sebastian Haffner, *Defying Hitler*

Prologue

In October 1922 Mussolini led a Fascist march on Rome. The Italian government collapsed, and a month later the King granted Mussolini dictatorial powers. A decade later, in January 1933, Hitler, leader of the National Socialist or Nazi Party, was appointed German chancellor and within months was given dictatorial powers by the German parliament. Both these dictators were committed to a brutal policy of expansion, Hitler for *lebensraum* (living space) to the east, Mussolini to re-establish the old Roman Empire. Together, but in an unequal partnership, they led Europe into war.

From 1935 Hitler began developing the forces needed for expansion. Conscription was introduced to enlarge the army, an air force was created from scratch, and Britain agreed to an increase in the Germany navy. Each of these moves breached agreements included in the 1919 Treaty of Versailles. A more flagrant breach was Hitler's occupation of the Rhineland in March 1936. British and French protests were muted and ineffectual, though the French Foreign Minister presciently declared, 'If you do not stop Germany by force today, war is inevitable.'[1] In March 1938 Germany annexed Austria, a move presented as the *Anschluss* (union) of two German peoples, and German troops were cheered as they moved in. It was reported to Hitler that Mussolini 'accepted the whole thing in a very friendly manner', and Hitler responded, 'I will never forget him for this.'[2]

In September 1938 Hitler was threatening Czechoslovakia, which Chamberlain dismissively described as 'a quarrel in a faraway country between people of whom we know nothing'.[3] Chamberlain's personal diplomacy produced the Munich Agreement, allowing Germany to occupy immediately the German-speaking Sudeten areas of Czechoslovakia, and German annexation of the rest of western Czechoslovakia followed six months later. The Munich Agreement brought the very opposite of 'peace with honour' or 'peace for our time' which Chamberlain claimed.[4]

Mussolini's expansionist drive to recreate the Roman Empire was symbolised by the four maps, made of marble and displayed on

Rome's Capitol, which showed the extent of that earlier empire. His first ambition was in Africa, where Libya, Eritrea and Somalia were already Italian colonies. The last two of these bordered the much larger Ethiopia, which on 3 October 1935 was invaded by Italy. The move was presented as part of Italy's 'mission to civilise the black continent',[5] but this civilising process included the use of mustard gas. The League of Nations condemned Italy as an aggressor and imposed sanctions but without enforcing them, and crucially excluding oil. This gave Mussolini the opportunity to claim that Italy, represented by himself, had triumphed over the 52 nations of the League.

By 1939 both Germany and Italy were eyeing the Balkans as targets. Hitler needed Romanian oil, and Mussolini declared that the Balkans were part of Italy's living space, essential for providing food and raw materials. It was still not clear what impact the widening war would have on the Balkan countries, including Greece. But a portent of the future was Mussolini's invasion of Greece's northern neighbour Albania in the spring of 1939.

1

The Albanian Gateway to Greece

Between 6 and 7 o'clock on the evening of 7 April 1939, which was Good Friday, King Zog of Albania abandoned his palace in the capital Tirana. Accompanied by a fleet of official cars carrying strongboxes which contained his personal wealth, he headed south towards the Greek border. Zog's young wife Geraldine, a Hungarian princess, who had given birth to their first-born Prince Leka just two days earlier, had left with the baby 24 hours before Zog. At about 5 o'clock that morning Italian troops had begun landing in Albania at the port of Durres, only 15 miles west of Tirana, meeting practically no resistance. This was the prelude, and in some ways a rehearsal, for Italy's attack on Greece 18 months later. It was a rehearsal whose lessons Mussolini failed to heed.

Albania had existed as an independent state for less than 30 years. The Balkan War of 1912 had effectively pushed the Ottoman Empire out of the Balkans. The London Conference at the end of that year was held to settle Balkan rivalries, and on 20 December 1912 agreed to create an Albanian principality. In 1925 Ahmed Zogu, having crushed his political opponents, was elected president for a seven-year term, and three years later was proclaimed King Zog. He declared, on taking the oath of office on 1 September 1928: 'I, Zog the First, King of the Albanians [...] swear before Almighty God to maintain the national unity, independence and territorial integrity.'[1] But by 1928 any semblance of Albanian national independence was already a vanishing dream.

Italy had always wanted control of Albania. Mussolini believed that dominance of this small, feud-ridden and newly created state would give Italy mastery of the entrance to the Adriatic – only 50 miles of the Strait of Otranto separated the two countries. It would also serve as a base for resisting incursion from other states, in particular Yugoslavia, which could then threaten those 50 miles of water, and it would provide a springboard for further Italian expansion in the Balkans – including, of course, into Greece.

Mussolini's first moves were through lira imperialism. In 1925 Zog as president had agreed, with some reluctance, to the creation of a national Albanian bank wholly controlled by Italy. Thus for the first time Albania had a national currency – but one redeemable only in lire. Coupled with this arrangement was a five-year loan, equivalent to £2 million at the time and more than double Albania's national revenue. These funds were to be administered by a company which was supposedly independent but was in fact an arm of the Italian finance ministry. Zog needed the money for the development of the country, and he needed it personally – attached to the agreement was a substantial secret gift to him. He had to accept the deal.

Mussolini followed this with a diplomatic initiative. In November 1926 Zog, under pressure from a revolt of his own people and fearful of incursion from neighbouring states, was forced into another humiliating concession in the Pact of Tirana with Italy. The pact, accompanied by further payments to Zog, declared that any disturbance of the Albanian status quo was contrary to both countries' interests, and that to safeguard those interests they would give each other mutual support. The Italians described this as a 'Pact of Friendship and Security', but it was a great deal more than that: it gave Italy grounds for moving into Albania in the event of any threat – real, imaginary or if necessary faked – to the country's stability. Combined with the bank deal and the loan, it meant that Albania was now virtually an Italian protectorate. In Rome a special ministry for Albanian affairs was set up which in effect ran the Albanian economy, and in Albania an Italian, Count Francesco Jacomoni, was appointed governor-general.

So far Italy's subjugation of Albania had been by economic and diplomatic means, but after ten years of uneasy Italian–Albanian relations it was time for the military option. In the spring of 1938 Count Galeazzo Ciano, Italy's foreign minister and Mussolini's son-in-law, proposed to Mussolini that, in compensation for letting Hitler take Austria, Italy should annex Albania. The ground for invasion was prepared by Jacomoni, the governor-general. Ciano wrote:

The operation is beginning to take shape clearly: assassination of the King – it seems that Koçi [Zog's private secretary] will undertake this for reward of ten millions – riots in the streets, descent from the mountains of the bands we can trust [...] appeal to Italy to intervene politically and if necessary militarily, offer of the throne to the King Emperor [Italy's Vittorio Emanuele] and a little later annexation. Jacomoni guarantees that all this can take place without trouble at a month's notice.[2]

In the event, these elaborate, farcical and criminal ploys were not needed. On 25 March Mussolini's envoy presented Zog with a list of further demands for Italian control of Albania, on the grounds that Germany, soon to be Italy's Axis partner, was advancing into the Balkans, so acceptance by Albania was absolutely necessary. These demands were to be agreed as a whole – there was no room for negotiation. They amounted to a complete surrender of Albanian sovereignty, and Zog could not possibly accept them.

Mussolini had said, 'Either Zog accepts the conditions which we lay before him, or we shall undertake the military seizure of the country.'[3] Zog prevaricated as long as he could, and was still playing for time when the first Italian troops landed early on the morning of Friday 7 April. That afternoon he spoke to the nation on the radio:

Italy has made demands of Albania which would have deprived her of her independence. I and my Government will never accept such conditions. In the face of aggression, I invite the whole Albanian people to unite today, in this moment of danger, to defend the safety of the country and its independence to the last drop of blood.[4]

But there was virtually no resistance to the Italians, and by that evening Zog had fled.

Ciano's chief assistant commented sarcastically 'If only the Albanians had possessed a well-armed fire brigade, they could have driven us back into the Adriatic.'[5] This may have been meant as a jibe at Albanian weakness, but was in truth a devastating comment on Italy's lack of preparation. Though the Albanian invasion had been in prospect for a year, military plans had been left to the last minute. The Italian operational commander Alfredo Guzzoni had only a week's notice of the invasion, and the air force only two days. Conscripts were given only a few hours' warning, were given no training, and were sent to totally inappropriate units – to motorcycle companies when they had never ridden one, to signals when they did not know Morse code. The navy had not been told that Albania's main ports could not take deep-water ships, and there was no air reconnaissance at all. These failings could be ignored when the outcome was an easy victory, but it was a different story when Mussolini turned his attention to Greece.

What happened to the unhappy Zog and his family? On the day after his flight he arrived red-eyed and unshaven at Flórina in north-west Greece, some 10 miles from the Albanian frontier, where Geraldine and the baby were already installed in an unfurnished house. The Greek government allowed him a short stay in the country but, anxious not to provoke Italy, banned him from any political activity. After touring Europe in search of sanctuary – Turkey, Romania, Sweden, Paris, rural France – he and his family and entourage were allowed to settle in England, where he tried unsuccessfully to interest the authorities in his plan to raise and lead a band of guerrillas in the Albanian resistance. But Albanian partisans had no love for Zog, and when their leader Enver Hoxha took Tirana in November 1944 he barred Zog from the country. The royal group settled in Egypt from 1946 to 1953, but when Egypt recognised the Hoxha government Zog became an unwelcome guest. His final years were spent on the French Riviera, where he died in 1961.

Zog can seem a venal and semi-comic figure, from Ruritania rather than reality, but there was more to his credit than that. He had consistently made efforts, though with limited success, to advance this backward country by improving the infrastructure, reforming the law and education, and bettering the lot of women. He lost control of his country because it was wholly unable to withstand Italian aggression – economic, diplomatic and military. Perhaps Zog best deserves to be remembered as the first European ruler to refuse to bow to demands from the Axis powers. An even more emphatic refusal was to come from the Greek Prime Minister Ioánnis Metaxás.

For his invasion of Albania, Mussolini received extravagant praise from his toadying supporters. The Italian ambassador in London wrote that Mussolini had started on a path that would lead Italy through the Balkans to the conquest of the Orient, and that Italy had now established a complete dominion over the eastern Mediterranean.[6] But the response from other countries was more sobering. Within days of the invasion of Albania, Britain and France had promised total support for Greece, as well as Romania and Turkey, if they were attacked. As Britain's Prime Minister Neville Chamberlain said in the House of Commons on 13 April 1939, 'In the event of any action being taken which clearly threatened the independence of Greece [...]. His Majesty's Government would feel themselves bound to lend the Greek government all the support in their power.'[7]

Mussolini brushed this aside. Greece, he claimed, was entirely dependent on the good graces of Italy, and the British could not be so unrealistic as to believe in the sanctity of treaties. Nevertheless, European war was clearly imminent. Mussolini needed to be a partner on the winning side, and equally clearly Germany would win against the effete democracies. Thus on 22 May 1939 Italy and Germany signed a formal alliance for war – the Pact of Steel. This committed each party to fight alongside the other, with all their forces and no time limit, in any war, whether defensive or offensive. The belligerent-sounding Pact of Steel had no immediate effect. Germany did not need Italian help to overrun western Europe, and Italy stayed neutral, not declaring war on Britain and France until 10 June 1940, when France was already on the brink of capitulation. But the pact gave both leaders what for the moment they wanted: Hitler an assurance that Italy would not provide a Mediterranean base for the Allies, and Mussolini a secure place on the winning side. Now Mussolini needed a military triumph of his own, something much more impressive than the walkover in Albania, to establish his position as an equal partner with Hitler in the Axis.

Mussolini believed that Germany was successful because Hitler ran military affairs personally. Mussolini went further. As well as being commander-in-chief and prime minister, he was head of five different ministries – interior, colonies and the three armed service departments – and no minister could take even minor decisions without his express agreement. Mussolini ignored warnings that such concentration would lead to inefficiency. Later events showed that indeed it did.

Mussolini vacillated wildly over whether to attack Greece. In September 1939 he instructed Emanuele Grazzi, Italy's ambassador in Athens, to work for a rapprochement with Greece, 'a country too poor for us to want'. But in August 1940, after Italy had declared war on Britain and France, he thought the Greek attitude was 'very unreliable' and he was considering 'a forceful gesture'. Later that month he moved Italian troops to the Albanian–Greek border, but in September moved them back. On 12 October he said: 'Hitler keeps confronting me with *faits accomplis*. This time I shall pay him back in his own coin; he shall learn from the newspapers that I have occupied Greece.'[8]

Mussolini finally declared his decision three days later, at a meeting on 15 October in his study at the Palazzo Venezia. Present were Ciano (foreign minister), Pietro Badoglio (chief of the general staff), Jacomoni (governor-general of Albania) and three other military commanders – though no representatives of either the navy or air force, whose co-operation would be essential. Mussolini told them that he had decided on a two-phase operation against Greece; in the first phase Italy would take north-west Greece (Epirus as far south as Préveza), the Ionian Islands and Salonika, and in the second would occupy the whole of Greece. The operation would start on 26 October and 'must not be postponed even by an hour' (it was in fact postponed by two days). Some hesitant objections were brushed aside. In support of the plan Mussolini was told that the Greeks were indifferent to the prospect of an Italian invasion, that British intervention could be excluded, that Albanian bands would fight with the Italians and that the operation 'has been prepared down to the most minute details and is as perfect as is humanly possible'.[9] Every one of these statements was completely wrong.

At this meeting Mussolini demanded an 'incident', if necessary an arranged one, to justify Italy's invasion. Two incidents, just inside the Albanian frontier and so attributable to Greeks, took place two days before the invasion: a bomb explosion in Governor-General Jacomoni's office, and a sham attack by covert Italian troops on an Italian border post near Koritsa.[10] No matter, said Mussolini, if nobody believed them genuine, and nobody did.

The Italian ultimatum to Greece was delivered at three in the morning on Monday 28 October 1940. The bearer was Grazzi, the Italian ambassador in Athens. Grazzi had been taken by surprise: he had not been told of the planned invasion and Mussolini's previous statements to him had been pacific towards Greece. His own reports that the Greeks would resist had been ignored, and he knew the ultimatum gave Greece no choice but to refuse it. He was painfully embarrassed by his mission.

Grazzi respected and liked the recipient of the ultimatum, the Greek Prime Minister Metaxás. In August 1936, after a period of political turmoil, Metaxás had been appointed prime minister by King

George II and had immediately dissolved parliament, suspended civil liberties articles of the Constitution and imprisoned political opponents. He was characterised as a dictator, was proud to say that his regime was totalitarian, and he attracted much criticism as a result. There was little of the dictator in his personal appearance and style: he was short, plump and bespectacled, and he lived simply in a modest villa 5 miles or so from the centre of Athens. He was 69, and already weakened by the illness that would kill him in a few months. He was woken from sleep by Grazzi's arrival and met him wearing dressing-gown and slippers.

The ultimatum, in French, first listed a string of flimsy allegations of Greek provocation of Italy and then demanded that the Italians be permitted 'to occupy some strategic points on Greek territory'.[11] The ultimatum expired in three hours' time, at 6 a.m. Zog had been given time to attempt negotiation, the Greeks were not, but as with Zog it was an ultimatum that was designed so that it could not possibly be accepted.

Metaxás asked which strategic points Italy wished to occupy and Grazzi, even further embarrassed, confessed that he did not know. Metaxás' widow Léla later recorded what she heard of the encounter from outside the room, and in her account:

> Their conversation began calmly, but soon I heard an animated exchange, and an angry tone in my husband's voice followed by a loud bang of the palm of his hand on the top of the desk. It was the exact moment of the 'ochi' (NO), and there followed Grazzi's departure.[12]

The conversation between Metaxás and Grazzi was in French, like the ultimatum, and not in Greek, so probably Metaxás never uttered the famous 'Ochi' ('No') but said, 'Alors, c'est la guerre.' Georgios Vláchos, in the following week's issue of his paper *Kathimeriní*, wrote an editorial which ended:

> Today there is no Greek who does not add his voice to the thunderous OCHI. OCHI, we will not hand over Greece to Italy. OCHI, Italian ruffians will not set foot on our land. OCHI, the barbarians will not desecrate our Parthenons.[13]

At a stroke Metaxás had been transformed from reviled dictator to national hero.

2

Mussolini's War on Greece

M ussolini's preparations for war on Greece were as chaotic as those for Albania. At a conference in February 1940 he was warned of the practical difficulties of going to war. Mussolini glibly brushed these aside, and not a single major decision was taken in the eight months before the invasion to increase the army's strength. Nevertheless the two men who would be directly responsible for the attack on Greece were arrogantly confident of success; these were Jacomoni, governor-general of Albania, and Count Visconti Prasca, commander of Italian forces there. Self-delusion had gripped all the Italian leaders, and Jacomoni and Visconti Prasca 'formed a perfect couple for the disastrous campaign; they formed a perfect counterpart to that other couple in Rome, Mussolini and Ciano'.[1]

This quartet of fantasists believed that three factors would favour them in the campaign against Greece. First, it was thought that the Albanian minority in Tsamouria – north-west Greece as far south as Préveza – would fight with the Italians in the cause of uniting Tsamouria with Albania. There was no evidence that this would happen, and it did not. Second, there was a plan to bribe certain Greek military leaders to come over to the Italian side. Money may have been dispensed for this purpose, but there is not a shred of evidence of Greek treachery. Third, there was reliance on Albanian bands supporting the Italian army. However, as soon as fighting began they deserted en masse.

Two weeks before the invasion began, Mussolini ordered an army demobilisation, releasing 600,000 reservists, a process not halted until 10 November, and after the first setbacks those released had to be recalled. The only possible explanation for this bizarre decision is that Mussolini, propaganda oriented as always, wanted to create a feeling of normality at home. When the invasion began, troops did

2   Italian and German invasions

not have enough ammunition or transport, the port at Durres could not handle the flow of supplies from Italy, and units were detached from their divisions and put under unfamiliar commanders. To make matters worse, on 26 October the weather changed to torrential rain with thick clouds, and the temperature dropped.

The Greeks were much better prepared. They had been well aware of a possible Italian invasion ever since Italy massed troops on the Albanian–Greek frontier in August 1939, over a year earlier, and Italy had declared war on the Allies in June 1940. A further incident increased Greek forebodings. On 15 August 1940 the aged Greek cruiser *Élle* was in the harbour of Tínos attending the island's annual celebrations of the Feast of the Assumption of the Virgin. Three torpedoes were fired from a submarine, one sank the *Élle*, killing one person and wounding 29, and the other two torpedoes hit the harbour mole. It was widely believed that an Italian submarine was responsible. The Greek government played down the incident to avoid provoking Italy, and Italy denied the allegations, but later documents proved that they were completely true.[2]

Greek troops were called up, but not by a general mobilisation order which Italy could have regarded as provocative. Instead each reservist was given a code derived from his unit and date of original call-up: T47 for certain anti-aircraft units, V18 for infantrymen and so on. Press, radio or sometimes notices on walls would announce the call-up of a particular code so no outsider could tell what these cryptic announcements meant and mobilisation remained secret.

The Greeks had a number of advantages over the Italians. Their lines of supply and communication were shorter and easier – they had no Strait of Otranto to cross – and there was no bottleneck as at Durres. The question of the number of troops on the two sides has been hotly debated; each side has tended to magnify the strength of the other, the Italians to excuse defeat and the Greeks to enhance victory. The best estimate seems to be that total numbers were roughly equal at about 100,000 men, though the balance varied in different sectors. In theory, the Italians had two advantages over the Greeks: they had air superiority and they had tanks. But the arrival of bad weather soon limited the use of their air force on the battlefields. Italian bombers instead attacked Greek towns, including Salonika, Patras, the outskirts of Athens and, to the particular disgust of the Greeks, Corfu town on Christmas Day 1940. Tanks could achieve nothing on the few unpaved roads, which soon became a sea of mud.

In command of the Greek forces was Aléxandhros Papágos. After service in the Balkan Wars and in the disastrous 1922 Asia Minor campaign, in 1936 he was appointed inspector general of the army by Metaxás and later chief of the general staff. He was responsible for the strengthening of the Greek military in the Metaxás years and its preparation for war, including the building of a road between Métsovo and Ioánnina which would be vital for supplying Greek forces once the Italian invasion began. A month before the Italian invasion, Papágos had drawn up the Greek forces in two arcs: the first, 5 to 10 miles from the Albanian border, ran from opposite Corfu up to Flórina, and the second, 40 to 50 miles from the border, from Préveza along the river Aliákmonas almost to Salonika. The crucial point was in Papágos' orders to the army: 'The destruction or excessive weakening of these forces must be avoided even at the cost of territorial losses. Therefore the operations of the forces in Epirus must follow the principles of elastic defence.'[3]

Elastic defence meant in practice that the Greek first line would offer little resistance more than skirmishing, allow Italian forces through the gap, and then close the gap and trap them. In the first days of the fighting this is what happened on the Greek left, and Italian forces crossed the river Kálamas, with great difficulty as the river was now in violent spate. Italian forces had been concentrated on the Greek left, so Papágos pushed forward across the Albanian border on his right, towards Koritsa. Thus within a week the axis of the battle lines had tilted to south-west and north-east: the Italians were on the river Kálamas in Greek territory, while the Greeks were on the river Devoli in Albania. But it was the Greeks who were in a better position to advance.

It was clear to Prasca that the offensive which he commanded had failed, and by 2 November he was reduced to issuing frantic orders to his troops 'to attack, always to attack, without worrying about their flanks. Every column must attack, even with only a single man.'[4] His failure was also obvious to Mussolini. On 9 November he was demoted to a lesser command, two days later he was also relieved of that, and at the end of the month he was released from active service and put on permanent leave. His successor as commander-in-chief of the Italian forces was General Ubaldo Soddu.

Meanwhile, Greek forces were advancing on Koritsa, 10 miles inside Albania. Fierce attacks began on 14 November, and the following day the Italian commanders reported deep and dangerous breaches opened by the Greeks. On 22 November the Italians abandoned Koritsa, to jubilation throughout Greece. The next day Georgios Vláchos wrote in *Kathimeriní*: 'Koritsa has fallen. The Italians have fled. Shall we ever live through another day like yesterday?'[5] The jubilation was echoed by wildly cheering crowds in Athens, and by Greeks and their supporters as far away as New York, Alexandria and Sydney, as well as in Britain's House of Lords.

Bad winter weather in Albania and north-west Greece could have been expected, though this did not concern the Italian planners, who thought they would be victorious in a fortnight. But it could not have been expected that this Albanian winter would be the worst for 50 years, and the conditions in which both sides fought were appalling. A Greek soldier recorded his experiences:

> Eventually we reached a place where we could set up our camp. It was all thick mud. We cut branches from the trees to lay on the mud, so that we could sleep relatively dry. But it wasn't dry, just mud.

And of another occasion he wrote:

> We pitched our camp on a hill. Snow! We had set up our tent over a trench which had been lined with rocks. We were exhausted. During the night, the snow fell heavily on our tent and collapsed on us. If we hadn't woken up we would have all died. We then dug the snow out and went under the tent.[6]

It was the same for the Italians: 'The columns moved forward in the dark under the driving rain. Boots sank in the mud, puttees were soon wrapped in a thick yellow crust, horses and mules kicked up showers of slush at every step.'[7] When puttees were soaked they weighed pounds, but it was even worse when they froze and gripped the legs as in a vice. The two sides became indistinguishable: 'Men with long beards and torn and tattered brown uniforms swarming with lice delivered attacks on men in equally tattered gray-green uniforms and broken boots who furiously defended themselves.'[8]

Mules were the main carriers of supplies for both sides, and many of them died. In mid-December an Italian officer recorded that 'more than ninety mules are lying along the road, either singly or in groups of two or three at various intervals; they collapsed from exhaustion and were abandoned on the spot with all their load.'[9] Some Italian soldiers adopted a grisly but effective means of warming their heads, smashing the heads of mules dying from exhaustion and putting the still warm animal brains inside their helmets. There were fewer horses, and one Greek officer could never forget the look in his horse's eyes as he had to leave it dying:

> My grey got stuck in a ditch, covered with so much snow that it was invisible. I jumped off the saddle. The horse tried to get up, couldn't and fell down further. Starving, drenched to its bones, tortured by the endless running on the rocky ground, it was doomed to stay there. I stroked the back of its neck a little and kissed it. Then I set off. After a few paces, I turned to look at it one last time. It had been my companion in war; we had faced death so many times together. And I saw it looking at me as I left.[10]

The Greek supply lines worked better than the Italian, but the Greeks too had problems. In the first weeks of the war food, blankets and clothes were carried up to the troops by women, children and old men. Women also transported back-breaking loads of cannons and ammunition, only getting up the rocky slopes with the help of a rope round their waists, hauled by a man standing above. The Italians' situation was worse, and even after more than a month of war the supply report on 4 December read: 'Reserve rations, nil. Equipment, minimal. Woollen clothing, zero. Infantry ammunition, none. Artillery ammunition, insignificant. Arms and artillery, all supplies exhausted. Engineering equipment, practically nil. Medical equipment, inadequate.'[11]

The lack of medical supplies had terrible results. Treatment was needed not only for wounds, often needing amputation, but for the many cases of frostbite, followed by gangrene when there was no disinfectant. Untreated gangrene was horrible: 'Legs swelled above the ankle, all feeling disappeared from the foot, the flesh changed colour, turned purple and then blackish.'[12] The wounded were treated under lorry tarpaulins, in the ruins of cottages or in snow-covered tents near the fighting. When the battlefront moved, these field hospitals had to move too, often across swollen rivers whose bridges had been destroyed, the medical equipment and beds transported by ropes and pulleys, the doctors and nurses crossing on horseback (if they were lucky) or by wading across.

Amid the horrors of war there are instances of sympathy for the enemy. On Christmas Day 1940, 50 taxi drivers from Salonika made the long journey to the Albanian front, bringing crates of brandy and Christmas presents. On the instruction of a Greek officer, one taxi driver who spoke Italian took some of the brandy to the Italians opposite, his car carrying a large white handkerchief of truce. After delivering his load he set off back with a final cheerful 'Buono Capo d'Anno', to applause from both sides. There was compassion at more sombre moments too. One Greek soldier recorded in his diary:

> When day came we buried the two Italians in the snow. We cried over our own dead. We felt sorry for the two Italians as well, victims of people with paranoia and foolish ambitions. They too had mothers waiting for them.[13]

After their celebrated capture of Koritsa on 22 November 1940, the Greek forces pushed on further, capturing Pogradeç at the end of November, Porto Edda, Gjirokastër and Himara in December and, on 10 January 1941, Klisura, their last significant gain. It was at this high point in Greece's fortunes that Metaxás died on 29 January, but not in a triumphant mood, as his diary shows. He clearly foresaw an attack by Germany which Greece would be powerless to stop. His successor as prime minister, Aléxandhros Korizís, had to face this attack with no heroic option available, and paid dearly as a result.

After Koritsa had fallen to the Greeks, Soddu, the new Italian commander in Albania, pulled the Italian forces back to a defensive line beyond Koritsa and some 30 miles inside Albania, too far from most of Greece's later gains to contest them. The front now became static, in mountainous country blanketed by snow and in freezing conditions. The Italians were exhausted and demoralised, while the Greeks benefited from Albanian hatred of Italy and were 'in a friendly environment, in which every house constitutes a refuge, every mountaineer a guide, and in which every help is given him'.[14] But in this frozen landscape it was harder for Greeks to advance than for Italians to defend, and Greek supply lines were becoming dangerously stretched. For the moment there was an uneasy equilibrium.

Soddu's failure was now as apparent as that of his predecessor Prasca. On 4 December he was ordered to share command in Albania with Marshal Ugo Cavallero, who had replaced Badoglio as chief of the general staff. On 30 December Soddu was relieved of his command for so-called health reasons. Cavallero was now sole commander in Albania, as well as his other role. Cavallero was something of a buccaneer, and his reliability and integrity had often been questioned. But he had qualities that matched the hour: a natural optimism, which helped Italian morale, and a readiness to accept realities. Also in two breaks in his military career he had worked in industry and knew how supply lines worked. Italian supply systems were never perfect, but under Cavallero were greatly improved from their disastrous position in early December.

Mussolini's reaction to the debacle in Albania was bellicose. At the beginning of January 1941 he wrote to Cavallero: 'After sixty days of being the anvil, we will become the hammer', and a fortnight later: 'There is only one way out. Attack!'[15] Cavallero obeyed and devised an assault through the mountainous region north of Klisura with the aim of recapturing Klisura itself. Mussolini arrived in Albania on 2 March to tour the Italian positions and oversee the expected Italian advance. He was enthusiastically cheered whenever he passed a camp, demonstrations which may or may not have been spontaneous. Early on the morning of 9 March Mussolini took his position to watch the Italian offensive from an observation post on the 2,500-foot Mount Kommarit, which looked south down the river valley between the mountains towards Klisura.

The Italian attack began with a massive artillery barrage, firing 100,000 rounds in a couple of hours. The Italian air force, now strengthened, was in action during the fine weather which lasted only that morning. However, the Greeks knew all about the Italian plan from documents found on a captured Italian officer. A bitter and bloody struggle ensued for possession of these desolate heights, the main weapons being the bayonet and the hand grenade as in World War I. Most Italian gains were lost again by immediate Greek counter-attacks. By the end of the first day Mussolini, more realistic than usual, said: 'If an offensive has not succeeded after two or three hours, it does not succeed at all.'[16]

The Italian offensive lasted a week, with fierce fighting – the Italians suffered 12,000 casualties – but no Italian gains. Mussolini, as so often, fell back on rhetoric. On 12 March he proclaimed that military victory was absolutely essential and on 13 March he told Cavallero, 'Things have gone very well today. I think the Greeks wavered, as I said they would.'[17] On 15 March Cavallero told Mussolini frankly that 'If success is not in sight, we must not continue to feed the struggle, but break it off.'[18] On 16 March the offensive was abandoned, and five days later Mussolini returned to Italy, having witnessed the failure of a prestige attack designed to rescue what had always been a prestige campaign.

While Greek and Italian soldiers fought and died in the mountains of Albania, international alignments were shifting.

The first and most vital concern of the Greek government, under both Metaxás and his successor Korizís, was to avoid a German invasion and occupation of Greece, a catastrophe which Metaxás had long feared. One way of achieving this would be by a Greek–Italian armistice guaranteed by Germany, with Greece keeping all territory gained and a neutral buffer zone held by the German army. Tentative proposals on these lines – at the level of ambassadors and military attachés, not of government – were first put forward by Germany through several different channels in mid-December 1940. This would have given Germany control of Greece without the need for an invasion. It is not clear if these discussions ever reached government level, but in any case nothing came of the idea either now or later.

A second way of preventing a German invasion was for the Greek government to accept the offer of British military aid. Neville Chamberlain as prime minister had made this offer in April 1939 after Italy invaded Albania, and Churchill repeated it when Italy attacked Greece, writing to Metaxás: 'We will give you all the help in our power. We will fight a common foe and share a common victory.'[19] With the agreement of the Greek government Britain immediately took over the defence of Crete, but there were as yet no British forces in mainland Greece.

The question for the British government was what troops could be spared. Churchill initially believed that the front in North Africa was static and troops could be diverted from there: 'No one will thank us for sitting tight in Egypt with ever-growing forces while the Greek situation and all that hangs on it is cast away. Loss of Athens far greater injury than Kenya and Khartoum.'[20] But on 8 November Anthony Eden, then British war minister, returned from a tour of the Middle East and told Churchill in person – the information was too secret to be telegraphed, even in code – that the static phase was over and within a month Operation Compass would launch a massive Allied attack westward across the desert. Any help to Greece would now be severely limited.

The Greek government too faced a dilemma: how much British aid should it accept? Too much could provoke a German attack, too little would not deter, let alone resist, such an attack. On 22 February Eden (now foreign secretary), General Wavell (Allied commander-in-chief Middle East) and Dill (chief of the imperial general staff) were in Athens to discuss British military aid with Prime Minister Korizís and Papágos. On 4 March two agreements were reached, which were endorsed by the British War Cabinet three days later. First, Wavell would send to Greece as soon as possible 100,000 men with artillery support, and this process was begun when British troops sailed from Alexandria ten days later, though the total number was never reached.

The second agreement was on the line to be held by the combined Greek and British forces. Papágos was currently holding the Metaxas Line, which stretched east for some 100 miles from the junction of the Greek, Yugoslav and Bulgarian frontiers along the border with Bulgaria. It was now agreed to concentrate the combined forces further back on the so-called Aliakmon Line, running in a loop west and north from the mouth of the river Aliákmonas through Véria and Édhessa to the Yugoslav frontier 15 miles north-west of Édhessa. This line was only 60 miles long, not 100, offered good defensive positions and made military sense against an attack through Bulgaria, though not one through Yugoslavia west of the line. However, it meant Papágos withdrawing some Greek forces from ground heroically gained in Albania, and not even trying to defend a large swathe of Greek territory east of Salonika or, crucially, Salonika itself. Papágos, extremely reluctant to make such sacrifices, procrastinated, and Greek forces were still holding the Metaxas Line when the invasion began.

Until March 1941 Hitler had achieved virtually all he wanted in the Balkans by diplomacy, not armed force. In September 1940 Romania had asked for a German military mission, and German troops and technical experts had moved in, giving Germany control of the vital Ploeşti oilfields. On 1 March 1941 Bulgaria signed the Tripartite Pact with Germany, Italy and Japan.

Yugoslavia had remained neutral and was under the government of the Anglophile Prince Paul, acting as regent for the young pro-British King Peter whose father Alexander had been assassinated in 1934. Germany had put relentless pressure on Yugoslavia to join the Tripartite Pact but Prince Paul and his government had tried to placate Germany while resisting every German demand. Churchill described Prince Paul's position as 'that of an unfortunate man in a cage with a tiger, hoping not to provoke him while steadily dinner-time approaches'.[21] However, by spring 1941, with German troops in

Romania, and Bulgaria and Italy perennially hostile to it, Yugoslavia eventually signed the pact on 25 March. There was an immediate reaction. On the night of 26–7 March an army coup took over the government in a clear rejection of the pact and installed King Peter, still only 18, as monarch. Crowds in Belgrade cheered the Allied cause and decked the streets with British and French flags. The Yugoslav volte-face was hugely popular in the country, but was to prove ultimately quixotic.

The Yugoslav coup tipped the scales. Both Yugoslavia and Greece could now offer the Allies bases to threaten Germany's southern flank as well as airfields for bombing the oilfields of Ploeşti. Contingency plans for a German invasion of Greece had been signed by Hitler the previous December. Hitler now ordered an immediate revision of the plans to include Yugoslavia, which the super-efficient German high command achieved in a few days.

Final attempts were now made to avert the disaster. The Greek government tried, through the German ambassador in Athens, to revive the idea of Germany acting as mediator in the Italian–Greek war. The German government, unsurprisingly, made no response. Georgios Vláchos published a passionate appeal to Hitler in an open letter which became famous. Vláchos wrote that Greece wished only to live in peace and had done nothing to provoke the Italian attack, even keeping quiet about the sinking of the *Élle*. Greece, with no other allies, had no option but to accept British aid, spontaneously offered in spite of Britain's own perilous position, and it was the Italians not the Greeks who had brought British forces to Greece. Vláchos appealed to the honourable traditions of the German army. But, he warned Hitler, if invasion came, the Greek army of free men would fight to the death in Epirus or Thrace or wherever the battlefield lay. And, he concluded magnificently, 'We taught the world how to live; we must now teach it how to die.'[22] But disaster could not be averted. In spite of the defiant words of Vláchos, the Greeks were overwhelmed by the German invasion which was launched at dawn on 6 April 1941.

3

The German Invasion

In the same hour as German forces launched their invasion of Greece, they attacked Yugoslavia. Would Yugoslav resistance help the Greek and Allied forces in the defence of Greece?

Unhappily, Yugoslav resistance quickly crumbled. On paper the Yugoslav army had close to a million men but it was far from a modern army, its transport depending on horses, oxen and mules. Even this antiquated force had not been mobilised. The coup of 27 March had been by anti-German Serb officers, and they believed that pro-German Croats and Slovenes would resist a call-up until a German invasion actually happened. By then, of course, it was too late. Furthermore, the Yugoslavs faced enemies across four of its frontiers: two to the north, from Germany through Austria and from the Axis adherent Hungary; to the west from Italy through Albania; and to the east from Bulgaria and Romania. The Yugoslav forces were spread along 1,000 miles of frontier, too thinly to protect any of them, and Papágos thought they should have been concentrated in the centre. As Frederick the Great said, 'He who defends everything defends nothing.'

On 6 April, the day of the invasion, the Germans launched a devastating bombing raid on the capital Belgrade, killing at least 3,000 civilians and destroying most of the 450 planes of the Yugoslav air force. Churchill, who had likened the Regent Prince Paul to a man in a cage with a tiger, grimly recorded that the animals of Belgrade's zoo were now literally out of their cages:

Out of the nightmare of smoke and fire came the maddened animals released from their shattered cages in the zoological gardens. A stricken stork hobbled past the main hotel, which was a mass of flames. A bear, dazed and uncomprehending, shuffled through the inferno with slow and awkward gait down towards the Danube.[1]

In quick succession the main Yugoslav towns were captured by the invading forces: Skopje in one day on 7 April, Niš on 9 April, Zagreb and Ljubljana on 10 April and on 13 April Belgrade itself. Yugoslavia surrendered unconditionally on 17 April, and the short reign of the young King Peter ended with his evacuation on a British sea plane. That was the outcome of the anti-German coup of 27 March, which has been described as 'one of the most unrealistic, if romantic, acts of defiance in modern European history'.[2]

The crushing of Yugoslavia gave the German forces two great advantages. One, logistic, was that they now had control of the Yugoslav railway system which, unlike Bulgaria's, connected with those of Austria, Hungary, Romania and Greece, thus simplifying German troop movements. The other advantage was strategic: they could now advance through the major road and rail junction at Bitola only 10 miles north of the Greek border, a route known as the Monastir Gap from the old Turkish name for Bitola. This led them into north-west Greece and down Greece's west coast, giving them the opportunity to get behind the defenders and encircle them.

The Allied ground troops in Greece were under the command of Lieutenant-General Sir Henry Wilson, known as Jumbo Wilson from his portly figure, and at least nominally subordinate to Papágos. These forces consisted of three elements: British, New Zealand and Australian. The British contingent was about 15,400 strong, commanded by Brigadier Charrington. It was supported by some 100 light tanks brought over from North Africa which were already in poor condition and short of spares. The British were first deployed in the Édhessa region on the Aliakmon Line.

The Australian troops eventually numbered around 17,000 men, though about a third of them were still at sea on their way from Africa when the invasion began. They were commanded by Major-General Mackay and were originally positioned at Véria, about 20 miles south of the British.

The New Zealand forces, also about 17,000 strong, were based further east, mainly south of the Aliákmonas river and near the Aegean coast. One New Zealand unit was in reserve further back, to hold the Olympus Pass to the west of the mountain and the coastal road on its east side. The New Zealanders were commanded by Major-General Bernard Freyberg. The combined Australian and New Zealand contingents were under Lieutenant-General Thomas Blamey.

There were thus four elements of the forces available to resist the German invasion: the Greeks on the Metaxas Line and in Albania, the British and Australians on the Aliakmon Line and the New Zealanders further east and south. The campaign story is of resistance at four separate lines progressively further south – the Metaxas Line, the Aliakmon Line, the line fixed on 8 April, and finally the Thermopylae Line – and of eventual withdrawal from each of them.

The Greek people gave the Allied troops an ecstatic welcome. One officer wrote: 'I felt more like a bridegroom than a soldier with my truck decorated with sprigs of peach blossom and my buttonhole with violets.' Some officers tried to communicate with the villagers in Ancient Greek, with predictable lack of success.[3]

The Allied troops had to be supplied by sea, which could not have been done without two earlier successes of the British navy and Fleet Air Arm against the Italian navy. On the moonlit night of 10/11 November 1940 the British attacked the Italian fleet in its port at Taranto. In an hour, half the Italian battle fleet had been destroyed or disabled with the loss of two British planes; as Churchill saw it, 'By this single stroke the balance of naval power in the Mediterranean was decisively altered.'[4]

The second British naval success was three months later off Cape Matapan at the southern tip of the Peloponnese. There a British fleet attacked an Italian fleet on the morning of 28 March 1941 and disabled the Italian battleship *Vittorio Veneto* and an Italian cruiser. Continuing the battle in a risky night attack, British destroyers accounted for the rest of the Italian fleet, bringing the Italian death toll to 2,400. The British forces lost two planes, but not a single ship was damaged. Though Italian vessels were still present in the Mediterranean, the victories at Taranto and Matapan made supplying Allied forces in Greece possible.

The Greek forces, nominally of 18 divisions, were dispersed. In support of the New Zealanders were two Greek divisions, and a third division was placed north of Salonika, in the plain of the river Axiós (called Vardar in Yugoslavia) to defend against parachutists. Three Greek divisions held the Metaxas Line on the frontier with Bulgaria. The remaining 12 Greek divisions were in Albania, holding on to the hard-won gains from the Italians. Many of these Greek divisions were under-strength, under-supplied and under-trained. A glaring example was the Greek 19th Motorised Division, said to consist of 'just over 2000 quite untrained and recently enlisted garage hands, with no possible prospect of fighting usefully as a mobile force, having only a few Bren carriers, motor cycles and small cars.'[5]

The Greek and Allied forces on Greek territory, some nine divisions in all, faced dauntingly superior numbers. Estimates vary, but broadly speaking they were threatened from Yugoslavia by a German army under Maximilian von Weichs of ten divisions and from Bulgaria by Wilhelm von List's 11 divisions. So they were outnumbered by roughly 21 divisions to 9, more than two to one. They were also outnumbered in Albania, where 12 Greek divisions faced 21 Italian on a temporarily static front.

There was even greater disparity in the air. The Royal Air Force, under Air Commodore D'Albiac, had some 80 aircraft against 800 German and about 300 Italian. One of the two RAF Wings supported the Greeks in Albania from a forward airfield at Ioánnina, or from Athens, which was just within range of the front. The other Wing operated from bases hastily improvised near Lárissa after Allied troops were committed, on ground still soggy from the winter rains. To add to their disadvantage, the Allied forces were weak in anti-aircraft artillery and the Greeks had virtually none.

The first encounter of Greek and German forces was on 6 April, the day of the invasion, on the Metaxas Line. This line consisted of a few forts and tank barriers, but mainly of pillboxes and trenches, so was no Maginot Line, and would have needed far more than the three under-strength Greek divisions to hold it. There was heavy artillery shelling from both sides. Greek resistance was fierce, but two of the forts were lost in the first day, and on 9 April the Greek forces surrendered. The Germans paid tribute to Greek courage, and Field Marshal Alexander spoke of their outstanding gallantry. The way south was now open to the German forces, and they took Salonika on 9 April, the day of the Greek surrender of the Metaxas Line. The line of defence was now the Aliakmon Line, where the British and Australian forces were concentrated.

After the collapse of Yugoslav resistance the Greeks had little option but to withdraw from Albania; otherwise their line of retreat would have been cut by German forces pushing south. On 9 April Koritsa, captured to such jubilation six months earlier, was abandoned. The next day Greek troops left Pogradeç, their most northerly capture, leaving some 60 men behind as a doomed rear guard. Two of these men decided to leave for the south, and one recorded his adventures on the way: his companion suffering from frostbitten feet and having to be left behind in a friendly village; in another village being given civilian clothes which deceived the Germans he met; a lift from a German officer who needed an interpreter; finally Athens, and a bath which at last got rid of his lice.[6]

On 12 April Papágos ordered that the retreat from Albania should be general. The Greek soldiers, including senior officers, were furious at having to give up their heroically won gains, and the order provoked near mutiny. The command was ultimately and reluctantly obeyed, with the Greeks still skirmishing with the Italians who were, in effect, merely keeping up with a retreating enemy which had been beaten not by them but by the Germans.

As the German forces pushed forward on the ground, they dominated the air. On the day of the invasion the Luftwaffe launched a devastating bombing raid on Piraeus, the main port of the Allied convoys, setting fire to docked ships and to the surrounding buildings. In the middle of the following night the British ship *Clan Fraser*, with 200 tons of explosives on board, blew up, and an Australian sailor described the results:

> The sight was terrible. Nearly every ship in the harbour was alight and sinking. Two hundred yards away from us was a large Greek ship loaded with oil blazing furiously and every few minutes oil drums would explode in her. The water was one mass of flame where burning oil had spread over the surface and upon this were all sorts of small fishing boats, wrecks and debris on fire and drifting about starting more fires. I could count at least fourteen capital ships afire. Beside us were two Greek hospital ships on fire one sinking by the stern. Helpless men were seen trapped and their cries for help going unheeded for nothing could be done for them.[7]

The same day, 6 April, brought an attack on the forward RAF airfield at Ioánnina, some 80 miles from the Yugoslav border, by 60 German bombers and 30 fighters, against which the RAF had only 12. After a vicious air battle the Germans had lost 15 planes and the RAF 10 of their 12, and as bombing had completely wrecked the airfield the remaining two were withdrawn to the south. Further disasters followed. On 13 April six bombers set off to block the Monastir Gap, and not one returned. On 15 April at the Lárissa airfields 16 RAF bombers and 14 fighters were destroyed on the ground. On 19 April five of the remaining 15 RAF fighters were lost in an air battle over

Athens. It was now no longer possible for Allied planes to support their ground troops by fending off Luftwaffe attacks.

While the Allied air defences were being depleted, by 8 April the situation on the ground had become distressingly clear. The Metaxas Line had not held, and the Germans were crushing Yugoslavia and could now attack through the Monastir Gap. It was also clear that, despite fierce resistance by the British and Australian troops, the Aliakmon Line could not be held. It was therefore decided that the Allied forces including Greek divisions would pull back from the Aliakmon Line some 40 to 50 miles to a line running north-west from Mount Olympus through Kozáni to Kastoriá. Crucially this new 8 April line was well west of the Aliakmon Line and so was in a position to resist a German assault through the Monastir Gap.

This attack came three days later on the morning of 11 April. It began with German mortar and machine-gun fire, followed up that afternoon with tanks and infantry patrols. In this mountainous region the temperature dropped below freezing. Truck drivers clutched their steering wheels with numb fingers, and troops slept in stony hollows covered only with a ground sheet. The German attack was met with fierce resistance, and continued the following day. But it was obvious that the Allied forces were 'committed to tasks which they had not the numbers to fulfil. Every position they occupied would be too thinly held, with few or no reserves.'[8] On 15 April the order was given to retreat to a front far to the south at Thermopylae, only 30 miles north of the Gulf of Corinth, where the New Zealand units had already taken up position. It was here in 480 BC that Leonidas and his 300 Spartans had died resisting the Persians, and to Churchill the historical association was a call for heroism: 'Why not one more undying feat of arms?'[9]

It was now some ten days since the German invasion had begun, and during that time the Greek troops had ceased to be an effective fighting force. The defenders of the Metaxas Line had been killed or captured or had escaped from the ports to the east on the Aegean. The Greek units retreating with the Allied troops disintegrated, and Christopher Buckley, in Athens at the time, wrote of them with some sympathy:

> The Greeks, like the soldiers of many other nationalities, do not move with our formality and precision. Their withdrawal would naturally be carried out in small groups bearing little semblance of purpose and

order even if they were ready and willing to respond to the next call for action. The primitive and varied types of transport were bound to slow down the march, causing traffic blocks and delay.

And of the Greek forces in Albania he wrote:

> To retreat from an enemy they had beaten along a single road packed with transport vehicles of every kind and swarms of refugees, constantly dive-bombed and machine-gunned from the air, and to maintain their cohesion and fighting spirit through it all was not to be expected.

Refugees were indeed everywhere: 'They were mainly on foot, but also on donkeys, in ox-carts, in antiquated buses and ramshackle cars, the vehicles covered with a medley of bedding, furniture and pots and pans lashed to roofs, mudguards and running-boards.'[10]

With the collapse of the Greek army and the retreat of Allied troops, the Greek government accepted the inevitable. On 17 April Papadhímas, the Greek army minister, declared further resistance impossible and gave the generals a free hand to do as they saw fit. This was later contradicted, but to no effect, by the King's broadcast on 22 April calling on Greeks to fight to the end. On 18 April in Athens, after a depressing military report from Papágos, Prime Minister Korizís retired to his study and committed suicide by shooting himself in the head, seeing no other honourable way out. On 21 April General Georgios Tsolákoglou, commander of the Greek forces in Albania and north-west Greece, offered to surrender, and this offer was formally accepted two days later. On 19 April Wavell had arrived in Athens to reach a decision on whether Allied forces should leave Greece. Churchill had stipulated that this could be only with the full consent of the Greeks, and on the same day the King and government gave that consent. The question was no longer about resistance but about withdrawal. On 22 April the order was given for evacuation, which was to take place between 24 and 27 April. On 23 April the King and members of his government were flown out to Crete by Sunderland flying boat.

At this point the Allied forces were still struggling back to the Thermopylae Line. They were under attack from the air:

> In the absence of any anti-aircraft batteries the German bombers had it all their own way. They would circle overhead, select a target,

and then dive. Sirens screaming, they swooped down amid a rattle of ineffectual small-arms fire from the ground. A crash or thud as bomb after bomb burst about the road was followed by the roar of the approaching fighters who swept along the column to machine-gun their all-too-visible targets.[11]

On the ground the main problem was the bottleneck at Lárissa. Both of the usable roads to the south led through it, one from Salonika on the north side and the other from Grevená and Tríkala on the west. Lárissa had been damaged by an earthquake in March, and German bombers continued the destruction. Nevertheless the retreating Allied convoys continued to crawl through the debris-strewn streets, and a British military policeman was seen calmly controlling the night-time traffic at 4 a.m.

Once through Lárissa their progress to Lamía and beyond depended on the holding of the Thermopylae Line for as long as possible until the inevitable order to retreat was given. The New Zealanders were already there, and were joined by the withdrawing British and Australians and the remnants of the Greek army. All were in position by 20 April. They had been severely weakened in a number of ways. Their tanks had been reduced by losses in battle or mechanical failure to a mere 14, and the tank units were pulled back to Thebes or Athens. The troops on the Thermopylae Line no longer had air support. The remaining 20 or so fighters of the RAF had been withdrawn to Árgos to cover the evacuation, and there on 23 April the Luftwaffe destroyed them all on the ground. Furthermore there were threats other than direct assault on the Thermopylae Line. German troops had landed on the offshore island of Évvia to the east. The Germans advancing down the west coast of Greece could threaten Athens by the road from Delphi, or could cross the Gulf of Corinth at the narrows near Návpaktos and head east to seize the Corinth isthmus. Troops had to be withdrawn from the battle front to counter all these threats.

Depleted in numbers and without air support or tank units, the troops on the Thermopylae Line faced vastly superior German forces. The two days of 22 and 23 April saw artillery bombardments from both sides as the Germans prepared their assault, advancing their infantry, digging gun pits, and bringing in troops and supplies by transport planes from their airfields at Salonika. On 24 April the main assault began. In the morning the artillery duel was intensified and German dive-bombers attacked the troops on the ground. In the early afternoon the German tanks moved forward and came under heavy fire which destroyed at least 15 of them. German infantry probed forward from the neighbouring hills and down the railway line from Lárissa, supported by heavy mortar shelling. In the early evening the Allied forces were ordered to withdraw, and after driving 80 miles through the night reached Mégara soon after dawn next morning on 25 April. The Thermopylae Line had been held for three days, providing vital time for an orderly retreat and departure.

The evacuation was to be from four areas: from the fishing ports of Rafína and Pórto Ráfti east of Athens, from Mégara on the Gulf of Corinth west of Athens, from Návplion and Tolón in the northern Peloponnese, and from Kalamáta far to the south. In the event there was a final evacuation from Monemvasía, also in the far south. To speed up the turn-around, troops were to be taken first to Crete for later movement to more distant Egypt. To avoid air attacks embarkation was to be at night, though it would be daylight and dangerous once the transport vessels left.

East of Athens over 5,000 men were evacuated from Pórto Ráfti and two days later over 3,000 from Rafína. West of Athens the road from Thermopylae had been comprehensively wrecked by Allied troops, which was described as one of the best demolition jobs of the campaign. This slowed the German advance and allowed nearly 5,000 troops to leave from Mégara. In the Peloponnese at Návplion and Tolón over 5,000 men plus 150 hospital nurses were taken off.

The support of the Greek people for the Allied troops, so colourfully expressed on their arrival, was just as warm on their departure. 'We know you will return,' said the villagers, girls tossed flowers to the weary soldiers, there were shouts of *Níki! Níki!* (Victory! Victory!), and the thumbs-up sign, picked up from Allied troops, was everywhere. An officer on General Wilson's staff, leaving Athens by car without food, went into a confectioner's shop. The pretty girl gave him a whole box of chocolate bars, and the manageress added a ribboned box suitable for a mother-in-law. The Greeks refused payment, said how grateful they were that the Allies had come, and threw the last of their flowers through the car window as it left.

The commanders as well as their troops were being withdrawn. Carrington (British forces) was one of the last to leave from Rafína. Blamey (combined Australian and New Zealand troops) and Mackay (Australian) were flown out on 24 and 25 April. That left Freyberg (New Zealand), who refused to leave and was given command of troops remaining in the Peloponnese, and still with him was Wilson the overall Allied commander.

So far evacuation had gone relatively smoothly, but it was now disrupted by a lightning German attack by parachutists on the Corinth canal bridge and the troops guarding it. At 6 a.m. on 26 April, a bright and windless morning, the Germans attacked from the air, first with high-level bombing and then with dive-bombers and fighters. Soon afterwards German troop-carriers appeared, having flown from Lárissa, and dropped some 800 parachutists from a height of about 200 feet. Their objective was to seize the bridge intact, but the bridge had already been wired for demolition. Two young British officers, Phillips and Tyson, took cover under heavy fire 200 yards from the bridge and aimed their rifles at the explosive charge. Their second shot appeared to hit it and the bridge came crashing down. This feat is disputed as impossible, and the explosion is credited to a stray British shell, but both Phillips and Tyson were awarded the Military Cross.

The Germans soon installed an emergency bridge and had now cut off the retreat of the Allied troops who were still north of the canal – perhaps a third of the original total. By the one remaining wireless link Freyberg arranged their evacuation from Pórto Ráfti two days later. They waited there next day, driving back German attacks on the ground and being bombed and machine-gunned from the air, and early on the morning of 28 April some 3,400 were on the way to Crete.

In the Peloponnese the British navy continued the evacuation. From Návplion and Tolón about 4,300 men were rescued, and on 27 April Wilson was flown out from there to Crete, leaving Freyberg in sole command. At Kalamáta where most of the troops in the Peloponnese had now assembled, 8,000 were taken off on the night of 26/27 April. The remaining 7,000 were to leave on the following night, and the navy's ships were already off the harbour when an order came from Wavell in Egypt that all ships must rejoin the main fleet without delay because of a reported threat from the Italian navy, a report which later turned out to be false. Next day, 29 April, the Germans seized Kalamáta and took most of the 7,000 prisoners. The last major contingent of Allied troops reached Monemvasía, from where 4,000 were taken off on the night of 28/29 April, the last boatload carrying Freyberg. Of the remainder a few left Yíthion by caique, some reached the island of Kíthira off the southern Peloponnese and some got to the island of Mílos 80 miles out in the Aegean. The evacuation was complete.

There is still debate about whether the British decision to send troops to Greece was justified. Cyril Falls wrote in 1948, of British involvement in Greece and Crete, 'The whole episode now appears a sorry tale of political and strategic frivolity.'[12] Was this fair?

The battle for Crete is covered in Chapter 4. In Greece the military losses were certainly severe though figures are not precise: probably about 3,000 British and Commonwealth troops killed or missing and 9,000 captured. Also some 8,000 vehicles were lost, plus 100 or so tanks, over 200 aircraft and a variety of artillery. Churchill, to emphasise that the British bore their full share of the burden, shows that British losses were three times those of either Australia or New Zealand. To set against these losses, the military gains were very small: the invasion of Greece had been held up for only a few weeks.[13]

It is also sometimes maintained that involvement in Greece weakened Allied forces in North Africa. But Wavell said that the reverses in North Africa were due to the arrival of Rommel and the enemy superiority in tanks, and Eden maintained that even if the 100 or so tanks lost in Greece had been available it would not have made much difference.[14] It has also been argued, on the other side, that there was an indirect gain because the diversion of German forces to Greece delayed from May to June 1941 the start of Barbarossa, the German attack on Russia, with disastrous results for Germany. But it is probable that the main reason for that delay was the weather. The German advance against Russia had to begin across northern Poland. Even in normal years this area was a morass, with muddy roads and overflowing rivers, and the previous winter had been exceptionally severe. So even without their involvement in the Balkans the Germans would have had to delay Barbarossa.[15] In any case Hitler had signed the directive for the attack on Greece months ago, on 13 December 1940, and for Barbarossa five days later on 18 December, so involvement in Greece had already been built into the Barbarossa plans. Also the Allies knew nothing of Barbarossa until it was launched, so the delay of Barbarossa cannot be any justification of the decision to support Greece.

Ultimately that decision was a matter of honour. Chamberlain had promised support for Greece in April 1939 and Churchill repeated the pledge in November 1940. There was no going back on these offers after the 4 March 1941 agreement with the Greek government by Eden, Wavell and Dill that troops would be sent, an agreement about which Churchill continued to harbour doubts on military grounds and which was fiercely criticised by the Australian Prime Minister Robert Menzies.[16] But how could Britain stand as champion of the free world if it did not stand by pledges to support Greece, the one other European country prepared to resist the Axis? The decision to do so was essentially political and, as Falls conceded 'not necessarily wrong for that reason'.[17] There was also a particular political reason. The United States had passed on 11 March 1941 the Lend-Lease Act providing Britain with essential supplies. It was vital that the United States, where isolationism was still strong, should continue support for Britain. The likelihood of this was strengthened by the British action in Greece, which was praised by Roosevelt as 'not only heroic but very useful work'.[18] So Churchill was able to end his British broadcast on 3 May, which was specific about recent reverses, with a heartening quotation from Arthur Hugh Clough: 'But westward, look, the land is bright.'

4

The Battle for Crete

The battle for Crete lasted a remarkably short time. The first German parachutist attack on the island came at dawn on Tuesday 21 May 1941. One week later Churchill's War Cabinet agreed that the island should be abandoned. In the early hours of Sunday 1 June the last evacuation of troops by the Royal Navy took place, leaving many thousands of Allied soldiers behind. The whole episode had lasted less than a fortnight.

Brief as it was, the battle for Crete generated as many controversial questions as any event of the war. Had Wavell, commander-in-chief Middle East, failed to prepare Crete to resist invasion? Did Freyberg, given command of Allied forces in Crete after his escape from Greece, sensibly deploy his forces? Could information from ULTRA, the intercepted German communications that were deciphered and summarised at Bletchley Park, have been better used? The one thing not in doubt was the fighting spirit of the forces engaged – of British, New Zealand, Australian and Greek soldiers, of the Cretan population, and indeed of the Germans. An account of the battle and its preliminaries will show how the controversies arose.

Six months before the battle Britain, by agreement with the Greek government, had taken over the defence of Crete, and the first British troops landed there on 1 November 1940. Crete, with Malta, commanded the sea routes of the eastern Mediterranean, and the harbour of Soúdha Bay on Crete's north coast was a vital refuelling station for the Royal Navy. In the months before the invasion Churchill constantly emphasised to Wavell the importance of holding Crete: 'We must at all costs keep Crete!' (12 February 1941), and 'We shall aid and maintain the defence of Crete to the utmost' (17 April).[1]

So what was done to prepare for the defence of this vital outpost? The answer has to be: not nearly enough. First, and perhaps the source of all the other problems, there were constant changes in the

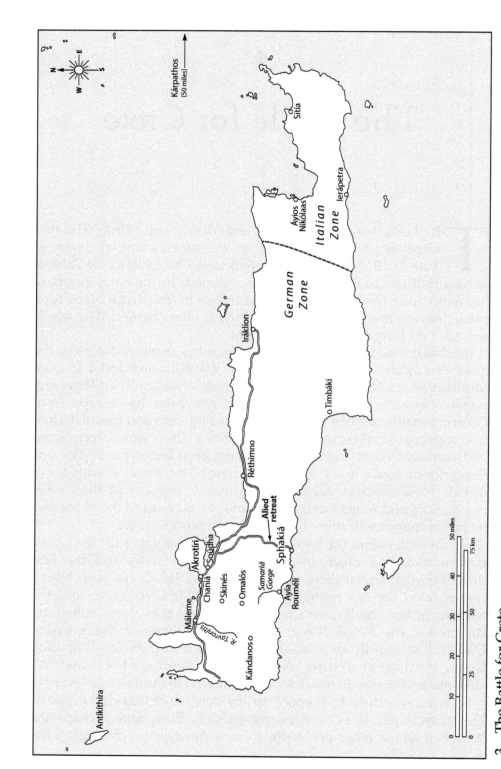

3 The Battle for Crete

overall command in Crete, sometimes almost at weekly intervals. A succession of generals, brigadiers and colonels were appointed. Tidbury (November 1940 to 10 January 1941) was followed by Gambier-Perry for three weeks, then Mather as a temporary appointment until Galloway took over on 19 February. Galloway was succeeded by Mather again until Chappel relieved him on 19 March, who was in turn replaced ten days later by Weston. Finally Freyberg, evacuated from Greece to Crete on 29 April, was next day given the command. The only possible justification for this chaotic procedure is that the officers relieved were transferred to posts which Wavell considered more important. But Wavell was well aware of the situation on Crete, visiting the island in November 1940 and again on 30 April 1941 when he appointed Freyberg. Even Wavell's sympathetic biographer Ronald Lewin says that Crete was Wavell's blind spot, and that the command muddle was 'a damning error of oversights by a normally alert commander'.[2]

From the time that Britain took over the island, the German intention to take Crete had been made clear with relentless air attacks by the Luftwaffe, which dropped bombs and machine-gunned troops and civilians on the ground. On the day that the first British troops landed, 1 November 1940, the port at Soúdha Bay and the nearby town of Chaniá were bombed, and raids continued daily. On 22 April 1941 after the fall of Greece, Princess Frederica, wife of the King's younger brother and heir-apparent Paul, reached Crete from Athens by flying boat with her two children, Sophie aged two and Constantine not yet one. On arrival they were bombed and took cover in a ditch shared with a Cretan policeman. Frederica put her hands over Sophie's ears and sang 'Baa, baa, black sheep' to her while the nurse cradled the baby. 'They dropped about 50 bombs around us,' wrote Frederica, 'but we got through all right, awfully proud to have been under fire.'[3]

The RAF had pathetically small forces to oppose this threat from the air. The largest number of RAF planes ever on Cretan airfields was 36, none of them in a really satisfactory condition, to face an estimated Luftwaffe strength of 'over 300 long-range bombers, between 200 and 300 dive bombers, and over 300 fighters'.[4] On Monday 19 May, the day before the German assault began, the last six of these RAF planes were flown away to Egypt. Any further air support had to come from there, over 350 miles away. A small number of bombers managed to reach Cretan airfields during the battle but far too few to be any use.

There were other weaknesses in the provision for the defence of Crete. There were not enough anti-aircraft guns – only about 50, mostly captured Italian guns, and it was estimated that at least another 50 were needed. The tanks sent from Egypt were in a shocking state, described as 'battered ancient hulks, without proper cooling systems for the guns, drawn from the workshops without being properly refitted or even having their wireless equipment installed'.[5] Wireless sets were also in short supply elsewhere, were unreliable and were useless when their batteries ran out. One of Freyberg's officers believed 100 more were needed. The only other means of communication were field telephone lines strung along telegraph poles, which could be cut by the enemy or destroyed by bombs. The last resort was a runner.

Finally, there was the problem of roads. The only good road in Crete was a 100-mile stretch along the north-west coast, and the only substantial harbour was close to that road at Soúdha Bay. Ships bringing supplies or reinforcements to Soúdha from Egypt had to sail round to the north coast, either running the gauntlet of the narrows at Antikíthira at the western end, threatened from German airfields in Greece, or using the passage past Kásos at the eastern end which was under air attack from Kárpathos. Could the south coast have been used instead? That coast was safer, and Admiral Cunningham said he wished the island could have been turned upside down. There was a harbour at Timbáki, but little more than a track from there to the north coast. The failure, in the six months when invasion was threatened, to upgrade it for motor transport has been condemned as foreseeably disastrous.

Thus Churchill writes, of the six-month preparation for the defence of Crete, that all should have been in readiness: 'There had been however neither plan nor drive.'[6] And Freyberg sent a signal to Wavell on 1 May, the day after his appointment, saying:

Forces at my disposal are totally inadequate to meet attack envisaged. Unless fighter aircraft are greatly increased and naval forces made available to deal with seaborne attack I cannot hope to hold out with land forces alone, which as a result of campaign in Greece are now devoid of any artillery, have insufficient tools for digging, very little transport, and inadequate war reserves of equipment and ammunition.[7]

In terms simply of numbers of men, the forces at Freyberg's disposal were substantial. A precise listing gives a total of 25,614, made up of the original garrison (5,200), roughly equal proportions of British, Australian and New Zealand troops from Greece (19,950 in all), and reinforcements from Egypt (3,464). To this must be added some 15,000 Greek troops.[8] They were deployed to protect the vital points on the north coast: the Soúdha Bay area (mainly British) and the three airfields at Máleme (mainly New Zealand), Réthimno (mainly Australian) and Iráklion (mainly British) with a number of Greek troops in each sector. Some forces were charged with guarding the coast against seaborne landings.

These danger points were the obvious ones and had been identified by Crete's first commander, Brigadier Tidbury, as early as December 1940. This assessment was confirmed a week before the battle began by secret information from ULTRA. The crucial summary of ULTRA information, labelled OL302, reached Freyberg on 13 May. It stated that the Germans intended, 'as from day one', to make parachute landings to seize all three airfields. This would be followed by troop-carrying planes landing on the airfields, and by a seaborne contingent bringing more troops and supplies.[9]

To keep secret the existence of ULTRA, which was vital in every theatre of the war, the rules imposed on Freyberg and other commanders laid down that the information from it could be shared with only a very few senior officers, that any document containing it must be read and then destroyed, and, crucially, that no action must be taken based on ULTRA alone. Freyberg later told his son that ULTRA information, which he was not allowed to use, had shown him 'that his forces were in the wrong position to counter the greatly increased German airborne assault against the airfields'.[10] But his forces were already deployed to protect the airfields, on the basis of common sense and of Tidbury's original assessment, and it is hard to see what significant changes he could have made if given free use of ULTRA. It seems that the only crucial bit of ULTRA information which he could not use to forewarn his troops was the precise date of the German attack.

The troops brought to Crete from Greece arrived at the crowded harbour of Soúdha Bay in poor shape. One group's ship had been torpedoed and they had been told to leave boots and rifles and then jump, so reached Crete unshod and unarmed. On the quay was an open cook-house at which snaked a queue of thousands of troops, many to be disappointed. Units had been split up, and with no food and no shelter some initially roamed the island, 'many armed with rifles, living like tramps on the hills and olive groves'.[11] Gradually some order was introduced and tents and rations provided. Nevertheless Freyberg, on assuming command, reported that his preparations were hampered by 10,000 other ranks without arms and with little or no employment other than getting into trouble with the civilian population. It is a tribute to officers and men that this disorganised collection of troops was transformed in a few weeks into a formidable fighting force to face the German assault.

The German decision to invade Crete was not taken until 21 April, just a month before the attack, and the directive to do so was issued on 25 April. As the ULTRA intelligence had stated, the assault was to be on all three airfields. It would be led by parachutists, followed by troops either in gliders, to be crash-landed, or in Junkers 52 troop-carriers to land on captured airfields. A fleet of freighters and motorised caiques would bring in reinforcements and supplies.

German parachutists had successfully attacked before the Cretan operation: at the Belgian fort at Eben-Emael in May 1940 – but this had been with the support of troops already on the ground – and, as we have seen, at the Corinth Canal on 26 April – but this had been against a disordered Allied army in retreat. Hitler was doubtful about the Cretan proposal, commenting 'It sounds all right, but I don't believe that it's practicable.'[12] It has been suggested that Hitler finally agreed to the plan as a sop to Göring, whose Luftwaffe would have only a supporting role in the forthcoming Barbarossa campaign; but the Alice in Wonderland world where all must have prizes seems a far cry from the ruthlessly efficient German high command.

The operation was under the overall command of General Alexander Löhr, while General Kurt Student, commander of XI Air Corps, was responsible for ground troops and their transport by air. In the first weeks of May some 12,000 of these men travelled by rail from their training grounds in northern Germany to Salonika and then by bus to the Athens airfields, a 13-day journey of 1,000 miles. Secrecy was essential: they travelled only by night, wore no badges, and were even forbidden to sing their regimental songs.

Other preparations were equally meticulous. The parachutists were provided with protective clothing for their landing and pistols for their descent, rations for two days and water-distilling apparatus. But there were two mistakes made by the German planners. One was that they failed to estimate the number of troops on Crete, due to incomplete aerial reconnaissance. They initially believed that all troops from Greece had already left for Egypt and put the total number of defenders at about 5,000, less than a fifth of the actual figure. The figure was later revised upwards, but Student said later that the defenders were much stronger than he expected. The other mistake was a total misreading of the reaction of the Cretans. The Germans thought that the Cretans, being long-term opponents of the king, Metaxás and the Greek government, would actually assist the invaders or at least not hinder them. That the Cretans were above all patriots and would fight ferociously to defend their homeland was never considered.

The first of the 120 transport planes on Athens airfields took off at 5 a.m. on Tuesday 21 May. One of the parachutists, von der Heydte, later described his feelings in flight:

> Being dropped in battle is always a wonderful experience. You are, of course, anxious but still you feel you are over the enemy – I can't describe it otherwise because you're coming from heaven. And the enemy is on the ground and this gives you a sort of strength, a feeling of strength.

But he went on to say, 'This feeling, however, disappears the moment you are on the ground.'[13]

Reality struck even before the paratroopers reached the ground and were still descending from the planes. Soon after 8 a.m. the parachutists, 15 per plane, began to drop around the Máleme airfield. The parachutes were colour-coded – violet or pink for officers, black for other ranks, yellow for medical supplies and white for arms and ammunition – and were described as like handfuls of confetti. They were dropped from as low as possible, perhaps only 200 feet, but they were in the air for at least 20 seconds, and many were shot as they descended. 'It was just like duck shooting,' said one New Zealander.[14] Moreover parachutists had no lines to control their descent, as the parachutes were centrally attached to a yoke across the shoulder blades, and many landed in the middle of the defenders' positions.

Almost simultaneously with the parachutists, troop-carrying gliders began to arrive around Máleme. Their most dangerous concentration was on the west of Máleme airfield, where the ground fell away to the dry and rocky bed of the river Tavronítis, so they were largely hidden from defenders on the airfield. Crucially, there were no Allied troops west of the Máleme airfield because, as Freyberg said at the time, 'It had not been considered feasible for aircraft to land in the river-bed west of the Máleme aerodrome.'[15]

There were two plans by New Zealand troops to counter-attack and regain control of the Máleme airfield. The first, at about 5 p.m., was by infantry supported by their two tanks, but the guns of one tank jammed and the engine of the other broke down, so the troops, having no covering fire, had to withdraw. The second attempt was intended for that evening by a New Zealand company commanded by Lieutenant-Colonel Andrew, VC, but because communication was almost non-existent he wrongly believed that his other companies could not support him and felt he had to withdraw. Both of these moves were tragic examples of brave men being let down by faulty equipment.

In the course of this first day the Germans used parachutists and gliders to attack their other objectives along the north coast. At Chaniá about 2,000 were put down with severe losses, and though the survivors concentrated in an area south-west of the town, the so-called Prison Valley, neither the town nor the access roads to Soúdha were taken on the first day. At Réthimno 1,200 men were dropped but about half were lost, and neither town nor airfield was captured. At Iráklion 2,000 were dropped and again about half were lost. A few German troops got into the town and were resisted in fierce street fighting, but as at Réthimno they did not gain control of the town or the airfield. Thus none of the German objectives for Day 1 had been achieved, despite terrible losses of elite troops. Only at Máleme did they have a foothold on the undefended west side of the airfield, where one counter-attack had been repulsed and a second one called off. Student, receiving this news that night at his headquarters in the Grande Bretagne Hotel in Athens, had only one option apart from an unthinkable ignominious withdrawal. That was, in spite of already very heavy losses, to pour more troops into the one area of partial success – Máleme.

King George of Greece with his small entourage was still in Crete, at a villa a couple of miles south-west of Chaniá, though the rest of his family had already left for Egypt. Within an hour or so of the German air attack on Chaniá early on Tuesday 22 May it was clear that this was their major offensive, and that the King must make his pre-planned escape. It would be a great German propaganda coup if he was killed or captured – perhaps particularly the latter.

At 9.30 that morning the King moved off with his party – his cousin Prince Peter of Yugoslavia (briefly monarch), Levídhis the

King's equerry and old friend, Tsoudherós the prime minister and Varvaréssos the governor of the Bank of Greece, with a few servants. Their escort was Colonel Blunt, British military attaché in Greece, and a platoon of New Zealanders with some Greek policemen. The whole group numbered less than 40. They were to walk the 20 miles or so across the mountains to the tiny village of Ayía Rouméli on the south coast, where they would be picked up by a Royal Navy warship.

The first night was spent in a village some 5 miles from their starting point, where they were given a simple meal and slept on the stone floor. Wednesday was spent climbing, and that night they slept out in the bitter cold at about 7,000 feet. On Thursday they completed the journey down the Samariá Gorge, a testing experience even for today's visitors who have not walked for two days over the mountains to get there. The group reached Ayía Rouméli in the early afternoon.

The King's cheerful fortitude throughout was praised both by his companion Tsoudherós, 'The King did not for a moment lose his smile. With a majestic simplicity he shared with us all dangers, all privations, all hardships,' and by his escort Colonel Blunt, who said, 'His Majesty treated it like an outing.'[16]

The royal party was greeted at Ayía Rouméli by a distinguished delegation, suitable for a king's send-off, who had travelled round from Chaniá by boat. It consisted of the British minister to Athens Sir Michael Palairet and his wife, a British general and an admiral, and Harold Caccia, first secretary at the British Legation. As night fell they waited for a signal from a rescue ship. Only at 1 a.m. on Friday morning did they see a flash some miles out, but could not tell if it was from a friendly ship. Eventually the admiral and Caccia went out in a fishing boat to check, and an hour later came back to say that it was indeed HMS *Decoy*. Late that night the King and his entourage were safely landed at Alexandria.

Back at Máleme the results of Student's decision to reinforce were soon evident. At 9 a.m. on Wednesday 21 May, Day 2 of the assault, about 60 transport planes dropped 500 parachutists west of Máleme airfield. Soon afterwards Junkers 52 troop-carriers began to land under intense fire on the airfield itself to the amazement of the defenders: 'No man but a madman would obey an order to pilot an aircraft on to that steel-raked field,' said one.[17] For the German aircraft speed meant survival: they were down and away again in 70 seconds. The defenders were harassed by waves of fighter aircraft. By the afternoon of that day troop-carrying Junkers 52s were landing at a rate of three every five minutes. Early the following morning Freyberg threw all his available forces into a counter-attack from the east, but a shortage of transport meant that the attack was piecemeal, sometimes company by company. One group of New Zealanders actually reached the Tavronítis river bed, but the counter-attack could not break the Germans. Máleme was now lost and so, in effect, was Crete.

However, the Allied forces were far from giving up and the next four days, Thursday to Sunday 22–5 May, saw intense fighting in the other three crucial areas: Chaniá with Soúdha, Réthimno and Iráklion.

At Chaniá the civilians were evacuated and the town was heavily bombed and set on fire, leaving only the waterfront buildings standing. On Friday 23 May German troops landed on the Akrotíri peninsula, immediately threatening Soúdha. On Sunday 25 May the Germans attacked in strength, and a heroic counter-attack, described by Freyberg as 'one of the greatest efforts in the defence of Crete',[18] was at first successful but then repulsed, and next day, Monday 26 May, Freyberg had to accept that this position could not be held. At Réthimno the Germans were still being held back. At Iráklion the civilians were evacuated and the town bombed, as at Chaniá, but by 26 May it was still held. However, it was surrounded by an ever-growing number of German forces who thanks to air-drops were increasingly well armed.

A few RAF fighters and bombers had managed to reach Crete from Egypt, but too few to do more than briefly raise morale. The Royal Navy initially patrolled the north coast of Crete to counter seaborne arrivals of troops and artillery, but this was at the cost of six ships sunk and seven more severely damaged, victims of air attack. Admiral Cunningham wrote, 'Sea control in the Eastern Mediterranean could not be retained after another such experience.'[19] Thus by Monday 26 May the Chaniá and Soúdha position could no longer be held, and the loss of Réthimno and Iráklion was imminent. In the event, three days later on Thursday 29 May the Iráklion garrison of 4,000 was evacuated by the navy, again with heavy losses of ships and men before they reached Alexandria, and the following day the garrison at Réthimno surrendered.

Thus by the evening of Monday 26 May Freyberg had to accept the inevitable, and told Wavell that the military situation was hopeless, and that, though he would carry on if a gain of time would help the general Middle East situation, the only realistic option was evacuation. The next day evacuation was approved by Churchill and the War Cabinet.

Troops began to pour down the rough dusty road, in places only a track, towards the village of Sphakiá on the south coast. From there they were to be picked up by the navy – the island had in effect been turned upside down as Cunningham wished. The retreat was mostly chaotic, and Freyberg reported a 'disorganised rabble making its way doggedly and painfully to the south [...] never shall I forget the disorganisation and almost complete lack of control of the masses on the move.'[20] One New Zealander described his experience of the retreat:

> Still, the ravine wound up and down. Legs were like lead now, and you trudged in a foggy coma, conscious only of aching feet and the raw patch on your hip where the rifle chafed. The sweat ran down your face and stung your cracked lips. Sometimes a creaking wisecrack would come from somewhere down the column.[21]

However, some troops kept their cohesion:

> We saw units withdrawing in perfect order with their rifles and all their equipment [...] Their officers and NCOs ordered them when to scatter and when to reform. It was very heartening to watch the calm and competent way they went about it.[22]

Several factors helped the retreat. One was the last-minute arrival on 24 May by ship at Soúdha of fresh troops to fight a rearguard action. These were 200 British commandos under Colonel Robert Laycock, the so-called Layforce. A second was the determined resistance still being put up by New Zealanders and Australians a mile west of Soúdha and by Greek troops to the south of them. A third factor was that on the first day of the retreat the Luftwaffe was still concentrating on Réthimno and Iráklion which were still holding out – though on the next day raids on the retreating columns were resumed.

Air attacks on the exhausted troops continued once they reached Sphakiá, and they had to take cover under trees during the day while waiting for the evacuation ships to arrive at night. The road into Sphakiá ended in a 500-foot cliff, traversed only by a goat track, leading down to the narrow beach. This meant that designated units had to be brought forward after dark, often from a distance, and ushered down to the beach. It was obvious that not everyone could be taken off, and some gate-crashers tried to jump the queue. But the marshals managed to control the flow, and on each of the four nights of Wednesday to Saturday 28–31 May between 3,000 and 4,000 men were safely evacuated, a total of some 15,000. On the night of 31 May the remaining 5,000, knowing that this was the final night of evacuation, heard the sound of anchor chains through the hawser of the last rescue ship and realised that their chance was gone. Now they would either escape into the mountains of Crete and, if very lucky, get away in a small boat, or – the fate of most – be taken prisoner.

The losses had been very heavy on both sides. The Allied forces had lost, in round figures, 3,700 killed on land plus 2,000 of the Royal Navy, 2,200 wounded, and 11,300 captured before and after the evacuation. Among the rescued survivors were two New Zealanders who had won the Victoria Cross in Crete – Sergeant Clive Hulme and Captain Charles Upham. To the losses on land must be added loss and damage to ships, which severely weakened the whole Mediterranean fleet. The Germans had probably lost some 4,000 killed, most of them elite troops, 2,500 wounded, and a third of the aircraft committed.

Consequently, when a year later Student proposed an airborne attack on Malta, Hitler 'turned it down flat', saying 'The affair will go wrong and will cost too many losses.'[23] So it is fair to say that the lost battle for Crete was the salvation of Malta, and Churchill went even further, saying that without German air and ground losses in Crete the Germans might easily have gone on to take Cyprus, Iraq, Syria and even Persia.

These were justifications after the event, but at the time Churchill defended the decision to fight for Crete on more general grounds. In a speech to the House of Commons on 10 June 1941 he rejected 'the rule that you have to have a certainty of winning at any point, and if you have not got it beforehand, clear out'. He went on to say 'It is not only a question of the time that is gained by fighting strongly even at a disadvantage for important points, but also there is this vitally important point of stubborn resistance to the will of the enemy.'[24]

If Crete was to be defended whatever the outcome and whatever the cost, could it have been defended better? Much has been made of the theory that Freyberg might have deployed his forces differently if he had been able to make full use of ULTRA information, but – as we have seen – his forces were already in position to defend points identified by ULTRA. The ULTRA summaries seen by Freyberg did not reveal that the main attack would be on Máleme, and John Keegan suggests that the raw ULTRA data – still not publicly available – may have indicated this, but admits, 'We cannot know.'[25] In any case, it is a truism that no battle plan survives contact with the enemy. In the battle itself Freyberg, only recently appointed, did the best he could with what he had: troops, many of whom had been fighting in Greece until a few weeks earlier but nevertheless of great fighting spirit; a shortage of armament and equipment, and much of that faulty; and crucially without air support, which it was virtually impossible to provide.

The other principal figure in the battle for Crete was Wavell. It can seem invidious and even arrogant to sit, comfortably and with hindsight, in judgement on the actions of men under great stress. But one must have an opinion, and it appears that Wavell failed on a number of counts. The constant changes in command of Crete were a recipe for disaster. The tanks provided from Egypt were largely unserviceable. The only artillery sent were mostly captured Italian guns. Extra wireless sets were not provided. As the old rhyme says, for want of a nail the shoe, the horse, and eventually the kingdom were lost.

However, Wavell was then under extreme pressure, facing emergencies in five separate theatres. In North Africa Rommel's Afrika Corps had already captured Benghazi on 2 April, there were threats in Ethiopia, Iraq and Syria, and now Crete had to be defended. Wavell's generals resisted any transfer of resources to Crete. Churchill recognised Wavell's burdens, but after the Crete battle Churchill had lost confidence in him, and on 20 June 1941 transferred Wavell to be commander-in-chief India. His predecessor in India, Claude Auchinleck, replaced Wavell as commander-in-chief Middle East. Wavell was promoted to field marshal in January 1943, and later that year became viceroy and governor-general of India, finally handing over to Louis Mountbatten in 1947.

Outwardly, Wavell was the complete soldier, and as a general was praised even by Rommel, who said that of all the British commanders he fought 'the only one who showed a touch of genius was Wavell.'[26] His manner as a commander was taciturn; his standard response to any proposal was 'I see', often accompanied by polishing his glasses. It was said that he seemed, like Stevenson's Weir of Hermiston, to be going up the great, bare staircase of his duty. But another side of him was revealed by his book *Other Men's Flowers*, his poetry anthology with his own lengthy comments. It ran to over 400 pages of English poems, all of which he said he had at one time known by heart. The book was published in 1944, while Wavell was still grappling with the Japanese in the Far East; it was an instant success and was reprinted many times. Wavell personally replied to all the letters its readers sent him. There was, of course, a section headed 'Good Fighting', but his heading of the love poem section seems characteristic – 'Love and All That', revealing the romantic dismissive of his own romanticism. Freyberg said simply that Wavell was 'a man for whom I had affection'.[27] It is easy to share that feeling.

5

The Occupation Begins

The German forces entered Athens on 27 April, and two days later a collaborationist Greek government was formed. Its prime minister was Georgios Tsolákoglou, who had been the first to surrender, and his cabinet included three other generals. The country was given a new name, the Greek State (Ellinikí Politía), to emphasise its subservience. After the war Tsolákoglou was condemned to death for his actions, a sentence commuted to life imprisonment, and he died in prison in 1948. In his memoirs he strongly defended his decisions:

> I found myself before a historic dilemma: to allow the fight to continue and have a holocaust or, obeying the pleas of the army commanders, to assume the initiative of surrendering. To this day I have not regretted my actions. On the contrary, I feel proud.[1]

Occupied Greece was now divided into three zones. The Germans held the Athens–Piraeus area jointly with the Italians, but with the Germans dominant, and the Germans were in sole control of the other strategically important zones: Salonika and its hinterland up to the Yugoslav border, a buffer area next to the Turkish frontier, and the larger Aegean islands near the Turkish coast (Lémnos, Lésvos and Chíos). They also occupied western Crete while the Italians controlled the eastern part. Bulgaria occupied the area south of its frontier in north-east Greece as far as the sea, territory it had coveted since the time of the 1912–13 Balkan Wars, which had now, Bulgaria's King Boris III declared, 'returned to the fold of the Bulgarian Motherland'.[2] But there was nothing maternal about the Bulgarian occupation, which even the Germans described as a reign of terror. The Italians, generally the least oppressive of the occupiers, were responsible for the rest of mainland Greece and the Aegean and Ionian islands.

The German system for the administration of Greece had three branches. First there was the special plenipotentiary for Greece, initially Günther Altenberg, responsible to the Foreign Ministry. Second, the security services and police were answerable to Himmler. Third, there was the army under the conquering general von List, which itself had two branches, one for economic affairs and the other for military matters. The flow chart suggested a system of streamlined efficiency but it was very different in practice. The army often overruled the special plenipotentiary, disagreed with its own economic branch and clashed with the security services over responsibility for dealing with resistance. Sinisterly, four different agencies had responsibility for ordering reprisals against civilians. The system soon degenerated into what has been called 'authoritarian anarchy'.[3]

In a speech to the Reichstag on 4 May 1941 Hitler praised the Greeks for their bravery, and said, 'Towards the Greek people we feel a sense of genuine compassion.'[4] As the occupation began, von List's subordinate General Hans Speidel proclaimed: 'On taking over Athens we come not as enemies but as friends bringing peace to Greece.'[5] Fine words, but it was soon clear that they meant little in practice.

The first potential flashpoints were the triumphal parades of the victors through the streets of Athens. To avoid trouble during the German parade on 4 May 1941, 12 Athenian civic leaders were held hostage in the city hall from the evening before the parade until two hours after it ended, and Greeks were ordered to stay indoors. So the parade was through the empty streets of an enemy city. Similar precautions were taken for the Italian parade on 23 June, probably delayed to indicate that the Germans were the real conquerors and the Italians mere hangers-on. The Athenians regarded with a mixture of rage and scorn this procession of the defeated posing as conquerors. Subtle ways were found of ridiculing the Italians. An Italian officer entered one of Athens' smartest cafés, Phlóka, and, while he made a telephone call, left on a table his military hat with its distinctive cockerel feathers. When he returned and lifted his hat he found an egg underneath. The implication was that the Italian officers were just strutting cockerels, or perhaps that they were cowardly chickens. Phlóka was closed for two days while the victim of the joke interrogated the staff in an unsuccessful attempt to find the culprit.

German orders to the Greek people were fierce: no displaying of the Greek flag, no carrying of weapons, no help for Allied prisoners or fugitives. Any disturbance of public order 'would be met with the utmost vigour and without compunction, and the culprits would bear full responsibility for any innocent blood shed'.[6] Nevertheless resistance flourished in many forms, publicly or covertly, and by high officials, ordinary citizens or boys in the street.

One of the first public acts of defiance was by Chrísanthos, the archbishop of Athens and All Greece, who refused to swear in the collaborationist government of Tsolákoglou. He was replaced by Dhamaskinós, more diplomatic and conciliatory than Chrísanthos, who when the occupation ended became interim regent of Greece.

Other acts of resistance had a more direct effect. Ship owners refused to hand over their vessels to the Germans, and manufacturers refused to release men for work in Germany. Hospital staff refused to clear their beds of patients, many of them war wounded, and hand over the building to the Germans or Italians, and women refused to billet the occupiers in their homes. It seems that these individual acts of defiance were not punished, since at this stage the official German line was that they had come as friends to Greece

Support for Allied troops, now fugitives or prisoners, continued despite the risks. One safe house sheltered several dozen escapers, keeping them for two days and then passing them on for two days at a time to other houses until, it was hoped, they could get away to the Middle East. Near the safe house was a barber's shop, where a particularly skilful girl changed the men's hair style and gave them false moustaches to make them look like Greeks. But the organisers were soon caught by the Gestapo. Other efforts were made to help Allied troops who had been caught. Some were held in the museum, and Greeks brought cigarettes, biscuits and chocolate to the walls below the windows, from which the prisoners let down a basket on a string to collect the offerings. But this too was soon stopped by the Germans.

Listening to the BBC on the radio for accurate war news was harder to detect. The Germans had tried to seal all radios to block the BBC, but the seals were quite easily broken. Everyone who could listened in, closing all doors and shutters for the evening broadcasts between 8.30 and 9.00. When a Greek was suspected of committing a murder at 8.45 it was declared impossible – he would have been otherwise occupied.

All ages and all classes found ways of showing their antagonism to the occupiers. Boys went out at night to paint on walls 'Ochi' (OXI in Greek capital letters). One group in Salonika was surprised in mid task by a German patrol, leaving the tail of the X as a scrawl down the wall, and the next day everyone came to laugh at this misshapen symbol of both resistance and its hazards.[7] In Athens a group of even younger boys met a German soldier who had just bought some figs, which he offered to them. All refused except the youngest, five years old, who accepted some without understanding the implications. Moving away, the older boys told him off, and he tearfully went back and returned the figs to the no doubt surprised donor. It was usually the middle classes who recorded acts of resistance, but Greek prostitutes, considered the dregs of society, found their own means of defiance by refusing to serve Germans or Italians, lucrative as that would be for them in their poverty. Many years later a tribute to them was published in the newspaper *Kathimeriní*:

> Official history does not include them, and their names are nowhere recorded. I do not know if any of these noble Greek women still survive, but if one does I want her to know that history has not forgotten her.[8]

The German swastika flag flying from the summit of the Akropolis was particular anathema to the Greeks. It was said that, when the Germans came to replace the Greek flag with the swastika, the Greek guard wrapped the Greek flag round him and threw himself off the cliff to his death. The account was repeated in the London press and was a satisfying example of heroic self-sacrifice, reminiscent of the Greek women at the time of the War of Independence who threw themselves off a cliff holding their children by the hand rather than submit to the enemy. Unfortunately the story was probably untrue.

However, another episode involving the Akropolis swastika is well attested. Two young men aged 19, Manólis Glézos and Apóstolos Sántos, had discovered, by looking up 'Akropolis' in an encyclopedia, that on the north side there was a gulley running from the bottom to the top. On the night of 30/31 May – which happened to be the night when Crete finally surrendered – the pair climbed the gulley at 11 p.m. The flag should have been guarded, but by happy chance the German guards were a good way down the slope, having a party with some girls. Glézos and Sántos managed to undo the metal wires holding the flag and lower it. They then went down the gulley, first carefully leaving their fingerprints on the flag pole so that nobody else should be implicated. On reaching the bottom they cut up the flag, each kept a piece, and they threw the rest down a ravine. The

Germans never caught them, and their story was not told until 1945. Soon after this episode the swastika was replaced, with the Italian flag to one side and the Greek flag in the middle; 'Christ between two robbers' was the bitter comment. Glézos, a life-long communist, remained an activist, and in 2015, aged over 90, was prominent in protests against Eurozone austerity.

Some of these acts of defiance had an air of youthful skylarking, but they were done under a dark shadow and had serious consequences. Papágos, the hero of the Italian campaign, recorded that within days of the German arrival three young men were executed for displaying the Greek flag. In August 1941 a man in Salonika was condemned to death for helping Allied prisoners to escape, and three in Athens for carrying arms.

On Crete the dark shadow fell almost immediately. The island was divided into two occupation zones, the larger German one to the west and the Italian to the east, the dividing line being some 20 miles east of Iráklion. The Italians did not arrive until 28 May when German victory was already certain, and though the Italian propaganda claimed that they met fierce resistance, they actually took over their zone without a shot being fired. The Italian military governor was General Angelo Carta, regarded as being much more easy-going and humane than the German governor and architect of the German victory, General Student.

The Cretans were in a particularly dangerous situation because so many civilians had attacked Germans, armed with knives, farm implements, hunting rifles and even ancient guns last used against the Turks, and women and boys had joined in the attacks. The Germans regarded these civilians as guerrillas, not protected by any of the conventions of war. The printed instructions to the German paratroopers before take-off included: 'Against an open foe fight with chivalry, but to a guerrilla extend no quarter.'[9] On 31 May Student issued a chilling order. The civilian population, it said, had 'taken part in the fighting, committed sabotage, mutilated and killed wounded soldiers'. It was assumed that wounds on dead soldiers indicated mutilation, rather than attack with primitive weapons. The response, Student's order continued, was to be 'reprisals and punitive expeditions which must be carried through with exemplary terror' and would comprise 'shooting, fines, total destruction of villages by burning [and] extermination of the male population of the territory'.[10]

Sabotage included sheltering Allied soldiers who had been left behind, many of whom were still roaming the island. There were many instances of Cretans in villages and towns providing shelter for weeks or months despite the risk to themselves, and soldiers often left their refuge to avoid endangering their hosts. Hospitality could sometimes be overwhelming. One group was 'plied with so much food and wine that after three days we managed to continue on our way only by sneaking off in the dead of night during a lull in the hospitality'.[11]

The reprisals ordered by Student began almost immediately, concentrated in the area south and west of Chaniá. In the first days of June the village of Kándanos and three neighbouring villages were wholly or partially destroyed, and 180 men were shot. On 1 August Skinés was destroyed, and 147 people from Skinés and nearby villages were executed. In the first week of September 39 Cretan civilians and six British soldiers were shot near Omalós for attempted resistance.[12] It is a horrifying litany of brutality, and it continued until the Germans left Crete three years later.

In mainland Greece, by the end of 1941, a further threat was looming: economic catastrophe. In other occupied countries – Holland, Denmark and Norway – the Germans pursued a rational policy of maintaining productive capacity and controlling inflation, with the aim of creating stability. Not so in Greece, where economic chaos was imminent. Most examples of economic turmoil happen because the policy of the authorities has failed. In occupied Greece the policy, which might have been designed to produce catastrophe, triumphantly succeeded. By the end of 1941 Greece was facing the twin disasters of hyperinflation and starvation.

6

Hyperinflation and Starvation

Hyperinflation has been defined as a period in which inflation rises by at least 50 per cent *per month*, and ends only when it has been below that level for a year. For Greece that period lasted over four years, from June 1941 to January 1946. The Weimar Germany experience of 1922–3 is often taken as a prime example of hyperinflation, illustrated by the story of a man who took a wheelbarrow full of money to make a modest purchase, left it unguarded for a moment, and on return found the money was still there but the wheelbarrow had been stolen. However, the Greek hyperinflation on one reckoning exceeded that of Weimar Germany by a factor of 5,000. Also the 50 per cent a month level of increase seems generous; inflation would have severe effects at even half that level. The wonder is that money retained any purchasing power at all, however minimal. The economy was kept going by barter, usually of goods for food, controlled by the black market.

Inflation varied from time to time. Any Allied victory, or expectation of victory, raised hopes that Greece would be liberated sooner rather than later. Then with increased food supplies and a stable economy, food prices would fall, so food stocks were released before that happened. It has been said that 'when Rommel retreated in Africa, black market prices also retreated. When Rommel advanced, so did the black market prices.'[1] Purely local events might also affect prices. On the island of Sámos civil servants had not been paid for months, and when their back pay arrived from Athens local prices inevitably shot up.

The underlying reason for the Greek hyperinflation was that the collaborationist government was being squeezed economically from two directions. On the one hand its expenditure was vastly increased because it was required to pay the occupation costs of the Germans and Italians. On the other, its revenue was vastly reduced because of the great difficulty of collecting taxes.

The first move to get the Greeks to pay for being occupied came immediately and was simply by plundering. All stocks of olive oil, olives, raisins and figs were seized, as was the entire tobacco crop. The raw materials of the textile factories were appropriated, crippling the industry and leaving thousands unemployed. The mineral mines for chrome, bauxite, manganese, molybdenum and nickel, all useful for munitions, were handed over to German companies. Payment for requisitions was in newly created occupation currency – German Reichskredits, or Italian currency issued by the so-called Casa Mediterranea. But the values of these were set at an unrealistically high number of drachmas, so the value received was much lower than it appeared.

The system of occupation currencies did not last long. To have three parallel currencies in circulation – German and Italian occupation money and Greek drachmas – was a recipe for economic chaos, and the Italians were suspected of using the differing exchange rates between the currencies to their own advantage. So from August 1941, after less than three months of Axis control, the occupation currencies were scrapped and the occupying powers levied a monthly payment in drachmas from the Bank of Greece. These payments were to cover the costs of supplying the occupation armies, of goods sent to Germany, of Greek labour for the occupiers, and of transport improvements. About three-quarters of these occupation costs went to the Germans and the rest to the Italians. In practice these were simply thinly disguised methods of extracting resources from Greece.

However, these payments did not benefit the occupiers as they intended. Initially the amount was set at about 4 billion drachmas a month, and the table below shows in column 1 a rise from billions to millions of billions between 1941 and 1944. But column 2 of the table shows that the actual purchasing power of the payments fell, until by the end of the occupation they were worth only a quarter of the original amount. Occupying troops, paid in rapidly depreciating drachmas, also felt the effects of inflation, and it was said that 'for his monthly salary, a general [stationed in Greece] could pay for one midday meal in a good restaurant.'[2]

How was the Greek government to pay these occupation costs, which more than doubled its total expenditure? They could not be covered by taxation, which initially totalled only a quarter of occupation costs, let alone other government expenditure.

Table 6.1 Total occupation costs, average per month, in selected months

	In current drachmas (billions)	*Estimated purchasing power in pre-war drachmas (millions)*
August–October 1941	3.7	261
August–October 1942	22.7	93
August–October 1943	153.7	154
August–October 1944	1,122,127	64

The system for collecting taxes was in any case in disarray. There was a long tradition in Greece of avoiding or evading paying tax, over the centuries of not paying it to the Ottoman rulers, and later of not paying it to a government in Athens seen as remote and not concerned with the welfare of the whole country. Also Greece was a country of mainly small industrial units, from which it is much harder to collect tax than from large organisations. The same was true of agricultural units; since the Venizélos land reforms of 1917 which broke up large estates, most farms had become small peasant properties. After occupation the tax base too had shrunk: merchant shipping had completely stopped, and industrial production had been much reduced because raw materials and fuel were short. The one off-setting factor, though far from sufficient to solve the government's revenue problem, was that there were no longer the Greek armed services to be paid for.

The only solution was simply to print money. Thus by November 1941 there were nearly five times as many drachmas in circulation as at the end of 1939, and by September 1942 some 20 times as many.[3]

In October 1942 Germany attempted to halt this slide into financial chaos. A special economic mission was sent to Athens, led by Hermann Neubacher, whose remit was 'to sustain Axis operations in Greece without destroying the Greek economy'.[4] His first move was to discourage hoarding, by the radical expedient of simply not paying Greek businesses which were supplying the Axis. This forced them either to release stocks or to sell their gold for drachmas, which would put more stable-value gold into circulation.

The stratagem worked for a time, and the level of prices fell for some six months from October 1942 before rising again. In response to this rise Neubacher in November 1943 released more gold into the market by auctioning for drachmas the gold held by the Bank of Greece. However, these gold resources soon ran out, and Neubacher's requests for more gold from Germany were turned down. At the end of 1943 inflation resumed its relentless upward climb.

It is the uncertainty that goes with hyperinflation which causes shortages of food. This leads to hoarding, which Neubacher had tried to reduce. Why sell stock at today's price when tomorrow's price will probably be higher, and replacing stock tomorrow will cost more than the price you can get for it today? Nor probably does a fall in agricultural production explain food shortages. Some of the figures suggesting such a fall are suspect for two reasons. One is that they compare pre-war production for the whole of Greece with that of the German and Italian zones only – that is, excluding the fertile Bulgarian zone in north-east Greece. The second reason is that the figures are based on ten times the tithe exacted in cash or in kind by the government on declared production, which was of course regularly lower than actual production. One historian concludes, on the basis of specific evidence from different regions, that during the occupation agricultural production 'was probably as high as that of a normal year'.[5]

There were several reasons for the food shortages in Greece. Greece was not self-sufficient in grain, and in normal times imported 600,000 tons of grain a year, imports which were now completely stopped. Also the country was divided into a patchwork of disconnected areas, partly because there were few vehicles and little fuel to transport goods, and partly because the transfer between occupation zones of goods, especially food, was forbidden. This regulation is understandable by the Italians and Bulgarians who held the most productive areas, but for the Germans occupying mainly urban centres it seems very short-sighted. The result of this market fragmentation was that availability of food varied massively from place to place. The same was therefore true of prices: in summer 1942 haricot beans in Athens cost nearly three times as much as in Salonika, and tomatoes four times as much, and Athens prices were probably the highest in the country.

Food shortages could not be relieved by shipping in imports because of the Allies' naval blockade of occupied countries, a blockade policed by the British navy. The justification for this was that it was the responsibility of the occupying powers to feed the population of the country they had occupied, and in practical terms not to make the task of the occupying powers any easier. This policy was to become harder and harder to sustain. However justified it was, could an ally be left to starve?

A standard response to food shortage is rationing, and the Greek collaborationist government introduced such a system, but this proved totally inadequate. Between October 1941 and March 1942 in Athens–Piraeus, the worst period for the worst affected area, the daily bread ration averaged only a sub-survival 116 grams, falling to 84 grams in February. Figures for total calories from rations tell the same story: 327 per day in October 1941, falling to 204 in February 1942, compared with today's estimated daily needs of 2,500 for a man and 2,000 for a woman.

Food became increasingly expensive, and the American ambassador Lincoln MacVeagh recorded food prices rising from the start of the German invasion in April 1941. It also became increasingly hard to find food in the shops, and by March 1942 a housewife shopping for her family returned with only four oranges, a few pounds of apples, some rusks and a spinach pie. Most food, she said, came from her garden, and the regular diet was vegetables at midday and soup with lettuce salad in the evening. All food was precious. A young woman was seen carrying a small bottle of olive oil, but she stumbled and dropped it. The bottle shattered on the pavement, spilling the oil, and the woman was seen on her knees attempting with desperate cries the impossible task of retrieving it. At other times, commented the witness, spilling the oil would have been unremarkable, but now it was tragic.

Families went out to the countryside near Athens in the search for food, looking for plants, nuts, or anything else that was edible. They also collected another precious commodity, wood, as fuel for cooking and heating. Two brothers, then aged 10 or 11, remember going out with their father every day for three years to the forests of Pentéli to collect wood for sale. Some was taken home by their donkey, some in hand-carts, and one of the boys remembers carrying, he reckoned, half a hundredweight of wood on his back. They also saw Germans collecting wood and seizing wood collected by Greeks.

Young boys, the *saltadhóri*, got hold of food by jumping on grain-carrying trucks and taking what they could. They would grab whole sacks, or slash sacks with penknives while others picked up the spilled contents from the road. German patrols went out to round up gangs of *saltadhóri*, and at first the boys ran away, but later realised that if caught they would be fed twice a day and then sent out of Athens, perhaps to the Peloponnese, where food was more readily available than in Athens and where they hoped that conditions would be better. So they would wait or even ask to be arrested, and their parents would come and support them.

The main source of food quickly became the black market. In effect this was an informal and uncontrolled distribution system. It was also branded as illegal, not only by the occupying powers, which had banned the transfer of goods between zones, but also by the Greek government; as early as 8 May 1941 Tsolákoglou announced the establishment of special courts to try speculators. However, these prohibitions were fairly easily circumvented, sometimes by judicious bribery, sometimes because the occupiers or Greek government officials were themselves operating in the black market. The black marketeers' system was primarily to bring food from abundant to deprived areas and to exchange it not for rapidly depreciating cash but for things of lasting value – jewellery, household possessions or gold, the traditional Greek store of value.

Abundance close to deprivation was evident in all parts of Greece. The Mani town of Yeroliménas was short of food while it was plentiful 20 miles north. The island of Sámos had much better conditions than Chíos, 40 miles away across the Aegean. In 1941–2 the food shortage was the most severe in Athens, and the productive island of Évvia became a source of supply. Every day a cart would leave Kálamos on the mainland opposite Évvia at dawn, laden with black market produce and reach the Athens suburbs early in the morning. In one account there were frequent checks by the Germans, but the cart was not stopped, indicating how widely movement bans were ignored.

Exchanging one's possessions for food, however necessary, was a distressing business. A mother sold her gold rings for 9 pounds of grain. One family was burgled, and soon afterwards a black marketer, who looked like a bank clerk behind his pebble glasses, came to negotiate with the father for the rest of the family possessions. The father tried to bargain but the black marketeer was implacable, and everything was sold, in the father's words, for a biblical mess of pottage. In working-class districts the streets were lined with beds for sale, their owners' last possessions. A rhyme of the time summed up the almost universal experience:

It's in black market that I sell, and there I do my buying,
And whatever I, poor wretch, collect, it goes straight to my kitchen.[6]

By the end of 1941 conditions in Athens were appalling. That winter was unusually severe, as the previous one had been, and from mid-November the cold became intense. The destitute, in search of warmth, slept on the gratings above the Athens metro, and many were dead by morning. The death toll rose, and proper burial became impossible, so the dead were taken in carts to mass graves. One such cart, with blood seeping from the bodies onto the road, passed a crowd of hopeful shoppers in the suburbs, and nobody even turned to look. Deaths were often concealed so that the survivors could keep their ration cards. One witness wrote:

Every day around noon, if you walked from Omónia Square to Síntagma, the centre of the capital of Greece, you had to stop every few paces so as not to trip over those dying of hunger.[7]

Estimates of the total number of deaths in Athens–Piraeus during this period are variable: some too low because deaths were not recorded or deliberately concealed, some too high when used to campaign for relief. There is no doubt that in Athens–Piraeus the death rate massively increased; in the three months from December 1941 it was about six times the level of the year before. For the whole year from late summer 1941 the best estimate for the area is probably over 40,000 deaths in all.[8]

A nightmare picture of famine conditions at the time was given in a report to the International Red Cross. It described men, women and children standing for hours outside bakers' shops hoping to get a few ounces of horrible bread to last them for days. In the streets and at the stations women, old men and children begged in a low voice for a piece of bread. Rubbish was not collected, and you would see children and youths searching through it for food, competing with dogs. The report pointed out that starvation and the bitter cold of December and January took the weak first – the old, the ill, and sickly children. Men with pinched faces and dressed in stinking rags roamed the streets looking for any discarded food. In working-class areas, the report said, you would see barefoot children, skeletal and ashen-faced, sitting in the sun for a little warmth; lice had made them itch, and their skin was bleeding where they scratched it. Even the formerly prosperous now had a pitiful appearance, with a downcast look and shabby clothes, becoming old in a few months.[9]

Reports such as this were smuggled out of the country and fuelled a vigorous campaign, especially in Britain and the United States, for aid to be sent to Greece. Photographs of distress, by Voúla Papioánnou and others, were particularly effective. Relief efforts within Greece were too limited to have any real impact – a food-sharing scheme set up by the Church, or workers' canteens maintained by employers, who sometimes enrolled families as fictional employees so that they too could be fed. The obstacle to sending any international aid to Greece was the Allied blockade of the country.

There was intense debate in the British War Cabinet during 1941 about whether or not to maintain the strict blockade of Greece. Churchill had laid down the blockade policy in a speech to the House of Commons on 20 August 1940, the speech in which he famously paid tribute to the Few of the RAF. In this speech Churchill said in part:

> A matter of general complaint would be if we were to prolong the agony of all Europe by allowing food to come in to nourish the Nazis and their war effort. It is our intention to maintain and enforce a strict blockade not only of Germany but of Italy, France and all the other countries that have fallen into the German power. There have been many proposals, founded on the highest motives, that food should be allowed to pass the blockade for the relief of these populations. I regret that we must refuse these requests.[10]

However, by the summer of 1941, a year after this speech, the effect of the blockade on Greece was becoming clear, and calls for some easing of the blockade both in Britain and in the United States were more insistent. On the Axis side, while the Bulgarians, occupying Greece's largest wheat-growing area, refused to release supplies, the Germans maintained that Italy, holding most of the rest of Greece, should be responsible for feeding the Greek population. The Italians claimed that they did not have enough for their own needs. German propaganda insisted that the blame for Greek food shortages lay with Britain and its blockade.

The debate in Britain's War Cabinet was primarily between the two ministries responsible for blockade policy. Eden, in charge of the Foreign Office, favoured easing the blockade, while Hugh Dalton, minister of economic warfare, sought, in his own words, 'firm and total enforcement'.[11] The first attempt at a compromise solution was to allow 50,000 tons of food imports to Greece from Turkey, Turkey being within the blockade area.

The initial Turkish relief ship was called *Kurtuluş*, appropriately the Turkish for 'Salvation', and its first voyage, prominently displaying the Red Crescent symbol, was made on 13 October 1941. Its arrival in Piraeus was joyfully received as indeed salvation from starvation, and the Turkish crew were so appalled by the conditions they saw that they left their own provisions in Greece and made do with stale bread on the way home. But joy turned to disappointment when it was realised that the supplies carried by the *Kurtuluş*, paid for by the American Greek War Relief Association, were vegetables, not grain; any grain sent would have to have been imported to Turkey and so would have broken the blockade.

The Turkish relief effort met further difficulties. In December 1941 voyages were temporarily stopped because the army maintained that Turkey did not have enough foodstuffs for itself. The *Kurtuluş*, on a resumed voyage in January 1942, struck a rock and sank. A replacement vessel sailed in February, but by May conditions in Turkey had worsened and the bread ration there was actually smaller than that in Athens. The final Turkish relief shipment was on 24 August 1942. In total Turkish aid amounted to 14,031 tons, less than a third of the 50,000 tons originally envisaged, and at great expense; the Greek War Relief Association had paid out $1.4 million. The quantity of foodstuffs brought to Greece by Turkey was relatively small, an average of some 1,400 tons a month, less than a tenth of the amounts later provided by international efforts. But the main problem was that the Turkish shipments did not contain what was most needed: grain.

It was Britain which had imposed the blockade, and Churchill had explicitly committed the country to it. However, Britain could not ignore the demands to allow relief for Greece that were now coming from within the War Cabinet, from Parliament, from British public opinion, and not least from public opinion in the United States. A way had to be found to get food into Greece through the blockade without, at least nominally, lifting it.

The solution emerged from initiatives by the International Red Cross in Geneva and by the neutral Swedish government. In autumn 1941 Marcel Junod, a Swiss doctor working for the Red Cross, was in Athens and brought back to Geneva a horrifying account of conditions there, supported by a folder of photographs. At about the same time

Gunnar Cederschöld, a Swedish journalist and businessman, visited Athens and found conditions deteriorating even before the terrible winter of 1941–2. He published his report in a Stockholm paper:

> Never have I seen anything that shocked me as much as what I saw in Athens during the summer months of 1941. Everywhere I saw starving children. One orphanage had 1,200 children. Those that were still able to screamed continuously with hunger. The rest were apathetic, unable to utter a word.[12]

Cederschöld contacted the Swedish Red Cross and the government, proposing that Swedish ships should be used to take supplies to Greece, and wrote to the British government pressing his idea.

Lengthy discussions followed, involving Allied, Axis and neutral countries, on how this would work. A committee would have to be set up to organise distribution in Greece. Britain insisted that the committee should be Swedish as it distrusted the International Red Cross, believing that this body would leave everything to the Germans and staff the committee, as one British official wrote, with only a man and a boy. It was eventually agreed that the Joint Relief Commission, the JRC, should be headed by a Swedish chairman, with four other Swedes and four Swiss as members.

The Germans and Italians agreed that any local produce used by their troops would be replaced with food of equal calorific value, a commitment which they more than fulfilled. Three-quarters of the relief supplies was Canadian grain, paid for principally by the Canadian government and the American Greek War Relief Association. The Germans undertook not to attack the Swedish ships carrying it.

There were practical problems to be solved. The grain had to be milled into flour on arrival, and in Piraeus more mills had to be found than those at the harbour. All trucks carrying relief supplies needed an armed guard against the depredations of the *saltadhóri*. Ships returning empty needed ballast to survive the rough waters of the Atlantic, and the only solution was for them to carry ballast on the outward voyage too, reducing the space for supplies. In September 1942 the first Swedish ships arrived, and between then and March 1944, when the United Nations Relief and Rehabilitation Administration (UNRRA) took over, supplied 623,000 tons of food, an average of 20,000 tons a month. Athens was the main beneficiary, and at soup kitchens supplied by the JRC nearly a million people were registered by September 1942, a third of them children. To achieve this the JRC in Athens employed around 2,000 administrators and 2,900 workers and drivers.

Swedish ships also took supplies directly to Crete, Corfu, Sámos, Chíos and Lésvos. JRC delegates were stationed there and in the main towns of the mainland, and a separate section of the JRC dealt with relief to the provinces. Perhaps inevitably the allocations in the countryside and the islands were somewhat irregular and haphazard. A Swedish delegate commented that 'provisions go to whoever shouts loudest rather than whoever needs them most.'[13] By March 1944, in the last months of the occupation, 3 million Greeks, nearly half the population, were receiving regular food rations from the JRC.

There were some surprising aspects of this great humanitarian effort. Relations between the Swedish and Swiss members of the JRC were marked not by the harmony of shared philanthropy but by bitter dissension. The Swedish members considered themselves answerable only to the Swedish government, leaving the International Red Cross and the Swiss marginalised and powerless. The Swiss responded that, while they themselves were professionals in the aid business, the Swedes were amateurs, lacking the necessary discretion and tact. As late as June 1944 the Swiss were warning of a possible scandal because of the failings of their Swedish colleagues.

Another perhaps surprising aspect of the JRC story was the behaviour of the Germans and Italians. They stuck to the agreements that they would not take any of the relief supplies for themselves and that any Greek produce they used would be replaced by food of equal calorific value. In the event they brought in more than they consumed, and in the last two years of the occupation imported 20,000 tons of grain and 90,000 tons of dried vegetables, sugar and potatoes. JRC reports repeatedly stressed the co-operativeness, particularly of German commanders, who came down hard on any of their troops interfering with relief operations.

The aims of the blockade had been to prevent the occupying powers using relief supplies for their own forces and to lay on them the responsibility for feeding the people of the occupied country. The agreements attached to the relief effort for Greece ensured that all supplies went to the Greek people, and that the occupiers made at least a contribution to feeding them. Thus the easing of the blockade, as well as saving Greece from starvation, turned out to be much more effective in achieving its objectives than strict enforcement had been.

7

The Emergence of
the Communists

The term 'wartime resistance' has a noble ring to it, of dedicated opposition to foreign invasion, occupation and brutality. It is also seen as heroic: the civilian, often ill-trained and poorly armed, faces the might of a regular army. But resistance has a wider significance. The more successful it is, the more it shapes or even controls the country once the war is over. When in July 1940 Churchill established the Special Operations Executive (SOE) to promote resistance in occupied Europe, he said its task was to 'set Europe ablaze'. As the war progressed, the question increasingly became: what will arise from the ashes?

In Greece it was the resistance led by the Greek Communist Party which was first in the field, Communists who increasingly dominated resistance activity, and Communists who formed one side of the conflict over the shape of postwar Greece. To see how the Communist Party of Greece, the KKE, reached this powerful position, we need to go back to its origins.

The period from 1918 to 1941 can be seen as the first phase in the development of the KKE, a period marked by constant shifts in Greek politics and in the KKE itself. In November 1918 the first nationwide meeting of Greek Socialists was held in an Athens hotel and established the Socialist Party of Greece, the Sosialistikón Kómma Elládhos, known as the SKE. Its programme could have been supported by any Fabian idealist: freedom of assembly and of the press, assurance of personal liberty, an eight-hour working day and no curbs on the right to strike. In 1920 the SKE joined the Communist International, the Comintern, and its language became less specific but more aggressive; the main aim was now 'the final overthrow of the bourgeoisie by all possible means'.[1] In 1924 the socialist SKE formally changed its name to the Communist Party of Greece, the KKE, and elected a new Central Committee. Eight former members of the Central Committee were blamed for the party's poor showing in the previous year's elections and were expelled as opportunist or extremist. The chilling justification was that 'the knife of the Central Committee has begun to cut off the rotten parts of the body.'[2] This set the pattern; after every setback the party found scapegoats to denounce.

From January to August 1926, under the short-lived dictatorship of General Theódhoros Pángalos, the KKE was banned and leading members were briefly imprisoned. But in the parliamentary election a few months later in November 1926 the party, campaigning as the United Front, had its best result so far: 41,982 votes or over 4 per cent of the vote, and ten members elected. Votes had been translated into seats because for the first time the election had been held under the proportional system, not first past the post which disadvantaged parties with widely dispersed support.

These ten Communist members were in a surprisingly strong position, since the two main parties had 143 and 127 seats, so the ten Communists plus six independents held the balance. However, nine of the ten were moderates, and the hardliners of the Central Committee set out to subvert them. The method was to link the ten to the unpopular, and in many eyes treasonous, Communist policy of independence for Macedonia and Thrace, a policy which for tactical reasons had been kept out of their election campaign. The ten were then charged by the government with undermining the constitution and their parliamentary immunity was removed, though none was prosecuted. Internal KKE rifts had thrown away the chance of parliamentary influence.

Over the next five years the KKE continued to tear itself apart and its influence in the country sank. In the election of August 1928, now under the majority system, the party received only a third of its 1926 vote, and won no seats. In December 1928 seven former members of the Central Committee, including three of the members of parliament elected in 1926, were expelled from the party as Trotskyites. The government increased the party's difficulties when in June 1929 it passed a law making agitation against the social order a criminal offence. In August that year the party's call for a general strike was almost completely ignored, and a demonstration in the summer of 1931 attracted only 150 people. Party membership was under 2,000.

Thus the KKE began the 1930s bankrupt and politically isolated. As the party itself conceded, it was 'estranged from the masses, beaten and broken by the criminal factionalist struggle'.[3]

The fortunes of the KKE began to change when in 1931 the Comintern appointed a new KKE leader, Níkos Zachariádhis. Born in 1902 at Izmit in Turkey, he spent three years of his early twenties at the KUTV, the Russian school for training in Communist theory and tactics. In 1926 he came to Greece, became a leading member of the Salonika Communists, and was imprisoned for agitating for a separate Macedonian state. On release he spent three more years in Russia until his return to Greece and appointment in 1931 to lead the KKE. He was an extreme hardliner, and wrote:

> The members of the KKE and even more so the party officials belong totally and exclusively to the Party. This means that (a) the interest of the Party is the primary and highest consideration; (b) our personal life is organized in such a way that the Party and its struggle will benefit most. And (c) every action or word must be weighed in the scales of party interest.[4]

Zachariádhis instituted two major changes in the KKE, one in policy and the other in organisation. The policy change was to concentrate on appealing to the everyday concerns of the workers, to talk to them 'about bread, about wages, about their problems',[5] problems intensified by the widespread unemployment and economic disruption following the Wall Street crash of 1929.

The organisational change was the revival and rejuvenation of the system of Communist cells. This had been formally adopted as far back as 1924, but had been largely ineffectual. A Communist cell was a small group of no more than five people, who had no knowledge of other cells and no contact with the Communist Party except through one of its members, the secretary. In 1932 the need for secrecy was made even more explicit: 'The cell is above all illegal, that is, it exists and operates underground,' and a member must not appear as a party member but as an 'ordinary factory worker.'[6] Crucially, the cell system was to be run by special teams of propagandists and agitators, to be paid from the annual contribution of the Comintern to the KKE. The effects of these changes in policy and organisation showed in the growing support for the party at elections. In 1928 it had under 15,000 votes, but in the elections of 1932 and 1933 over 50,000 and in 1935 nearly 100,000. But 1935 and 1936 brought a radical shift in Greek politics and the fortunes of the KKE.

In November 1935 King George II, after 12 years in exile, was reinstated by a plebiscite that was overwhelmingly favourable but widely regarded as rigged. The King now had the constitutional power to form a government. In January 1936 a new election was called, only seven months after the previous one, and once again under the proportional system. This gave the Communists 15 seats, so that they held the balance between the royalists (143 seats) and their pro-Venizélos opponents (141 seats). The King tried to reconcile the two major parties and avoid a government controlled by the minority Communists, and in March 1936 the two major parties agreed to a non-political government – that is, one not composed of parliamentary deputies. In this government the prime minister was Konstantínos Dhemertzís, and his deputy the more dynamic Ioánnis Metaxás.

These manoeuvres totally failed to resolve the political crisis. On 9 May 1936 there was a massive strike in Salonika, initiated by the tobacco workers and joined by textile workers and other unions. At 11 a.m. the police, in danger of being overwhelmed by the crowd, fired into the demonstrators, killing or fatally injuring 12 people and seriously wounding over 30 others. The KKE declared that 'only a universal revolt, on the lines of Salonika, can impose the united and sovereign will of the People,'[7] and the riots were seen by its opponents as a dress rehearsal for a Communist seizure of power.

A month earlier, on 13 April 1936, Prime Minister Dhemertzís had died and the King had appointed his deputy Metaxás in his place. At the end of that month Metaxás received an overwhelming parliamentary vote of confidence in his government – 241 members out of 261 in favour. Parliament was adjourned, ostensibly until September, but in fact it did not meet again until after the war. In response the Communists called for a general strike on 5 August, but on the day before the strike Metaxás, with the King's approval, was granted emergency powers, enabling him to use the army to quell civil disturbances. In his battle with the Communists Metaxás had got his retaliation in first, and the Salonika strike was quickly ended. The Metaxás regime of 4 August 1936 was now established.

The Metaxás period is commonly labelled a dictatorship or even a tyranny, but a better description is authoritarian paternalism.[8] Metaxás realised, exactly as the Communists had done, that the main threat to any regime was the discontent of ordinary people.

The Communists set out to exploit this, Metaxás to alleviate it. Thus he began a major series of public works, declared a moratorium on countryside debt, and for industrial workers guaranteed a five-day working week with set wage rates and hours. The price for these measures was the curtailment of civil liberties, the outlawing of strikes, and government control of the press. As with other dictatorial regimes, freedom was sacrificed for efficiency, but unlike other such regimes this one had no rigid ideology or racist dogma and has been described as 'one of the mildest regimes of its kind'.[9]

The Communists would not have thought so. Metaxás' minister of public security, Konstantínos Maniadhákis, immediately moved against them, arresting and imprisoning Zachariádhis in September 1936 and virtually all the other party leaders soon afterwards. Maniadhákis then proceeded to undermine the Communist movement by two techniques: the system of 'declarations of repentance', and the infiltration of the party by police agents.

A declaration of repentance (dhilosí) secured the release of anyone arrested on suspicion of Communist activity. For those, men or women, who admitted to being a Communist the declaration was a signed statement containing a chronological account of their Communist activities, with the names of those who initiated them in Communist ideology, an account of all party meetings they had attended, the position they occupied in the party hierarchy, and any of their non-party activities.[10] For those denying they were Communists, the statement read, 'I have never been a Communist, nevertheless I denounce Communism and I recognise Metaxás as a great Premier of the Greek Kingdom.'[11] But Maniadhákis soon banned this second version as idiotic, a transparent way of forcing people to declare allegiance to Metaxás. The declarations caused the KKE great difficulty: should those who had signed be allowed back into the party? Some said none should return, others that only those considered to have signed in a moment of cowardice could be forgiven. Maniadhákis had achieved his aim of shattering the party's trust in individuals and breaking up its internal cohesion.

Maniadhákis' other tactic was to develop the practice, already in use for some years, of infiltrating police agents into the party. Working through local party organisations, which were by now established from Salonika to Crete and from Ioánnina to the Aegean islands, he contrived his own Central Committee, known as the Temporary Administration. At the same time there was a rival group, aiming to represent the committee elected in December 1935, and known as the Old Central Committee. Each committee published its own version of the party newspaper *Rizospástis* – with, of course, conflicting messages. Maniadhákis had in effect created his own Communist Party.

In 1939, as the threat of an Axis attack on Greece became more apparent, the confusion created by these conflicting messages increased, and was intensified by statements from Zachariádhis, still in prison, and by the future party leader Georgios Siántos, briefly out of prison between 1937 and 1939. The disagreement was over what the party's prime enemy now was: a foreign invader or the Metaxás regime. Thus one statement proclaimed that 'the primary enemy of our independence and territorial integrity is Monarcho-Fascism' – that is, the King and Metaxás – while according to Siántos a Comintern directive laid down that 'the first duty of the KKE is to defend the independence of the country. Since the Metaxás government is fighting against the same danger, there is no reason for you to pursue its overthrow.'[12] Zachariádhis appeared to back this second version in a published letter: 'In this war, directed by the Metaxás government, we shall all give every ounce of our strength without reserve.' However, this letter was denounced as a forgery by the non-Maniadhákis Old Central Committee, which instead declared that 'the war was provoked by the King–Metaxás gang on orders from the English imperialists'.[13] Only those with total commitment to the KKE party line, whatever it was and however often it changed, could remain loyal in this chaos of instructions.

By the end of the 1930s the KKE was not only attacked and infiltrated by the government and racked by internal dissensions. It was also lacking widespread popular support because of two unfortunate pieces of baggage it was carrying. One was its subservience to the Comintern; those aware of this would obviously not support a Greek political party ultimately answerable to the Soviet Union. The other hampering piece of baggage was KKE support for an independent Macedonia and Thrace – that is, their detachment from northern Greece.

The question of independence for these regions had been bloodily troublesome for many years. Since the 1880s there had been violent conflict between Greek nationalist groups and independence groups, of which the International Macedonian Revolutionary Organisation (IMRO) was the most prominent. Independence for Macedonia and Thrace was one of the main issues of the Balkan Wars of 1912–13 from which Greece emerged victorious, securing both regions as part of Greece. But the independence question was not dead, and at a KKE congress in 1924 there was a unanimous vote in favour of independence for Macedonia and Thrace as a matter of principle on which there could be no disagreement. The policy's justification had nothing to do with minority rights; it was urged on flimsy grounds as an anti-imperialist move:

> The new imperialist war is approaching the Balkan peninsula with gigantic steps. As long as the present dismemberment and oppression of Macedonia and Thrace continues, we cannot avoid imperialist wars [...] That is why we fight for the unification of the three sections of Macedonia and Thrace [that is, an end to their division between Greece, Yugoslavia and Bulgaria] and for their becoming independent.[14]

The issue was recognised as an electoral liability and was as far as possible removed from the party programme. It was not mentioned in the 1926 election and in 1935 was replaced by an emollient call for complete equality for minorities. The Macedonian question is alive to this day, and underlies the Greek belligerent insistence, bizarre to outsiders, that the former Yugoslav republic of Macedonia is called just that, FYROM, not Macedonia, which could imply possible future rule of Greek Macedonia from Skopje.

As well as the Communists' specific difficulties – unpopular policies, Soviet influence, government oppression, internal disputes – they suffered the drawback of being in so many ways wholly alien to the Greek spirit. In the view of Chris Woodhouse, who had seen Communism at first hand,

> [Communists] are required to be everything that a Greek is not. A Greek is patriotic, religious, emotional, loyal to his friends, hot-blooded but quick to forget a quarrel; he is loaded with *philótimo*, for which 'self-respect' is a feeble translation; however poor, he has a strong sense of private property; and he is passionately devoted to democracy. And of all the nonsense in Communist dogmatism, perhaps none seemed more ludicrous to the ordinary Greek than the notion that the Party is always, by definition, infallibly right. When a Greek disagrees with his political party, he leaves it, or breaks it up and forms a new one. When a Communist does so, he invites the Party to destroy him.[15]

How then did the KKE survive at all, let alone become a major factor in wartime and postwar Greece?

One part of the answer is that there were many ways in which the KKE did appeal to Greeks. It was the only party which consistently attacked the government, which was seen as corrupt, dominated by self-seeking politicians and the rich, and indifferent to the welfare of the people as a whole. It offered new political ideas, attractive to intellectuals and to the young. As one student wrote:

> The charm of Marxism affected us all, not just those who were accepted or recruited into left-wing parties. We all willingly succumbed to the intellectual excitement aroused by philosophical and sociological analyses, such as those of Marx and Engels, or tough and belligerent propositions such as those of Lenin. Youngsters in the final classes of secondary school or the first year of university learnt suddenly that the world of ideas was not so monotonous, sterile, dry, and boring as made to appear by slogans or proclamations.[16]

Girls as well as young men were drawn to the left-wing programme of the Communists. One girl, a teenager during the occupation, later wrote: 'Of course we (me and my friends) were in support of the poor people, and those wronged by society, and we wanted a kind of social justice to reign [...] that people should not be oppressed by people with more power.'[17] By the end of the civil war which followed the occupation, about a quarter of the Communist army was made up of women or girls.

Moreover the party offered some sort of rule by the people, though it was not clear what form this would take. The full-blown Soviet model would hardly be attractive. In a 1942 document in which the Communists set out their postwar aims, the call was for freedom of speech, of the press and of assembly, a new constitution which 'will enshrine the people's will', and a general amnesty. It all sounded good. The sting in the tail was that 'a government will be constituted from the leadership of the entire people's national liberation struggle.'[18] That would mean, of course, a government by Communists irrespective of the will of the people. It was implied though not specifically stated that this government would be provisional, but in the event how temporary would it have been? As the French say, 'Rien ne dure comme le provisoire.' Nevertheless the declaration's high-sounding democratic principles were enough to satisfy many, at least for the moment.

Further strengths of the Communists lay in their organisation. Greek political parties were by and large clientelist, that is they were centred on an individual leader, and his followers expected favours from him in return for their support. By contrast the Communists had a structure, an ideology and a programme, however vague in parts. Also they had forceful leaders. As Chris Woodhouse conceded, Zachariádhis, Siántos and their colleagues 'were not negligible men'.[19] Perhaps the Communists' most important advantage was that, after years of being suspect, hounded by the government or banned, they knew very well how to operate as an illegal clandestine underground organisation – exactly what was needed in a country under foreign occupation.

This was the Communists' troubled past and potential for the future when Germany invaded in April 1941.

8

Early Resistance

The mountain *andártes* are seen as the reincarnation of the heroic Greek fighters of the War of Independence, a link which they themselves often invoked. Many of their leaders were colourful figures. They claimed to be fighting not only against the foreign occupiers but also for social justice. And, of course, they had a far-reaching effect on the shape of postwar Greece.

However, for Greeks in the towns, urban resistance to the occupation was just as important. Some of it was organised by Communist organisations, some by small groups on their own initiative. The dangers were in many ways greater than in the mountains: the risks of being caught by the ever-present occupation troops or of informers from among their own countrymen betraying them. Urban resistance produced some dramatic results.

Most urban anti-Axis activity ceased in the harsh winter of 1941–2, especially in starving Athens, but some of the resistance techniques of 1941 were continued or developed. Two underground newspapers, *Néa Zoí* (*New Life*) and *Dhimokratikí Siméa* (*Democratic Standard*) were produced daily for evening distribution. One young man recalled taking them round by bicycle, with his brother sitting behind him, the safest place for distribution being near a German brothel where any German troops had other things in mind. The writing of graffiti was now promoted and organised by the Communist youth movement, who used green paint while the main Communist Party used red. One way of writing unobtrusively was for a young man and a girl to stand by a wall, apparently in a loving embrace, while the girl held the paint pot behind her with her free hand and the young man used the brush with his.

Much of the urban resistance was a good deal more serious. Clandestine bomb attacks, now associated with terrorism, were then a matter of patriotism. In early 1942 such an attack was planned on the German airfield at Elévsis, about 10 miles west of Athens, and the plot was masterminded by Aléxandhros Zánnas. Zánnas had a remarkable career. He was born in 1892 and in 1916 as a young air force officer he was appointed as head of a committee of inquiry into the conduct of a general. In the disastrous Asia Minor campaign of 1919–22 he commanded a fighter squadron, and after the defeat took part in a coup against the royalist government and was briefly exiled. In 1930 he became minister of aviation under Venizélos. In 1941 he was chairman of the committee responsible under the International Red Cross for the distribution of relief food supplies.

The Elévsis airfield plot began when two young men approached Zánnas and asked him whether they should take jobs at the airfield. Zánnas encouraged them and told them what information about German operations he needed, which he could then pass on to the British in Egypt. One of the young men, Níkos Nikolaídhis, had lived in Germany and spoke German, and Zánnas described him as sharp as a needle. Nikolaídhis got a job in the airfield's command office and the other, Stávros Margarítis, worked in the officers' mess.

After three weeks the pair came back to Zánnas with a plan to plant bombs in officers' briefcases on planes. Zánnas managed to buy four Russian bombs from what he called 'a Communist organisation' and paid the substantial sum of 280,000 drachmas. Two planes were the targets. One was destroyed on the ground. On the other the fuse for a more powerful bomb was set for half an hour after the planned take-off, but the plane was delayed and the bomb exploded while it was still on the ground, causing massive damage – according to Zánnas, 87 planes destroyed, 93 men killed and 150 injured. Zánnas sent the two young men away to Egypt via Smyrna, with $1,000 each and suitable introductions. Zánnas was arrested and sentenced to 18 years in prison, but was allowed on health grounds to serve it under surveillance in a hospital in Italy. Planning, daring, the right contacts, a great deal of money and a bit of luck had achieved what was so far the biggest act of sabotage in Greece.

Some six months later, in September 1942, there was another major bomb attack on the occupation forces, this time in the centre of Athens. The target was only 100 yards from Omónia Square, a building where the upper floors housed the headquarters of a body with the bland name of the Ethnic Socialist Patriotic Organisation (ESPO). In fact it was run by the Germans to recruit Greeks to serve on the Eastern Front or to work in German factories – women as well as men. Across the whole of the front of the building was a banner reading 'Greek girls, join the pioneers of the New Order', a slogan more effective as provocation than as recruitment.

The leader of the group planning to blow up the building was Kóstas Perríkos, like Zánnas a former air force officer, and the rest of the group was made up of two technicians, four students and two young women. In June large quantities of explosives were stolen from the German army, reportedly over 2 hundredweight of dynamite, 300 detonators and 100 yards of fuse wire. The time chosen for the attack was late Sunday morning, for two reasons. On a Sunday the Greek shops and offices on the ground floor of the building would be empty, so the innocent would not be harmed. Also the weekly meeting of ESPO officials ended at about 11 a.m. on Sunday, so after that security would be minimal. The date was to be Sunday 29 September 1942.

That morning one of the young women, Julia Bíba, carried from her house a 28 lb bomb in a bag covered with vegetables and handed it to two of the group, a technician and a student, while the rest kept watch outside with revolvers hidden under their coats. The bomb was carried up to the first floor and placed outside the main office, the fuse set for six minutes delay. Shortly before noon the bomb exploded.

The building was wrecked, and among those killed were 43 German civilians and soldiers, including the head of ESPO, while 55 German soldiers and 27 Greek informers were wounded. ESPO never recovered and not long afterwards the programme to recruit Greek workers was abandoned.

The bombers initially got away but were later caught, betrayed by informers who were paid either two or three gold sovereigns per denunciation. It was a tempting reward – a gold sovereign would feed a family in the country for a month. One of the group, the technician who had planted the bomb, managed to escape although in chains, and went on to other sabotage. Julia Bíba, who had carried the bomb, was executed in Germany, reportedly beheaded with an axe. The leader Perríkos was killed by firing squad in the following February. On the day of his execution he wrote a moving letter to his children:

For you that remain, work for the ending of wars and the uniting of all mankind. I leave the world without hatred and without malice. Those who condemned me are also fighting for their own country. Let the shedding of my blood help to reconcile us with the enemies of today.[1]

As in the towns, the early acts of resistance in the countryside were by small groups on their own initiative. The first recorded guerrilla action was in July 1941 near Kozáni in mountainous northern Greece, when a group of demobilised Greek soldiers fired on German troops and two villages were burnt down in reprisal. In July a band of 120 guerrillas attacked and looted a Greek police post at Nigríta, 50 miles east of Salonika; in reprisals for supporting this band two villages were destroyed and 202 men executed. German sources show that in the month of October 1941 a total of 488 hostages were executed and another 164 arrested for supporting guerrillas.

In the summer of 1941, only a few months after the occupation began, a revitalised Communist Party began moves to organise resistance. The Communists had somewhat paradoxically benefited from the German invasion. Many of their imprisoned leaders were released from jail in Athens on German orders, as political prisoners of a defeated regime, others escaped in the general confusion, and those in exile were able to return. Zachariádhis, the pre-war leader, was not so fortunate, remaining in Greek jails until 1942, when the Germans transferred him to Dachau, from which he was eventually released in 1945. His absence left the way open for a new leader, Georgios Siántos. Siántos had been imprisoned in 1939 for Communist activity but had escaped in 1941 and was now living freely in Greece. He became in effect the party leader in November 1941, a position formally confirmed two months later and which he held throughout the war.

The Communists' first step was the establishment in late September 1941 of EAM, the National Liberation Front. Three other small political groups joined, but it was dominated by the Communists. Its main function was to foster strikes and demonstrations in the towns, and its first success in April 1942 was a massive strike – the first in occupied Europe – by communication workers, initially in Athens and within days in Salonika as well. The strike was ostensibly against the collaborationist government for higher wages, and workers for the Germans and Italians were not called out. So the occupation authorities regarded the action as simply economic and not, as later strikes and demonstrations obviously were, directed against them.

The military arm of EAM soon followed. In the winter months after EAM's foundation in September 1941, Communist agents were sent into central Greece to investigate the possibilities of guerrilla warfare, and on 10 April 1942 guerrilla bands were officially approved. This was the beginning of ELAS, the National Popular Liberation Army, and the first time that the word Army (*Strátos*) had appeared in the title of a Communist organisation. In May the first ELAS band, of only 15 members, was formed by Áris Velouchiótis.

Áris Velouchiótis was the *nom de guerre* of Thanásis Kláras. He had become a communist in the 1920s and was imprisoned by the Metaxás regime, being released in 1939 after signing a 'declaration of repentance', possibly on instructions from the KKE. He was well educated, and could impress village audiences with quietly spoken but forceful speeches, outlining Greece's successive descents into slavery under the Turks, the monarchy and Metaxás, and proclaiming that 'Our sole object is to help the people to live better.'[2] He combined a silver tongue with a streak of violent sadism, as his later treatment of opponents showed.

The other main guerrilla group was EDES, the National Democratic Greek League, and was led by the flamboyant Napoleon Zérvas. EDES was strongly Venizelist and anti-monarchy, as 'Democratic' in its title signified. Its manifesto denounced King George as a traitor, and its nominal head was the absent General Nikólaos Plastíras, a distinguished and popular soldier who had led pro-Venizélos coups – successfully in 1922 and unsuccessfully in 1933 and 1935 – and was now living in exile in France. Zérvas later readily changed his anti-monarchy stance to accommodate the views of the British.

Zérvas, like his nominal leader Plastíras, was an army officer, and like him had been involved in several coup attempts until he was imprisoned by Metaxás, being released in 1941. He was reluctant to leave Athens for the mountains, and did so only when he was threatened by SOE contacts with exposure to the Germans. Once there he adopted a highly personal style, reminiscent of War of Independence heroes; his slogan was 'Faith in the leader. All for the leader. All from the leader.'[3]

Thus after a year and a half of occupation resistance in the mountains consisted of relatively small groups independent of each other, under different leaders and with different philosophies. That was to change with the arrival in autumn 1942 of a handful of British agents parachuted directly into the mountains.

9

SOE, the Andártes and Gorgopótamos

The Special Operations Executive, SOE, had been established in 1940 with the broad objective, as Churchill put it, of setting Europe ablaze. Its active agents were recruited from the armed services and were soldiers not spies, but civilians in the occupied countries provided them with often vital information. In September 1942 in Cairo a small group of such active agents was formed to parachute into Greece to join and if possible organise the resistance. It was led by Eddie Myers, a Royal Engineer brigadier in his thirties, described as quiet and methodical. His second in command was Chris Woodhouse, still only 25, a classics scholar who had learnt Modern Greek, had taken part in the battle for Crete and had stayed on there during the winter of 1941–2 helping stranded Allied troops and gathering information. Myers and Woodhouse picked ten others to go with them: three sappers, three captains in the commandos, three wireless operator sergeants and Themistoklís Marínos, a young Greek army lieutenant whom Woodhouse had met before and respected. Only four of the 12 – Woodhouse, Marínos and two of the commandos – spoke Greek. The rest, including Myers, did not.

The group was under the command of SOE in Cairo, and SOE's operational instructions were clear: Myers and his men were to disrupt German supplies from northern Europe through Greece to Africa by blowing up one of the three railway viaducts, about 10 miles south of Lamía. These viaducts were the Asopós, the Papádhia, and – the largest – the Gorgopótamos.

However, the briefing on which Greek resistance leaders they would meet was a good deal less clear or helpful. They were given three names. One was Zérvas of EDES, the second was a Greek who in fact commanded no forces at all, and the third was Karalívanos, who turned out not to be a resistance leader but simply an uncooperative bandit. Áris Velouchiótis and ELAS were not mentioned, and until their arrival in Greece neither Myers nor Woodhouse had ever heard of them.

Only Myers had parachuted before, and that was in training years ago, so the rest had to learn in a hurry. Time was pressing because drops could be made only when the moon was full, as it would be for the next few days and then not for another three weeks. There was time for only one practice night jump, in which Woodhouse damaged his back but managed to conceal it for fear of missing the operation.

These 12 men, sketchily briefed, few of them speaking Greek, and beginners as parachutists let alone parachuting at night carrying weapons and equipment, were made ready to drop into Greece and fulfil in one part of Europe Churchill's huge ambition for SOE. Three Liberators took off from the Cairo airfield after dark on the evening of 28 September 1942. Each carried four of the party, one of whom was a wireless operator. Myers was leader of one group, Woodhouse of a second, and John Cook, one of the commando captains, led the third. They had been told, via the Greek agent of SOE in Athens, that fires in the shape of a cross would mark the drop zones, and were ordered not to jump unless they could see them. On the first flight over Greece no fires were spotted, and all three planes returned to Cairo. On a second attempt two nights later Cook's plane again found no fires and returned, waiting three weeks for a full moon and a successful drop at the end of October. However, both Myers and Woodhouse saw a group of three fires more or less in the right area and decided to make the jump. Both groups came down in the mountainous area near Ámphissa, but about 15 miles apart.

Woodhouse landed perfectly – 'It was no harder than stepping off a table,' he wrote.[1] Myers was less fortunate, carried by the wind into the branches of a tall mountain fir which entangled his parachute, and on releasing the harness he rolled out of control down a slope into a second tree. But there was no one to greet him and all was quiet. 'I realised', he wrote, 'that for the moment anyhow I was alone in the mountains of Greece.'[2]

During the first few days Myers was found by the other three of his group, and on a plateau above a village they endured persistent rain under a bivouac of branches and parachute material. Fifteen miles away Woodhouse's group were luckier and had been shown a low narrow cave just below a mountain peak, where after a week they were joined by Myers and his group. They were given food by villagers who were ready to help but fearful of detection by the Italian troops.

Outstanding among the helpful villagers was Nikólaos Béis, known as Barba Niko. In his mid-fifties – hence 'Barba' or 'Uncle' – he had lived in the United States and spoke a fractured but intelligible American. Barba Niko led the whole party to a much better cave above the village of Strómi, described as palatial, where he brought food from the village below, prepared it – he was a butcher by trade – and cooked it. When asked why he took so much trouble for them, he replied, 'I heard that God had sent us Englishmen from heaven, so it was my duty to keep them.'[3] Myers and Woodhouse both said that they would not have survived without him.

The next task of Myers' party was to find the Greek resistance leaders and their andártes. Karalívanos had proved useless. There was talk in the villages about Áris and ELAS, but no one knew where Áris was. The only firm lead was to Zérvas and EDES. One of SOE's Greek informants in Athens, known as Prometheus, sent a message by runner that Zérvas was 80 miles to the north-west, between Agrínion and Árta, and named the village where he would meet them. So on 2 November Myers sent Woodhouse, with Barba Niko as guide, to find Zérvas. He was told to return with Zérvas' forces by 17 November so that the chosen viaduct could be attacked during the next full moon.

To walk 10 miles a day – 80 miles there and back in 16 days – may seem straightforward, but in the Greek mountains it was punishing. On the third day Woodhouse sent Barba Niko back to the cave at Strómi, partly to save him from further exhaustion and partly so as not to slow his own progress. On 10 November Woodhouse met Zérvas and was warmly greeted with 'Welcome to the Angel of Good Tidings.'[4] They set out for Strómi to be joined by the EDES andártes two days later, and after a further two days were joined by Áris and ELAS troops. Woodhouse now learnt what had happened to John Cook's party in the third plane. They had finally been dropped on the last night of October near Karpenísi into the outskirts of an Italian garrison town, had evaded the small-arms and mortar fire which greeted them, had been sheltered by Áris' forces and were now on the way to the Strómi cave.

By 17 November, the last day before the deadline for return, Woodhouse, Zérvas and Áris, with 60 andártes from EDES and 90 from ELAS, were close to Strómi. Woodhouse pressed ahead, arriving

15 minutes late at a quarter past midnight. But Woodhouse, in a twist reminiscent of Phileas Fogg's miscalculated 80 days, pointed out that, though 15 minutes late by Greek time, by British time he was 45 minutes early.

Myers now met for the first time Zérvas and Áris, whose co-operation with him and with each other would be vital. Of Zérvas he wrote:

> Zérvas had a short and rotund figure. When he laughed, as he so often did, his whole body vibrated and the merry sparkle in his eyes belied the black, hairy fierceness of a heavily bearded face. The moment he stopped smiling, his large brown eyes immediately gave his round face and full, generous mouth a serious, yet understanding expression. An unpolished 'Sam-Browne' belt around his ample waist supported a small automatic pistol and a jewelled dagger whose sheath was liable to stick out from his stomach at a jaunty angle when he sat down. I was immediately struck by his outstanding personality.[5]

This was more generous than the Foreign Office opinion of Zérvas, which was pithier: 'Zérvas was a rogue in his youth and remained a rogue in his old age but a most charming rogue.'[6] Áris, however, made a different impression on Myers:

> He was a small man of a wiry build. His long black beard, which balanced his Cossack cap of black fur, could make his face look benign and almost monk-like. But his eyes were deep-set and, except when he smiled, there was much hardness in his features. Only when mellowed by alcohol did he ever relax. Silent and inclined to be dour, he always gave me the impression of being on guard against someone or something.[7]

It is clear that from the start Myers was not comfortable with Áris.

Before Woodhouse left for his trek, Myers had reconnoitred the three viaducts and decided that Gorgopótamos, the least well guarded, was the one to attack. The original 12 of SOE had now been reunited, their equipment and in particular the plastic explosives had been largely recovered, and they had been joined by enough Greek fighters to deal with the viaduct's Italian guards. The whole party with their equipment had moved from the cave at Strómi to far more comfortable cottages in the village of Mavrolithári a few miles away, where Zérvas had already established himself. Áris, Zérvas and their andártes were still untried but otherwise everything was ready for the operation.

The attack on the Gorgopótamos viaduct was planned for 11 p.m. on the night of 25 November 1942, when there would be an almost full moon. The viaduct, about 7 miles south of Lamía, carried the north–south railway line across the deep gorge in which the Gorgopótamos river, now in full spate, flowed roughly from west to east, 100 feet below. The viaduct was 674 feet long, and its two spans were supported by four stone and two steel piers. The more vulnerable steel piers were the targets. The four girders of each pier were thought to be L-shaped and the plastic explosives, rather like fudge, were moulded accordingly – but, as it turned out, mistakenly.

The attacking force was divided into six groups: four of SOE and two of andártes under Zervás and Áris. Áris had agreed to take part, on his own initiative and against orders from Athens, to prevent Zervás getting all the credit. Two groups were to attack the Italian guards at the north and south ends of the viaduct, and another two were to blow up the railway line to the north and the south and cut the telephone wires beside it to delay any Italian reinforcements. One group led by Tom Barnes was to carry out the demolitions and in that group were Arthur Edmonds, the sapper captain, and the Greek-speaking commando Denys Hamson. Finally there was the command post of Myers, Woodhouse, Zérvas and Áris, with a reserve force to be deployed in case of trouble.

This battle plan, as always, did not long survive contact with the enemy. By 11 p.m. on the appointed night Myers and the command group had crept forward to the edge of the ridge overlooking the viaduct, and for ten anxious minutes nothing happened. Then pandemonium broke out at the north end of the viaduct as the andártes attacked the Italian guards, but after 20 minutes it was clear that the attackers had been beaten back, and the reserve force was sent in. For a further 20 minutes the firing continued, and Zérvas was ready to withdraw his forces by firing the green flare for retreat. Fortunately the only flare pistol had gone with the reserve group, and was quickly retrieved and safeguarded from Zérvas by Woodhouse.

The attack on the guards at the viaduct's southern end, led by Zérvas' second in command Astérios Michalákis, was more successful, and after an hour the white flare went up, signalling that the position had been taken. Though the north end was still a battleground Myers ordered Barnes and his group into the ravine to begin demolition, yelling 'Go in, Tom' above the noise of firing and the roar of the river. It was now that Barnes discovered that the steel girders were not L-shaped but U-shaped, and it took about 20 minutes to remould the plastic explosive. Then Barnes blew the whistle for everyone to take cover, and as Myers recorded 'There was a tremendous explosion, and I saw one of the seventy-foot steel spans lift into the air and – oh what joy! – drop into the gorge below, in a rending crash of breaking and bending steel-work.'[8]

Soon after the explosion, which no doubt unnerved the Italians, the north end of the viaduct was at last taken. There was still the second steel pier to be blown up, and Myers, after walking across the viaduct as far as its jagged end, learnt from shouted exchanges that this would take another 40 minutes. At that moment an outbreak of firing further north signalled the approach of Italian reinforcements by rail from Lamía, giving the demolition party only 20 minutes at most. In a quarter of an hour the second explosion happened, further distorting the wreckage of the viaduct, but there had only been time to fix explosives to two of the pier's four girders, and the pier and the span it supported still stood. Myers' force could do no more, and Woodhouse fired the green flare for withdrawal. In small groups they made their way to the agreed rendezvous at forest huts 4,000 feet up on the mountain slopes, where the indefatigable Barba Niko had a hot meal for them. Two days after the attack they entered Mavrolithári in triumph.

The Gorgopótamos operation had been a resounding success, but what did it achieve? It came too late, at the end of November 1942, to have impact on the Allied campaign in North Africa. The Battle of El Alamein had started on 23 October, the Italian forces in Africa had been defeated by early November, and by 20 November Rommel was already in retreat. When Montgomery was asked later if the Gorgopótamos operation had contributed to his campaign, he declared ungraciously that he had never heard of it. Nevertheless during the six weeks it took the Germans to repair the viaduct – a remarkable achievement – supplies to the Axis forces in North Africa were disrupted, and German records show that the flow of war materiel to other parts of Europe was reduced by 3,000 tons, more than 40 per cent.

Probably the most important result from Gorgopótamos was psychological. The Italian occupying forces were cowed, and thereafter made no attempt to intercept groups of British and EDES troops. 'Mountain Greece', wrote Woodhouse, 'was already in effect liberated.'[9] The operation had also shown what could be achieved by British and disparate resistance forces acting together, a unity which in Greece was unhappily never to be repeated.

Two myths to the discredit of the British were later propagated. One was that it was Áris who had planned the operation and commanded it, which was simply untrue – Myers had done both. The other myth was that the BBC in its broadcast of the success had named EDES but not ELAS. Though there is no recording of the broadcast, it is almost certain that the BBC referred unspecifically to 'national bands', as its instructions were never to name resistance leaders or their forces. These myths were part of the war of words of the communists against the British, which was eventually to become a shooting war.

The British and Greek forces had come through relatively unscathed – none killed, only four out of over 100 wounded. But others paid the price, and in reprisal 16 Greek hostages from the neighbourhood were executed at the viaduct, where a memorial to them now stands. Though wireless communication with SOE Cairo was very erratic, Myers had managed to get one message though, asking for leaflets to be dropped after the operation warning that any reprisals would be treated as war crimes and be severely punished after the war. There is no knowing if this would have been effective because SOE passed the request to the Foreign Office, where the permanent secretary Sir Alexander Cadogan vetoed it, perhaps on the grounds that to treat all reprisals as war crimes was a commitment too far.

Myers recommended a number of awards for those who had taken part at Gorgopótamos, and the following February got news of the recipients. Tom Barnes, Arthur Edmonds and Denys Hamson, who had all played major parts in the demolition, were awarded the MC, and so was Michalákis, whose group had subdued the Italian guards to the south. Myers and Woodhouse were given the DSO, and Zérvas and Áris the OBE. To Myers' particular satisfaction their unfailing helper Barba Niko was awarded the MBE.

10

Village and City

From the beginning of 1943 life in rural Greece was increasingly dominated by the two resistance bands which had taken part in the Gorgopótamos operation – ELAS and EDES. EDES under Zérvas held most of Epirus (Ípiros), the area of north-west Greece stretching south from the Albanian border to Préveza and Árta. ELAS under Áris controlled most of the rest of rural and mountainous Greece north of the Gulf of Corinth.

The numbers in each band were in hundreds before Gorgopótamos, but in the following year expanded enormously as oppression by the occupying powers increased and the spirit of resistance to it grew. EDES reached a total of 4,000 combatants in October 1943. ELAS, partly through absorption of other bands, reached some 5,000 by spring 1943 and 35,000–40,000 by autumn, reaching on one estimate 200,000 in 1944.[1] What were the motives of those who joined the bands in such numbers?

The common thread was without doubt patriotism. There was universal scorn for the Italians, whom the Greeks had already defeated, hatred of the Germans for their harsh regime and brutal reprisals, and pride in Greece with trust in its eventual liberation. There was only one way to express these passionate beliefs and that was by joining one of the resistance bands. No senior officer in the armed forces gave a lead, nor did any of the pre-war politicians, while the absent King was widely distrusted and his government in exile was regarded as wholly out of touch. 'The first time I felt like a man', said one andárte, previously a garage mechanic, 'was when my brother and I joined EAM and went to the mountains.'[2] Even those who initially joined EAM, and later left in disgust at its methods, had no regrets. 'Even if I had known at the time', said a schoolmaster, that the Communist party had masterminded EAM, I would not have cared in the least. Someone had to take the first step. Although I have broken with them now, I must remember that it was EAM which first allowed me to live with a clear conscience.[3]

A further incentive for joining the resistance was that by the summer of 1943 the mountainous areas of central Greece were effectively free. 'The whole central massif that forms the backbone of Greece is absolutely and entirely independent of the influence of or contact with the occupying Powers or the Quisling administration in Athens. In it you are in perfect safety.'[4] So the life of an andárte was now much easier, a comparatively safe occupation with plenty of glory, and recruiting, especially among young men, became a simple matter.

The Central Committee and its immediate adherents in the towns understood and believed in the theory of Communism but very few of the rank-and-file andártes did. Whether they joined ELAS or EDES depended on which was dominant in their area. EDES had little to say about its political ideas beyond a vague commitment to social justice, but ELAS had long advocated rule by the people (laokratía) and now began to put this into practice in the mountain villages.

Woodhouse, though generally critical of the Communists, wrote glowingly of their system of local government:

July 1943 was a month of hope and excitement as well as wonder and fear in the mountains of Greece. The benefits of civilization and culture trickled into the mountains for the first time. Schools, local government, law courts and public utilities, which the war had ended, worked again. Theatres, factories, parliamentary assemblies began for the first time. Communal life was organized in place of the traditional individualism of the Greek peasant. EAM/ELAS set the pace in the creation of something that the government of Greece had neglected: an organized state in the Greek mountains.[5]

This passage was published in 1948, when there were still few firsthand accounts of ELAS rule in the villages. It seems an overenthusiastic assessment. Factories? Think workshop rather than industrial plant. Theatres? Think am-dram skit rather than La Scala. Woodhouse later gave a much more guarded assessment in his 1976 book.[6]

ELAS certainly introduced changes in rural Greece. New village councils were set up, sometimes by a show of hands in the presence of armed ELAS andártes, and sometimes simply imposed. The council could not refuse demands from ELAS; in one village it offered ELAS 60 per cent of the village crop reserve, and when this was not enough had to hand over all its cash as well. People's courts were established, to save villagers from long journeys into town and payment to bourgeois lawyers. However, such impromptu justice was often undermined by existing village feuds and animosities, and any deviation from support of ELAS became punishable as treachery. The dominant figure in the village became the *ipévthinos*, the responsible one, appointed by the Communist Party. He was head of the village council, always one of the judges for the people's court and according to one British observer was often the roughest man in the village.

In his book *Eleni*, his life of his mother, Nicholas Gage gives a picture of the impact of ELAS on the small village of Liá, in the far north-west of Greece and close to the Albanian border. Communist ideas had reached Liá in an unusual way. In the 1930s, at Kalpáki near Liá, the Greek army had established a military camp specifically for soldiers suspected of Communism. These soldiers met and talked with the students at the local academy, three of whom were from Liá and who were impressed by Communist ideas. All three became schoolteachers, which gave them status and influence. By spring 1943 they had formed a band of 20 as part of ELAS and summoned the people of Liá to the village square, announcing that Liá was now controlled by ELAS which would bring in a democratic new order based on justice.

ELAS brought some immediate benefits. Local brigands were controlled, and for the first time in centuries villagers could travel freely, provided that they held ELAS passes. Also ELAS offered new opportunities:

ELAS gave the people of Lia a new purpose and hope in the dark hours of the occupation. Villagers who could not even read or write found themselves with important jobs: collecting cheese to sell for money to buy black-market guns, conscripting mules for the guerrillas' use, levying taxes on each farmer's harvest. There were committees for administration, security, justice, supplies and recruitment, and many who had never thought of joining the resistance were flattered to be put in charge of them.[7]

There were entertainments organised by ELAS, and Nicholas Gage, then four years old, remembers laughing, cheering or hissing as appropriate at the skit about Zérvas, who was shown as collecting sovereigns from the Churchill figure, kissing the boots of the King, whispering secrets to Hitler, and finally being seized by ELAS and having a sack of goat dung dumped on his head.

However, the promised justice could be highly uncertain. In a long-running feud over field boundaries a young man brandished a stick and was accused of having an unauthorised gun. The beating ordered by the new justice system left him unconscious and soaked in blood. It was quickly realised that the punishment was a complete mistake, and ELAS offered the victim money in compensation; he threw it on the floor in disgust.

Later, justice became even less a legal matter. In autumn 1943 EDES defeated ELAS and briefly supplanted it in control of Liá and the nearby villages. EDES held a memorial service for the comrades who had fallen in the recent battle with ELAS. When ELAS regained control it rounded up those who had attended the EDES service and tortured them to reveal other names, beating them on the soles of the feet, the *phálangas*, and clubbing them heavily on the body. Justice had become arbitrary, brutal and political.

While much of rural and mountainous Greece was virtually free and unaffected by the occupation forces, things were very different in Athens. Arrests were frequent and unpredictable. They might be for some flimsy reason – one woman was arrested because two or three cap badges of Italian officers were found in her house, which an Italian soldier who was an admirer had sent to her sister. Owning a functioning wireless was a crime. One man was charged with stealing petrol and a spare tyre from a German's car, and the number of locksmiths listed in the meticulous German prison records suggests that pilfering, actual or suspected, of German stores was often the reason for arrest. A more substantial charge was helping Allied soldiers, often escaped prisoners of war, to get away by boat to Turkey. But often arrests were completely arbitrary and en masse.

One evening in December 1943 a man was walking through Omónia Square and found it completely deserted. One of the ragged boys who begged by day and slept on the metro warm air vents at night told him that there had been a round-up, known as a *blóko*, in the station below. After a few more paces he stopped, struck by two dangers, one that he too might be rounded up, and the other that if a Greek saw him walking free he would be suspected of being in

German pay. He turned off into a side street and in future took a long way round to avoid Omónia, wearing out his shoes in the process. This was an instance of the corrosive fear that these arbitrary arrests could generate. As one contemporary wrote, 'Haïdhári prison was set up for its effect on those outside, not those inside.'[8]

Anyone arrested would commonly be first interrogated and then sent to this Haïdhári holding camp outside Athens before transfer to one of the Athens jails. Interrogations needed Greek interpreters, and some later paid the price for collaboration; one was tried and sentenced to 20 years in prison, another was dragged into the street and killed. The questioning might be no worse than intrusive: 'Open your mouth [...] You have gold teeth [...] Where did you get the gold sovereigns to pay for them?' If information was to be extracted more brutal methods were used, on women as well as men. A common practice, known as *opisthokrémasma*, was for victims' hands to be bound behind them, a rope on a pulley attached to the binding, and the prisoner hauled into the air face down, causing excruciating pain across the shoulders. Beatings were with whips made of twisted wire. It could get much worse. One 17-year-old, after repeated *opisthokrémasma*, was subjected to elaborate and perverted torture of the genitals.[9] As Sigmund Freud said after his experience of the Gestapo, 'In good times they are our patients, in bad times they are our jailers.'

The Haïdhári holding camp for prisoners was an old military barracks, about 6 miles west of Athens near the Byzantine church at Dháfni. Men were put in one barbed-wire enclosure, women and children in another. When a young boy recognised his father beyond the wire and ran towards him, a guard shot the boy in the leg. Men were put to work breaking stones or digging unnecessary trenches, and any misbehaviour could land them in a crammed isolation cell, up to 50 men in the space of a small living room. On arrival the prisoners' possessions and most of their clothing was removed, and one task of the women was to pack these in boxes, to be sent to Germany and cynically labelled 'A gift from the people of Greece to the heroic people of Berlin'. After morning roll-call the camp commandant would read out names at random from a list. These were the day's hostages who were to be shot in reprisal for sabotage.

The Italians as well as the Germans created terror in Athens, especially the secretive Italian CS or Counter Sabotage unit. One contemporary said of the CS, 'It was a truly astonishing organisation, and compared with its perfection the famous Gestapo was innocent and harmless.'[10]

It is a relief to find examples of humanity among those who imposed this regime. A girl prisoner described one Italian guard, old enough to have fought in the 1914–18 war, a Neapolitan with five children whose photographs he would show to the prisoners. One evening he broke down in front of the girl.

> My eldest son is at the front, I haven't heard from him, he may be dead. A curse on the war! And you, poor young girl stuck in here! And all the women who are far from their homes and their children! The war – it is the same for all of us.[11]

In another episode a German officer was interrogating a Greek who was a professional actor. The Greek gave a false name backed up by a false identity card. 'No,' said the officer, 'I know your real name because I saw you as Hamlet in Frankfurt. As an artist, you must survive to encourage your compatriots.' The officer sent the Greek, with an escort, to meet a contact in central Athens, and he escaped via Turkey to Cairo. He learnt later that the German officer had been tried, condemned and executed as a traitor.[12]

The archbishop of Athens, Dhamaskinós, was widely praised for his support of prisoners. He visited them in their cells, especially on the night before execution, he supported their families, and did all he could to prevent the killing of hostages. On one occasion, shown a list of those to be executed, he presented the authorities with an alternative list, headed by himself and including all the Greek senior clergy. He was praised by Neubacher, the German economic commissioner who briefly halted Greek hyperinflation, for his intercessions on behalf of hostages, and Neubacher described Dhamaskinós as the most powerful political figure he had met in Athens.

Intervention in the German courts was handled by Iánnis Yeorgákis, the young legal adviser of Dhamaskinós. Until the end of 1942 he was able to appear in court on behalf of the accused, arguing often successfully on the basis of international law and exploiting the German respect for rules. After that he was banned from appearing, on the grounds that he had insulted the court, and all he could do now was accompany the condemned to their execution. This he did, heart-breaking as he found it, until it became impossible because executions were so numerous and so sudden.

Most executions were at Kaisarianí on the eastern outskirts of Athens. The condemned went defiantly to their deaths, loudly singing national hymns on their last journey, refusing to be blindfolded, and as their final words shouting '*Zíto I Elládha*' (Long live Greece).

11

The Destruction of the Jews

The Nuremberg Laws, promulgated on 15 September 1935, were in two parts. The first part, the Reich Citizenship Law, defined a Reich citizen as a state subject 'who is of German or related blood', that is, Aryan in Nazi terms. The second part, the Law for the Protection of German Blood and German Honour, stated that 'purity of German blood is the essential condition for the continued existence of the German people' and dealt with the Jews.[1] Jews were categorised according to whether they had three or more Jewish grandparents (full Jew), two Jewish grandparents (full or half Jew depending on other factors) or one Jewish grandparent (quarter Jew). Jews were forbidden to marry Aryans, or to have extramarital relations with them or even to employ as domestic servants Aryan females aged under 45. Charts were distributed illustrating the different classes of Jews, and showing couples, one Aryan and the other Jew or part Jew, approaching a Registry Office but meeting a barrier with a large 'Verboten' sign.

These Nuremberg Laws could be seen as an expression of intemperate and irrational prejudice and nothing worse, but what they would lead to soon became clear. The events of Kristallnacht, on 7 November 1938, were sparked by the fatal wounding of a German diplomat in Paris by a 17-year-old Polish Jew, and retaliatory attacks on Jews were encouraged by Hitler and by Goebbels. In Munich, Berlin and other German towns, and in recently occupied Vienna, over 100 synagogues were burnt down, Jewish businesses were wrecked, Jewish homes were broken into and ransacked in front of terrified children, and 91 Jews were killed.

Once war had broken out and German forces occupied the countries of eastern and northern Europe, the killing of Jews was intensified, either by gratuitous violence or in reprisals. In some places there was a quota of 100 hostages to be shot for every German killed. By the end of 1941 around half a million Jews in occupied territories had been killed by the German army, the SS and paramilitary groups.

Also many Jews were being deported to camps, along with political prisoners, gypsies and homosexuals. These were ostensibly labour camps, but to cope with the numbers of inmates mass killing was begun. Initially this was done by packing up to 60 victims at a time into a specially built airtight van and pumping in the fatal exhaust fumes. However, in July 1941 a chemical pesticide called Zyklon-B was shown, owing to the chance death of an unfortunate cat, to give off lethal fumes when warmed. At Auschwitz, which was established as a labour camp in April 1940 and destined to become the largest mass killing centre in history, this was the method used. The victims were packed up to 1,200 at a time into sealed gas chambers, Zyklon-B pellets were lowered through holes in the roof in wire-mesh baskets, and the body heat of those in the chamber released the gas. Some of the condemned were advised by other inmates to stand near the vents and die quickly without having to witness the deaths of their comrades. Within 20 minutes they were all dead.

These measures were still not enough, and at the beginning of 1942 there remained over 2 million Jews in Germany and the occupied countries. On 20 January 1942 a conference was held at Wannsee near Berlin with the explicit purpose of finding 'the final solution of the Jewish question'.[2] Those present at Wannsee were senior officials from the ministries of the interior and of justice, from the Foreign Office and the SS. Göring, formally in charge of Jewish affairs, was not present, and nor were other major policy makers. Ostensibly the Wannsee Conference was about procedures rather than policy, a meeting of managers rather than directors.

Emigration before the war had removed some Jews from Germany, including some 9,000 children on the Kindertransports to Britain, and further emigration was discussed but considered impractical in wartime. At Wannsee the sterilisation of Jews was proposed, voluntary or as an alternative to deportation, but it was accepted that sterilisation would have to be forced. Deportation to camps was the only option remaining, where many would die of hunger, overwork and disease. As the conference record put it, 'doubtless a large proportion will be eliminated by natural causes.' As for the possible final remnant, they 'will have to be treated accordingly'.[3] There could be no doubt, then or later, what this meant; it was a commitment to mass murder.

The Wannsee Conference also agreed that, in the hunt for Jews, Europe would be combed from west to east. This meant that the Jews of Greece, hitherto undisturbed, were now targets of Nazi policy.

In 1941 Salonika held the largest population of Jews in Greece, some 56,000 or nearly three-quarters of all the Jews in the country. In Salonika, unlike elsewhere in Greece, they were concentrated in particular areas rather than being dispersed among the population. Many spoke not Greek but Ladino, a form of the Spanish which Jews had brought with them when expelled from Spain in 1492, or they spoke Greek with a Ladino accent, so how they spoke identified them as Jews. Some Salonika Jews were prosperous, but the majority were not, and even in normal times some 70 per cent had a card which entitled them to public assistance.

The Germans entered Salonika on 9 April 1941, and took immediate steps against the Jews, though nothing as yet to indicate how extreme these measures would become. The press, including the three Jewish papers, was closed down except for the pro-German *Apoyevmatiní* and a new and anti-Semitic publication, *Néa Evrópi*. Jewish houses were singled out for requisition. In June a German commission arrived to seize Jewish books, manuscripts, archives and artefacts and remove them to Frankfurt.

The Germans in effect also took over the Jewish Council. All the council members in Salonika were arrested and those away on a mission to Athens, including Chief Rabbi Cevi Koretz, were picked up there soon afterwards. In their place the Germans selected one council member, Saby Saltiel, as president not only of Salonika's Jews but of all Jews in Greece. Saltiel was fiercely criticised by other Jews. It was conceded that he was fundamentally honest, but he was condemned for forgetting the infamous source of his powers and was called an operetta-president and an idiot-king, 'a dictator to the Jews and a subaltern to the Germans'.[4]

These comments are from Michael Molho's book *In Memoriam: Homage to the Jewish Victims of the Nazis in Greece*, published in Salonika in 1948–9. The book was compiled under his direction, with contributions from himself and others, and it is reasonable to assume that Molho was in sympathy with any views expressed. Molho was a Salonika rabbi during the occupation, and took part in many of the negotiations between the Jews and the Germans. So his book is written soon after the event, and from the perspective of an official representative of the Jews.

A parallel account, this time from one family's viewpoint, is Erika Kounio Amariglio's *From Thessaloniki to Auschwitz and Back*. It was written 50 years after the war, partly to counter Holocaust denial, partly to memorialise those who did not come back, and partly as a result of asking herself whether she should write it and answering with a simple 'Why not?' She had thus had a lifetime to reflect on, and try to understand, what happened.

Erika Kounio was born in 1926 and brought up in a house giving directly on to the waters of Salonika's harbour – there was then no intervening road. Her Jewish father owned and ran a successful photographic shop, and on a visit to the annual Leipzig photographic exhibition met and later married a German girl. Erika and her family were thus in a relatively unusual situation: her German mother, married to a Jew, was classified by the Nuremberg Laws as a full Jew, while Erika and her brother, having only two Jewish grandparents (paternal) and two German (maternal) were classed as half Jews. A more significant result of the German connection, as it turned out, was that all the family spoke German.

In the first months of the occupation food became short but otherwise life for the Jews went on much as before. A German officer and his orderly were billeted in Erika's house, but they were polite and did not bother the family at all. 'You see,' said Erika's German grandfather who was now living with them,

> it is unnatural for Germans to behave badly. They are civilized, they are cultured. A nation that gave us Beethoven, Goethe and Heine could not be savage. It is only the SS who act brutally, and they are only a handful of people.[5]

Erika overheard her parents say, 'You see, they leave the Jews undisturbed. Fortunately the Nuremberg law does not apply here.'[6] In January 1942 the Germans released Koretz and reinstated him as chief rabbi of Salonika, with Saltiel still as his nominal superior.

The first clear portent of what was to come was on 11 July 1942, when all Jewish men between 18 and 45 were ordered to assemble in Elevtherías Square, next to the harbour and only a few hundred yards from Erika's house. A callous piece of theatre followed, designed to humiliate the Jews and crush any spirit of resistance. The men were forced to stand in rows without moving, under a baking sun, from eight in the morning till two in the afternoon.

They were allowed neither to shield themselves from the sun nor – a considerable deprivation – to smoke. Those who collapsed were doused with water and kicked until they stood up. They were made to do humiliating knees-bend callisthenics, and when finally released they were ordered to run the first 150 yards or go on all fours. The next day's issue of *Néa Evrópi* gleefully published photographs of the event with anti-Semitic comment.

Two days later the men were summoned again, and German intentions became clear. The men were to be sent to other regions of northern Greece to do forced labour in mines and quarries or on road-works, and over the next four days they were allocated to the various tasks. Their working conditions were appalling. Though there was no effective protest from the Jewish leaders Koretz and Saltiel, a commission of a Jewish representative and two German officials reported in the following September on the plight of the forced labourers. Most of them, it said, were quite unsuitable for the work, sleeping and sanitary arrangements were deplorable, food was completely inadequate, disease, particularly malaria, affected some 60 per cent, medical care was absolutely insufficient, and after two and a half months 12 per cent had died. After protracted negotiations the Germans agreed to release the labourers on payment by the Jewish community of 3.5 billion drachmas. This German experiment in conscripting forced labour had failed, but at great human and material cost to the Jews.

Early in the following year the next blow fell on Salonika's Jews. On 6 February 1943 Dieter Wisliczeny arrived, sent by SS officer Adolf Eichmann to oversee preparations for the deportation of the city's Jews, and on the same day an official notice was issued by Max Merten, head of Salonika's military administration, stating that the Nuremberg Laws now applied. Another fond hope of Erika's family was shattered. All Jews were to wear a yellow star whose shape and dimensions were precisely defined, they were to move to the ghetto area, all Jewish businesses and homes were to be prominently marked, those premises outside the ghetto being of course abandoned and open for looters. Jews were not allowed to be outside the ghetto after sunset, so Erika, now living in the ghetto, had to hurry home from school, and once riskily removed her yellow star and went for a last look at her old house by the sea. Later, Jews were forbidden to leave the ghetto at all.

Fascist ideology was not anti-Semitic as Nazism was, and the Italians did all they could to help the Jews. In areas under sole Italian occupation – that is everywhere except Salonika and its hinterland and Athens – it was said that every man in the Italian army, from humble soldier to superior officer, gave aid and protection to Jews.[7] In Salonika the Italian consul Castrucci provided Italian passports for Italian Jews married to Greeks and therefore technically Greek Jews, and to their children who were 'minors', elastically defined as up to age 35. Many an Italian officer escorted a Jewish woman, supposedly his wife, to Salonika's railway station, offering his arm 'in a spirit of perfect chivalry and with exquisite courtesy and delicacy.'[8]

Erika and her family had made their own way to the ghetto, but other Jews were taken there by German soldiers. Níkos Kokántzis, of a Christian family, was deeply in love with a Jewish girl whom he calls Gioconda who lived next door, and though both were teenagers they were lovers in the full sense. The day came when a lorry arrived, with three German soldiers and an officer to take away Gioconda and her family – father and mother, six children and an aged grandmother. Níkos and his parents were there to help and to say good-bye. His father had earlier offered to keep Gioconda in hiding, but she had refused to leave her family. Possessions were hurriedly packed, and after a last tearful embrace of the two young lovers the lorry drove away. The Germans had been patient, polite and almost apologetic, and at the end the officer incongruously stood to attention and saluted. Neither Gioconda nor any of her family survived.

On 10 March 1943 Erika and her family were ordered to move to the ghetto area known as Baron Hirsch which was near the railway station. The area was packed, and Erika's family spent two cold, damp and hungry days in the corner of an abandoned building with a leaking roof. They were told that they were going to Poland, and were offered, in exchange for drachmas, Polish zlotys for their life there. Though they could have delayed, they decided to leave on the first group of cattle-trucks, Erika's mother saying, 'Whatever will be, let it happen as soon as possible. Let's leave at the first opportunity.'[9]

They spent a week in their cattle-truck, 70 people in each crammed into a space designed, as a notice said, for 40 soldiers or eight horses. There was no light, very little water, food was one sack of biscuits, wormy figs and olives, the latrine was a communal bucket, and at night it was freezing cold. On 20 March 1943 they arrived at Auschwitz-Birkenau, and Erika, her parents and her brother were separated from the rest as the only ones out of 2,800 who spoke German, and so were needed as interpreters and clerks. Of the remainder, 2,191 were sent immediately to the gas chambers. 'Coincidences had saved us,' Erika wrote – the coincidence that they had taken the first transport, and that they were the only ones among several thousand on it who spoke German. All four survived.[10]

Auschwitz was also the ultimate destination of many other Jews, from Athens and elsewhere. At first, Athens was a much safer place for Jews than Salonika. In Athens they were dispersed among the rest of the city's population, so could not be identified by where they lived. The Athenian Jews did not speak Ladino, but spoke Greek like everyone else, so accent was not a marker. In Athens too it was easier to escape, either to the EAM bands which were active not far from the city and welcomed Jews, or by caique to Turkey or Palestine. Perhaps most important, by the time the Germans moved against them in September 1943, the Athens Jews and their sympathisers knew of the fate of Salonika's Jews and could not cherish any illusions that only petty restrictions would be applied to them.

On 20 September 1943, Dieter Wisliczeny, having completed the destruction of the Salonika Jews, arrived in Athens on the same mission there. The Germans were now in sole control of the city since Italy had switched allegiance to the Allies 12 days earlier. On 4 October Wisliczeny issued, through the German police chief Jürgen Stroop, a set of orders to the Athens Jews. They must return to where they had lived on 1 June 1943, and not move house. They must within five days register with their religious centre, or if in the suburbs with the local Greek authorities and present themselves there every day. They must stay indoors overnight from 5 p.m. to 7 a.m. They must wear a yellow star. Any Jews disobeying these orders, and anyone helping them, would be shot.

However, Wisliczeny found himself frustrated at every turn. Registration was a farce, as only one-seventh of the city's 8,000 Jews registered, and only about 60 in the initial five-day period. Rabbi Barzilai, president of the Athens Jewish community, was summoned to Wisliczeny's office and ordered to hand over all Jewish records. Barzilai claimed that they were incomplete and that he needed three days to update them. Within that time he had destroyed them all, and at the end of it joined EAM in the mountains.

The Athens Jews also had powerful supporters outside their own community. Six months before the arrival of Wisliczeny, Archbishop Dhamaskinós had sent a forceful letter on behalf of the

Jews to Konstantínos Logothetópoulos, successor to Tsolákoglou as collaborationist prime minister from December 1942 to April 1943. The letter was also signed by 19 distinguished Greeks from the worlds of business, academia, the arts and the law. The letter pointed out that under the terms of the armistice all Greek citizens were to receive equal treatment, irrespective of race or religion; that Greek Jews were law-abiding and there was no justification for any accusation that they were a threat to occupation forces; and that the Orthodox religion believed as a matter of faith that, in St Paul's words, 'there is neither Jew nor Greek.' The letter went on to protest against the deportation of Salonika's Jews, which was already in progress. A similar letter was sent to Altenberg, the German plenipotentiary in Athens.[11] This was a bold stand by the Archbishop and his co-signatories, but unhappily neither letter had any effect. Logothetópoulos did nothing, and Altenberg claimed that Salonika's Jews were only being sent to Poland to work.

Dhamaskinós went further than sending protest letters. He offered to baptise Jews, and municipal rolls were altered so that over 500 Jews were now registered as Christians. He also instructed the Orthodox clergy to tell the faithful that they must do all they could to help the Jews. Dhamaskinós was threatened by Stroop that if he continued to help the Jews he would be shot, and splendidly replied – recalling the fate of Patriarch Grígorios V at the hands of the Turks in 1821 – 'Greek bishops are not shot, they are hung.'[12]

The Jews had another effective supporter in Ángelos Évert, head of the Greek police in Athens. He ordered his men to give Jews false Greek identity papers, and issued them himself, telling the recipient to be sure to go to the Orthodox church on Sundays. Most of them acquired the new name of Papadhópoulos. Also EAM in the autumn of 1943 issued a proclamation supporting the Jews:

> The condemnation of their race is absurd [...]. We shall fight with every possible means against the persecution of the Jews [...]. We shall help the Jews, and shall hide their children [...]. We must all do our utmost to help these new victims from among the Greek people.[13]

Athenian residents of all classes sheltered Jews, though they could be shot for doing so. One evening the celebrated poet Ángelos Sikelianós brought an eight-year-old Jewish boy to a family he knew and asked them to shelter the boy until he could get a fake identity card. Sikelianós, nearly 60 and unmarried, could not shelter the boy himself without arousing suspicion. The family agreed, and the boy survived. Another distinguished helper of the Jews was Princess Alice, the English wife of the King's uncle Andrew and mother of the Duke of Edinburgh. Like Sikelianós, she was now nearly 60 and alone in Athens, but sheltered a Jewish family for a year in an unused floor of her apartment, resolutely maintaining that they were all English. This family also survived.

The ordinary Athenians too sheltered Jews, as Elia Aelion discovered when he and a group of other Jews from Salonika reached Athens. Elia's background helps to explain his wartime experiences. Before the war it was privileged. His father was president of the synagogue and head of a company producing spirits and liqueurs. One uncle was a wealthy doctor, and another had established and now ran a successful textile business with contacts in Athens. When the Italians invaded in 1940 Elia was a 22-year-old army sergeant stationed in northern Greece. After the collapse of the Greek army he and some friends walked the 300 miles south to Návplion, eventually getting back to Athens, and from there to Salonika on a bus on which the fare for the journey was a 5-gallon can of petrol. So Elia had already experienced a life of hardship and improvisation as well as a comfortable one.

Within weeks of the German invasion in April 1941 the danger to Salonika's Jews became clear, and Elia's uncle in the textile business decided that his stocks of material should go to Athens for safety. It was Elia's job to take them there, putting them in safe warehouses en route and selling cloth for gold. He met other Salonika Jews in Athens where, he said, they all lived openly as Jews. Fourteen of them moved into a house together and were looked after by two neighbours, 'a remarkable woman' Eléni Nikolaídhis and an Armenian lady Yula Yazitsian, 'another generous soul'.[14] But by autumn 1943 the fate of Salonika's Jews was well known, and Elia and five others decided to flee to the andárte bands in the mountains. They contacted an EAM agent who provided andárte escorts, they changed some gold for drachmas, the village currency, and set off on a week-long trek into the mountains.

Life with the andártes was not the sanctuary they had hoped for. Their andárte escorts were 'mostly poorly educated villagers, some of whom were very rough'.[15] On the way they met a fugitive girl, obviously a prostitute, whom the andártes wanted to execute as a presumed collaborator, but Elia and his party with difficulty dissuaded them. Eventually, in a village some 20 miles from Thíva (Thebes), they met the andárte leader Orestes and his men.

> They were basically illiterate, fanatical types, professing to be Communists. In reality, however, they knew little or nothing of the precepts of Communism, and were more or less products of the ferment of the times – men who had embraced a symbol around which they could unite.[16]

Italy had by now changed sides, and the whole countryside was under German occupation. The andártes wanted to shoot German patrols and Elia and his friends tried to prevent them, warning of the repercussions, but without success. A group of Germans was ambushed and killed, and a few days later, at four in the morning, the Germans arrived at the village to inflict reprisals. The women and children fled – all the men were out fighting – and Elia and his group fled with them. After a hazardous journey, in danger from wolves as well as Germans, they got back to Athens, and were again sheltered and looked after by Eléni Nikolaídhis and Yula Yazitsian.

In Athens they survived the remaining year of the war. They were at risk from their Ladino accents and were in constant fear of informers. However, they had their false identity cards from Salonika, went out in the streets as little as possible, and did not apply for ration cards. Their main safeguard was that they had plenty of money, presumably from continuing sales of their textile stores; as late as August 1944, Elia says, 'my money belt was full of gold.'[17] Money and dedicated helpers had saved them. One of the girls in Elia's group was Rachel Saporta and they became engaged, holding a celebration at the house of their protectress Eléni Nikolaídhis.

This group of Jewish refugees from Salonika were more fortunate than the resident Jews of Athens, whose fate had only been delayed. In January 1944 Eichmann, annoyed at the inactivity of Wisliczeny in Athens, replaced him with Toni Burger, who moved quickly. On 24 March 1944 Burger ordered all male Jews to assemble at the synagogue on Melidhóri Street, just north of the Akropolis, and a notice outside said that there would be a free distribution of flour for the traditional Easter unleavened bread. Some 300 of the 1,200 registered Jews went into the synagogue, but immediately the doors were locked; there was no sign of flour, and they were told that they were being sent to Germany to work. Some were allowed out to fetch their families, some were spontaneously joined by families anxious for their relatives, and by midday the number had grown to 700. That afternoon they were taken to the Haïdhári camp, where over the next few days they were joined by those caught in a general round-up of Jews in Athens and another 600 from Préveza, Árta, Agrínion and Patras. They were then taken to the station and into closed cattle-trucks for the journey north. At Lárissa and at Salonika over 3,000 more Jews were added to the grim convoy, so that in all 5,200 deportees in 80 trucks reached Vienna. There some were marched on foot to Bergen-Belsen but the vast majority were sent on to Auschwitz.

When Erika Kounio Amariglio and her family arrived in Auschwitz and were at least for the moment saved from the gas chambers, her father and brother were sent to one block for office work and Erika and her mother to another. Jews had to wear the yellow star, and the other inmates of the camp had badges of different colours: green for criminals, pink for homosexuals, black for 'antisocial persons', and a Z for *zigeuner* or gypsies. The two women had their heads shaved, a number tattooed on their left arms, and they were clothed in striped prisoners' uniforms and wooden clogs. Living conditions, later somewhat improved, were initially dreadful; they had sores on their feet from the clogs, suffered from lice and diarrhoea and were fed once a day on watery soup and one piece of bread. Erika and her mother were put to work in the office which maintained the lists of the dead, on which those killed in the gas chambers were marked, with cynical euphemism, as S.B., standing for *Sonderbehandlung* or Special Treatment.

Other Jewish prisoners had more immediately grim tasks: taking corpses from the gas chambers, removing anything of value, and cutting off women's hair before taking the bodies to the crematoria to be incinerated. One prisoner told Erika about the work he had to do.

You cannot imagine what is going on there. Piles of fur coats, winter coats, dresses, glasses, jewellery, gold, coins, shoes, all in separate piles. They sort them after they have examined the seams, the stitching, the sides, the heels of the ladies' shoes to find anything that might have been hidden there and then send the items to Germany. Hundreds of baby carriages tied together in bunches of five have been sent to Germany.[18]

Some prisoners were selected for the infamous medical experiments of Joseph Mengele, designed among other things to find the most effective method of sterilisation. Other prisoners, women as well as men, were marched out of the camp each day as labourers, on work which was often useless – moving stones from one place to another, or moving a heavy roller. Twice a day a roll-call and a selection were carried out, those selected being sent to the gas chambers as no longer useful, so to stand upright and look confident was a matter of life or death.

Meanwhile transports of prisoners continued to arrive, and four new crematoria had been built to incinerate even more corpses. In 1943 the prisoners came mainly from Germany, Yugoslavia, Poland, Belgium and France. In May 1944 transports began to arrive from Hungary, bringing thousands every day who were marched directly to the gas chambers. In June there were new arrivals of Greeks, from Athens, other mainland towns and the islands of Corfu and Rhodes. In the autumn of 1944 the holding camp at Theresienstadt near Prague was closed, and another 2,000–3,000 people arrived at Auschwitz, few of whom survived.

By January 1945 the Russian army was approaching from the east, and their guns could be heard in the camp. The Germans had rushed to finish their work of destruction, and now rushed to destroy the evidence of it. Prisoners who had worked in the crematoria were themselves killed. Documents were stuffed into cardboard boxes and driven away on trucks. Many non-Jews had died in Auschwitz of hunger, hardship or disease, not in the gas chambers, and their bones and ashes had been kept in heavy urns, to be offered to their families with an insincere letter of condolence. There were some 6,000 of these urns, and Erika with other women worked for three days loading them on trucks for removal.

It was clear that the Germans were eliminating witnesses to Auschwitz, and those still alive expected to be killed now. However, on 18 January 1945 the women in the camp were assembled and marched out of the gates, told to walk fast and keep lines parallel, and that any who fell behind would be shot. For four days they were marched west some 100 miles through the winter snow, freezing in barns at night and subsisting on the loaf of bread issued to each of them at the start. They finally reached the railway station at Leslau and there, their numbers much diminished, they were put on trains, packed 60 to 80 in each wagon, and transported to the Ravensbrück camp some 50 miles north of Berlin. There on 5 May 1945 the Russians reached them. Against the odds, they had survived.

The survivors were profoundly troubled by their experiences, and even years later were still trying to understand and come to terms with what had happened. Elia Aelion from Salonika, whose fortunate circumstances had enabled him to survive in Athens, stayed on in the city with his companions for the winter of 1945 and witnessed with dismay the Communist rising. He was engaged to Rachel Saporta but did not want to marry. 'The wars were over, but I had lost my mooring. The future loomed before me like that of a black hole and I stepped into it as one who falls into an abyss.'[19] Other survivors whom Elia met tried to free themselves from their memories: 'It won't stay this way forever'; 'I can't make my life with dead people'; 'If I don't get a grip on myself, I'll be gone too.'[20] Rachel urged Elia to go back to Salonika, arguing that as long as he was torn by doubt or driven by ghosts they would not be able to get on with their lives. When he did go to Salonika memories became even more painful. Their family house had been sold, and the new tenants gave him the family photograph album, found in the house, compiled by Elia's brother who had died in Auschwitz. When Elia visited his father's winery he was given a box containing the wedding rings and other jewellery of the families who had been partners in the firm. He was also given a trunk which he could not bring himself to open until years later. When he did so he found many of his family's possessions, including wedding dresses and trousseaus. 'Once more', he says, 'I was plunged into misery.'[21]

Elia returned to Athens, Rachel eventually overcame his procrastinations, they were married and emigrated to California. One ends his story with the feeling that the good fortune that had enabled him to survive the war was matched by his good fortune in finding Rachel.

After liberation, Erika and her mother returned to Salonika, and so did her father and brother, of whom they had sometimes caught glimpses in the camp. Her German grandfather, when left alone, had gone to the Gestapo, shown them his 1914–18 medals, and asked to be allowed to join the family. The Gestapo complied, and Erika imagined him thinking how very civilised the Germans were. He never came back.

Even 50 years later Erika was still asking herself how it had all happened. In particular she wanted to give an answer to her 25-year-old grandson, who could not understand or condone why so many thousands of people let themselves be herded like sheep to the slaughter. Her explanation was that the Jews of Salonika had no presentiment of how bad things could get, unlike Jews in Athens and elsewhere who had been warned by Salonika's example. In Salonika the German noose had been tightened imperceptibly.

> I remember saying, and hearing other people say: 'So we shall have to wear a star: it is not so terrible.' And then: 'So we will have to declare our assets, let this be the worst and nothing else. So we have to move to a smaller house and live with all the Jews together, it doesn't matter. It will be good to have all the families together.' But the orders came one after another, without giving us time to figure out what was happening.

Even as they boarded the transports to Auschwitz they believed that they were going to Poland to work. 'It would not have been possible', Erika concluded, 'for the Jews to have reacted any differently.'[22]

In the memories of survivors different things stood out: sometimes hatred of the Germans, or the deep remorse that as victims they had learnt to hate, sometimes questions about why others did not do more to help or about why God had allowed this to happen, but always the continuing pain of recalling their own experiences and remembering those known and unknown who had been lost. Perhaps the most surprising judgement was that of Erríkos Sevíllias, a Jew from Athens who survived Auschwitz. Those killed, he reasoned, had lost their lives, as we all must sooner or later, but the perpetrators had lost their humanity. 'I do not understand', he wrote, 'what the real aim was of those who carried out something so unjust and wicked. Nevertheless I believe that it is those who did this evil deed who are the victims, the true victims.'[23]

12

The Fractured Resistance

The Gorgopótamos viaduct had been blown up on the night of 25 November 1942, and Myers' instructions from SOE before he left for Greece had been to evacuate most of his 12-man party once the operation was completed. Only four were to remain and be attached to Zérvas: Woodhouse, the young Greek officer Themistoklís Marínos, and two wireless operators. Myers signalled to SOE in Cairo that his group would be ready to be picked up by submarine on one of the four nights 22–5 December, from a point about 5 miles south of Párga on the west coast.

On 1 December both groups, Myers with those to leave and Woodhouse with those to stay, left the Gorgopótamos area, accompanied by Zérvas, to trek across Greece from east to west. After eight days they reached Zérvas' stronghold, the village of Megalochári about 10 miles east of the Gulf of Árta, where Zérvas and Woodhouse's group remained. Myers' group, after a welcome day of rest, pushed on to the west coast. By now hungry, cold and exhausted, they waited there for the expected submarine. On the first three nights, 22–4 December, no submarine appeared. On Christmas Day they were ready for the final opportunity when a runner arrived with a message from Woodhouse. SOE Cairo had told him that no submarine would now be sent. It was a bitter blow, and even Myers' usual resilience deserted him.

> I was by now too weak and tired to succeed in instilling a measure of humour into this group of bitterly disappointed volunteers, who had gallantly carried out their part of the bargain. Apart from the fact that their morale was by then so low, they were all feeling the effect of poor and inadequate food, the lack of proper rest on our outward journey and the hard days and nights, half starved, during our way to the coast.[1]

On 3 January Myers and his party were back in an even more exhausted state at Zérvas' headquarters in Megalochári, where a few days later Myers received new instructions from SOE. This was the start of a stream of instructions from SOE Cairo, initially to Myers and subsequently to Woodhouse who replaced him in August 1943. By April 1943 much more efficient wireless contact between Cairo and the Greek mountains had been established, and the instructions became even more frequent. These instructions were sometimes countermanded, as with the cancelled submarine evacuation, sometimes based on sketchy knowledge of the Greek situation and hence wholly unrealistic, and sometimes infuriating to the recipient. To explain this it is worth looking back to how SOE was established, what its constraints were, and in particular how SOE Cairo developed.

On 1 July 1940, within a year of the outbreak of war, the foreign secretary Lord Halifax chaired a high-level meeting to discuss irregular forms of warfare. Present were three other ministers, including Hugh Dalton the minister of economic warfare, and Churchill's private secretary. It was agreed that the direction of all subversion in occupied countries, a hitherto divided responsibility, should be handled by a single organisation, headed by 'a controller with almost dictatorial powers'.[2] This was the birth of the Special Operations Executive.

The next day Dalton wrote to Halifax reinforcing and elaborating the decisions of the meeting, stressing the need for the new organisation to be entirely independent of the War Office machine and the importance of absolute secrecy. A fortnight later on 15 July Churchill invited Dalton to be head of SOE, with the stirring and apparently straightforward instruction, 'And now set Europe ablaze.'[3]

Meanwhile the so-called founding charter of SOE was being drawn up by Neville Chamberlain, appeasement now firmly behind him, who had resigned as prime minister in May and was soon to succumb to the illness which killed him in November. Chamberlain's document indicated even at this early stage that SOE's task would not be straightforward, and that its head would not have dictatorial powers: 'All subversive plans, whether SOE's or others' were to be approved by its chairman, he in turn was to secure the agreement of the Foreign Secretary and of other ministers if interested, to major plans of SOE's.' The paper added: 'It will be important that the general plan for irregular offensive operations should be in step with the general strategic conduct of the war.' Dalton therefore was to keep the chiefs of staff informed, while they in turn gave him a 'broad strategic picture'.[4] In short, SOE's plans would need the agreement of the foreign secretary and sometimes other ministers, and at least the assent of the chiefs of staff. The potential conflict between the requirements of foreign policy on the one hand and of the military on the other was thus built into SOE from the start. On 22 July 1940 Chamberlain's document was approved by the War Cabinet. There it remained, following Dalton's demand for absolute secrecy, unlike the usual charters which are widely promulgated to tell everyone what the organisation is for. It seems that nobody outside the War Cabinet, and certainly neither Myers nor Woodhouse, ever heard of the charter until after the war.

Dalton, initially the minister responsible for SOE, was moved in February 1942 from the Ministry of Economic Warfare to the Board of Trade. He was succeeded, as minister for economic warfare with responsibility for SOE, by Lord Selborne. Executive head of SOE from September 1943 to the end of the war, after three predecessors had been and gone, was Colonel Colin Gubbins.

SOE operations in Greece were originally intended to be run from Crete, but after the fall of Crete SOE for Greece and the rest of the Balkans was established in Cairo. In autumn 1942, when Myers' group was parachuted into Greece for the Gorgopótamos mission, head of SOE Cairo was Lord Glenconner. His chief of staff, from whom SOE agents in Greece received their instructions, was Brigadier Keble, described perhaps charitably as 'eccentric but ruthlessly efficient'.[5]

Woodhouse could not stand him, though it was only some 40 years later that Woodhouse put his criticisms in print. Woodhouse had met Keble before, at a training course in Swanage in autumn 1941, and described him then as 'a tubby little major whose eyes almost popped out of his head with lust for killing'. The briefing for the Gorgopótamos operation, signed by Keble, was 'a highly imaginative document', showing various andárte bands, and their locations and numbers, all fictitious. Keble's briefing also included the totally unrealistic order that if one night's attempt on the viaduct failed they should try again the next night.[6]

Giving misleading briefs to agents and issuing unrealistic orders were not the only shortcomings of SOE Cairo. There were constant changes of leadership – Glenconner was the fifth head of SOE Cairo in two years. New leaders would introduce changes in structure, which seemed to occur every August. Initially the sections of SOE

Cairo had been by country, one section being responsible for all SOE activity there. In August 1941 the new head reorganised the sections by function, basically one for operations and one for political issues. After a year this had become clearly unworkable, and when Glenconner arrived in August 1942 he changed the system back to country sections.

Furthermore SOE Cairo was overstretched. In the spring of 1943 it was running 27 missions in the Balkans, of which ten were in Greece, and six months later the total had trebled, mainly due to the ruthless drive of Brigadier Keble There were not enough girls to handle wireless signals, the circulation of which was often delayed so that SOE was accused of being unnecessarily secretive. Also, although SOE was technically independent of the War Office as Dalton had originally proposed, it was heavily dependent upon the armed services. The army supplied its few and initially unreliable wireless transmission sets – only later did SOE get its own production of sets. SOE depended on the RAF for planes to drop agents and supplies, and on the navy to provide submarines for evacuation. The planned submarine rendezvous for Myers and his group had been cancelled because the navy, having lost one submarine on a similar mission, had decided late in the day not to risk another. All three vital supplies – wireless sets, planes and submarines – were urgently needed elsewhere, and it was not easy for SOE to obtain them. SOE certainly did not have the envisaged dictatorial powers.

Finally, the fact that SOE Cairo was based in such a distracting city cannot have helped the formation of well-considered judgements. Officers on leave from the Western Desert thronged the smart restaurant-nightclub the Auberge des Pyramides, the famous Shepheard's Hotel and the Gezira Club with its own racetrack and swimming pool, and were welcomed by the multinational Egyptian elite. At a house named Tara after the legendary palace of Irish kings, the exiled and glamorous Polish countess Sophie Tarnowska threw legendary parties. The Tarnowska name was already notorious. In 1907 in Venice Maria Tarnowska had two lovers, one of whom shot and killed the other, allegedly at her instigation, and the subsequent trial revealed a scandalous tale of drug-fuelled orgies. Girls from Britain arrived in Cairo in increasing numbers as part of the armed services or as secretaries and cipher clerks. Woodhouse, commenting on the large number of people involved in decisions on Greece and their distractions, said that 'perhaps nowhere in the world do their discrepancies become more aggravated than in the unwholesome atmosphere of Egypt.'⁷ Political pressures on SOE Cairo greatly increased when in the spring of 1943 King George of Greece and his government in exile moved from London to Cairo, accompanied by a new British ambassador, the forceful Reginald Leeper.

While SOE in Cairo struggled with its problems, some of them of its own making, Myers and Woodhouse were in the Greek mountains coping with the situation on the spot. In January 1943, soon after Myers and his group had returned to Zérvas' headquarters at Megalochári after the failed submarine evacuation, Myers received his new instructions from Cairo. Now the whole group was ordered to stay on in Greece as the British Military Mission, with Myers in command, to co-ordinate and develop further andárte activity. Myers, realising how demoralised some of his men were by the reversal of the original promise to bring them out, told them that he wanted only volunteers to stay, which all but three did, and he promised to do all he could to evacuate the others.

The other part of SOE's new instructions was that Woodhouse should go to Athens and make contact with a group of officers known as the Six Colonels who might, thought SOE, take control of the andárte bands in the mountains. It was reasonable, on a general view, for SOE Cairo to ask what contribution army officers could make if fighting was to be done, and two army colonels, Stéphanos Saráphis and Dimítrios Psarrós, were already leading two of the smaller resistance groups. However, in these circumstances SOE's proposal was out of touch with reality. The Six Colonels were supporters of the King – under Metaxás only royalists had been allowed to rise above the rank of captain. The King, the Greek government in exile, and General Papágos, the hero of the repulse of the Italians, had all discouraged officers from joining the resistance. Even if they had joined, ELAS would never have served under them. A further part of the instruction was even less realistic: Woodhouse was to stay permanently in Athens. Even a brief visit to Athens was highly dangerous, since as Myers pointed out Woodhouse, however well disguised, 'was over six feet tall and had red hair, whereas most Greeks are five foot nothing and have black hair'.⁸ But orders were orders.

Woodhouse, with a guide provided by Zérvas, left Zérvas' headquarters at Megalochári for Athens on 9 January and reached it in the last days of the month. Woodhouse was taken to a supposedly safe house, where he stayed cooped up all day and ventured out only during the night-time curfew. A meeting with the Six Colonels was arranged for 30 January, but none of them turned up. For a second planned meeting two days later two of them appeared, but had no interest in guerrilla warfare; they feared the consequences of the resistance movement in the mountains and wished it had never begun. As might have been predicted, the Six Colonels were no help at all.

Woodhouse also, on his own initiative, contacted the Central Committee of EAM, the Communist political controllers of ELAS, and had two meetings with them. The first on 31 January was with five of its members, and the second, two days later, with the secretary general of the Communist Party, Georgios Siántos, and Andréas Tzímas. Woodhouse thought Tzímas was 'certainly the ablest and clearest thinker in the Communist party' and said that Tzímas 'was the only leading Greek Communist with whom it was an intellectual pleasure to argue'.[9] Woodhouse tried to persuade the EAM Central Committee to join ELAS in the mountains. In theory this would have made it much easier for the British to control ELAS, instead of ELAS receiving instructions from distant Athens and referring all major decisions back there. However, Siántos refused and agreed only to send Tzímas to the mountains, ostensibly on a tour of inspection but in fact as political commissar to ELAS. The other significant outcome of these meetings was Siántos' proposal that an EAM representative should go to Cairo to meet the British and Greek authorities there. This proposal bore fruit in the following August, with major repercussions for all concerned.

On the day of this second meeting with EAM Woodhouse received the disastrous news that his main contact in Athens, careless of security, had been captured by the Germans in the middle of a wireless transmission, undoubtedly located by direction-finding apparatus. As all this contact's files had also been seized the Germans now knew a lot about Woodhouse, who had to get out. Tzímas sheltered him for two days in a properly safe house – 'Communist security was truly professional,' commented Woodhouse – and provided false papers.[10] Woodhouse left Athens after dark on 4 February and after a 15-day journey on foot through the mountains rejoined Myers.

While Woodhouse had been in Athens Myers had been struck down by a bout of pneumonia, during which he had been moved, half delirious and wrapped in blankets on the back of a mule, to escape an Italian raid. Initially he was bled by the village doctor using the ancient remedy of cupping, but fortunately Zérvas was able to provide some M and B tablets, an early antibiotic only recently available, and Myers quickly recovered.[11]

It was now becoming clear to Myers that ELAS aimed to absorb or eliminate all other resistance bands, with an eye to power in postwar Greece. On 4 March ELAS attacked and captured the rival leader Saráphis and his officers. Myers sent a strongly worded signal to Cairo calling for an ultimatum to ELAS – release Saráphis and his men, or no more British supplies – but it is not clear if this ultimatum was ever delivered. Myers hastened to ELAS headquarters, believing Saráphis was in imminent danger of being shot, but was astounded to find that Saráphis had switched allegiance from EDES to become commander-in-chief of all ELAS forces in the field. The Saráphis affair also led to ELAS making threats against Zérvas and EDES. ELAS claimed that Zérvas was sheltering some of Saráphis' men and threatened to 'drive Zérvas and all his forces into the sea' unless these men were handed over.[12] Myers and Woodhouse, on the evening of the day they heard of this, decided to act on their own initiative and to draw up an agreement which would stop the resistance bands attacking each other, and in particular restrain ELAS.

The document, put together on 14 March 1943, came to be called the First Military Agreement. Under it, all resistance bands were to be known as National Bands, allocated to different areas. All bands would co-operate with each other. No band would attack another or enter its territory. Any Greek could choose which band to join, and could hold any political views, but should not even mention politics in public. Pressure would obviously have to be used to get general agreement, and this pressure would be applied by the threat of cutting off all supplies to any group which broke the agreement. The controlling role of the British was not highlighted but it was considerable. The leadership of any band had to be agreed by Myers, British officers could order one band to assist another, and a British officer's agreement was needed for any execution. It was British officers who would decide whether there was non-compliance with the agreement, and if there was would stop supplies. Not surprisingly these provisions caused trouble.

Myers and Woodhouse spent much of the next four months trying to get acceptance of this agreement, if necessary with variations. But the British mission was also involved in two military operations. The first, in May and June, was the destruction of the Asopós railway bridge a few miles south of Gorgopótamos. The second, in

June and July, was the widespread sabotage in Greece code-named Operation Animals.

Asopós was an even more difficult operation than Gorgopótamos had been. The track down the gorge was never more than 10 feet wide, and sometimes only two or three, and was drenched by waterfalls, some of them 40 feet high, which formed deep pools. The attacking group had to wrap five bundles of explosives in waterproof capes and progressively lower them by rope or carry them above their heads through the pools. Moreover the viaduct was guarded by Germans, not Italians.

At the first attempt on the night of 24 May the demolition party got two-thirds of the way down the gorge and could get no further, so they left the charges in a safe place for a second attempt at the next full moon on 20 June. This time they got to the bottom of the gorge, found their explosives intact, and – largely thanks to a ladder carelessly left behind by a workman – were able to climb 30 feet up to a platform from which they could place the charges on the three main girders. This work took an hour and a half, being interrupted by periodic sweeps of German searchlights. The one German guard who approached them was hit on the head and tipped into the river below. The fuses were lit and the party was halfway back up the gorge when a deafening explosion brought the whole central span crashing down. It took the Germans four months to repair it with forced labour, and this time it seems there were no reprisals against the Greeks. The Germans were convinced that the destruction of the bridge was due to treachery, and shot all 40 of the garrison guarding it.

The Asopós operation was carried out solely by the British. Initially Áris had offered to co-operate with 1,000 ELAS andártes, but this was forbidden as too dangerous by Tzímas, now in the mountains after Woodhouse's visit to Athens. Tzímas had a point: the Asopós operation proved extremely risky. Instead ELAS proposed blocking the railway tunnel at Tírnavos, some 20 miles north of Gorgopótamos. This they did at the end of May, blowing up both ends of the tunnel after a train had entered it. The train crashed into the debris at the far end and caught fire, burning alive not only the trainload of Germans but also the 40 Greeks placed in the front carriage to deter sabotage. The line was closed only for a week. ELAS tactics had produced a limited success but at a high cost in Greek lives.

Myers' other military task was Operation Animals. This was a plan for widespread sabotage in Greece to fool the Germans into thinking that the next move of the Allied armies of North Africa would be to Greece and not to Sicily. Myers received his instructions for it on 29 May, and on 23 June the sabotage began.

In a little over two weeks there were, by Myers' reckoning, 44 major sabotages of rail and road, of which at least 16 were of railways, and telephone wires were cut throughout Greece. The north–south rail and road links between Salonika and Lárissa were disrupted in many places, as was the east–west road between Athens and Agrínion. The most important road disruption was of the road from Kalambáka to Ioánnina across the 5,500-foot Métsovo Pass, the only route in northern Greece by which the Germans could move troops from the east coast to the west. Here every culvert was blown up and every bridge destroyed.

All the andárte bands played a part in Operation Animals, but separately and never in co-operation. By now there were just three such groups: ELAS under Áris, EDES under Zérvas, and EKKA (National and Social Liberation), the smaller non-Communist resistance group under Colonel Dhimítrios Psarrós, which in May had been saved from elimination at the hands of ELAS only by British pressure.

On 11 July Myers learnt that Sicily had been invaded the previous day, and Operation Animals was ended. It had achieved it purpose. German documents later showed that Allied landings in western Greece had been expected daily. Two German divisions were moved to Greece from Yugoslavia and six from the Russian front, and Rommel was even transferred briefly to Salonika as commander-in-chief.

Myers sent warm messages of congratulations to the andárte bands. He had had to conceal the ultimate purpose of Operation Animals from them, but they had carried out important sabotage themselves and provided safe areas in which the British could operate. However, Myers was no closer to his aim of bringing the bands under unified and ultimately British control. A matter which was now becoming increasingly important, not only for Myers in the Greek mountains but also for SOE, the Foreign Office and ultimately both Churchill and Roosevelt, was the question of King George of Greece.

13

The Question of the King

The monarchy in Greece had had a turbulent history from the time of the Bavarian Prince Otto, installed as king in 1833 after the War of Independence, to a series of royal abdications, exiles and returns in the twentieth century. For clarity, it is worth summarising the reigns of the kings of Greece since independence, with their various departures and returns:

Otto (Óthon)	1833–62	resigned
George I	1863–1913	died
Constantine I	1913–17	abdicated
Alexander	1917–20	died
Constantine I	returned 1920–2	abdicated
George II	1922–4	then to exile
George II	returned 1935–47	died

The British, accustomed to their own long-established, stable and for centuries uncontested monarchy, took some time to appreciate that the Greek monarchy was a very different institution.

The first king of Greece after independence, the young Prince Otto of Bavaria, stepped ashore at Návplion on 6 February 1833 as King Óthon of Greece. He was only the second choice of the allied powers, Britain, France and Russia, who controlled Greece's destiny. The first choice was Prince Leopold of Saxe-Coburg, widower of George IV's daughter Charlotte, but he eventually refused the offer and instead became king of Belgium. Furthermore Otto would not be 21 until 1835, and until then a three-man regency of distinguished Bavarians acted in his place. Their rule was autocratic, and so was Otto's when he came of age.

Otto resigned after a revolt against him in 1862 and was replaced, again through the influence of the allied powers, by the son of the future king of Denmark. He ruled from 1863 as King George I of the Hellenes, his title signalling that he was king of Greeks everywhere, not just those in Greece, and that he backed the Great Idea, the *Megáli Idhéa*, of a greater Greece with Constantinople as its capital. The long reign of George I was ended when he was assassinated while walking on the seafront in Salonika, and he was succeeded by his eldest son as Constantine I. A Byzantine Constantine had lost Constantinople in 1453. Would a new Constantine regain it?

The 1914–18 war brought the biggest crisis yet for the monarchy, the National Schism, the *Ethnikós Dhikasmós*. King Constantine I believed Greece should remain neutral, but his sympathies were clearly with Germany. He was married to the sister of Kaiser Wilhelm of Germany, and like many Greek officers had been trained in Germany. Elevthérios Venizélos, prime minister since 1910, strongly supported Germany's opponents, the Triple Entente of Britain, France and Russia. In June 1915 the King ordered Venizélos to resign, and in the following September Venizélos set up a rival government in Salonika. In 1917 Constantine was forced to abdicate in favour of his son Alexander, but would be allowed to return after the war. In 1920 Alexander died of septicaemia, bizarrely caused by the bite of a pet monkey, and in 1920 Constantine returned to the throne, after a plebiscite which gave him a suspiciously high 99 per cent support.

The postwar Versailles Conference gave Greece territorial concessions which promised the fulfilment at last of the *Megáli Idhéa*. Smyrna and its hinterland on Turkey's Mediterranean coast were placed under Greek administration, and Greek troops moved into Turkey, almost reaching Ankara. But disaster followed and the Greek forces were driven out of Turkey, leaving the town of Smyrna in flames behind them. The event became known as the Asia Minor Catastrophe.

Those held responsible for it suffered a heavy penalty. In late 1922 a revolution, of which General Plastíras was one of the leaders, forced Constantine, who had returned to the throne only two years before, to abdicate again. He did so in favour of his son who became George II, the king whose position was to be such a bone of contention in the 1940s. Eight of the political and military leaders of the Asia Minor Catastrophe were tried by court martial for treason. Though nothing worse than incompetence was even alleged, six were executed by firing squad and the other two sentenced to life imprisonment. Constantine's brother Prince Andrew, who had commanded an army corps in the campaign, was condemned to banishment for life. It was Prince Andrew's son Philip who became Britain's Duke of Edinburgh, as consort of Queen Elizabeth II.

The first reign of George II was short lived. A Revolutionary Council in effect governed Greece from the time of the 1922 Plastíras revolt, and in October 1923 demanded that the monarchy be abolished. Under this threat George II left Greece in December for 11 years as an exile in England, and the monarchy was formally ended in the following March.

The 11 years 1924–35 brought, by one reckoning, 23 government changes, one dictatorship and 13 coups. By 1935 even staunch republicans had swung to support for the monarchy. As one of them said in a speech to parliament:

> Everybody knows that I was one of the warmest supporters of the republic and was among those who fought for its establishment. But after eleven years' experience of a republican regime, I now see that instead of internal peace it has brought us civil war, the undermining of respect for the State, spiritual anarchy. So what would you have me advise the Greek people? I shall say to the Greek people that the only thing to do is to bring back the well-tried system of constitutional monarchy.[1]

In 1935 a plebiscite on the return of the monarchy produced another suspect 98 per cent in support of George II and he returned to the throne. As we have seen, elections in the following year gave the Communists the balancing power in parliament, and on 4 August 1936 the Metaxás regime began.

Thus by the time George II returned to the century-old monarchy in 1935, a number of issues had bedevilled the institution. It was not forgotten that both of the first two kings, Otto in 1833 and George I in 1863, had been in effect imposed by foreign powers, and all the successors of George I were his descendants. The titles of George I, who was in fact Danish, included Glücksburg, and Communist orators of the 1940s often referred to George II as Glücksburg, with the disparaging implication that he was both foreign and pro-German.

A second issue was the *Megáli Idhéa*, the dream of a greater Greece. The King's association with it at first worked in his favour, but the failed attempt to realise it, the Asia Minor Catastrophe, was a disaster for the monarchy.

Finally, the National Schism of 1916 brought about by Venizélos had never been mended in spite of the King's efforts at reconciliation on his return in 1935, and the two sides continued at loggerheads through the Metaxás years and the occupation. In terms of personal loyalties they were labelled as royalists against Venizelists, and at the political level as monarchists against republicans. The outcome of this continuing struggle was that both Constantine I and George II had been exiled and then returned, and for a decade the monarchy had been abolished altogether.

What sort of man was King George II to whom this troubled legacy fell? Not long after the King's death in 1947 Woodhouse gave a largely sympathetic assessment of his character. The first point Woodhouse made was that George II was not a Greek. He had no Greek blood in his veins. By temperament and from his years of exile in England he thought and felt like an Englishman, or at least an educated Western European. He valued objectivity, consistency, balance and coolness – not characteristically Greek qualities. Reginald Leeper, British ambassador to the Greek government in exile, added to this picture in a 1943 report, stressing the King's austere aloofness, especially in the company of Greeks: 'Amongst these vivacious, talkative and intensely political southerners he is very much the reserved northerner who damps the ardour of those who might otherwise acclaim him.'[2]

Despite the King's powerful sense of having a sacred duty to Greece, he often thought of giving up the crown, perhaps by abdication once the monarchy was re-established. Leeper noted in 1943 that the King faced the future without enthusiasm and never talked of it, perhaps from a lurking hope that the Greeks would reject him after all. His personal life was also a factor. His marriage to Princess Elizabeth of Romania, never happy, ended with divorce in 1935, and he now had an English mistress, Joyce Brittain-Jones, referred to only as J, with whom he wanted to settle in England.

The King's stubbornness in carrying out what he saw as his duty, combined with his aloof manner, often antagonised the British on whose backing he depended. While in London between 1941 and 1943 he constantly demanded assurances that he would be restored to his throne, if necessary by force, and accused everyone, including the Foreign Office, of being hostile to him. His relations with Foreign Office officials were not improved when his mistress J, perhaps unwisely, told them of the King's belief that, if he did not return to Greece, this would largely be the fault of the Foreign Office and its agents. Once the King was in Cairo, Leeper became so used to the King's constant complaints about the British that he was taken aback when one day the King came to him and with a cheerful smile said, 'Today I have no grouses to bring you.'[3] Uneasy lay the head that wore the crown, but also uneasy lay the heads of those who in varying degrees tried to keep that crown in place.

As we have seen, King George II of Greece and his party had made a hazardous escape from Crete in May 1941 when German parachute troops were already landing on the north of the island. They reached Alexandria on a Royal Navy ship, and then moved on to stay at the Greek legation in Cairo. However, it was soon clear they were not welcome as guests to King Farouk and his pro-Italian prime minister, and at the invitation of the British government King George, Prime Minister Tsoudherós and his government in exile sailed for England on 27 June 1941. After a three-month journey via the Suez Canal and the Cape, they docked at Liverpool on 21 September. When their train reached Euston Station their welcome was as grand as it could possibly be; on the platform to greet them were Churchill and his Cabinet, with King George VI and Queen Elizabeth. The King of Greece moved into Claridge's Hotel, and his government to a block of flats in Park Lane.

Initially the King had the unequivocal support of the British government. Churchill took the view that 'we had a special obligation [to him] as the head of a State which had fought as our Ally.'[4] Eden thought the same. On 29 October he wrote, 'I fully agree that our policy is to support the King of Greece and the present Greek Government. In fact we are pledged to see them through to the end.' But in the same note he acknowledged that many Greeks 'now harbour suspicions that the King and the present government intend to restore the [Metaxás] dictatorship'. The King and his government must therefore 'do all they can to dissipate the mistrust which undoubtedly exists as to their political intentions'.[5]

It might seem that a simple statement by the King that he would restore the constitution would do the trick, but it was not as easy as that. For one thing, a pledge to restore the constitution would be an acknowledgment by the King that the Metaxás regime and his own position as head of it were both illegal, an admission he refused to make. Secondly, the Greek government in exile would also be illegal, since it was a continuation of the Metaxás regime. Also many of its initial members were Metaxás' ministers, including the reviled anti-Communist Maniadhákis, and the last of these ministers was not removed until January 1942. Finally, it was not at all clear what restoring the constitution meant.

Greece had had three constitutions since the beginning of the century. The 1911 constitution was monarchist, a revision of the 1864 constitution which had established King George's grandfather on the throne. In 1923 King George II was exiled and in 1927 a republican constitution was introduced. In 1935 the King returned, under a new monarchist constitution, but this crucially was subject to revisions which were never carried out. This meant that technically the 1935 monarchist constitution had never come into effect, and restoring the constitution meant adopting its predecessor, the 1927 republican one. But for King George II and his British supporters the restored constitution had of course to be the 1911 monarchist one.

The arguments over how and in what way the King should clarify his position went back and forth for months between the King's prime minister Tsoudherós and the Foreign Office. Eden quickly wearied of it, writing in a somewhat twisted metaphor only a month after the King's arrival, 'Greek politics is a hot and sticky porridge and I abhor the idea of putting my finger into this mess.'[6] Eventually a formula was found to bridge the gap. The 1911 monarchist constitution would remain in force *for the time being*, but after the war a new constitution under the King would be established *subject to popular approval*. The King signed a Constitutional Act to this effect on 4 February 1942. Thus the King had conceded that the monarchist 1911 constitution would only be temporary, and the British had accepted that the King's return would be subject to some form of popular approval.

The 'sticky mess' of the constitutional issue was quickly followed by another. Did 'subject to popular approval' mean a decision by the Greek people in a plebiscite on whether the King should return? Back in June 1941, the month of the German invasion, the American ambassador to Greece, Lincoln MacVeagh, had told Washington that he expected a demand for a postwar plebiscite on the monarchy. In the first months of 1943 the attitude of the resistance groups towards the King and his return became clear. The views of Zérvas and EDES were opportunist rather than principled. Initially Zérvas was anti-monarchist. The nominal head of EDES, the now exiled General Plastíras, was a republican, and the founding charter of EDES opposed the return of the King except after a free expression of the will of the

Greek people. However, it soon became clear to Zérvas that his own survival depended upon support against ELAS from the British, and he switched to total commitment to the British policy of backing the King. He announced this in a telegram of 9 March 1943 to the King and the government in exile which said:

> If King returns here result free opinion our people we will be first to welcome and consider Greece constitutional quarrels ended. If England for wider reasons and even without people's wishes wants return of King we fighting for liberation will not oppose at all.[7]

In other words, Zérvas would prefer a plebiscite, but would go along with the British whatever they did.

At the same time as the Zérvas telegram Woodhouse was reporting that EAM was insisting on a plebiscite. EAM obviously expected the King to be firmly rejected, and reports reaching London from November 1941 onwards confirmed this impression. One such report claimed that 80 to 90 per cent of Greeks were opposed to the return of the King, and another that nobody supported the King except a few with personal ties to him and a handful of royalist officers. These reports were undoubtedly skewed. They largely originated from areas dominated by ELAS in northern Greece and took no account of opinion in the traditionally royalist Peloponnese, where there was then no British Military Mission to send back reports.

A further question about the King was where he and his government in exile should be based while the war continued. If he was to return to Greece with his troops at liberation, as Churchill strongly favoured, he should be with them meanwhile and not living in luxury at Claridge's over 2,000 miles away. The Greek army in Egypt consisted of some 18,000 men, of whom one-third were former officers. They formed three infantry battalions, one made up of Greek nationals living in Egypt and the other two of soldiers who had escaped from Greece at the time of the occupation. They were a discontented lot. They had nothing active to do, and there was hardly any training because equipment for it was scarce. It is no surprise that political intrigue was rife, with conflict between the mainly royalist officers and the mainly Venizelist and anti-monarchist other ranks. As early as July 1941 some of the rank and file were refusing to serve under royalist officers associated with Metaxás. Each group, royalists and Venizelists, formed its own political organisation, and in early March

1943 there was a short-lived mutiny by the Venizelist other ranks which was suppressed by the British army. In this encounter four British military policemen were shot. It was not to be the last mutiny of the Greek forces in Egypt.

Up to now only one member of the Greek government in exile, Panayiótis Kanellópoulos, had been in Cairo. Both the King and the British Foreign Office were now in agreement that the King and all the rest of his government in exile should leave London for Cairo, and it was hoped that their presence would end the disputes in the army. They arrived there in March 1943, within weeks of the mutiny. They were shortly followed by Leeper, the new British ambassador to the Greek government. He was to play a major role in what followed and was considered by some to be effectively the prime minister of Greece.

On 21 March 1943, soon after his arrival in Cairo, the King made a tour of inspection of the Greek battalions, each now under the command of a British brigadier. It went off quietly, though the King had his own doubts about whether his presence among the troops might seem to condone their mutiny. On 4 July 1943 he made a broadcast to the Greek people, which was in effect a public statement of the little-known Constitutional Act which he had signed in February of the previous year. The broadcast, as summarised by SOE, said:

> As soon as Greece is free, you will decide by popular and free vote the institutions with which Greece must endow herself to take her place in Europe. As soon as military operations allow, free and general elections will be held for a Constituent Assembly, in any case within six months. I am sure that no Greek, least of all myself, will fail to respect the Assembly's decision. Until then the monarchist constitution of 1911 will be in force. As soon as the seat of Government can be transferred to Greek soil, the present Government will resign, in order that a fully representative Government may be formed, whose composition will guarantee the freedom of the elections.[8]

This was all very well as far as it went, and Churchill maintained that it was an adequate statement of the King's position. But it left unresolved two crucial questions. One was whether the King would return with his troops at the time of liberation, and many thought the implication was that he would. If he did, he would greatly enhance his prestige, and would be in situ when a decision on his future was made. It is much more difficult to throw out an unwanted guest than to prevent him attending in the first place. The other unresolved question was whether the King's future would be decided in government or by a plebiscite of the whole Greek people on this specific issue. A plebiscite was not mentioned in the broadcast, and again many assumed that the King was ruling it out.

This was the state of affairs when the delegates of the resistance bands arrived in Cairo on their long-anticipated visit in August 1943.

14

The Cairo Conference, August 1943

In the early months of 1943 Myers had three principal responsibilities, two military and one political. The two military tasks were, as we have seen, the destruction of the Asopós railway bridge and the Operation Animals sabotage designed to make the Germans expect an imminent invasion of Greece. Both were successfully completed in June and July. Myers' political task as instructed by SOE was to unify the resistance as National Bands, but this proved much more difficult. As Myers wrote, 'political problems were the greatest ones which faced me.'[1]

The first step towards the formation of National Bands was the so-called First Military Agreement, drawn up by Myers and Woodhouse on 14 March 1943. Its principal features were that bands in different areas would co-operate with other bands, and certainly not attack each other; that all bands would be under British control; and that British supplies would be cut off from any band breaching the agreement.

First responses from the two main groups were promising. Zérvas for EDES signed at once. Tzímas for ELAS said that he personally had no objection to the agreement in principle but would need to go to Athens to discuss it with the EAM Central Committee. Tzímas left for Athens in early April and returned on 16 May, bringing EAM's forcible objections. EAM wanted all references to British officers removed, and proposed that ELAS should thus be controlled not by British officers but by a general headquarters consisting of Tzímas as political adviser, Saráphis as military commander and Áris as popular leader. All three must agree on any operation, and they would 'be pleased to accept general instructions from Middle East Command'.[2]

However, they would not obey those instructions unless their wishes were carried out – that is, unless there was a public commitment to a plebiscite on the future of the King before he was allowed to return. Myers sent to SOE Cairo a version of the agreement revised on these lines, and on 26 May SOE unsurprisingly told Myers on no account to accept the revised version. It looked like stalemate.

Meanwhile ELAS launched attacks on both EDES and EKKA. Myers could in theory prevent these by playing his ace of withholding supplies, but found that he had to continue supplies to ELAS in spite of its attacks because ELAS support was vital to Operation Animals. Also his ace could be trumped by the retort that attacks would continue *unless* supplies were resumed. Myers came face to face with his political problems when he addressed a group of some 250 ELAS andártes and their political advisers, in an attempt to stop their current attack on other bands and to promote the original version of the military agreement. He was aggressively heckled, subjected to what he considered insulting behaviour, and had to be escorted away for his own protection.

Myers tried again to get an agreement from the resistance bands. ELAS had demanded a general headquarters of its three leaders, Tzímas, Saráphis and Áris. On 4 June Myers called a conference of these three together with Zérvas for EDES, himself and Woodhouse, and proposed a *joint* general headquarters consisting of Áris for ELAS, Zérvas for EDES, and himself. The ELAS response was that all three ELAS leaders must be members, and all decisions made by vote. As this meant that Myers and Zérvas would always be outvoted by three to two, neither of them could accept it.

Myers sent an account of the conference to SOE Cairo by wireless and asked for instructions. These reached him on 17 June and, with the start of Operation Animals only days away, gave him a free hand to get the best possible terms out of ELAS, assuring him that any decision he made would be backed by Cairo. Myers made some minor alterations to the ELAS version of the agreement, and ELAS signed it. So did Zérvas, under pressure from Myers but with grave misgivings. So too some weeks later did Psarrós for EKKA, an organisation too weakened by ELAS attacks to have played any part in the prolonged negotiations. A few days later an announcement by General Wilson, commander-in-chief of Middle East Command, said that: 'It is therefore now an accomplished fact that all Greek andarte bands, irrespective of their political or other tendencies, have been welded into a united and co-ordinated instrument for the furtherance of the Allied struggle.'[3] This optimism was sadly unfounded, as the visit to Cairo by EAM-ELAS representatives in August soon made clear.

A month later on 14 July 1943 Major David Wallace arrived in north-west Greece as Eden's representative, to be political adviser to Myers and to report to Eden on conditions there. Wallace was a remarkable young man. He was the eldest child by her first husband of the glamorous, flamboyant and five-times married society figure Idina Sackville. He was born on 3 October 1914 at his parents' house in Park Lane and grew up surrounded by wealth, privilege and prestige. He became familiar with the world of politics through his father Euan Wallace, a Conservative MP and government minister, and Anthony Eden was a family friend. Wallace rebelled against this background: 'How empty, barren, rotten this home life is [...] with all this artificiality, selfishness, utter blindness that cannot see or feel the needs of others.'[4] He determined to become a celibate Christian socialist priest and spent time with a religious settlement in south-east London and with down-and-outs on the Embankment. But while Wallace was at Oxford reading Classics this aim was given up and replaced by a passion for Greece as it was now, which he saw as embodying a set of beliefs and a way of life for which he could live and die fighting. After a then rare first class degree he went to Greece in 1937 on a research fellowship, met and married Pru Magor, who was also a rebel against an affluent background, and remained in Greece until the German invasion. So when he arrived back in Greece in 1943 as a political adviser he had already spent four years there, knowing the language and the country, familiar with British politics, temperamentally ready to challenge official views, and free of any previous judgements on the protagonists.

Wallace began his report with a picture of life in Greece, and said he was astonished to find how much of it was free. The whole central part was completely independent of the occupying powers or the collaborationist government, and you could travel in perfect safety from Flórina in the far north to Athens with nothing more than an ELAS pass. In Kardhítsa in central Greece, only a few miles from a large Italian garrison, British officers freely went shopping – in uniform.

Wallace went on to assessments of the resistance groups and their leaders. EAM, the political arm, was clearly just a cover for the Greek Communist Party, the KKE. ELAS, the military arm, had about 15,000 men, as opposed to 5,000 in EDES. However, the ELAS andártes were ill-trained and ill-disciplined, and few of them had any serious intention of fighting the occupying powers. They were scallywags officered by schoolmasters, of little military value. The Greek people distrusted ELAS and EAM, hated their violent methods and would give anything to be rid of them. 'They have no fear that the Italians or Germans will remain in Greece much longer; but they are terribly afraid that EAM will.'[5]

Wallace believed that until about March or April of that year EAM had definitely been working on a policy of a violent Communist seizure of power. This policy had now changed, mainly from the realisation that their popular support was being lost by their attacks on other bands, and that they were wholly dependent on the British. The new EAM policy was at all costs to appear respectable. Thus past errors were denounced, ELAS members were supposedly given freedom of political opinion, and any who questioned British good faith would be expelled. Was this policy switch sincere? Yes, thought Wallace – but only for the time being.

Wallace's opinions of some of the EAM and ELAS leaders were trenchant. Siántos, the EAM general secretary, was a calculating opportunist. Tzímas, Wallace believed, was an idealist who sincerely accepted the new conciliatory policy and would be prepared to carry it out to the end. Saráphis, defector from EDES and now ELAS commander-in-chief, was vain, ambitious, stupid, obstinate, unpleasant and ill-mannered.

The position of EDES was simpler. Everything hinged on Zérvas, who had committed himself to British policy, though Zérvas saw clearly that it would be impossible for him to co-operate with ELAS. Wallace had high praise for Zérvas' second in command Piromáglou as a sincere, honest and able man, in whom Wallace had much more confidence than in any other resistance leader. EKKA too was built round one personality, Colonel Psarrós, whom Wallace praised as simple and honourable, and the most efficient officer in the whole resistance.

Wallace was extremely sympathetic to the British liaison officers under Myers. They had gone to Greece to fight, but found themselves almost entirely occupied in trying to keep the peace among the Greeks and were doing their job 'with a devotion, skill and patience that is beyond all praise'.[6] About SOE, which had sent them there, he was scathing. Through SOE Wallace while in Greece had sent 13 telegrams to Leeper in Cairo and not one had been delivered, which Wallace believed was a piece of deliberate deception. SOE, said Wallace, was running armies of tens of thousands of men without in practice being answerable to anyone, and it must become directly responsible to the secretary of state for war and the foreign secretary.

Wallace also advocated a much tougher line both with the King and with EAM-ELAS. The previous policy smacked of Munich appeasement. He thought the British government should state firmly that the King's 4 July broadcast was the last word about his position and there would be no further discussions or concessions. After the Cairo Conference Churchill, with Roosevelt's support, did take this line but the King's broadcast, as we have seen, left unresolved the two vital questions of the plebiscite and the timing of the King's return.

With EAM-ELAS Wallace thought that the British Military Mission should 'develop the habit of saying "No" firmly and categorically, and of then sticking to it [...] supplies must be cut off without hesitation whenever we are not satisfied with their attitude.'[7] This of course was an implicit criticism of Myers, and Wallace made this explicit in recording his questions to Myers about the wisdom of constant concessions to EAM-ELAS.

Back in 1827, before the Battle of Navarino, Admiral Codrington had explained his method of dealing with a difficult foreigner, his French fellow admiral de Rigny. 'In order to ensure his yielding to me whatever I considered essential, I embraced every opportunity of giving way to him in matters of minor importance.'[8] Wallace clearly thought Myers had taken this principle too far.

However, Wallace was warmly sympathetic to Myers over the position in which he had been placed:

Eight months ago he was given his new commission, to develop the guerrilla movement. He was then left to do it. He was given no advice how to do it, and he was given no expert staff to assist him. By the time I joined him he had wrestled with all these problems for seven months on his own, and his mind was made up. A week earlier he had achieved in the National Bands Agreement the goal of several months of effort. In his own mind he was committed to a policy and he knew he was right [...]. In fact he has been left with responsibilities that it would be unfair to expect any man to bear without error. He has entirely by his own efforts and influence so far saved Greece from serious civil war. The credit for this is his. The blame for the terrible price he has paid to achieve this end belongs to those who gave him no help and no advice.[9]

The idea of a visit to Cairo by representatives of the resistance had been discussed intermittently since February, when the Communist general secretary Siántos suggested it to Woodhouse in Athens. In May Myers proposed a visit to Cairo by Greek politicians, including EAM and EDES representatives, and Leeper agreed.

The group that actually went was put together somewhat haphazardly. In early July, after the successful completion of Operation Animals, Myers told SOE that he wanted to come to Cairo for instructions on the next phase, and SOE replied that they would be delighted to see him. During July first Tzímas, then Piromáglou (Zervás' second in command representing EDES) and a bit later Kartális (representing EKKA) asked if they could come too. Myers agreed and so did SOE. With Myers and Wallace, it would be a party of five. All agreed with Myers' proposed modest-sounding agenda for the talks in Cairo on the next phase: that recruiting by each resistance band should be limited, that civil administration should be strengthened and that there should be closer links between the Greek government in exile and the resistance.

The party was to be flown out on an RAF Dakota, and a large airstrip was cleared and levelled at Neraídha in central Greece. The work was done by over 1,000 Greeks, including many women, under the direction of a British officer. To conceal its tell-tale shape from German aircraft, a large number of fir trees were felled and stuck upright in the ground.

On 8 August the party was ready to leave the following night except for Tzímas, who had gone to get instructions from an EAM emissary. Then Tzímas appeared accompanied by Siántos and three other members of the EAM Central Committee, and Siántos demanded that either these three should also go to Cairo with Tzímas or none of them would go. Myers had to bow to Siántos' ultimatum – a visit without EAM-ELAS would be pointless – and he signalled his decision to Cairo. The party, now of eight for whom there was just room on the plane, took off on 9 August and was in Cairo early the following morning. Myers was put up in Lord Glenconner's flat and wrote that after a delicious hot bath and breakfast on the veranda 'for the first time for almost a year I relaxed completely'.[10] Unfortunately his euphoria was to be short lived.

Two days after their arrival the Greek delegates led by Tzímas had a meeting with their government in exile and cast aside the agreed agenda. They now demanded a statement from the King that he would not return until after a plebiscite in his favour, and that the resistance movement should be given three seats in the exiled government as ministers for the interior, war and justice.

Leeper was very aggrieved at being taken by surprise. He said that he had not anticipated that the delegates would be mainly interested in raising political issues, though the slightest knowledge of the Greek resistance would have told him that this was likely. He seems to have felt that a diplomat's work should at all times proceed in a smooth and immaculately prepared manner. When Leeper complained that he was living on the edge of a volcano, Churchill retorted by asking 'Where else do you expect to live in times like these?'[11]

From now on Leeper's attitude to Myers changed completely, as Myers wrote, 'from one of cordial co-operation to one of suspicion and unjust accusations'.[12] Even before the conference Leeper had decided that Myers was in the wrong, writing: 'Myers has no political acumen and does not see beyond his nose or, should I say, the noses of his guerrillas. He is not astute enough in dealing with EAM and I am sure he exaggerates their political importance.' When Myers arrived in Cairo, Leeper did not want to listen to him, and wrote that Myers

> Keeps on telling me that he must have hours and hours of conversation with me in order to convince me. I have avoided as many of these hours as possible, but even so I am completely convinced that he is a very dangerous fool.

In short, Leeper considered Myers 'a complete disaster'.[13] Criticism of colleagues is common enough, but these vituperative strictures, from one senior government servant about another, were extraordinary.

Meanwhile the delegates' two demands were on the table. One was for three ministerial portfolios, and this was firmly rejected by the Greek government in exile. The other was that the King should state that he would not return before a plebiscite, and here there was more room for manoeuvre. Leeper was in favour of such a statement until the Foreign Office instructed otherwise, saying, 'If the King now pledges himself not to return to Greece until after a plebiscite he is in fact signing his abdication.'[14] Prime Minister Tsoudherós and the Greek government also backed no return before a plebiscite.

The King asked for advice from Churchill and Roosevelt, who were then meeting in Quebec. Churchill rejected the demand that the King should not return before a plebiscite, and replied that he was looking forward to the King's return at the head of his army, with a plebiscite to come later. He added that the British government would give the King the maximum support. Roosevelt, though somewhat more cautiously, backed Churchill. Roosevelt's support for the Greek monarchy was strange, as it was against the advice of his State Department and against the violently anti-monarchist opinions of most Greek Americans and their newspapers. It seems most likely that in Quebec Roosevelt came face to face with the full force of Churchill's persuasive powers and bowed to them.

The Cairo Conference had thus been a total failure, with no agreement on anything and no meeting of minds. The only question now was how quickly the delegates could be sent back to Greece, where Churchill thought they could do less harm than in Cairo. The delegates wanted to stay, believing that their demands had not been properly discussed. They were due to fly out on 22 August, but at the last minute asked, as Greek subjects, for a meeting with their prime minister Tsoudherós, and Tsoudherós secured a delay. On 16 September, their aims frustrated and their trust in the British much diminished, they finally left for Greece.

In many different ways the Cairo Conference was a turning point. It ended the illusion that military and political objectives could be kept separate and showed that these aims were incompatible: the Communist-dominated EAM-ELAS had to be supported because it fought Germans, but needed to be emasculated to prevent it seizing power in postwar Greece. The conference also made clear that the British policy of support for the King's immediate return with the army of liberation, to be followed by a later plebiscite, was becoming extremely difficult to sustain, and within a year it was abandoned. The irony is that, if the policy had been abandoned at the time of the Cairo Conference, it would have deprived EAM-ELAS of one of its main propaganda claims – that the British wanted to impose the King on Greece without regard to the wishes of the Greek people.

The conference also caused a convulsion in SOE. The Foreign Office was already deeply suspicious of SOE, referring to its 'ramps' and its preference for the cranky and unorthodox. Leeper blamed SOE for creating the fiasco of the conference and argued that SOE should be completely subordinated to the Foreign Office. In London the government's Middle East Defence Committee demanded that SOE Cairo should in effect be abolished, with its military operations passed to Middle East Command and its political activities to the Foreign Office. However, SOE Cairo was saved by Churchill and survived, though with its wings severely clipped.

Glenconner was dismissed, as was Brigadier Keble. Glenconner was described as 'by far the best chief whom SOE Cairo ever had'[15] but was accused first of undermining British support for the Greek King – a charge he refuted – and then for failing to control his subordinates, meaning Keble and his over-ambitious expansion. Glenconner, the civilian, was replaced by a professional soldier, Brigadier Stawell.

In mid-September Myers left Cairo for London to try and persuade the British authorities of the true situation in Greece. He had a frosty reception from the Foreign Office, where he was accused of putting the delegates up to demanding three ministerial posts and of exaggerating the military importance of the resistance. He met King George VI, whom he found extremely well briefed and most interested in Myers' views. He lunched and spent a long afternoon with Churchill at Chequers, when Churchill was genial but non-committal. Churchill's true opinion of Myers was made clear in his later comment that Myers was 'the chief man who reared the cockatrice brute of EAM-ELAS'.[16] The cockatrice was a fabled creature from the Old Testament, born of a cock's egg, represented as having the body of a cock with a barbed serpent's tail, and whose mere glance could kill. It was a characteristically Churchillian use of an obscure but sonorous term.

In October Myers was back in Egypt and learnt from SOE Cairo that he would not be returning to Greece. Again there was a parallel between Myers and Admiral Codrington: both were shabbily treated, on the flimsy grounds that they had exceeded their instructions, by the governments which they had devotedly served. Woodhouse had already been appointed in Myers' place, though Woodhouse had supported all Myers' decisions since they arrived in Greece and continued to do so. Myers returned to the army and later served with distinction at Arnhem. But in October 1943 he was, as he wrote, 'miserably disappointed because I was being denied the opportunity of completing the task which I had begun among the people whom I had grown to love and whom I believed I understood'.[17]

After the Cairo Conference Wallace remained for a time on Leeper's staff. Leeper thought highly of him and dedicated his own book on Greece to Wallace with the epigraph, borrowed from Dr

Johnson, 'Nullum quod tetigit non ornavit' (He adorned everything he touched). Wallace returned to Greece in July 1944, again as Eden's personal representative, this time to report on the situation in the Epirus area controlled by Zérvas and EDES. He spent some days with Nigel Clive, the senior British liaison officer in Epirus, and discussed with Clive his new report. Wallace now found ELAS much more formidable, no longer mere scallywags. He believed that, as he had suspected a year earlier, their professed co-operation then had been only tactical and temporary, and that now 'the indications are that ELAS definitely intends to try for the seizure of the monopoly of power.' He argued that

> unless Allied troops arrive in the country to take over the main centres from the Germans, or we reinforce Zervas to a point where he can take offensive action to protect the population in territory at present controlled by ELAS, there will be a most bloody slaughter ending in a Communist dictatorship.[18]

It comes as a jolt to find that in the end Wallace despaired of the Greeks. He concluded his report by saying:

> Our effort in Greece, in men and money, has not only been out of all proportion to the results we have achieved against the Germans, but also to the value of the Greek people, who are not capable of being saved from themselves, nor for themselves worth it. This is also the opinion of all British liaison officers, who have been long in the country.[19]

Clive said that he strongly disagreed with this, the only part of Wallace's report that he questioned. Wallace's statement can be taken as an example of his uncompromisingly hard-headed judgement, or perhaps of the tendency to lurch to extreme positions which had always characterised him.

A few days after leaving Clive, Wallace went to observe an operation of EDES against the Germans. At the start of the skirmish he was hit by a stray bullet and killed instantly. Anthony Eden wrote his obituary in *The Times*, saying that 'He was destined to be one of the leaders of his generation. Had he lived to take up that political career upon which he had set his heart, no position would have been beyond his reach.'[20] His death was one of the many tragic losses of talent and promise through the mischances of war. It was reminiscent of Kipling's angry lament for a young British officer killed on the North-West Frontier:

> Two thousand pounds of education
> Drops to a ten rupee jezail,
> The Crammer's boast, the Squadron's pride,
> Shot like a rabbit in a ride.[21]

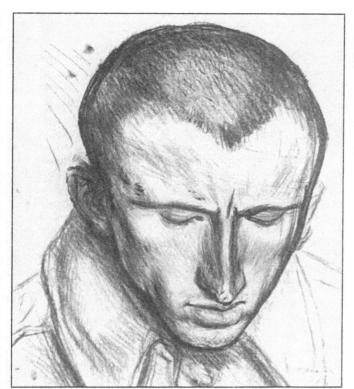

1 A Greek soldier at the time of the Italian invasion

2 'Return of the heroes' from the Italian front

3 General Tsolákoglou, the first Greek prime minister under the occupation, with a German officer

4 British troops leave
Greece, 3 May 1941

5 Father Iánnis
Alevizákis of Alónes,
Crete. He and his sons
were a great help to the
SOE agents

6 German parachutists land at Máleme, Crete, 20 May 1941

7 Cretans refuse to leave their village before it is destroyed in a German reprisal

8 Kidnapped and kidnappers, Bill Moss, General Kreipe and Leigh
Fermor in the Cretan mountains, May 1944

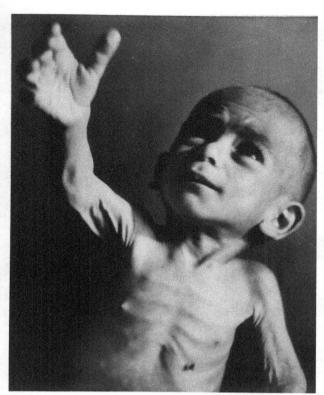

9 a & b Starvation in
Athens, winter 1941–2

10 a & b The Gorgopótamos viaduct before and after demolition

11 Napoleon Zérvas, EDES leader

12 Áris Velouchiótis, ELAS leader

13 Young widow with her children, Dhístomo, 1945

14 Hyperinflation. 500,000,000 drachmas for an egg, November 1944

15 Mourners after the demonstration in Síntagma Square on 3 December 1944. The partly obscured banner reads: 'When the people are in danger of tyranny, choose either chains or arms. E.A.M.'

16 a & b Bombarded streets during the battle for Athens, December 1944–
January 1945

17 Churchill and Dhamaskinós in Athens, 30 December 1944. Churchill's
earlier suspicions of the archbishop had by now evaporated

18 King George II of Greece

19 Queen Frederica in the mountains of Greece

20 a & b An older
and a younger
woman andártissa in
the Democratic Army

21 Children at one
of Queen Frederica's
pedhópolis

22 The end of the civil
war. Young andártes of
the Democratic Army
captured near the
Bulgarian border

15

The Italian Armistice and the First Communist Offensive

The months from September 1943, when the delegates to the fruitless Cairo Conference returned to Greece, until the following spring brought the first open attempt by the Communists to achieve dominance in Greece. It is often labelled the First Round of what was to be a long drawn-out conflict. The immediate trigger for this First Round was the collapse of Italy, and its switch first to an armistice with the Allies and then, just over a month later, to a declaration of war on Germany.

By July 1943 Italy's war on the side of the Axis was effectively lost. In the previous November the combined German and Italian forces in North Africa had been decisively defeated at El Alamein, with the capture of tens of thousands of Italian troops. The Allies had invaded Sicily on 10 June 1943 and were now poised for an attack on the Italian mainland. For Mussolini's colleagues in government, the time had come to remove him.

On the afternoon of 24 July 1943 the inner cabinet of the regime, known as the Grand Fascist Council, met to consider a resolution which declared that 'the immediate restoration is necessary of all State functions' and invited the head of government, meaning Mussolini, to request King Vittorio Emanuele 'to assume, together with the effective command of the Armed Forces [...] that supreme initiative of decision which our institutions attribute to him'.[1] It was politely worded, but if accepted it would clearly mean the end of Mussolini's rule. Some of Mussolini's colleagues opposed the resolution and tried to support him, though Mussolini did little to support himself. At about 2.30 the next morning, after the meeting had lasted over nine hours, the resolution was put to the vote. It was passed by the votes of 19 out of the 28 council members present.

Mussolini was arrested and confined in a hotel on the high Appenine plateau of Gran Sasso some 20 miles west of Pescara. The King appointed the elderly Marshal Badoglio as head of government, and Badoglio immediately opened negotiations with the Allies for an armistice, though continuing to the end to assure the Germans that Italy would carry on the struggle at their side. The Italian armistice was signed on 3 September, to come into effect five days later. After a further five weeks and under pressure from the Allies Italy took the final step, and on 14 October 1943 declared war on Germany.

Italian troops were now in a highly precarious position wherever the Germans were in control, not least in Greece. Their situation was particularly confused and dangerous during the five weeks between the armistice coming into effect on 8 September and the declaration of war against Germany on 14 October. In the days following the armistice the Italian government, its disarray increased by a move from Rome to Brindisi, issued a string of contradictory instructions. Badoglio announced that 'the war would continue', but did not say on which side. The Italian War Office laid down that Italian troops were to act against Germans only if attacked, and that only if attacked should they 'make common cause' with the resistance or the Allies. But a few days later, on 10 September, Italian forces were ordered to 'treat the Germans as enemies and fight them with all force available'. On the German side Hitler ordered that all Italian troops fighting against the Germans should be treated as guerrillas with no rights as prisoners of war and should be shot as they surrendered.[2]

One of the most appalling events resulting from this confusion was on the Ionian island of Kephaloniá. It was garrisoned by an Italian division under General Antonio Gandin, which greatly outnumbered the Germans on the island. On 9 September, the day after the Italian armistice was announced, Gandin was amazed to receive orders from his Italian superior in Athens to hand over all Italian weapons to the Germans. He was aware from his staff that if he gave this order the bulk of his troops would refuse to obey, and in any case the order was contradicted the next day by the instruction to fight the Germans with all force available. Gandin was still undecided when two days later the Germans gave him an ultimatum: surrender within the day or be attacked.

Gandin spun out discussions with the Germans, but on 13 September two small boats full of German troops tried to enter the main harbour of Argostóli. Italian troops on their own initiative sank one of the boats, and soon afterwards attacked German positions on Kephaloniá. The following day the German General Hubert Lanz arrived on the island, declared that the sinking of the troop-carrying boat was an act of hostility and demanded that Gandin surrender immediately. Gandin knew that his men would not obey, and three Italian officers who tried to organise a surrender were shot by their troops. Gandin refused to capitulate and hostilities began on 15 September.

Fighting continued for a week, but on 22 September Gandin, his ammunition nearly exhausted, had no option but to surrender. Hitler's general instruction that hostile Italians were to be treated as guerrillas was reinforced by a specific order to massacre all Italian soldiers who had fought on Kephaloniá. As the Italians surrendered the Germans mowed them down with machine guns, sparing only doctors and chaplains. Those not killed at their posts were imprisoned in a town hall near Argostóli, and taken from there to be shot singly or in groups, Gandin being the first to die. The corpses were loaded on rafts to be sunk in the sea, and the 20 Italian sailors forced to do this were shot when they had finished. An estimated 4,750 Italian officers and men were deliberately killed by the Germans after the surrender.[3]

There can be no doubt that this was a war crime, and General Lanz was tried and convicted for it at Nuremberg, though his stout defence led to the comparatively mild sentence of 12 years' imprisonment. The Germans were correct in saying that Italian troops had attacked them, and technically correct in saying that the Italian army, at that point, was not in the service of a state which had declared war on Germany. The Italians were in desperate confusion because orders from above were hopelessly contradictory. None of this in any way justifies the massacre, which was one of the last of the disasters, for both Italy and other nations, resulting from Mussolini's long career of heedless self-aggrandisement.

In mainland Greece after the Italian collapse all the combatants – the Germans, the resistance groups and the British officers attached to them – had two main concerns: first, if possible, to persuade the Italians to fight with them, and if not to get hold of their weapons. The Germans moved quickly. On 9 September, the day after the armistice was announced, General Alexander Löhr, the German supreme commander in the Mediterranean, told the Italian commander in Athens that all Italian forces must lay down their arms immediately, after which they would be sent home. The Italian commander complied, believing that resistance would be useless. One small unit joined the German side, but the rest either handed over their equipment to the Germans or sold it to Greeks. Those who surrendered were not sent home to Italy but assembled at the railway station in Athens, where long columns of them were seen marching through the streets under German escort. From there they were sent to camps in occupied Europe, as internees with none of the rights of prisoners of war.

Before the armistice there had been over 170,000 Italian troops in Greece, but by the beginning of October all but 40,000 had either surrendered, joined resistance groups or simply disappeared among the Greek population. The bulk of these 40,000 were in the Pinerolo Division in Thessaly, concentrated in and around Tríkala, Lárissa and Vólos, and were commanded by General Adolfo Infante.

The Italian capitulation had been foreseen for some weeks before the actual armistice, and negotiations with General Infante had begun even before the delegates left for Cairo on 9 August. The newly established joint general headquarters of the resistance did not make these approaches together, but each member of it – the British officers, ELAS and EDES – opened separate negotiations with Infante, each trying to get control of the Italian troops and weapons. It was Infante who resolved the issue, stating that he would make an agreement only if it was guaranteed by Woodhouse as acting head of the British (as it still was) Military Mission, and would make no agreement with the andárte leaders alone.

The agreement was made on 12 September, and signed by Infante, one representative each from ELAS and EDES, and Woodhouse. Woodhouse, though deeply suspicious of ELAS motives, had no option but to sign and so guarantee the agreement. If he had not done so the Italian weapons would have fallen into German hands. The terms were that Italian troops willing to join the struggle against Germany would keep their arms, and be incorporated in Greek formations, operating 'in small units of companies'. All other equipment (this would include artillery) would be used by the Greek forces. All Italians not willing to fight the Germans would surrender their arms and all equipment, again to be used by the Greek forces.[4]

The crucial weakness of the agreement was that Infante's Pinerolo Division was all in Thessaly, an area in which ELAS was completely dominant, so in practice all Italian fighting units and all equipment went to ELAS and nobody else. The other significant weakness was the reference to the Italians operating 'in small units of companies'. This might be taken to mean small units *of company strength*, but ELAS chose to interpret it as small units *drawn from companies*. ELAS split the Italians into small and widely scattered groups from whom weapons could be borrowed and never returned, or simply seized. By the end of September, only weeks after the agreement was signed, the Pinerolo Division had ceased to exist except on paper, and by mid-October the last units had been disarmed. By these tactics ELAS had acquired an estimated 12,000 small arms, as well as artillery, mortars and machine guns, and were ready to launch a major attack on their resistance rivals.

ELAS and their political masters EAM saw this as an ideal moment to make a decisive move against Zérvas and EDES, and to establish their dominance in post-liberation Greece. There were many signs that liberation was imminent. Allied forces were now fighting in mainland Italy and the British had occupied several Dodecanese islands (temporarily, as it turned out). Italy was out of the war, and consequently the Germans were moving some units out of Greece to bolster other fronts. This looked like a general withdrawal, especially as the Russian army was advancing from the east and could isolate German forces in the Balkans. Also ELAS was now better organised into divisions, brigades and battalions, and they had a military training school from which 136 officers had already graduated. They claimed that they were no longer guerrillas but 'disciplined troops who knew how to fight'.[5] Finally, they now had the Italian weapons.

The orders to ELAS to attack Zérvas were issued on 9 October, and by the end of November ELAS had succeeded in pushing Zérvas and EDES into Epirus, west of the river Aráchthos. But within days of the first ELAS attacks on Zérvas one of the key Communist assumptions proved false. The Germans were not leaving Greece, but launched determined offensives against both ELAS and EDES.

The pressures on all parties to the conflict now became complicated. ELAS needed to survive German attacks while trying to achieve its original aim of destroying EDES. The Germans wanted to weaken the resistance, which could be more easily achieved if the rival resistance groups were fighting each other and not them. Zérvas' need to survive coincided with the German intention that he should.

Given this coincidence of aims it is not surprising that there were discussions between EDES representatives and German officers about a truce between them, at least a temporary one. For Zérvas such a deal would be like those made by his ancestors, for their own advantage, with the Turks during the Greek War of Independence. The word for these was *kapáki* or cover, and in Greece today to make a *kapáki* with someone means to outsmart him. Zérvas strung out the discussions, never meeting German officers himself but sending representatives who would arrange some later meeting. In late October Zérvas did halt all EDES actions against the Germans but this was because he had his hands full resisting ELAS. Zérvas was accused of collaboration, but that is clearly the wrong description of his actions. The ELAS commander Áris Velouchiótis shared Zérvas' view of such arrangements, saying that 'only pharmacists, notaries, and milkmen never made truces, since they never made war.'[6]

The situation was further confused by the appearance of the recently formed Security Battalions (*Tágmata Asphalías*). With German encouragement Ioánnis Rállis, who had succeeded Logothetópoulos as head of the collaborationist Greek government in April 1943, announced the formation of the first of these units on 29 June. Their purpose was to attack the resistance, particularly EAM and ELAS, and they were presented as fighters against Communism. Five Security Battalions of about 1,000 men each were concentrated in the Peloponnese, the most anti-Communist area, and another four in central and southern Greece. Their record was appalling. In Athens in November 1943 they dragged from their beds hospital patients who were suspected of Communism and took them off to prison. After a fight with the resistance on Évvia the Security Battalions pillaged the nearby village, seizing large quantities of olive oil and cheese as well as sewing machines and dowry collections, needing 60 mules to carry it all away. In March 1944 their plain-clothes assassination squads killed 50 ELAS supporters in the Vólos area. They took part in German reprisals, and in the same month shot 100 of the 200 hostages taken after the killing of a German general.

The fighting between ELAS and EDES continued, sometimes sporadically, from October 1943 to February 1944. After EDES had been pushed back into Epirus at the start of the conflict there was stalemate for the next few winter months. In early January 1944 Zérvas attacked and recovered most of his lost ground east of the river Aráchthos, only to lose it again to ELAS at the end of the month. On 4 February an armistice was agreed and was signed on 29 February at the Pláka Bridge which symbolically straddled the river Aráchthos. Under the agreement the cessation of hostilities between ELAS and EDES was to be final, and each side would occupy the territory it then held. A pious hope was expressed for the unification of all the Greek resistance. The agreement would be supervised by a committee of representatives of ELAS and EDES, plus EKKA which was still considered significant. All three groups signed the Pláka Agreement, as well as the Allied Military Mission, which the British Military Mission had become after American officers joined it, Woodhouse signing for the British and Major Wines for the Americans. Unhappily, every commitment in the Pláka Agreement was to prove no more than temporary.

One thing all parties to the Pláka armistice could agree on unreservedly was condemnation of the Security Battalions. On 19 February, ten days before the Plaka agreement, they signed a denunciation of the Battalions, who they described as 'enemies of the nation, war criminals, responsible to the nation for acts of treason.'[7] Woodhouse was very aggrieved that this commitment, seemingly endorsed by similar Allied statements, was later ignored. The post-liberation Greek government, whose responsibility it was to act, never pursued the matter. No doubt, as with Myers after Gorgopótamos, the naming of war criminals was seen as none of the business of commanders in the field.

EAM and ELAS had tried to achieve dominance by eliminating their rivals, but the Pláka Agreement marked the failure of this military offensive. They now turned with remarkable speed to a political initiative. At the Pláka discussions they had proposed the formation of a Preparatory Governmental Committee, but this had been rejected. On 26 March 1944 they announced the formation of their own version of it, the Political Committee of National Liberation, known as the PEEA from its Greek acronym. This assumed all the characteristics of government, with departments for its various functions, each under a Secretary. It issued decrees, in intelligible demotic not official *katharévousa*, which it claimed had the force of law.

Some members of the PEEA were Communist, including Siántos the KKE general secretary, in charge of the all-important Department of the Interior, and Emmanouíl Mandhákis representing ELAS in Crete, but steps were taken to make the PEEA more broadly inclusive. Its first president was a former member of EKKA, which repudiated him. He was soon succeeded by Greece's most prominent Socialist, Aléxandhros Svólos, professor of constitutional law at Athens, a man later described as having 'little political experience but with great prestige and even greater dreams'.[8] Others of broadly liberal views supported the PEEA in the naive hope that they could separate its moderate elements from its committed Communists. This inclusiveness gave the PEEA a claim to be more representative than the official Greek government in exile.

The PEEA also organised elections in April 1944 for a National Council, but these were a travesty. EAM selected the candidates, and ballot papers were distributed to and collected from voters' homes, so opponents could be identified. Even though voters could write in other names, and sometimes did, the EAM candidate always won. In practice the establishment of the National Council proved to be pointless. Within a month it had ceased to meet, and it was formally wound up in November after the liberation. But the exercise did give EAM the pretext for claiming that the National Council was 'the elected parliament of Greece'.[9]

Once again EAM had made a tactical switch from belligerence to co-operation, just as David Wallace had noted in the previous summer, and once again it was no more than a show. The PEEA was supposed to be a coalition of equal partners, with democratically elected supporters, but in fact it was a political machine under the domination of EAM and the Communists.

16

The Resistance in Crete

A t first sight the resistance in Crete might seem very like the resistance on the mainland. In both areas British and other Allied agents were active during most of the war, in both there were Communist and non-Communist resistance forces between whom the Allied agents tried to keep the peace, and in both resistance activity could bring dreadful reprisals.

However, the differences between Crete and the mainland were more striking than the similarities. First, their initial tasks were different. On the mainland covert operations began with the demolition of the Gorgopótamos viaduct in November 1942 some 18 months after the German invasion. In Crete the first need was to evacuate Allied troops left on the island after the fall of Crete in May 1941, and the work began immediately.

There were probably about 5,000 British, New Zealand and Australian soldiers left behind in Crete, though estimates vary. Of these, many surrendered as they were authorised by their officers to do, and were taken prisoner, but the improvised German camps were ringed only with a single strand of barbed wire and it was not difficult to escape to the hills. Numbers are uncertain, but there were soon about 1,000 men roaming the wilds of Crete.

Life for these wanderers was often extremely hard. In the summer of 1941 the escapers could sleep in the open, but when the harsh Cretan winter set in they had to move into caves or into the houses of welcoming Cretan villagers. These villagers were unstinting in their hospitality, providing food from their own often meagre supplies, with copious wine and the fierce spirit drink *raki*, as well as information about German patrols. The Cretans were taking a great risk; they could be shot for assisting Allied soldiers, and their villages destroyed. The risk was magnified because, as among mainland Greeks, there were Cretan informers who had been either

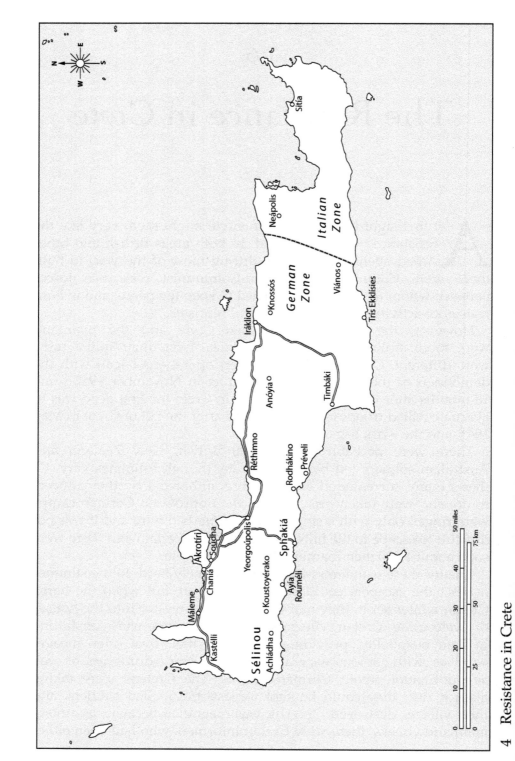

4 Resistance in Crete

coerced or lured by gain. Some stragglers left their shelter in the villages to save their hosts from further danger, some because the food and wine, impossible to refuse, had become too much for them. Nevertheless there were some who stayed in the same village house for over a year. Those on the run had to feed on snails, mountain grass, ground acorns and dandelion roots. An added problem was sickness, commonly jaundice or malaria, and some returned to prison camps for treatment, or simply to be fed.

One way of escape for the stragglers was to get hold of a small boat and escape to North Africa over 200 miles or so of the Libyan Sea. Finding a boat was not easy. The Cretan owner of the boat had to be paid – after all it was his livelihood – and the money was raised by subscription from the local villagers. Caiques with motors needed fuel. Other vessels, little more than rowing boats, had to be fitted with blankets as improvised sails. Some boats needed repair, but even so began to sink as soon as they set out. Once at sea navigation, without compass, was by the sun and the stars, and there were the added dangers of storms, of running into a minefield, of being attacked by German planes, or of finally landing in German-occupied North Africa. It is amazing that some of these hazardous voyages were successful.

Such escapes by boat, especially in the early days, were on the initiative of small groups, sometimes of only one or two individuals, but evacuations soon began to be organised from Cairo. On 26 July 1941 Francis Pool, a Royal Navy commander, was put ashore from a submarine to collect and evacuate stragglers. He landed at Trís Ekklísies on the south coast, but soon learnt that many were being sheltered in the monastery at Préveli about 40 miles to the west. There Pool assembled 130 men, and on 22 August left with them on another submarine, establishing, it was thought, a record for the number of men crammed into one submarine.

At the risk of getting ahead of the story, it is worth describing some of the more notable agents who served in Crete during the war. Initially these agents arrived and left by submarine on the south coast of Crete and later mainly by caiques or navy motor launches from harbours along 450 miles of the North African coast between Alexandria and Darnah. These vessels also brought in arms, gold sovereigns and the all-important wireless sets. Parachute drops were rare and uncertain because the only secure areas were on the rocky hillsides of Crete's mountains. The frequent traffic by sea between North Africa and Crete also meant that agents, and some Cretans, went in and out fairly regularly, whereas on the mainland Myers was head of the mission from the end of 1942 until the summer of 1943, and thereafter Woodhouse until the occupation ended.

Even before the invasion there was a singular and famous figure on Crete, John Pendlebury. Pendlebury was an archaeologist who had spent 12 years in Crete, knew its mountains 'stone by stone', as he said, loved the Cretans and they loved him: 'I have been carried shoulder high round five towns and villages and have been blessed by two bishops.'[1] His self-appointed mission, first as British vice-consul and then as a liaison officer, was to create a Cretan force to resist the expected invasion and he roamed the mountain villages to gather support. He would leave his glass eye on his Iráklion desk to show that he was away, and a swordstick, which he claimed was the best weapon against parachutists, added to his air of piratical braggadocio. On 21 May 1941, the day after the invasion of Crete, Pendlebury was badly wounded in a clash with German troops and was placed by the Germans in a nearby house under the care of two women. That evening he was treated by a German doctor. Next day a group of German paratroopers arrived, took Pendlebury outside and shot him against the wall of the house. German correctness had been overtaken by German brutality.

The first two agents sent into Crete to do more than organise evacuations were landed, again by submarine, on 9 October 1941. One was Jack Smith-Hughes of SOE, returning after his rescue by Pool, and his instructions were 'to unite the various small [resistance] bands into one great organisation'.[2] The other arrival was Ralph Stockbridge of the Inter Services Liaison Department or ISLD, charged with collecting intelligence on enemy dispositions. Stockbridge was the operator of the wireless set they had brought with them, and for the first time there was direct, even if frequently interrupted, wireless communication between Crete and Cairo.

Both Smith-Hughes and Stockbridge left Crete after two months, on the caique which had brought in Smith-Hughes' successor. Stockbridge returned to Crete, as a wireless operator, and Smith-Hughes ran the SOE Cretan desk in Cairo for the rest of the war. This was a great benefit to the SOE agents in Crete. It meant that they were controlled by a man who had been there, done their job and knew what he was talking about, and did not issue wholly unrealistic instructions like those sometimes given to SOE agents on the mainland. Smith-Hughes believed that everyone at a desk in Cairo should have served in the field, and they in turn should all spend some time in Cairo, a prerequisite, he thought, for mutual understanding. As a result agents rarely spent more than six to eight months in the field before a temporary return to Cairo.

Smith-Hughes' successor as head of the Cretan mission was Woodhouse, who had been in Crete with the army at the fall of Crete in May 1941 and had been evacuated on the last ship to leave. He returned to Crete by caique on 18 December 1941 to replace Smith-Hughes and left on 15 April 1942, to go later to mainland Greece for the Gorgopótamos operation and to stay on afterwards.

When Woodhouse left Crete in April 1942 he was in turn replaced by Tom Dunbabin. Dunbabin was Australian, a highly respected archaeologist, friend and professional rival of Pendlebury. He had already spent some 12 years in Greece and Crete, latterly as director of the British School of Archaeology in Athens, and he spoke the Cretan dialect fluently. In the early days the responsibility for each of Crete's three regions – west, central and east – lay with a British agent who operated virtually independently, but from September 1943 Dunbabin was made head of all Cretan resistance activity and was well chosen. He was described as 'an almost unnaturally modest man' but with the look of a brigand: 'In ragged breeches and black fringed turban, with his overgrown corkscrew moustache, he looked like a successful sheep-thief.'[3]

Xan Fielding landed in Crete from a submarine on the night of 11/12 January 1942. Fielding had walked across Europe in the 1930s, as Patrick Leigh Fermor had, and when war broke out was running a bar in Cyprus. He joined the army there, but loathed military life: 'I dreaded the companionship of adjutants and quartermasters more than the threat of shells and bullets.'[4] He was therefore delighted to be recruited by Smith-Hughes, now at SOE Cairo, for service in Crete.

His first attempt to reach the south coast of Crete in a motor launch which left Alexandria on 31 December 1941 had to be abandoned because of gale-force winds and mountainous seas. The second attempt, by submarine ten days later, was successful but extremely hazardous. The weather was as bad as before, and when Fielding came out on the deck of the submarine a blast of wind struck him in the face 'as though I had just leant out of the window of a fast train travelling at full speed'.[5] He and a companion were meant to land in collapsible canoes, but as soon as these were assembled and launched they were smashed against the submarine's sides. The only recourse was a saucer-shaped rubber dinghy, which when put over the side rose and fell precipitously but was briefly lifted level with the submarine's deck. That was the moment for Fielding and his companion, with a paddle each, to jump in. Sitting astride the dinghy's sides and using their legs as outriggers to control it, they eventually reached the shallows where they were tossed face down into the water. Thus, soaked and frozen, they landed in enemy territory.

Patrick (universally Paddy) Leigh Fermor landed in Crete by caique on 23 June 1942. Initially he was in charge of the eastern area occupied by the Italians, but in the following August took over the western area from Fielding when Fielding left for leave in Cairo. Leigh Fermor had two striking personal successes. One, after the Italian armistice of September 1943, was the evacuation of the commander of the Italian forces, General Angelo Carta. The other was the dramatic abduction on 26 April 1944 of the German commander of the Iraklion area, General Heinrich Kreipe.

This list of those who served in Crete is far from complete, and in particular says little of the wireless operators who had perhaps the most wretched time of all. They were stuck in remote locations because their heavy equipment could not easily be moved, with a dreary diet and no company but Cretans whom they could barely understand, and after the daily exchange of messages with Cairo had nothing whatever to do.

One further name should be added to the list, that of the New Zealander Dudley Perkins, known of course as Kiwi Perkins. One of the Allied soldiers left behind at the fall of Crete, he was captured, escaped from the prison camp and was then on the run for a year in the Sélimou area of the far south-west of Crete. He spent most of that year in unsuccessful attempts to obtain a boat. He was eventually taken off by submarine to Egypt, served for a time with his unit in the desert, was recruited by SOE in April 1943 and returned to Crete in July. He was landed in the Sélimou area which he knew well, and soon recruited a band of Cretans who were devoted to him. Thus unlike any other SOE agent he became captain of his own force, not a liaison officer. This position soon involved him, as we shall see, in a terrible incident near the Sélimou village of Achládha.

Among the Cretans too there were a vast number who made a contribution to the resistance, but some can be singled out. The elderly and portly abbot of the Préveli Monastery, Father Agathángelos Langouvádhas, sheltered over 100 men who were taken off by submarine in August 1941, and was later himself evacuated. Involved in many incidents were the three brothers of the Paterákis family from Koustoyérako in the south-western Sélimou area. In 1943 Kóstas Paterákis with other villagers temporarily saved Koustoyérako from German reprisal patrols. The Germans had set up a machine gun in the square to kill the village women and children, and Kóstas from a bluff above the village shot the machine-gunner, reputedly from a range of 400 yards. The Germans fled, but only to return soon afterwards and burn the village to the ground. Andónis Paterákis was the Cretan leader of the local guerrillas under Kiwi Perkins. The third brother, Manóli Paterákis, was Leigh Fermor's constant companion, joining him in an undercover visit to Iráklion to prepare, fruitlessly as it turned out, for destruction of the shipping in the harbour. Manóli also took part in the evacuation of the Italian General Carta and was one of the Cretans involved in the abduction of General Kreipe.

The vital job of communication between agents was done by Cretan runners, of whom the most famous was George Psichoundhákis. Leigh Fermor described what a runner did:

> The job of a wartime runner in the Resistance Movement was the most exhausting and one of the most consistently dangerous of all. It entailed immense journeys on foot at full speed over some of the most precipitous country in Europe, carrying messages between the towns and the large villages and the secret wireless stations in the mountains; humping batteries and driving camouflaged explosives and arms, and, occasionally, a British straggler in disguise, on the backs of mules through heavily garrisoned areas. He was in the game from the start to the very end.[6]

Psichoundhákis was a joker and would produce the letters he had carried 'with a comic kind of conjurer's flourish, after grotesquely furtive glances over the shoulder and fingers laid on lips in a caricature of clandestine security precautions'.[7] Though barely educated, he had written and would recite for over two hours an epic poem about the current war, and also by contrast an 'Ode to an Inkspot on a School Mistress's Skirt'. He asked endless questions about the outside world he had never seen: how whisky was made, what Churchill was like, how many sheep the average Englishman owned, religion, steam rollers and astronomy. Inventive, inquisitive and courageous, he was the epitome of a Cretan. This was what Stockbridge wrote of the Cretan contribution:

> If anything of value was achieved by the British in Crete, they owed this to the Cretans themselves, without whose protection and help of every kind no British officer could have survived more than twenty-four hours. All of us who had the honour to serve in Crete are well aware of this and consider Crete as their second country and Cretans as their brothers.[8]

There were four main tasks for the SOE agents and the Cretan resistance. The first was to evacuate the stragglers, the last of whom did not get away until the summer of 1943. The second was the collection of information about the dispositions of the occupying forces on Crete. This information, the most comprehensive collected in any part of Europe, was impressive in its detail:

> It covered: telephone systems; the state of every gun position, whether machine-gun nest, flak battery or heavy coastal artillery; satellite airfields; military roads; and the grid reference and defence details of each garrison and guard post with their strengths and armaments. Every aircraft in and out of the main airfields was logged with its direction of departure. Every ship or caique, loading and unloading in the harbours of Heraklion, Rethymno and Canea, was noted with its cargo. Landing beaches and dropping zones were reconnoitred.[9]

The Cretans hoped and believed that this information was to be used for an Allied invasion and were bitterly disappointed when it did not happen. But the information was not wasted. When the Germans built a splendid new airfield at Timbáki on the south coast it was bombed by the RAF on the day the runways were completed.

The third task was a negative one: to avoid overt and unprovoked attacks on the occupiers. These would lead to reprisals, causing damage out of all proportion to that inflicted on the enemy. But inevitably there were clashes when guerrilla bands launched attacks on their own initiative or resisted reprisals, and villages might be chosen for destruction because they had helped guerrilla bands or executed a Cretan traitor. The catalogue of these reprisals is appalling. Villages were burnt to the ground and the men of the village, sometimes virtually all, and those from the surrounding area were shot. From 1941 to 1944, apart from the winter, there were German reprisals in almost every month. In August 1944 alone nearly 1,000 Cretans were killed in such raids, and the total was in many thousands.

SOE agents in Crete were not required to create diversions like Operation Animals on the mainland, designed to make the Germans believe that the Allies would invade Greece and not Sicily. Nor were they directly involved in sabotage. There were no railways on Crete to be disrupted as on the mainland, and Soúdha Bay was too heavily guarded for any sabotage attempt as Leigh Fermor's reconnaissance showed, but airfields and petrol dumps were targets. These were attacked each summer from 1942 to 1944 by raiding parties of the Special Boat Service. In June 1942 the raiders destroyed 18 German aircraft at Iráklion and three at Kastélli in the far west. In July of the following year the Kastélli airfield was again attacked, and just south of Iráklion a large petrol dump blown up. The third raid, in July 1944, concentrated on petrol dumps, blowing up one near Chaniá and another near Iráklion, destroying over 2,000 barrels of fuel. SOE provided the information which made these raids possible, but the Cretans vigorously opposed such sabotage operations because of the reprisals which followed. Reprisals for the actions of your own people might be a price which had to be paid, but reprisals for the actions of others were intolerable.

The final part of the SOE agents' instructions was that they should unite the various guerrilla bands on Crete, but it quickly became clear how difficult this would be. Fielding's first meeting with a guerrilla leader was with Colonel Andréas Papadhákis, who had helped Stockbridge establish his wireless station and so seemed a good initial contact. He claimed, 'I'm the only man in Crete, who can offer you true service,'[10] and had set himself up as head of a Supreme Liberation Committee. This had four members, all elected by himself, and was recognised by nobody. Papadhákis refused to give details of his organisation, refused to co-operate with other bands, and they in turn would have nothing to do with him. In Smith-Hughes' succinct judgement, he was an impossible person and was removed to Egypt in August 1942.

Although the Cretan resistance was made up of many separate bands under their own leaders, ELAS was the first to create a broader coalition. Its leader was an army general, Emmanouíl Mandhákis, who in 1938 had been among those involved in a failed Cretan revolt against the Metaxás regime. Fielding first met him in early 1942:

> In his hooded cloak and baggy breeches he looked like a successful peasant proprietor, well-fed and massive, but far from flabby, for he had been on the run ever since the occupation started. Yet he did not give the impression of being a hunted victim, perhaps because he was attended by a retinue so overawed by military rank as to be reduced to a state of servility bordering on adulation.[11]

When Mandhákis left Crete for the mainland at the end of 1943 to become the military member of the Communist provisional government, the PEEA, his place was taken by a dubious character, Yánnis Bódhias, who had been in prison for attempted murder.

There was at first no counterweight to ELAS like EDES on the mainland, so the SOE agents needed to create one. Their choice to lead what became EOK, the National Organisation of Cretans, was Manóli Bandouvás, leader of an independent guerrilla band. As Fielding described him, he was 'a dark burly man with sad ox-eyes and a correspondingly deep-throated voice in which he was fond of uttering cataclysmic aphorisms such as "The struggle needs blood, my lads."'[12]

EOK was formally established in April 1942 on Fielding's initiative and with Bandouvás as leader. His band quickly drew in new recruits, and EOK established cells in every village. But Bandouvás' taste for blood was the undoing of himself and many other Cretans. In September 1943, days after the Italian armistice which was wrongly expected to lead to an Allied invasion of Crete, Bandouvás ambushed a German force of two companies near Viános close to the south coast. The German casualties were 113 killed, 71 wounded and 13 captured. Four days later the inevitable reprisals followed, in which seven villages were burnt down and an estimated 1,000 Cretans killed. At the end of October Bandouvás was evacuated to Egypt to return only at liberation, and after he left EOK became an amalgam of guerrilla bands under separate leaders.

There were frequent clashes between the two arms of the resistance, ELAS and EOK, and on 7 November 1943 Fielding brokered a non-aggression agreement between them. Only isolated skirmishes followed, including a failed attempt to kill Bódhias on the actual day of the liberation of Iráklion. This agreement is sometimes credited with saving Crete from a later civil war, but the mainland experience showed that civil war could not be prevented by any number of such agreements. Postwar conflict in Crete was probably avoided because the divisive political issues in distant Athens – the return of the King and the composition of the government – were far less important in Crete, and because ELAS was never dominant enough to start a civil war.

Life for the SOE agents was extremely tough. Leigh Fermor called it a troglodytic one, and it was not much different from that of the early stragglers. After an often dangerous landing they would climb into the mountains to establish a base, sometimes in an abandoned hut but more often in a cave. In winter it was impossible to light a fire because of the give-away smoke, or even to step outside and leave tell-tale footprints in the snow. There were permanent look-outs watching for German patrols, but since their location quickly became known, and sometimes betrayed, there were constant moves to another cave. This was very different from the mainland, where agents could base themselves in reasonably comfortable houses in secure areas. Also it meant that the agents shared the lives of the guerrillas with whom they worked, and they faced directly some of the harsh experiences and hard choices of guerrilla warfare.

Fielding faced such a choice in the summer of 1943. He was with a band of guerrillas who one day brought in a young German claiming to be a deserter. Fielding interrogated him and thought he was probably genuine, but could not risk him being a spy, could not endanger the band by keeping him under guard, and was too far from the coast to evacuate him. The only alternative was to kill him. A deep hole was found among the cliffs into which his body would fall, and Fielding decided he must fire the fatal shot himself. Next morning, with the Cretans, Fielding, increasingly distressed, led the German after a two-hour climb to the edge of the hole, pretending that they were on the way to the south coast. Fielding fired, wounding but not killing the German, who fell not into the hole but down the side of the cliff. A minute later they found him still conscious but with his body torn from the fall and both legs broken. He looked interrogatively from one to the other and tried to speak but could not, and one of the Cretans fired the fatal shot to the head. Fielding wrote, 'I knew only too well that I had bungled the killing. Had I made a clean job of it I might soon have forgotten the expression in the German's eye.'[13]

In October of 1943 Kiwi Perkins had a similar decision to make, and an experience if anything more horrific. In the plain of Achládha in the Sélimou region Perkins and his band, which included the three Paterákis brothers, attacked a group of Germans who were stealing sheep. The Germans took cover in a hut and after a long battle surrendered, nine being taken prisoner. Perkins reluctantly agreed that they had to be killed, especially as other German patrols were approaching. The band had a machine gun. The nine prisoners, tied together with parachute cord, were lined up on the edge of a chasm some 75 feet deep, and the plan was for the machine-gunner to kill them virtually simultaneously and let the bodies fall into the chasm. However, when the first two had been shot they fell back dragging with them the others, still alive and screaming. Andónis Paterákis was lowered on knotted parachute cord to finish the execution, but a knot slipped and he fell, with his leg damaged, among the Germans. Perkins, in spite of having had a bullet painfully removed from his back the day before, insisted that he should now go down. He killed the Germans who were still alive, then tied the injured Andónis Paterákis to the lifeline, and was finally hauled up himself.

All over the southern war zone, including Crete, the Italian armistice of September 1943, and a month later declaration of war against the Axis, had major repercussions. Eastern Crete was held by the 32,000 troops of the Italian Siena Division under General Angelo Carta, an easy-going commander, with headquarters at Neápolis. His right-hand man was the much more resolute Lieutenant Franco Tavana. Carta's concern was to avoid useless bloodshed, while Tavana, who had long been anti-German, wanted Italian forces with Cretan guerrillas to take control of eastern Crete. SOE's aim was to prevent the Italian forces combining with the Germans. The Italian armistice had been anticipated, and Tavana opened negotiations with SOE in August. Leigh Fermor moved quickly to eastern Crete, joined Bandouvás' band, the main guerrilla force in the area which might be needed to support Italian opposition to the Germans, and arranged an arms drop for Bandouvás on 20 August.

The German response was prompt and uncompromising. The Italian troops were given the choice of continuing to fight with the Germans, or to surrender their arms and support the Germans as non-combatants, or to be interned. Any who sold or destroyed Italian weapons or who deserted their units would be shot. General Carta endorsed these orders.

Most of the Italians submitted, many of them now happily drunk believing that their war was over. Two battalions took to the hills, but soon surrendered for lack of food and shelter. Tavana tried to infiltrate Italians into the German forces as fifth columnists and to organise sabotage, but these efforts failed and he was evacuated in October. His final service to SOE was to destroy any documents that might help the Germans, and to give Leigh Fermor those that might be useful to the Allies.

Leigh Fermor smuggled Carta and a few of his staff out of their Neápolis headquarters on 16 September, and a week later reached the rendezvous with a naval motor launch at Trís Ekklísies. There they found Bandouvás, a wanted man after his foolhardy attack on the Germans at Viános, also demanding evacuation. Leigh Fermor was on the launch handing over the documents, and so was Carta, when the weather worsened and the launch had to set out to sea, leaving Bandouvás on Crete for another month. So in the end the Italian collapse in Crete was of little benefit to the Allies, and the only objective achieved was General Carta's, that of avoiding pointless bloodshed between Italians and Germans.

The idea of kidnapping a German general on Crete had been discussed by SOE as early as June 1942, but had never been attempted. Leigh Fermor, after his successful removal of General Carta, decided that it was now possible. The original target was General Heinrich Müller, the brutal German commander of the Iráklion area, but he was transferred to another area shortly before the operation and the target became his less aggressive replacement, General Kreipe. Leigh Fermor returned to Crete by parachute on 4 February 1944, and Bill Moss, his second in command for the venture, arrived by sea two months later, and they began their preparations. The story of the Kreipe abduction has become famous from Moss' book *Ill Met by Moonlight* and the subsequent film, which added its own dramatic twists.

Kreipe was living at the Villa Ariadne near Knossós, a house originally built for the archaeologist Sir Arthur Evans, but Kreipe regularly visited his headquarters 5 miles to the south, returning in the late evening accompanied only by a driver. The plan was to stop the General's car when it slowed on a slope before a road junction. Leigh Fermor and Moss were to impersonate Kreipe and his driver, German uniforms having been stolen for their disguise, and they had 11 Cretan guerrillas in support.

Darkness was essential to the plan and for three nights the General's car appeared in daylight or not at all, but on the fourth night, 26 April, it came into view after dark. Leigh Fermor waved the car down and demanded 'Papier, bitte schön'. When Kreipe reached into his breast pocket Leigh Fermor seized him and dragged him out of the car, where he was handcuffed and then pushed behind the front seats, hidden and kept silent by three of the Cretans. The driver was knocked unconscious by Moss and taken away by the rest of the Cretans.

Now came the riskiest part of the operation: getting the car and the General past the Villa Ariadne, through the German checkpoints in Iráklion and out to the west. Moss drove, arrogantly hooting his way through the crowded Iráklion streets, and Leigh Fermor sat beside him wearing the General's hat. At most checkpoints the car and the pseudo-general were recognised and waved past the barrier, though once, when the barrier was kept down and an investigation looked imminent, Leigh Fermor barked 'General's Wagen'. Moss accelerated, and just in time the barrier was lifted.

They drove to a spot near the north coast about 20 miles west of Iráklion and there abandoned the car. With the car they left a letter for the Germans, signed by Leigh Fermor and Moss, which said that they were by now on their way to Cairo, and continuing:

> We would like to point out most emphatically that this operation has been carried out without the help of CRETANS or CRETAN partisans and the only guides used were serving soldiers of HIS HELLENIC MAJESTY'S FORCES in the Middle East, who came with us. Your General is an honourable prisoner of war and will be treated with all the consideration owing to his rank. Any reprisals against the local population will be wholly unwarranted and unjust.[14]

Leigh Fermor had also asked for planes to drop leaflets reinforcing the message that reprisals would be unjustified, but for some reason this was not done. This group then set off to walk south to Anóyia, a centre of resistance, where they were joined by the other Cretans of the abduction squad. There they learnt that the German driver, concussed and barely able to walk, had been considered too great a risk and a burden to his captors and they had cut his throat. Leigh Fermor feared that the driver's death had cursed the whole enterprise.

The whole party then set off on a 50-mile trek westwards across the mountains to Rodhákino on the south coast where they hoped – but wireless signals being intermittent could not be sure – that a motor launch would collect them. It was a time of scrambling over the mountain rocks or along the edge of precipices, relying on the

Cretans for food and sleeping in abandoned huts or out in the open. Kreipe was treated with consideration as promised, except once when he expressed satisfaction at news of a German reprisal. A surprising episode was regularly included in Leigh Fermor's accounts of the exploit. One morning Kreipe looked up at the peak of Mount Ida and murmured, half to himself, 'Vides ut alta stet nive candidum Soracte.' Leigh Fermor wrote:

> I was in luck. It is the opening line of one of the few odes of Horace I know by heart (*Ad Thaliarchum,* I.ix). I went on reciting where he had broken off and so on, through the remaining five stanzas to the end.

'It was very strange,' he added, 'as though for a long moment, the war had ceased to exist.'[15]

The abductors with Kreipe eventually made contact with the rescue boat on 14 May and returned in triumph to Cairo. But was the exploit justified? Bickham Sweet-Escott, then with SOE in Cairo, thought it should never have been undertaken:

> I was asked whether I thought we should let this operation go ahead. I made myself exceedingly unpopular by recommending as strongly as I could that we should not. I thought that if it succeeded, the only contribution to the war effort would be a fillip to Cretan morale, but that the price would certainly be heavy in Cretan lives. The sacrifice might possibly have been worthwhile in the black winter of 1941 when things were going badly. The result of carrying it out in 1944, when everyone knew that victory was merely a matter of months [away] would, I thought, hardly justify the cost.[16]

Very heavy reprisals did indeed follow, partly linked to the Kreipe abduction. SOE's instructions to the Cretan resistance forces had consistently been that they should not attack the Germans but wait to support an Allied landing which never happened. However, it was unrealistic to expect any resistance, perhaps especially Cretan, to do nothing against their occupiers but wait quiescently for some distant event. It was certainly contrary to the spirit of Churchill's 'fight them on the beaches' speech.

There were basically three forms of resistance in Crete and on the mainland. One was to attack the occupying troops, but it could be argued that killing a few enemy soldiers had little or no effect on the outcome of the war, though these attacks might be useful diversions such as Operation Animals. A second form of resistance was to attack the enemy's resources, such as planes or petrol dumps, or disrupting communications as at Gorgopótamos. These had a direct effect, but still limited and usually only temporary, as Gorgopótamos showed. The third type were basically stunts, such as the removal of the swastika from the Akropolis in the early days and the abduction of Kreipe. Their value lay in boosting resistance and civilian morale and demonstrating to the occupiers that they could not have everything their own way. All three forms of resistance had a further value in tying down troops as an occupying force which could otherwise be used on the battlefield. All three nearly always provoked reprisals.

On this basis the Kreipe abduction was as justifiable as any other form of resistance, and Leigh Fermor, like Myers at Gorgopótamos, had done all he could to prevent reprisals. Sweet-Escott was not criticising the operation as such but only its timing, on the grounds that by 1944 raising morale had become less important. Whether he was right or not can only be a personal judgement.

In the second half of August 1944 the Germans carried out a final series of destructive reprisals, designed to deter the Cretans from attacking them during the imminent German withdrawal. Iráklion was liberated on 11 October and Réthimno two days later, the same day that the Germans abandoned Athens. The Germans only partially withdrew and still hung on in a strip of the north-west coast, some 40 miles long by up to 10 miles deep, stretching from Kastélli to Yeorgoúpolis and including Máleme, Chaniá and Soúdha Bay. A six-month stalemate followed marked mainly by clashes between ELAS and EOK, some serious but none conclusive. Finally on 23 May 1945 the last Germans surrendered, and the whole of Crete was free at last.

Of those who took part in the resistance two who were killed were Pendlebury, shot by the Germans on the day after the 1941 invasion, and Kiwi Perkins, killed by a German patrol in the spring of 1944. Of those who survived Smith-Hughes became a diplomat and Stockbridge joined the military intelligence organisation MI6. Dunbabin died in 1947, Moss married Sophie Tarnowska, his fellow resident in Tara, the romantically named Cairo house, and Leigh Fermor and Fielding became well-known writers.

Of the Cretans Psichoundhákis had the most difficult and complicated postwar life. Because of a bureaucratic blunder he was arrested as a deserter from the Greek army, spending months in mainland Greek prisons, and when released he had to spend two more years in the army fighting the Communists. Back in Crete he worked as a navvy on roadworks, living in a nearby cave where, in his off moments and at night, he wrote his book *The Cretan Runner*, published in 1955 with Leigh Fermor's help and in his translation. On returning to his family village Psichoundhákis found it involved in a ferocious blood-feud and had to keep away, so scraped a living as a charcoal-burner in the southern mountains. Psichoundhákis finally found some stability in his life in the 1970s when he was employed to work in a cemetery – the German Cemetery near Máleme. The irony of it would have appealed to his irreverent sense of humour.

17

Upheaval in the Greek Government

On 26 March 1944 EAM and ELAS had announced the establishment of their own form of the government of Greece, the Political Committee of National Liberation or PEEA. It had many of the characteristics of a government: it had departments for different functions, it issued decrees, it held elections of a sort. It could claim to be the de facto government of the large area which it controlled and, though Communist dominated, to be more broadly based than the government in exile in Cairo. But to gain legitimacy it needed to be accepted by, and then become part of, the official and constitutional Cairo government.

From the beginning the Greek government in exile had been shaken by discontent among the Greek forces in Egypt, and division between monarchists and republicans. In early March 1943 these conflicts had led to a short-lived mutiny which was suppressed by British troops, but a year later there was more serious trouble.

On 31 March 1944 an army committee presented Prime Minister Tsoudherós with a petition asking him to form a government in coalition with PEEA. 'It has been established', writes one historian firmly, though he does not say how, 'that they did not receive any instructions from EAM in Greece on this question, and that their final decision was completely their own,'[1] though instructions from EAM were naturally suspected. As a counter to this demand from the army, invitations were issued by the government in exile to all the guerrilla bands, both Communist and non-Communist, to discuss their inclusion in the government. This was very different from an exclusive arrangement with PEEA.

The government in exile had undergone marked changes since leaving Greece at the time of the German invasion. Then it was a recognisable heir of the pre-war military-dominated Metaxás government. A general and an admiral were deputy prime ministers, three generals served as ministers of the armed services and other posts were held by three of Metaxás' civilian ministers, including Maniadhákis the scourge of the Communists. Every member of this government was a committed monarchist. However, from the earliest days there was agitation for the government to be more broadly based and to include republicans. The first step in this process was the removal of the three Metaxás ministers, two in June 1941 and the third in the following January. There followed a steady accretion to the government of republican politicians who had escaped from occupied Greece.

Woodhouse gave an illuminating explanation of why these escapers were welcomed, and why they tended to be republican and not monarchist. There was, he wrote, 'admiration towards every Greek who endured the torment of the occupation, coupled with a faint, ill-defined, but nevertheless real contempt for those who did not'.[2] These escapers were mostly of the left rather than the right because they were generally men who were suspect to the Germans for what they had done or might do, and were ready to leave when they could and to face the hazards of escape by caique across the Aegean to Turkey and then overland to Egypt. By contrast, those unmolested by the Germans had no motive to risk the journey. 'The kind of Greeks who found it easiest to get on with the Germans were the kind of Greeks who found it easiest to get on with the old regime and therefore with the monarchy.'[3] Thus broadly speaking it was monarchists who stayed in Greece and republicans who left.

The government ministers were divided on the issue of recognising PEEA. Though the government now included a number of republicans, the royalists, who included Prime Minister Tsoudherós, still had powerful influence. The Venizelist republican ministers asked Tsoudherós to step down in favour of Sophoklís Venizélos, the son of Elevthérios. Tsoudherós was ready to resign, but could not formally do so because the King was temporarily in London. On 5 April all the members of the government offered their resignations, but remained in office until the King's return. Leeper recommended that Venizélos should immediately become prime minister on an acting basis in order to calm the army, but Churchill would have none of it.

On 7 April he cabled Leeper setting out what should be his priorities, after discipline in the armed services and the King's safety. 'Thirdly every effort to be made to induce Tsouderos to hold office until the King returns and has had time to look around; fourthly try to get Venizelos to remain with Tsouderos.' The final priority was to celebrate Easter Sunday in a manner pious and becoming. Leeper was also urged, in a veiled rebuke for his vacillation, to show those 'qualities of imperturbability and command which are associated with the British Diplomatic Service'.[4]

The King returned to Cairo on 11 April 1944, and three days later resolved the government issue by appointing Venizélos as prime minister, an office which Venizélos now accepted in spite of an earlier refusal. Venizélos had not inherited either the character or the political skills of his famous father and was little help in dealing with the unrest in the army, which had by now reached a more serious level. Leeper considered him full of good will but weak and easily influenced, and he believed that his great name was 'the only asset of this very little man'.[5] A later historian writes:

> I can think of very few Greek politicians who were less deserving of responsible positions in government than was Sophocles Venizelos. A weak man, devoid of imagination and initiative and an example of much that was wrong in the bourgeois political world.[6]

The unrest in the armed forces had now moved from petitions to open revolt. Nearly all units of the army and navy declared openly in favour of PEEA's inclusion in the government though the air force was uncommitted. The army's First Brigade, which was being prepared to move to Italy, destroyed all the new equipment with which it had been issued. Sailors in one of the Greek ships at anchor in Alexandria harbour arrested their officers and threw them overboard. Clearly it was the British and not the Greek government that would have to take the initiative against the mutineers. Churchill had no doubt that they should do so. In a cable to Roosevelt when the mutiny was at its height, he said that the lawfully constituted Greek government headed by the King

> cannot be discarded to suit a momentary surge of appetite among ambitious émigré nonentities. Neither can Greece find constitutional expression in particular sets of guerrillas, in many

cases indistinguishable from banditti, who are masquerading as the saviours of the country while living on the local villagers.[7]

The British authorities intended that as far as possible action against the mutineers should be taken by the Greeks themselves, and to deal with the navy a party of trusted Greek officers and sailors was collected to board two of the ships in Alexandria. The attack was launched, after some dithering by Venizélos, on the night of 23 April. It was successful, though at the cost of 50 dead or wounded, and the other ships soon surrendered. On the day after the naval attack the army mutineers also laid down their arms.

In the aftermath the British completely reorganised the Greek forces in Egypt. Out of a total of 18,500 men about 2,500 who had not joined the mutiny were formed into the Third Mountain Brigade, which after distinguished service in Italy moved to Athens after the liberation to confront the ELAS forces. Another unit of loyalists was the commando Sacred Battalion of company strength. Of the rest, 8,000 or so, nearly half the total, were interned, and about 2,000 were taken back into the armed forces but only for unarmed garrison duty. Of the ringleaders 18 were sentenced to death, though the sentences were commuted by the government in the following October in a gesture of post-liberation reconciliation.

The military crisis had been settled, and the political crisis was now resolved in an unexpected way by the arrival of Georgios Papandhréou, who reached Cairo from Athens on 15 April 1944. Papandhréou, born in 1888, was a long-time supporter of Elevthérios Venizélos and was with him in Salonika when in 1916 Venizélos set up a rival pro-Allies government there. Papandhréou served as minister of four different government departments in the 1920s and 1930s, was exiled by Metaxás in 1936 and returned to Greece in 1941. During the occupation, for three months of which he was imprisoned by the Italians, he sent regular dispatches from Athens to the government in exile in Cairo.

In these dispatches Papandhréou expressed a belligerent stand against EAM and ELAS, which he believed were aiming to establish a postwar Communist dictatorship, and as late as February 1944 he was urging that it would be a political blunder to accept EAM and ELAS participation in any new government. He saw the conflict in Greece, and indeed in the world as a whole, as one between pan-Slavist communism and Anglo-Saxon liberalism. He had not given up a lifetime of republican views, but believed the question of republic versus monarchy was altogether secondary to this wider conflict and could easily be resolved if the King agreed – as seemed likely though still not certain – that he would not return to Greece before a plebiscite.

However, by the time Papandhréou reached Cairo in April 1944 his view had changed. He now accepted that the solution to the problem of EAM and ELAS lay not in outright rejection of them but in the inclusion of all guerrilla bands, including ELAS, in a national army under the orders of a single government – that is the legally constituted government and not the rival Communist PEEA. For this plan to work all guerrilla bands must be represented in the government, and delegates from all the bands brought together in a conference and their agreement obtained. In the course of April all the bands had accepted the invitations to send representatives to such a conference, and the King in a statement on 12 April had encouraged them to do so. PEEA also asked to attend and Venizélos during his brief premiership had agreed, a decision supported by Leeper. Thus the agitators who had demanded recognition of PEEA had to that extent succeeded.

Papandhréou entered the confused arena of Greek politics in Cairo as a breath of fresh air. He had impeccable credentials as a sufferer under the occupation. He was a republican, but not stridently anti-monarchist. He was an eloquent and persuasive orator. Unlike any of the other politicians he had a plan – a unified national army controlled by a broadly based government – and the energy to push it through. 'We all turned to him', wrote Leeper, 'as the man of the hour.'[8]

In fact not everyone turned to Papandhréou. The government ministers in Cairo did not, and initially not one of them agreed to serve with him, after the King appointed him prime minister on 26 April 1944. As Leeper wrote, 'The first Government of Papandreou, in those still mutinous days in Cairo, was literally Papandreou.'[9]

The proposed conference was quickly assembled and ran for four days from 17 to 20 May 1944. It was held in a hotel, the Grand Hotel du Bois de Boulogne, in a remote village outside Beirut in Lebanon, and Lebanon was chosen to distance the delegates from the political turbulence of Cairo. The PEEA delegation of three was led by Svólos, the non-Communist president of PEEA. There were three more representing EAM and ELAS, of whom two were Communists, and three from Zervas' EDES. EKKA, which sent one representative, was still in precarious existence with British support. This was in spite of an attempt by ELAS to eliminate it in April, which had led to the death of its leader Psarrós, purportedly in a private quarrel with an ELAS officer. The remaining half-dozen or so delegates represented the politicians and army officers. Leeper, the only diplomatic representative, installed himself in another hotel halfway between the conference venue and Beirut, where he met all the delegate groups in turn. It was very clear that the Lebanon Conference was backed by the British.

Papandhréou opened the conference with a forceful attack on EAM, ELAS and PEEA. As Leeper summarised it, he said:

> It is the responsibility of EAM that they did not only look towards the liberation struggle, but wished to prepare in advance for their own domination after the war. Therefore their first aim was to monopolise the national struggle. They did not allow anyone else to take to the mountains and fight the invader. They prevented Greeks from fulfilling their patriotic duty. They made themselves a State within the State, and considered their opponents as enemies of the country. Such a condition of affairs only occurs in a Fascist system in which the Party is identified with the State.[10]

The representative of the battered EKKA condemned the Communists even more harshly. The EAM and PEEA delegations, blamed both for the attack on EKKA and for instigating the recent mutinies, were in a weak position.

The outcome of the conference was the Lebanon Charter of eight points. Six were relatively uncontroversial: terrorism whatever its source must cease; the people's decision on the constitution should be made as soon as possible; relief should be organised, and reconstruction; traitors should be punished; and Greece's frontiers should be secured. The significant points were the first two. One looked to the return of the Greek military forces to Greece after liberation and stated that 'The army will carry out the orders of the government, and cannot possess political opinions.' The other point dealt with the immediate situation: 'All guerrilla bands in free Greece must be unified and disciplined under the orders of a single Government.'[11] However, it was accepted that this could not happen yet, and the form of this unified force was to be decided later by the Greek government in consultation with the Allied commanders in the Middle East.

The Lebanon Charter thus mainly looked to the future. More important was a separate commitment by Papandhréou to include immediately all signatories to the charter in a government of national unity. All the delegates had agreed to sign the charter, and all did so except the representatives of PEEA, EAM and ELAS. These were denounced for exceeding their instructions in agreeing to sign by the Communist leadership in Greece, which put forward a string of new demands.

The first set of these reached Cairo on 29 June, the most significant ones being that an ELAS officer should be commander-in-chief of the new national army and that in the Papandhréou government they should have five ministries, including the crucial ones of the interior, justice and labour. Papandhréou publicly rejected these demands on 6 July. Three weeks later the Greek Communists dropped all their earlier points and agreed to join the government but on condition that Papandhréou resigned as prime minister. Papandhréou offered to do so, but soon withdrew the offer under British pressure. Churchill declared, again using his favourite term for the Greek Communists, 'We cannot take up a man as we have done Papandreou and let him be thrown to the wolves at the first snarlings of the miserable Greek banditti.'[12]

At this point a Russian mission arrived by air at ELAS headquarters in Neraídha, a village near Kardhítsa, 3,000 feet high in pine-clad foothills where a landing strip had been built. The mission consisted of three Russian colonels, headed by Popov, and five others. There to meet them were Siántos of the KKE, Svólos the president of PEEA, Nicholas Hammond, acting head of the Allied Military Mission in Woodhouse's temporary absence, and Hammond's American colleague Colonel West.

Before any serious business the Russians held a night-long drinking party for the Allied Military Mission in which Hammond was spared the worst excesses by passing out after the first three toasts. Policy discussions between the Russians and their Greek hosts began on 2 August, and though no records were kept it is virtually certain that the Russians made it clear that there would be no Soviet help for the Greek Communists, leaving them no option but to join the Papandhréou government.

This Russian initiative was in line with what became known as the Percentages Agreement. Some three months earlier, in May 1944, Eden had proposed to the Soviet ambassador in London that,

in Eden's words: 'Roumanian affairs would be in the main the concern of the Soviet Government while Greek affairs would be in the
main our concern.'[13] The Russians agreed, provided that the United
States also agreed, as they reluctantly did, on condition that the deal
was for wartime only and in any case should not be for more than
three months.

The actual Percentages Agreement was made later on 9 October
1944 when Churchill met Stalin in Moscow. Churchill wrote on
a scrap of paper his proposed spheres of influence. These were for
Romania, Russia 90 per cent and others 10 per cent; for Greece, Britain
90 per cent and Russia 10 per cent. Also on the list was Bulgaria:
Russia 75 per cent and others 25 per cent. Stalin put a blue tick on
the paper. Although the arrangement was informal and supposed
to be temporary, it lasted well beyond the end of the war and was
respected by the Russians as well as the British.

The Percentages Agreement was derided at the time, and has been
since, as an exercise in neo-colonialism. Some thoughtful and not
just doctrinaire nationalist Romanians believe to this day that the
Percentages Agreement was a betrayal of their country, condemning
it to decades of repressive Communist rule. But from a wider point
of view the arrangement was a recognition of reality. Neither party
had any wish to become embroiled in the other's sphere of influence.
Also Britain had no obligations to Romania or Bulgaria, which had
been formally or informally on Germany's side throughout the war,
whereas Britain had a debt of honour to Greece as an ally throughout
and in the early days Britain's only ally. Furthermore Greece in the
British sphere would provide security in the eastern Mediterranean
and protect Britain's links to the Middle East and India. In any case
Britain did not have the capacity to interfere in Romania or Bulgaria,
so was giving away nothing, whereas Greece was a valuable prize.
It was a surprisingly favourable deal for the British, provided that
Stalin kept his word, as in the event he did.

Siántos may have been persuaded that he was in a weak position
not only by the message of the Russian mission but also by another
event. In early August Hammond gave Siántos the impression that
large Allied forces would soon enter Greece, and did so by telling
him that the force would be small, which Hammond knew to be
the truth. As Hammond expected, Siántos, accustomed to years of
Communist deceptions, assumed that Hammond was lying, that the
Allied force would actually be large, Communist seizure of power

by force would be impossible, and the only option was to join the Papandhréou government.

Thus finally in mid-August the Communists dropped all demands and agreed to join the government. On 3 September the Communists took up their government posts. They were awarded five ministries, though not the three significant ones – interior, justice and labour – which they had demanded in June.

Papandhréou, with strong British support, had pulled off a remarkable success. In the six months since the March 1944 mutinies a weak, fractured and unrepresentative government had been transformed into a government of all shades of political opinion under a forceful and impressive leader. It is all very well to accuse Britain of meddling in national Greek affairs, but Britain was clearly going to be responsible for conditions in post-occupation Greece, and British lives would be risked and sometimes lost in the effort. Britain therefore had a legitimate and vital interest in promoting whatever might lead to order and stability. Greece now had a government which could return to the country at liberation with good claims to be a government of national unity. It did so, but unhappily without being able to fulfil the high promise that attended it.

18

Liberation

By the summer of 1944 the German troops in Greece and the rest of the Balkans were in grave danger of having any escape route to the north cut off by the advance of Russian armies from the east. On 30 August the Russians captured Ploeşti, the centre of Romania's oilfields, and the next day entered the capital Bucharest. By September German troops were evacuating Bulgaria, hitherto Germany's ally. On 6 September Russian forces reached the Yugoslav border at Kladovo on the Danube, and six weeks later on 20 October liberated Belgrade. The Germans had to get out of Greece now or be trapped.

The German withdrawal began in early September with retreat from the Peloponnese. They left behind them two violently opposed forces, the Security Battalions and ELAS. The Security Battalions, now numbering some 10,000 in the Peloponnese and outnumbering ELAS, controlled the towns and had co-operated with the Germans against ELAS. ELAS controlled the countryside and was the only resistance force in the Peloponnese, having absorbed or eliminated all its rivals. The aims of ELAS were to take revenge on the Security Battalions, and to gain control of the Peloponnese before British troops arrived. The aim of the Security Battalions was to survive until they could surrender to those British troops, but on no account to surrender to ELAS.

The Security Battalions had consistently been denounced as collaborators, as indeed they were, but those who joined them were frequently, as so often in the story of the Greek resistance, swayed by personal or local pressures much more than by ideological conviction. One Security Battalion commander was the brother of a man murdered by ELAS. Some recruits were said to be simply Piraeus street ruffians who wanted a square meal. One British liaison officer in the Peloponnese recalled that:

throughout that summer [of 1944] Greeks who were in trouble with
ELAS would come and talk about their plans to join the Security
Battalions, claiming that at the critical moment they would be able to
switch the Battalions over to the allied side. We of course always told
them not to, but they mostly did join.[1]

On 4 September the Germans pulled out of Pírgos on the west coast
of the Peloponnese, leaving the town in the hands of the Security
Battalions, and next day abandoned Kalamáta in the far south. ELAS
and the Security Battalions were now face to face. The aims of the
few remaining members of the Allied Military Mission were first to
prevent bloodshed, and then to secure the surrender of the Security
Battalions to the British with their arms, so that these did not fall into
the hands of ELAS.

The officers of the Allied Military Mission, with as yet no British
troops to support them, were in an extraordinarily difficult position,
made worse by confused orders from Middle East Command. On
8 September they were told not to meddle in Greek political affairs.
Two days later ELAS attacked the Security Battalions in Pírgos and
took the town with much bloodshed. The same day a British officer
cabled in desperation:

> For sake of humanity if nothing else either do something or give me
> power (to) act as intermediary. Have already been approached by
> officer ELAS 9th Regiment to act between themselves and Security
> Battalions trapped in Kopanaki. According to your instructions
> unable to. Great deal of blame attached to Allied Military Mission
> and position very unsatisfactory. General public watch sea night and
> day and in despair.[2]

A week later the first instructions were reversed, and this officer was
told to intervene.

Intervention was not always possible, and even if so was not always
completely successful. At Meligalás in the central Peloponnese no
Allied officers were present when on 13 September ELAS attacked
the Security Battalions holding the town. ELAS took Meligalás after
a three-day battle, and executed many hundreds of people. But at
Trípoli on 28 September a deputation, including Allied officers and
a minister in Papandhréou's government, plus 50 recently landed
British soldiers, negotiated the surrender of the Security Battalions to

the British – but ELAS got their weapons. A few days later at Patras a similar surrender was agreed, and this time the Security Battalions surrendered to the British and kept their arms.

All German troops had left the Peloponnese by the end of September, and during the previous months the Germans had been preparing to abandon the rest of Greece. Their reprisals became increasingly vicious, one of the worst being at Dhístomo some 10 miles east of Delphi, where 270 inhabitants were massacred.[3] The object of these reprisals, it seems, was to ensure that any German soldier tempted to desert during the withdrawal would know that he would receive no mercy from the Greeks.

To forestall ELAS attacks on their retreat the German forces in July launched their severest ever attack on ELAS, ferociously code-named Operation Steinadler. ELAS suffered some 2,000 casualties and lost large quantities of ammunition. German emissaries also had secret talks with Zérvas about a temporary truce with EDES. The whole episode is murky, but Woodhouse believed it likely that Zérvas, under orders from Middle East Command to lie low for the moment, made a temporary truce, which he denounced on 20 August.

That was the date on which Zérvas was ordered to prepare for Operation Noah's Ark which was intended to harass the German troops as they pulled out. Woodhouse, who was away from Greece during most of this period, thought at the time that the operation was a success, estimating German losses as 100 locomotives, 500 road vehicles and 5,000 men killed. However, a few years later he was much less enthusiastic: 'Greece was liberated because the Germans left, not because they were driven out; the difficulty was even to keep contact with their rear-guard.'[4]

With hindsight Operation Noah's Ark seems misconceived, and it is difficult to agree with William Mackenzie, the historian of SOE, that 'Noah's Ark paid a dividend much higher than the whole British expenditure on special operations in Greece.'[5] Noah's Ark was in conflict with the Foreign Office view that 'we do not want [the German forces] to collapse until we ourselves are ready to send in British troops.'[6] Also any short-term military success against the Germans was outweighed by damage to Greece's post-liberation infrastructure, with Woodhouse's estimated 100 locomotives wrecked, bridges blown up or roads sabotaged. It might have been better if Operation Noah's Ark had lived up to its name and been designed to rescue rather than to destroy.

Destruction was in fact sometimes averted by other initiatives. The German military commander for northern Greece, with headquarters in Ioánnina, was Lieutenant-General Hubert Lanz. Lanz was an unusual German commander. He was a devout Catholic who refused both to cut his public connections to the Church and to join the Nazi Party. On the Russian front he had insisted that Soviet political commissars who were non-military should not be shot, against Hitler's instructions. Lanz was held responsible for the killing on Kephaloniá of Italian troops who had surrendered, but here he acted with humanity. Before Lanz led the last German convoy out of Ioánnina on 15 October 1944 he had been ordered to destroy all stores and supplies and leave the earth scorched. Lanz simply disobeyed the order, and no civilian installations were destroyed.

Much of Athens too was saved from destruction. On 10 October General Helmut Felmy, on his own initiative, declared Athens an open city, that is one that neither side would attack, and both the Allies and the resistance respected Felmy's declaration. Otherwise the Parthenon, and other historic buildings, could have suffered much more damage than from the besieging Venetians' mortar shot in 1687.

A separate operation called Counter-Scorch was charged with saving installations from destruction, and the two most important installations were the Marathon dam supplying Athens with water and the Athens power station at Piraeus. At the Marathon dam the Germans laid explosive charges to destroy it, but by 20 September these had been removed and dumped in the lake. This may have been done by a combination of bribed Germans and intrepid Greek workers at the dam. However, Rállis, the last collaborationist prime minister, by then imprisoned in the Avérof, claimed that he had personally persuaded Felmy to remove the charges.[7] At the Piraeus power station the German manager, keen to ingratiate himself with the Allies, agreed that only non-vital parts of the plant would be damaged, and he kept his word.[8] However, the journalist Richard Capell heard a more dramatic story. The German destruction party, improbably not knowing where the power station was, asked directions from an old man who misdirected the Germans three times and was then shot. This gave the Greeks at the power station time to prepare, and they held off the Germans, 12 against 45, until ELAS forces arrived to support them. However it happened, the power station was saved, and Capell, used to newly liberated cities being totally darkened, was amazed when he reached Athens in October to find it ablaze with light.[9]

Waiting in the wings was Papandhréou's government of national unity, finally formed when the Communist representatives at last agreed to join it. On 21 August Papandhréou met Churchill in Rome, and Churchill convinced him that the Greek government should move from Cairo to Italy. Churchill told him that British troops would soon be taking part in the liberation of Greece, though he carefully avoided saying anything about their numbers or deployment in case these details were leaked. These troops would be under the control of General Wilson, now based at Caserta, just north of Naples. Therefore it would be a great advantage if the Greek government were established nearby. Papandhréou readily agreed, and by the end of the first week in September Papandhréou and his colleagues were settled at Cava dei Tirreni, a small town in the hills south of Naples. With them came Leeper and a new actor on the stage, Harold Macmillan.

Since 1942 Macmillan had been directly responsible to Churchill for political affairs in the Mediterranean theatre and had been based first in Algiers and then in Italy. In August 1944 he was appointed British resident minister to Allied Forces Headquarters now at Caserta, with particular responsibility for Greece. He was thus the political adviser to Leeper, as well as to three other ambassadors, who all, as Macmillan put it, 'found themselves acting more or less under my control'.[10] Macmillan and Leeper were both thoroughly in favour of the Greek government's move to Italy, Macmillan saying that they would thus be 'away from the poisonous atmosphere of intrigue which reigns at Cairo. All previous Greek Governments in exile have been broken in the bar of Shepheard's Hotel.'[11]

On 26 September a conference at Caserta agreed plans for the immediate future of Greece. Attending were Papandhréou and four of his ministers, as well as Leeper and Macmillan. Presiding was Wilson as supreme Allied commander for the Mediterranean theatre, who had invited the two main resistance leaders to attend, Zérvas for EDES and Saráphis for ELAS. Also present was General Ronald Scobie, who was to command all forces in Greece, Greek as well as British. Scobie had made his name in military operations, notably as leader of the break-out from Tobruk in November 1941. He had little experience of complex political situations, and as we shall see was also found lacking in the military sphere in Greece.

Under the terms of the Caserta Agreement, all guerrilla forces were to place themselves under the orders of the Greek government, which in turn would place them under the orders of General Scobie. There were special provisions on the all-important question of Athens. ELAS was to keep out; Greek forces there would nominally be commanded by the right-wing General Spiliotópoulos, but no action was to be taken except on Scobie's direct orders. More general items were that the Security Battalions should be treated as enemies unless they surrendered, and that Greek forces should put aside past rivalries, maintain law and order, help distribute relief and continue the Noah's Ark policy of harassing the retreating Germans. The Caserta Agreement was signed by Wilson and Macmillan for the Allies, and Papandhréou, Saráphis and Zérvas for the Greeks.[12]

The Caserta Agreement might seem to settle the question of how Greece was to be liberated, but it met a barrage of criticism from many quarters. Much of the British press, *The Times* as well as left-wing papers such as the *New Statesman*, were fiercely opposed to the plan, holding to the belief that EAM was the champion of social justice and democracy and spoke for the Greek people, and so should not face these restrictions. In September Churchill had to defend the policy against attacks in the House of Commons. The American press too was largely hostile, and the State Department's policy was that there should be no American involvement in Greece except for relief and reconstruction, a policy supported by Roosevelt although he was sometimes prepared to bend it to accommodate Churchill's wishes. These criticisms became fiercer as British involvement in Greece intensified.

The American ambassador to Greece, Lincoln MacVeagh, was also deeply suspicious of the British, as his diary reveals. On 5 June 1941, when the Germans invaded, MacVeagh had left Greece for other postings, and returned to Cairo on 7 September 1944, moving to Athens after liberation on 27 October. During the weeks in Cairo he wrote in his diary some damning criticisms of British intervention in Greece: 'England is going on with the Imperial Game, counting on us to help her out when she gets in trouble, but not consulting us before she does.' British forces being sent to Greece were inadequate, even though there were plenty in Egypt whose only task was 'sitting on the necks of the local population'. MacVeagh had his own solutions, though these were hardly coherent. 'If only the Military had been under American command, as I have always wanted it to be!' His idea was that British troops should be replaced by American forces, who would not be resented as the British were on suspicion of trying to reimpose the King. The following years made it very clear that any foreign intervention, including American, provoked Greek resentment. In general MacVeagh thought that a new world war could be avoided 'only if we will recognise the seeds of trouble as they are sown and destroy them before they sprout,' by publicity and international settlement. These were laudable sentiments, but this approach had signally failed to avert the world war which was now being fought to the end.[13] A diarist, recording personal fleeting thoughts, has perhaps no obligation to be fair or consistent, but these qualities should be evident in any man with MacVeagh's responsibilities.

MacVeagh's criticisms of the British were surpassed in virulence by reports from Americans in the Office of Strategic Services based in Cairo. They said that, according to Greeks in Cairo, British procedures involved 'an intolerable diminution of Greek sovereignty' and the relation between Papandhréou and the British was equated to 'that between the quisling Premier Rallis and the Germans'. The British aim, it was said, was to install a Greek government which would 'not oppose the establishment of British bases on Greek soil'. SOE activities in Greece had been 'cynically opportunist' and had 'sought to maintain an equilibrium by setting Greeks against each other'. SOE officers were 'incapable of forming true judgements of the Greek political situation'. The chief offender was Woodhouse, a 'polished Oxonian' and a congenital Tory 'not sufficiently mature to have evolved a different attitude'. By contrast, 'the best informed man on Greek matters' was the Cairo-based Colonel O'Toole. As for communism, they found it hard to believe that communism could obtain a foothold in a country of small landholders with little industry, and an extraordinary statement is quoted from an American who had recently been to Greece: 'Communists are those who believe in the sanctity of private property, the Church, the family and the integrity of Greece's boundaries.' And as for Papandhréou, he 'has only an outmoded theatrical style of oratory to recommend him'.[14]

These comments are little more than Cairo tittle-tattle. They are worth quoting only because they were included in reports to the State Department and so presumably had an effect on US policy, and because they fully justified Macmillan's belief that it was essential to remove the Greek government from the poisonous atmosphere of Cairo.

In Athens during the summer of 1944 the Germans prepared for departure by increasing use of the round-up or blóko. These were carried out, on German orders, by the Security Battalions and by the German-sponsored Special Security branch of the police, though the Athens City Police under Ángelos Évert shunned and sometimes actively opposed them. The blóko was used mainly in the poorer outlying areas of the city where EAM was strongest.

As a blóko began, all the men between 16 and 45 were ordered by loudhailer to assemble in the square or other open space. One purpose was to pick out men suspected of anti-German activity. These were identified by hooded informers and immediately put up against a wall and shot. A second objective was to seize hostages, who were taken off to the Haïdhári prison. Some were eventually allowed to leave the blóko, but it was a nightmare experience as they were pushed into the separate lines for prison or for release. As one of them wrote, 'I lost all initiative and became a marionette, an automaton. The Germans put me first in one line and then in another, until finally they asked for my identity papers and let me go.'[15]

The young Mary Kavadhías was already in Haïdhári prison. She was from a distinguished family, daughter of King George's doctor and niece of a Greek admiral, and was later to marry the British diplomat Nicholas Henderson. In the summer of 1944 she was arrested because her brother's resistance activity had become known, and her formidable mother went to Haïdhári with her: 'If you are taking my daughter you'll have to take me too.'[16] Mary witnessed the fate of the hostages after the morning prison roll-call:

> The camp commandant called out names at random from a list. Those he called out always knew why – they were the day's hostages and would be shot in reprisal for bridges or railways blown up by sabotage forces. But then, we were all hostages, all condemned to death. It was just a question of time. After the hostages had been shot, just to make sure that 'the lessons had been learnt', their blood-stained clothes were distributed among us. Some of the poorer prisoners in tatters were glad even of these.[17]

In mid-September Mary and her mother were released from Haïdhári, by which time the German forces were leaving Athens. Every day six trains carrying German troops and equipment were seen leaving the Athens railway station, returning a few days later for another load. The remaining Germans were concentrated in separate pockets of the city, where some dug underground tunnels for shelter or possible escape. On 27 September Haïdhári was officially closed. Some like Mary and her mother had been released earlier, but the Germans packed those remaining into trucks and took them to the Avérof prison in central Athens. After ten days they too were released and five days later on 12 October the last Germans pulled out of Athens.

There was no delay in bringing the Greek government to Athens. On Sunday 15 October a flotilla of something over 100 British and Greek ships assembled in the harbour of Póros at the eastern tip of the Peloponnese and about 50 miles south of Athens. On board was Papandhréou and most of his government, though three ministers had reached Athens in advance, one of them the Communist Ioánnis Zévgos, a signal that the government included all parties. Also on board were Leeper, Macmillan and Scobie. Minesweepers led the way, destroying 45 to 50 mines with the loss of some British ships. Mines were either exploded or cut loose, when they became targets for rifle fire, a tricky business 'like trying to shoot rabbits in thick bracken', as Macmillan commented.[18] By Sunday night the leading ships were within reach of Athens at Pháliron Bay, but waited throughout Monday for news that the German demolitions in Piraeus had been cleared. To land on Tuesday was out of the question, as Tuesday was the day of ill omen on which the Turks had taken Constantinople in 1453. Thus Papandhréou and his government, with Leeper, Macmillan and Scobie, finally reached Athens on Wednesday 18 October.

The Athenians had already been celebrating their liberation. As one of them wrote,

> The centre of Athens swarmed with hundreds of thousands of demonstrators, with multicoloured banners, Greek and Allied flags, hammer and sickle and placards. The people celebrated, danced, sang, shouted, and went wild with joy and enthusiasm over the great event.[19]

The capital now gave Papandhréou a tumultuous welcome, 'one of the few times', commented another eyewitness, 'that all Greeks united in welcoming a politician'.[20] Papandhréou was greeted at Piraeus by a band playing the national anthem, and went on to the Akropolis where the Greek flag now flew alone. He then made his appearance on a balcony above Síntagma Square from which, with Scobie beside him, he spoke for nearly two hours to a large crowd, interrupted only occasionally by the hostile chanting of EAM slogans. His basic theme was a call for unity: 'Our aim is not only the freedom of the nation. It is also the uniting of *our* nation.'[21]

Other arrivals soon followed. Small units of British forces had reached Greece earlier, but now the main body of troops were brought in. These numbered about 8,000 (Churchill had agreed 10,000 with Roosevelt at the end of August) and Roosevelt had again bent the rules by approving the use of American transport planes to bring them in. Those destined for Athens consisted of 3,000 to 4,000 combat troops, and another 4,000 or so technicians and engineers to remove mines and repair damaged installations. A separate force of an Indian brigade was sent to Salonika, where they succeeded in co-operating with ELAS in a peaceful take-over of the city.

The Greek forces sent to Greece were the Third Mountain Brigade from Italy, now known as the Rimini Brigade from its distinguished part in capturing that city, and from Egypt the Sacred Battalion. These were the two loyal units salvaged from the mutinies of the previous March. Within a week Lincoln MacVeagh also arrived in Athens from Cairo. He was now seeing the situation on the spot and having almost daily meetings with Leeper. Unsurprisingly his views began to change, and by mid-November he was writing that civil war must be avoided and that Scobie's actions in the face of EAM threats were necessary. In his diary from now on the rancorous criticisms of the British are markedly absent, apart from a swipe at Eden: 'He seems the same old playboy, the Noel Coward of diplomacy, taking the same opportunist attitude toward affairs, trying to cure grave situations with haphazard expedients.'[22]

Notably missing from the list of arrivals was one of the protagonists, King George of Greece. The King kept pushing for an early return, preferably at the head of liberating Greek troops, but Churchill and Eden agreed that this must be resisted at all costs. His return now would play into the hands of those claiming that the King was about to be imposed on Greece by British bayonets. Churchill personally persuaded the King to accept delay, but Churchill's long-term support for him remained undimmed. It was Papandhréou's duty, Churchill maintained, to bring the King back as soon as his own government was established in Greece.

Amid the euphoria of liberation, and the hopes raised by the re-establishment of legality and authority, there were many signs of trouble to come. EAM was increasingly assertive and aggressive. A huge garish sign on the Akropolis rock spelt out 'EAM' in electric lights, and on the walls of the Stádhio the red-painted letters 'KKE' were 30 feet high. A graffito on the side of a smart block of flats in the wealthy Kolonáki district read 'Death to the bourgeoisie'.

Right-wing opposition to EAM was also emerging, particularly the organisation called X, the Greek letter chi. This was in effect a private army, founded and led by Colonel Georgios Grívas, whose aim was simply to fight Communists. A month before the Germans left, Chi was reckoned to number little more than 100, but it was now dangerous. During the liberation celebrations members of X fired on an EAM procession from a hideout in a small hotel, reportedly killing ten people and wounding over 80. Any suspected leftist who strayed into the Thesíon area, their base half a mile west of the Akropolis, was in danger of being attacked and killed, a murder which X immediately blamed on EAM.

This conflict between left and right also highlighted the question of the King's return. As fear grew of a Communist take-over of power, the King came increasingly to be seen as a counterweight to them. Papandhréou's earlier view, that the question of the King had become secondary, turned out to be wrong.

In the next few months these issues came to a head in a violent confrontation. The time of liberation was an episode, as Macmillan regretfully said, 'from the burdens and dangers of which our American allies were to stand aside'.[23] In the longer term the Americans found that standing aside was no longer an option.

19

Towards Sunday 3 December 1944

By the second half of October 1944 the Greek government and the British military and civilian authorities were established in Athens and were faced with three immediate problems. One was to bring in relief supplies to the shattered country. The second was to control inflation, which was now at a worse level than ever before. The third, and potentially most explosive, was the disarming of the resistance forces and their incorporation into a new National Army. For all three problems the initial attempts at solution were disrupted by the demonstration in Síntagma Square on Sunday 3 December and its repercussions, which became known as the December Events, the *Dhekemvrianá*. The demonstration turned violent, and weeks of conflict followed.

Since September 1942 relief efforts in Greece had been the responsibility of the joint Swedish and Swiss Joint Relief Commission, the JRC. In April 1944 this responsibility was passed to UNRRA, the United Nations Relief and Rehabilitation Administration. UNRRA had been proposed by the United States in the summer of 1943, and its charter was signed in November by 44 countries. The need for UNRRA in Greece was starkly obvious. The JRC, when it handed over to UNRRA in April 1944, had been distributing food to 3 million Greeks. The food situation had become worse in the six months leading to liberation as transport systems were wrecked during the German retreat and villages were destroyed in the last flurry of reprisals. It was now difficult to obtain supplies for distribution, and Macmillan and his advisers spent whole days sending cables calling for food and other commodities to be delivered to Greece.

Once British forces arrived in Greece, with responsibility for law and order and for ensuring the delivery of relief supplies, UNRRA and the British forces had to co-operate. In practice this co-operation meant that in the initial period UNRRA came under British military control, which was exercised through a body of officers, mainly British but including some Americans, known as Military Liaison. Military Liaison had a colossal burden and responsibility. Its tasks were multiple: in the short term to distribute food, clothing and medical supplies, to clear harbours and other installations of mines and booby traps, and in the longer term to revive farm production and fishing, and even to recover archaeological treasures. Not surprisingly the efforts to provide immediate relief were severely hampered by the shortage of supplies, of shipping to bring in those supplies and of transport to deliver them.

A further restraint was that Military Liaison had to operate on the principle that civilian relief must be harmonised with military operations. Thus military areas, those affected by army operations or in serious disorder, came under sole British control. Elsewhere the military had overall responsibility for relief with UNRRA acting as its agent. A degree of friction was unavoidable. UNRRA personnel felt that they were no longer answerable to the 44 countries that had signed their charter but to only one, Britain. Some suspected that the military, in breach of UNRRA's commitment to total impartiality, were withholding relief supplies from suspect areas, though no instance of this was provided. Some UNRRA staff complained that they were not being consulted, but others said that they were 'receiving the most cordial treatment and best evidence of respect and confidence' from their Military Liaison superiors.[1] In spite of these inevitable grumbles, this hybrid arrangement seems to have worked as well as could be expected in a confused and dangerous situation. By the end of November Military Liaison was able to announce an increase of the food ration for Athens and Salonika from 1,350 to 2,000 calories a day, the standard for postwar Europe.

On 18 December, after two weeks of violence in Athens which had begun at liberation, Scobie ordered the evacuation from Athens of all unnecessary personnel, including UNRRA. The staff of UNRRA moved to Cairo, to return to Greece in March 1945, this time with sole responsibility for relief and rehabilitation, and in the next two years distributed over $400 million worth of aid. UNRRA was back in business as an independent organisation.

At liberation the Greek economy was in chaos. Inflation had reached record levels, where even lower denomination drachma notes carried 12 zeros, and was rising further as the government continued to print money to pay its bills. The Greek Finance Ministry had hoped that liberation would bring stability and an increase in food supplies, so that prices would fall and inflation would stop of its own accord. The British Foreign Office agreed, stating at the end of October that 'the liberation would restore confidence in the drachma, that there would be a substantial fall in prices and that at least a measure of stability would be achieved.'[2] None of this happened.

Another illusory hope was placed in the currency with which British troops were paid, the British Military Administration pounds or £BMA. The British would determine the current value of the £BMA against the drachma, and it was thought that the £BMA would become the preferred currency, to be replaced after stabilisation by a new drachma. This did not happen either. The public, with memories of the short-lived German and Italian occupation currencies which had quickly become worthless, had no confidence in the £BMA, which was withdrawn in the following April.

To help devise an economic plan a group of experts from the British Treasury, headed by Sir David Waley, arrived in Athens on 27 October. Macmillan described Waley, a touch patronisingly, as 'a splendid little man, obviously a strong character, and a charming, even boyish, smile and sense of fun'.[3] Macmillan likened Waley to Sir Omicron Pie, Trollope's eminent doctor summoned, with Sir Lamda Mewnew, to the bedside of the terminally ill bishop of Barchester.[4] Like Sir Omicron Pie, Waley thought his patient would probably die.

Nevertheless Waley proposed a comprehensive plan for the Greek economy, which Macmillan called the 'Child's Guide to Stabilisation'. Waley's proposal had four main elements. It required that the Greek government should:

- cut its bloated pay bill, by reducing the number of its employees and by stopping the automatic linking of their pay to inflation;
- start collecting taxes;
- charge for relief supplies except to the destitute;
- stop printing money.

This would lead to stable conditions in which a new drachma could be introduced.

All four of Waley's main recommendations ran into trouble. On government pay there was prolonged argument between the British and Greek authorities over what the new pay rates should be. On the numbers of civil servants the Greek government was reluctant to sack employees, not least because many had been taken on during the occupation to save them from dire poverty. A fierce law was passed on 10 November requiring the removal of all civil servants hired during the Metaxás period or the occupation, that is eight years of recruits, and cancellation of all promotions made in that time. Not surprisingly, the law was too draconian and remained a dead letter.

Taxes were optimistically budgeted to bring in the equivalent of £15 million, but the budget gave no details, and in February 1945 government revenue provided only one-fifteenth of its expenses. Charging for relief supplies produced no net revenue after deduction of distribution costs. Finally, the Greek government continued to print money. Nevertheless on 11 November the new drachma was introduced, replacing old drachmas at the exchange rate of 50,000,000,000 old drachmas to one new one. However, because sufficient relief supplies were still not getting through, food prices continued their alarming rise, in Athens by 70 per cent between 11 November and the end of the month.

Waley's plan has been pronounced a failure: by May 1945 'the pretence at implementing the Waley reform was dead.'[5] But Waley had expected his patient, the Greek economy, to die, and it had not. With the new drachma, shaky as it was, the economy had taken a faltering step towards recovery and awaited further treatment under a new stabilisation plan later in 1945.

The third major problem, after those of relief supplies and currency stabilisation, was dealing with the resistance forces. Some five months earlier, in May, it had been agreed by all members of the Lebanon Conference, including those from ELAS, that at some future date 'All guerrilla bands in free Greece must be unified and disciplined under the orders of a single government.'[6] That future date had now been reached.

On 2 November Papandhréou proposed a plan to deal with the problem, which in fact had two related issues: the new police and the new army. The new police, the National Guard, was to replace the old gendarmerie – that is police outside the cities – and would incorporate EAM's own police force, the Ethnikí Politophilakí or EP. The new army, the National Army, would include two Greek army units, the Mountain Brigade soon to reach Athens and the Sacred Battalion currently in the Aegean islands, and would incorporate the ELAS guerrilla army. New blood for both the National Guard and the National Army would be provided by the call-up of successive age groups, beginning with those born in 1915 so now aged 29. The aim was perhaps to bring in the older and maybe steadier recruits before the more hot-headed youth. Dates were set for each step. The first call-up would be on 20 November and EAM's EP police would be dissolved on 27 November. All guerrilla forces were to be dissolved on 1 December, and four younger age groups would be called up on 10 December.

Papandhréou's proposals clearly threatened the existence of ELAS as an independent military force and would deprive EAM of the power to strike if or when that was needed. EAM's chief negotiator was Siántos, secretary general of the Communist Party, but he was willing to seek a compromise. Siántos proposed that the Mountain Brigade should be treated as a volunteer force and therefore disbanded on the same basis as ELAS. The 2,800-strong Mountain Brigade, which had reached Athens on 9 November, was a volunteer force only in the loosest sense that those who after the mutinies had joined it in support of the government were willing to do so, unlike their mutinous colleagues. Siántos' proposal was rejected, particularly firmly by Churchill: 'The disbandment of the Greek [Mountain] Brigade would be a disaster of the first order.'[7]

Further attempts at compromise followed. On 27 November EAM proposed that the new National Army should have two sections, one of the Mountain Brigade, the Sacred Battalion and EDES, the other ELAS of equal strength to the other combination, giving ELAS the preponderance over any other group. The next day Papandhréou proposed instead that one section should be the intact Mountain Brigade and Sacred Battalion, the other should be ELAS plus EDES in equal numbers, a marked reduction in the influence of ELAS. Both proposals were rejected by the other side. EAM was essentially seeking both the dissolution of the units loyal to the government and a dominant position in the new National Army. Papandhréou's government would accept neither. 'Thus the minimum demands of one side exceeded the maximum concessions of the other.'[8]

With compromise impossible the situation moved quickly to a climax. On 1 December Papandhréou's government ordered all resistance forces to report to demobilisation centres between

10 and 20 December, and in response the six EAM ministers in the government resigned. Also on 1 December Scobie issued a proclamation stating the British intention to protect the Greek people and its government 'against any attempt at a coup d'état or act of violence which is unconstitutional'.[9] On 2 December EAM called for a mass demonstration in Síntagma Square on the next day, Sunday 3 December, to be followed by a general strike on Monday. On the evening of 2 December Papandhréou's Cabinet, now without the EAM ministers, met to consider their response. Évert, the head of the Athens City Police, recommended that the demonstration should be allowed to go ahead, but the Cabinet decided otherwise and issued a statement to ban it.

The ban was ignored, and next morning, Sunday 3 December, the Communist newspaper *Rizospástis* carried a banner headline: 'ALL TODAY AT 11 O'CLOCK TO EAM'S DEMONSTRATION IN SÍNTAGMA. Down with the Government of Civil War. Forward to a Government of REAL national unity.'[10] Constant announcements through megaphones gave the same message. From early morning large crowds began to converge on Síntagma Square.

A number of observers, including foreign press correspondents, watched the developing scene from the balcony of the Grande Bretagne Hotel on the north-west corner of the square. If they looked half right they could see the square, and across it the Tomb of the Unknown Soldier and the old Royal Palace. If they looked immediately right they could see Amalías Street, up which the main body of demonstrators advanced. Immediately below them were the police. The police had been ordered to use only blank cartridges, which tallies with Évert's hope that the demonstration would not be violent, though it is possible that some police disobeyed instructions and armed themselves with live ammunition.

Until about 11 o'clock there was nothing worse in the square than scuffles between aggressive demonstrators and increasingly apprehensive police. Then came the spark that ignited the violence. According to William McNeill, the American military attaché in Athens:

When the demonstration had approached to within 100 feet of where they stood, panic ran down the single line of grey-clad police. At this moment a man dressed in military uniform, but not in the grey of the police, suddenly ran out from the Headquarters building, shouted 'Shoot the Bastards', crouched on one knee beyond the end of [the] wall, and began to fire his gun. The noise of gunshots and his example decided the wavering police. They, too, unslung their carbines, levelled them at the advancing crowd, and fired a veritable fusillade into the mass in front of them.[11]

This account raises a number of questions. First, was it true? McNeill was in Athens but not an eyewitness, though he may have heard this account from someone who was. It is not directly corroborated by any other source, but nor is it directly contradicted. On the other hand, McNeill was praised by Woodhouse as painstakingly impartial. He was not a man who would have invented the story, or repeated it unless he trusted the source.

Second, who was this unidentified man? It was later suggested that he was an EAM agent provocateur, inciting the police to violence to give EAM justification for responding in kind. He might possibly have been an agent of an extreme right-wing anti-Communist group, or he might have been a lone murderous maniac. Who he was remains a mystery.

The incident caused tragic casualties, and the third question is about their numbers. Various estimates give the number of dead as between seven (McNeill) and 21, and of wounded between 26 and 150. Who then was responsible? McNeill argues, from his figure of seven dead, that the police fusillade which he reported must have been with blanks or the number of dead would have been much higher. Some injuries that day were caused by hand grenades, of which ELAS had a store outside Athens but were not carried by the police. The Greek government report on the incident said that 'the first shots were fired by armed demonstrators, who were also supplied with hand grenades.'[12] So the question of responsibility also remains open.

In the aftermath of the shooting there were distressing sights in the square. The British officer Wilfred Byford-Jones wrote:

I shall never forget that scene. A young girl in a white blouse which was becoming red with blood near her breasts, a young man, with a mark that might have been made by a fish-hook, writhing for a moment, and then dying; a child screaming and clutching her head [...] I carried a girl of about twelve years, who was shot in the leg and had a superficial wound in the side of the head. She was pale and under-fed, and she looked up at me, smiling wanly.[13]

The girl died almost immediately afterwards. A British paratrooper was also seen, with tears in his eyes, carrying a little girl who had been hit twice and was bleeding. Later, when the square was empty, relatives of the dead came and placed small crosses, made from branches pulled from the trees, on the pools of blood on the paving. What happened in Síntagma Square on Sunday 3 December, whatever its cause, was a tragedy, and it initiated the greater tragedy of the weeks of violence which followed.

The wider question about the December events is about the aims of EAM and ELAS and behind them the Communist Party. Their objective was obviously to take over the government, which is after all the objective of any serious political group. The question is whether they intended to achieve this democratically or by force.

On one side it is argued that they favoured the democratic approach, as shown by their willingness to join the government as ministers, and to sign, albeit reluctantly, the Lebanon Charter in May and the Caserta Agreement in September, both of which placed all guerrilla forces under government control. It is also argued that there had been a golden opportunity for a Communist take-over of Athens by force in the few days of October between the final departure of the Germans and the arrival of the Papandhréou government. Woodhouse certainly thought so: 'Had the Communists wished to seize control of Athens in the period between the German withdrawal and the arrival of the government they would have succeeded and no available source could have expelled them.'[14] Macmillan agreed: 'This coup d'état […] would have been successful.'[15]

It has also been suggested that, because the Communist forces missed such a good opportunity to seize power by force, this had never been their intention.[16] But this argument is unconvincing. The fact that one fails to take an opportunity to achieve an aim in no way proves that one never had that aim.

Woodhouse and Macmillan were two of the best-qualified authorities to judge the potential effectiveness of an October *coup d'état*, but it has to be asked whether this opportunity seemed equally golden to the Communists. Some advance British troops were already in Athens, and an attempt to seize the city would have involved gun battles with the British, who were then being almost universally hailed as liberators. Furthermore the Communists did not know how many British troops they would be facing, since care had been taken that their numbers and deployment were kept secret from them. The window of this opportunity was in any case very short, a mere six days from the German departure on 12 October and the government arrival on 18 October, and neither of these dates could be predicted with any certainty.

The best interpretation of Communist tactics seems to be the simplest one: that they were opportunists. They would achieve power, at least cost, by peaceful and democratic means if possible, but by violence if not. They had been opportunistic throughout the period of the resistance, co-operating with the British when this seemed advantageous but attacking their resistance rivals when they had the chance. Moreover EAM counsels were divided, some such as Svólos and probably Siántos inclined to moderation, others such as most of the ELAS commanders in favour of aggression. On this view, what finally tipped the scales on the side of using force was the imminent emasculation of ELAS by its disbandment and incorporation with anti-Communist units in a National Army. If this went ahead their option to use force would be gone for good. It was clear to them, in the first few days of December, that they would have to strike now.

20

The Battle for Athens

By the evening of Sunday 3 December, after some noisy but non-violent demonstrations during the afternoon, Síntagma Square was quiet. But this was only a lull before the storm of the battle for Athens broke. The battle was in three inter-related fields. The first was the military action. The second contest was over public opinion in both Britain and the United States, much of it severely critical of what British troops were doing in Greece. Finally there was the political field, where the only lasting solution to the military problem lay.

Scobie was in command of British forces and of Greek troops loyal to the government. Directing ELAS was Mandhákis, formerly leader of ELAS in Crete, and he was directly answerable to the EAM Central Committee dominated by Siántos. On 5 December Scobie received forceful instructions from Churchill:

> You are responsible for maintaining order in Athens and for neutralising or destroying all EAM-ELAS bands approaching the city. Do not hesitate to act as if you were in a conquered city where a local rebellion is in progress. We have to hold and dominate Athens. It would be a great thing for you to succeed in this without bloodshed if possible, but also with bloodshed if necessary.[1]

Scobie had already ordered Mandhákis to withdraw ELAS troops from Athens as agreed at Caserta, and on the night of 3/4 December an ELAS battalion from Thebes was turned back from Athens by British soldiers. But on the night of 5/6 December 2,000 ELAS troops from the Peloponnese moved into Athens. Scobie was clearly not going to control the situation by issuing orders and quoting the Caserta Agreement. On 8 December Churchill sent further instructions to Scobie, including: 'The clear objective is the defeat of EAM. The ending of the fighting is subsidiary to this.'[2]

Initially ELAS did not directly attack British troops. Between 3 and 7 December it fought with the anti-Communist Chi (X) bands of Grívas, and captured 22 of the 25 Athens police stations. ELAS briefly attacked the government buildings round Síntagma Square but withdrew when they realised that British troops were among the defenders, and fired on the Greek Mountain Brigade. In response British forces occupied the EAM buildings in central Athens and held the Akropolis and a small area around it. The RAF launched air strikes against ELAS positions, first with Spitfires using machine guns and later with rocket-firing Beaufighters, and in the course of the whole battle over 1,600 air sorties were flown. Sniping was continuous from both sides.

Thus by 11 December the British were effectively under siege, the day on which Macmillan returned to Athens from Italy, and wrote:

At present the British forces (and the Embassy) are besieged and beleaguered in the small central area of Athens. We hold about 5–10 out of 50 square miles of built-up area (Athens and Piraeus). The airfield at Tatoi is lost and nearly 800 Air Force H.Q. and ground staff cut off in that suburb. Our airfield at Kalamaki is very insecure and the communications between it and the main body in Athens all under fire. We do not hold a port at all. In other words, we have no secure base anywhere from which to operate.[3]

Accompanying Macmillan to Athens was Field Marshall Harold Alexander, who only days earlier had taken over from Wilson as supreme Allied commander in the Mediterranean. Alexander immediately grasped the position: 'You are in a grave situation. I can put that right in time, but it may take a fortnight. It will need two fighting divisions to come from Italy.'[4] A brigadier on Alexander's staff reported that the main sources of trouble were 'a lack of experienced HQ or commander, confused orders, no unifying plan to co-ordinate operations, administration and the phasing-in of reinforcements'.[5] In short, military control of Athens would depend on bringing in both more troops and a more effective commander than Scobie. The new commander was General John Hawkesworth. Alexander wanted to sack Scobie on the spot and replace him with Hawkesworth, but was persuaded that this would be seen as a victory for ELAS. So Scobie kept his position while Hawkesworth took over operational command.

The new troops from Italy were brought in to Athens by air or by sea between 13 and 16 December, giving Hawkesworth some

50,000 men under his command. These men could be temporarily withdrawn from Italy because winter had brought a lull in the fighting there. Hawkesworth also had a plan of battle. Scobie's limited number of troops had meant that once they had cleared an area of ELAS they had to be withdrawn to fight elsewhere, so ELAS came straight back in. Hawkesworth's plan, with his larger forces, was much more coherent.

> British troops were only to capture areas the perimeter of which they could be certain of holding. Inside this area all houses would be searched and citizens who did not take part in the battle would be left. All those in any way connected with the fighting to be removed to PW (Prisoner of War) cages for screening. Thereafter as soon as possible the area would be taken over by a Greek unit under British supervision, and the British troops released to seize the next area. Immediately any such liberated area had been freed of incident, i.e. no rifle shots for 24 hours, hot meals would be served in the area by the British formation.[6]

The withholding and then provision of hot meals was a clever ploy to win co-operation, though UNRRA would certainly have disapproved.

It was to Hawkesworth, in Woodhouse's view, that the credit for winning the battle of Athens principally belonged, which was surely right, and Scobie was widely regarded as a failure. But Scobie had been put in an impossible position. He had belligerent instructions from Churchill to defeat ELAS whatever the cost, but had not been given sufficient forces even to begin to fulfil them. No political moves could be made until this illusory victory had been won. Scobie was not the first commander to be given a firm objective without being given anywhere near the means to achieve it.

While the battle for control was being decided on the streets of Athens, the battle for popular support was being waged in the court of public opinion, on both sides of the Atlantic. On 8 December, in the House of Commons, Churchill vigorously defended his Greek policy against a Labour move to censure it. 'We are charged', he said, 'that we are using His Majesty's forces to disarm the friends of democracy in Greece and in other parts of Europe and to suppress those popular movements which have valorously assisted in the defeat of the enemy.' But what was being opposed in Greece was not democracy:

The last thing which resembles democracy is mob law, with bands of gangsters, armed with deadly weapons, forcing their way into great cities, seizing the police stations and key points of government, endeavouring to introduce a totalitarian regime with an iron hand.

Churchill went on to contrast true and false democracy: 'Democracy is not based on violence or terrorism, but on reason, on fair play, on freedom, on respecting the rights of other people. Democracy is no harlot to be picked up in the street by a man with a tommy gun.' He concluded defiantly:

If I am blamed for this action I will gladly accept my dismissal at the hands of the House; but if I am not so dismissed – make no mistake about it – we shall persist in this policy of clearing Athens and the Athens region of all who are rebels against the authority of the constitutional Government of Greece – of mutineers against the orders of the Supreme Commander in the Mediterranean under whom all the guerrillas have undertaken to serve.[7]

The censure motion was comprehensively defeated by 279 to 30. Most Labour members abstained but continued to criticise Churchill's policy in Parliament. On 13 December the Labour Party Conference passed overwhelmingly a motion expressing regret at British policy in Greece, a vote triumphantly announced through ELAS megaphones in Athens. However, Churchill's government was strongly supported by Labour's Ernest Bevin, minister of labour in the coalition government, who strongly supported the Greek policy at the Trades Union Conference. Bevin, wrote Macmillan, 'both at this time and until the end of the rebellion, stood with rock-like loyalty against the wave of sentimentalist emotion'.[8] Bevin became foreign secretary in the Labour government elected in the summer of 1945, and his continuing tough stance on Greece was much more significant than the carping of the critics.

The British press almost universally damned the government's policy, especially *The Times* and the *Manchester Guardian*. The stance of *The Times* was made clear to Nigel Clive in January 1945, when, back in London from Greece, he met its editor, Robin Barrington-Ward, over a distinctly frosty lunch. Barrington-Ward maintained that:

Churchill had gone off his head – not for the first time in his political life – by ordering British troops to intervene in Athens. This showed that the war had taught him nothing. It was obvious that he was trying to impose a politically and morally untenable regime against the expressed wish of the Greek people. He had done so merely to satisfy a personal whim. The policy we were following in Greece showed Churchill's profound misjudgement of British interests.[9]

Clive's rebuttals were brushed aside in what he described as an utterly sterile debate.

The *Manchester Guardian* told the British soldier, as he read it under sniper and mortar attack in his comfortless mess, that he was 'fighting on one side of a miserable civil war' and that 'we had no right to abuse European countries'. The paper could also be uncharacteristically ruthless: 'Our business is to help Italians and Greeks to self-government and self-respect. If they have to cut a few throats in the process let it be their throats, not ours.'[10]

Public opinion in the United States was equally hostile to British policy in Greece, and repeatedly emphasised that the United States would not become involved. On 3 December the 'Voice of America' broadcast to Europe a statement by Secretary of State Edward Stettinius that 'the United States will make no attempt to influence the composition of any government in any friendly country. The American people have naturally viewed with sympathy the aspirations of the resistance movements.'[11] Ten days later Roosevelt sent Churchill a long message:

As anxious as I am to be of the greatest help to you in this trying situation, there are limitations imposed in part by the traditional policies of the United States and in part by the mounting adverse reaction of public opinion in this country. My one hope is to see this situation rectified so we can go along in this as in everything, shoulder to shoulder.

Roosevelt concluded with a practical recommendation:

I wonder if Macmillan's efforts [in Athens] might not be greatly facilitated if the King himself would approve the establishment of a regency in Greece and would make a public declaration of his intention not to return unless called for by popular plebiscite.[12]

The idea of a regency had been proposed before, but it was now steadily gaining ground.

In Athens the British Embassy was now under attack, and Macmillan, Leeper with his wife and daughter, and their staffs were in effect besieged. On 6 December, three days after the Síntagma Square incidents, Leeper's wife and daughter unwisely went out for a walk, got caught up in the fighting and had to take shelter in a friendly house. From then on Leeper ordered that nobody should leave the embassy without his approval. Even inside the embassy there was constant danger from snipers. Bullets lodged inside two of the bedrooms, and bullets came through the window of Macmillan's study, though as he said nonchalantly, 'there was a corner in which one could sit without undue risk.'[13] Leeper later counted 52 bullet holes in the wall beside that window.

There were some 50 people holed up in the embassy, and Mrs Leeper, as her husband said, became the manageress of a large-sized hotel. Meals were taken together in the central hall, and the food was army biscuits, bully beef and spam, to which British personnel were limited in order to leave all other food for the Greeks. These rations had to be fetched by regular car journeys under machine-gun fire from the army stores halfway between Athens and Piraeus. There was no electricity because ELAS now held the power station, and consequently no light and no heat, and no water because ELAS had drained the local reservoir.

However, the dangers and discomforts of life in the embassy were as nothing compared with the situation of the Greeks in central Athens. As Byford-Jones wrote:

Most of them went without water for days. Far more were without food, and pathetic creatures used to steal along the fire-swept streets like people who had crept out of hiding holes, whining and begging for food. The situation in hospitals became indescribably bad. Operations could only be performed at a certain period of the day, and then with difficulty, owing to the absence of electricity, and the original number of inmates, as at the Evangelismos hospital, were doubled and trebled by battle casualties. Patients lay on the floor and in corridors and the bodies were stacked in out-houses, because they could not be taken away to be buried.[14]

On 12 December, when the British position was at its most perilous, an ELAS representative met with Scobie to ask what were his terms for a truce. In reply Scobie said that all ELAS forces must leave the Athens area, as agreed at Caserta, and their armed supporters must give up their weapons. In reply ELAS offered a temporary withdrawal if the Mountain Brigade did the same. They also required the total dismissal of the gendarmerie, and that the British forces should play no part in the country's internal affairs. In effect Scobie was demanding that ELAS should hand Athens to him, and ELAS that Scobie should hand the city to them. Inevitably, both sides rejected the other's terms.

So the battle for Athens continued, at first marked by some ELAS successes. At 3 o'clock in the morning of 13 December they made their first, and only, large-scale attack on the British in central Athens. About 1,000 ELAS troops attacked an infantry barracks near Likavittós, only three-quarters of a mile from Síntagma Square, and after fierce fighting withdrew, taking over 100 British prisoners with them. On 17 December ELAS made a night attack on the Avérof prison which held some 800 suspected collaborators, including the occupation prime ministers Tsolákoglou and Rállis. The British guards let the prisoners out and ordered them to an assembly point outside the prison. The prisoners fled amid wild cries of horror and despair, and elderly generals were seen running at speed for safety. Most prisoners ignored the assembly point; some were captured later, but of the original 800 only 235, including the two prime ministers, were found and returned to prison. ELAS had demonstrated its military muscle, but its main effect was to free some of the suspected collaborators on whom ELAS wanted revenge. At the same time as the Avérof attack, ELAS seized the isolated RAF headquarters at Kifíssia north of the city, again taking prisoners.

However, Hawkesworth's plan was now taking effect and ELAS forces were being steadily pushed out of central Athens. Immediately after Alexander's visit on 11 December a massive airlift of supplies began, vitally needed because at one point the British had only two days' ammunition left. In the first two days 200 aircraft loads were flown in, and during the next two weeks a total of 1,650.

> Trucks were parked in a row like taxis on a rank. As each aircraft touched down, a truck peeled off from the rank, rushed to the aircraft, the truck crew loaded ammunition into their vehicle, took it to an ammunition dump, then returned to the rank.

As their commanding officer said, they all knew it was touch and go in Athens.[15]

On 13 December the RAF broke up a large ELAS formation in the Stádhio area, half a mile from Síntagma. On the night of 17 December British troops cleared ELAS from the Athens–Piraeus highway, moving steadily up from the south, providing an open, if still risky, link between central Athens and the main port. On 18 December ELAS moved its headquarters out of central Athens. An indication of the improved situation was that when Macmillan arrived in Athens on 11 December he had to travel to Scobie's office in a tank. By 17 December he was walking there once or twice a day. The military tide had turned, but the political problem, and in particular the question of the King, still had to be resolved.

21

Dhamaskinós, Churchill and the Varkíza Agreement

The military situation might have improved, but Alexander was convinced that ultimately there had to be a political solution. He had said so to Churchill on 15 December, and a week later gave Churchill his views with even more force:

> I am most concerned that you should know exactly what true situation is and what we can do and cannot do. This is my duty. Assuming that ELAS continue to fight, I estimate that it will be possible to clear the Athens–Piraeus area and thereafter to hold it securely, but this will not defeat ELAS and force them to surrender. We are not strong enough to go beyond this and undertake operations on the Greek mainland. It is my opinion that the Greek problem cannot be solved by military measures. The answer must be found in the political field.
>
> Finally, I think you know that you can always rely on me to do everything in my power to carry out your wishes, but I earnestly hope that you will be able to find a political solution to the Greek problem, as I am convinced that further military action after we have cleared the Athens–Piraeus area is beyond our present strength.[1]

Alexander was clearly right that it was impossible to gain control of mainland Greece by military means – which, as he pointed out, six to seven German divisions had been unable to do during the occupation. ELAS control there was now even more complete because on 18 December ELAS, led by Saráphis, had begun a drive to force the EDES of Zérvas out of their Epirus stronghold in the north-west, and by the end of the month nearly 10,000 EDES combatants and supporters had been evacuated to Corfu by the British navy.

The political solution to which Alexander referred was, as Churchill well understood, the establishment of a regent to replace the King as head of state until a decision could be made on the future of the monarchy. With a regency in place, the divisive issue of the King and his return could be moved out of the spotlight, and this would counter the damaging claims that Britain was trying to impose the King on Greece at bayonet point.

The idea of a regency had been under prolonged discussion since December 1943, always associated with the name of Archbishop Dhamaskinós. His standing as archbishop of Athens, combined with his record during the occupation of resistance to the Germans and help for the Greeks, made him the obvious candidate. In March 1944 Tsoudherós, then prime minister, urged the idea on the King in London, who rejected it: 'I find unacceptable the suggestion regarding the appointment at this time of Archbishop Damascinos as Regent.'[2]

When Papandhréou's government returned to Athens, the King had laid it down that there should be no regent but that in his absence from Greece a regency should be exercised by a council of Papandhréou's ministers. But the council had no authority, and this woolly arrangement was soon abandoned. By 11 December Leeper, Macmillan and Alexander were all agreed that Dhamaskinós must be appointed as regent. Three days later Macmillan met Dhamaskinós for the first time and wrote of him:

> I was impressed by the wide grasp of European politics, the good sense, humour, and courage of this ecclesiastic. He is willing to accept the regency, but realises the difficulties. He shares our view that there must be no reprisals and no counter-revolution.[3]

Roosevelt too supported the proposal of a regency, but Churchill replied that the King would not have it, and that it would be an act of constitutional violence if they finally took this course.

Churchill was also influenced by his totally wrong assessment of Dhamaskinós. He was convinced, according to Eden, that the Archbishop was both a quisling and a Communist. Churchill had heard that Dhamaskinós was very much in touch with EAM and was ambitious for political power. Churchill summed him up as a 'pestilent priest, a survival from the Middle Ages'.[4] Churchill's overall view of the Greek situation had always been of some medieval historical drama in which a king, hedged by something of divinity, defended his throne but was surrounded by scheming courtier-politicians while a despicable rabble clamoured at the gates. The wily ambitious cleric completed the picture.

On Christmas Eve, after the King had again rejected a regency and while bullets were still flying in beleaguered Athens, Churchill resolved, as he put it, to go and see for himself, and especially to meet Dhamaskinós. He cabled to Alexander, who was on his way to Athens, 'Two friends of yours, of which I am one, are coming out to join you.'[5] The other was Eden. About noon on Christmas Day they landed at Kalamáki airfield on the coast some 4 miles south of the city centre. They were met by Alexander, Leeper and Macmillan, with whom they had a three hour discussion on board the plane, ending with full agreement on the next steps. That evening the party was driven, escorted by armoured cars, the few miles to Piraeus and then to HMS *Ajax*, which was anchored off shore.

That evening the next day's conference was planned. It would be attended by Dhamaskinós, Greek politicians and representatives of ELAS. Churchill would open proceedings, in the presence of the British officials and three foreign observers: MacVeagh as American ambassador, Colonel Popov for Russia and the French minister in Athens. Then these would withdraw, leaving the conference to the Greeks with Dhamaskinós as chairman. On that same evening Dhamaskinós joined the British party on the *Ajax*, when Churchill met him for the first time and quickly began to revise his previous derogatory assessment. 'It was impossible to doubt', he wrote, that Dhamaskinós 'greatly feared the Communist combination in Greek affairs [...]. Generally he impressed me with a good deal of confidence.'[6]

Next morning, Boxing Day, the British party left the *Ajax* as shells fell in the water around them, and travelled by armoured car to the British Embassy. Churchill, meeting Dhamaskinós again, had by now completed his volte-face: 'I was already convinced that he was the outstanding figure in the Greek turmoil.'[7] At 6 o'clock the conference opened in the Greek Foreign Office. There was no lighting or heating, so the room was lit by hurricane lamps and the delegates kept their greatcoats on. At first no ELAS delegates appeared, which threatened the total failure of the conference, but Churchill began his opening speech without them. Five minutes later they appeared, incongruously but perhaps promisingly wearing British battledress.

After Churchill's address and some generally favourable responses from the delegates, the conference was left, as agreed, to the Greeks.

It went on until 10 p.m., rowdily according to Dhamaskinós, and resumed all the next day. Little progress could be made to end the fighting in Athens because ELAS was still making unacceptable demands, and this question was deferred for a further conference. But the delegates, including ELAS, were unanimous on one vital proposal, that there should be a regency and that Dhamaskinós should be the regent. ELAS delegates agreed because, it was thought, they expected that a new government under Dhamaskinós would be more ready to accept ELAS' truce terms. It now only remained for the King to be persuaded, at last, to agree to make way for a regency.

Papandhréou, by this time regarded as discredited and divisive, could clearly not continue as prime minister in a new government under Dhamaskinós. The nominee to replace him was General Plastíras, who arrived at the Grande Bretagne Hotel in Athens on 13 December at the end of a 12-year exile in France. As Byford-Jones described him, he was very thin, and wiry, and had a grim granite-like face, with a soldier's silvery waxed moustache. He was immaculately dressed, in contrast to the dishevelment of the other occupants of the Grande Bretagne.[8] He seemed a reassuringly impartial figure. He had been out of Greece since 1932, so had not been involved in the political animosities of the late 1930s and 1940s. He appeared to straddle both pro- and anti-monarchist views. In 1922 he had been one of the leaders of the coup that led to King Constantine's abdication, but during the German occupation he had been the nominal head of Zérvas' EDES, which had declared in favour of the King. On the day after his arrival he appealed to ELAS to lay down their arms, and stressed his inflexible insistence on democratic principles. Churchill is said to have growled, 'I am told we must put our trust in General Plaster-as. Let us hope that he does not have feet of clay.'[9]

Churchill and Eden arrived back in London on 29 December, and that evening called King George to 10 Downing Street. Churchill wrote afterwards: 'This has been a very painful task to me. I had to tell the King that if he did not agree the matter would be settled without him and that we should recognise the new Government instead of him.'[10] He also said that King George behaved like a gentleman with the utmost dignity, but it was not quite like that. The King's private secretary was in an adjoining room at Downing Street and wrote:

I could hear through the door the voices of Churchill and Eden, particularly the latter, raised in anger at the King. In the middle of this heated argument the door was flung open and the King stormed out, his face white and taut.

He had been given Churchill's ultimatum.

> In the car as we drove back to the hotel the King would not trust himself to speak; after recovering his composure he went back to Downing Street and informed Churchill and Eden that he had no choice but to acquiesce to their demands.[11]

This acrimonious meeting ended at 4.30 a.m., and later that day the King issued the necessary proclamation. 'Being ourselves resolved not to return to Greece unless summoned by a free and fair expression of the national will [...] we do now appoint you, Archbishop Damskenos [sic.], to be our Regent during this period of emergency.'[12]

The King's resistance had at last been overcome. Macmillan described the King as the villain of the piece, but it may have been loyalty to his chief that stopped him from adding that it was only Churchill's support which had made possible the King's prolonged and obstructive obstinacy.

Churchill's intervention had broken the Greek political log-jam and this adventure showed him at his best. He had many pressing concerns besides Greece. As Macmillan wrote before his arrival, 'Poor Winston! What with Greece, Poland and the German breakthrough on the Western Front, this is going to be a grim Christmas.'[13] Nevertheless, in the interests of both Britain and the Greek people, he undertook a journey of considerable discomfort and danger – though Churchill was always keen to sniff the scent of battle. He was remarkably quick to change his mind when faced with the true situation. Sneers suggesting that this was an ego-trip – for example that Churchill went to Greece 'to prove himself the peacemaker he wanted to be thought to be'[14] – can be dismissed. Even The Times, Churchill's inveterate opponent, described his initiative as an act of real courage and statesmanship.

The new government under Dhamaskinós was announced on 3 January, with Plastíras as prime minister. The six ministers under Plastíras were described as 'wholly Republican and moderately Left Wing'.[15] Only one under-secretary of state was from Papandhréou's government, and there was no place for Papandhréou himself.

The government's immediate priority was to bring about a truce to end the fighting in Athens. ELAS, its military position much weakened, withdrew its forces from the city on the night of 4/5 January and was now ready to negotiate. Scobie had offered truce terms on 12 December at the height of the fighting, in which the main condition was that ELAS should withdraw from Athens and its surroundings and from an area stretching about 35 miles to the north and west. In the changed situation these terms were superseded on 7 January by tougher ones. Scobie, encouraged by Macmillan, Leeper and Alexander, now required that ELAS withdraw some 70 miles to the north and west of Athens as well as from Salonika, the Peloponnese, and the Cyclades islands off the Peloponnese coast.

The ELAS representatives were prepared to accept these new terms, but were adamant on one issue. They would not return their civilian hostages, numbering between 15,000 and 20,000 and suffering under the harshest conditions. Scobie, Leeper and Macmillan reluctantly decided to defer this issue in order not to sabotage the truce. Dhamaskinós even more reluctantly accepted the decision, and in a public statement declared, 'I deeply regret that during the negotiations for truce it was not made possible to settle the question of hostages.'[16] Despite these misgivings, the truce was signed on 12 January and came into effect three days later.

It was now necessary, as Macmillan put it, to turn the truce into a peace, and this would require a new conference between the Dhamaskinós government and the ELAS representatives. Arguments over the conference's membership and agenda took up the rest of January. Dhamaskinós would obviously preside, but said it would be difficult to get the government to meet ELAS at all unless the hostages were freed first. Plastíras as prime minister would normally have led the government delegation, but he was proving increasingly belligerent, his attitude being 'Give me an armoured column for three days and I will smash [ELAS].'[17] He was clearly uninterested in a political solution, so the government side was led by the much more flexible minister of foreign affairs, Ioánnis Sophianópoulos. The ELAS delegation was led by Siántos, the Communist Party general secretary, and Macmillan thought his presence essential. Nevertheless Macmillan disliked the look of him – 'a set-faced, sly, shifty-looking man' – and his manner of speaking with an air of injured innocence: 'You felt almost convinced by the end that there had been no civil war, no insurrection, no disorders even.'[18]

In fact, as was now becoming clear, ELAS had been responsible for much worse actions. At first the reports of ELAS atrocities had been discounted as government anti-ELAS propaganda, but then journalists and others went to see the evidence for themselves in areas just liberated from ELAS. The BBC correspondent Kenneth Matthews saw one terrible scene, to which he went unwillingly but from a sense of professional duty. He was accompanied, at his insistence, by a university professor who was chief pathologist to the criminal courts. Matthews wrote:

> If ever there was a scene straight from hell, this was it. The bodies were being exhumed from a series of parallel trenches in which the diggers were still working. As each was uncovered, it was laid out on the lip of the trench, naked or half-naked, just as it had been buried. Scattered in small groups on the hillside, the womenfolk of the victims kept up a low wailing which rose from time to time to a blood-chilling shriek of lamentation. Over all a charnel smell making the air sick.

Matthews' companion, with professional detachment,

> passed along the line of corpses, pointing out the wire that bound the hands, the powder-burns on the scalp that betrayed a revolver shot from no distance, occasionally poking with his stick at the head or limb to show some appalling mutilation inflicted before death.[19]

It was not until some days later that Matthews felt the full shock of the scene, and broke down. He was comforted by his friend and fellow-journalist Richard Capell, who gave him two bleakly consoling lines from Shakespeare's sonnets:

> How with such rage shall beauty hold a plea
> Whose action is no stronger than a flower?

Others besides journalists found similar evidence. A British trade union delegation saw at least 250 bodies taken out from the trenches in which they had been thrown, many of them shot with their hands tied behind their backs. These atrocities caused not only revulsion among Greeks but also a shift in the reports in the international press and so in public opinion. ELAS could no longer be presented simply as a body of idealistic crusaders for social justice.

The peace conference finally assembled on 2 February, and continued for the next ten days. Its location was a villa at the seaside resort of Varkíza about 10 miles south of the centre of Athens. When the delegations separated to different rooms Dhamaskinós' secretary Yeorgákis, his trusted supporter throughout the occupation, went back and forth between them. There were many issues to be settled, besides the emotive question of the hostages who were now to be freed immediately. It was also eventually agreed that ELAS should be demobilised and hand over its weapons and other requisitioned goods. The quantity of weapons to be surrendered was specified, and in the event more than the specified numbers were handed in, though this was much less than ELAS actually possessed. Agreement was also reached on an amnesty for political crimes, with certain exclusions, on the formation of the National Army, and on the purging of collaborators from the civil service and the security services.

On 11 February one major question remained to be settled. This was the continuation of martial law, which gave the state the right to arrest without a warrant, in effect the suspension of habeas corpus. Siántos argued that any continuation of martial law would leave his supporters in terror of illegal arrest, and Macmillan took his point. In the end a compromise was reached: martial law would end immediately in Athens and Piraeus, and in the rest of the country after ELAS' disarmament was complete.

By 3 a.m. the following morning all points had been agreed, and the delegates were ready to go to bed, but Macmillan knew the propensity of Greek politicians to reject in the morning what they had agreed the night before. He therefore insisted that before the delegates dispersed they should sign at least a summary of the agreements. By 5.30 a.m. on 12 February this had at last been done, and at 7.30 that evening the full text of the agreement[20] was signed by the delegates at the Greek Foreign Office, in the room where at Christmas Churchill had presided in his greatcoat.

Two days later Churchill came to Athens on his way home from the Yalta Conference, and he and Dhamaskinós rode through Athens in an open car to a tumultuous welcome. When they appeared together in Síntagma Square on the terrace in front of the old Royal Palace, they were greeted by some 40,000 people in the square, and every house, window and roof was black with spectators. It seemed that the crowd was acknowledging and honouring the two leaders, Greek and British, who had brought an end to their troubles. The Varkíza Agreement seemed to offer hope of stability at last for Greece. Sadly that hope, like others before it, proved illusory.

22

The Government, the Communists and the Elections

The Varkíza Agreement had been signed in February 1945 promising stability, but the following year and a half was a period of conflict and change. There was a succession under the regency of short-lived prime ministers, reflecting the continuing fierce arguments between royalists and republicans. Two more attempts were made to reform the Greek economy, both with limited success. The Communist line hardened, while reciprocal violence by both left and right intensified. Finally elections for the government and a plebiscite on the monarchy were held. By the end of the period the Greek people were better fed thanks to UNRRA, but virtually nothing had been done about reconstruction, and the future was still highly uncertain.

In the course of 1945 Greece had five different prime ministers. The first was Plastíras, appointed at the beginning of January, but his early promise as a moderate and impartial figure was soon belied. It became clear that he backed a republic and opposed a monarchy. It also became clear that he wanted British troops to smash ELAS rather than seek a political solution, and in Leeper's view he simply despised politics. He packed the government ministries with his personal friends, ousting any moderates. On 5 April the final blow to Plastíras was the publication of a letter of July 1941 from Plastíras to Vichy France, in which he said, 'Greece was driven to suicide by the Royal Government which had consented with indescribable naiveté to take on two of the greatest military powers in Europe.'[1] A prime minister who belittled in this way Greece's resistance to Italy and Germany had to go, and on 7 April Plastíras resigned. Churchill's half-jocular foreboding had been proved right.

His successor was Admiral Pétros Voulgáris, who in April 1944, as head of the Royal Hellenic Navy, had put down the naval mutiny in Alexandria. This earnt him the confidence of royalists, but according to Leeper he believed that reasonable collaboration with republicans was the only possible remedy for Greece. On taking office he promised that his government would pursue no political ends, and that its sole mission was to return power to the people through early elections and a plebiscite. His government would be of no single political party and composed mainly of non-politicians – a service government in the service of the nation.

Voulgáris too soon ran into trouble. He tried but failed to get control of the army, whose higher positions he believed, with reason, were being taken over by royalist extremists. By August many of his ministers had resigned, and Voulgáris was ready to step down himself. On 6 October he made a last bid for credibility by announcing that the elections would be held on 20 January 1946. However, the republicans, socialists and Communists immediately said they would abstain, on the grounds that law and order had not been established and the voters' lists had still not been properly compiled. Their abstention meant that these elections would be a farce, and Voulgáris would be condemned as a tool of the royalists, who would obviously win. A few days later Voulgáris resigned, his premiership undermined by his attempts to be inclusive whereas Plastíras had failed by being belligerently exclusive.

For the rest of October Dhamaskinós was unable to find a politician willing to serve as prime minister and form a government, so assumed the premiership himself. After three weeks he appointed, on 1 November, the leader of one of the smaller republican groups, Panayiótis Kanellópoulos. But Kanellópoulos in office failed to win the backing of either republicans or royalists, he refused to commit himself to a date for the elections, and the Greek economy was now again in perilous decline. Kanellópoulos, wrote Leeper, was 'an honest and well-intentioned man but one partial to verbose discourse rather than vigorous action'.[2] On 22 November, after a three-week premiership, he made way for the fifth and last Greek prime minister of 1945.

This was Themistoklís Sophoúlis, the 85-year-old leader of the republicans. He formed a government which was of broadly republican sympathies but was more widely based than any of its predecessors, and significantly included younger men of the same age as his grandchildren. It lasted for four months, though shaken and shaky at times, until the elections were finally held. Age had not robbed Sophoúlis of decisiveness, but had brought him what might be called unflappability. Leeper wrote:

> During the four months that I had constant meetings with him I never saw him agitated or ruffled, and there was much almost every day to agitate and to ruffle. In the political life of Athens this calm was startling and almost uncanny, but it was very comforting.[3]

A bone of contention involving the British as well as the Greek politicians was the still unresolved question of when elections and a plebiscite on the monarchy should be held, and in what order. The Varkíza Agreement of February 1945 had laid down that the plebiscite should come first and be followed by the elections. The agreement also said that both were to be held as soon as possible and in any case before the end of 1945, though in the event neither was held until 1946. The monarchist politicians wanted the plebiscite first, as agreed at Varkíza, which they expected to win, giving them a better chance of also winning the subsequent elections. For the reverse reasons the republicans wanted the elections first.

The timing of both also had political implications. The monarchists wanted them as soon as possible while the memory of the battle of Athens and the attendant ELAS atrocities was still strong; anti-Communism meant support for the monarchy as a bulwark against it. Again for the opposite reasons the republicans wanted delay. The British simply wanted both to be held as quickly as possible, so that British troops could be withdrawn. Their presence was a drain on Britain's war-depleted resources and continued to provoke accusations of British neo-colonialism.

The issues over the order and timing of elections and plebiscite were partially settled in September 1945 by the initiative of AMFOGE, the Allied Mission for Observing Greek Elections. This group had been set up at the time of the Varkíza Agreement, with representatives from Britain, the United States and France. Russia had been invited to join but had declined, no doubt to avoid a precedent for Allied observation of elections in its own satellites.

The AMFOGE initiative followed a September meeting with Dhamaskinós in London and resulted in a statement signed on 20

September by the foreign ministers of all three participating countries. The statement said that the AMFOGE members unanimously 'hold the firm opinion' that elections should come first, if possible by the end of 1945, and that only then can stable tranquillity be established so that a free and genuine plebiscite can follow.[4] AMFOGE could not dictate, only 'hold a firm opinion'. Nevertheless after an AMFOGE visit to Athens in December Dhamaskinós issued a decree that the elections should be held on 31 March 1946. It was now settled that elections should come first, on a specified date, though no date for the plebiscite had yet been fixed. Thus the issue of republic versus monarchy remained the main divisive one for the Greek politicians.

There were two main groups backing a republic: the Liberals (Philelévtheri) led by Sophoúlis, and a new party, the United Patriotic Rally (Enoméni Parátaxis Ethnikophrónon), known as the EPE. This was formed in December 1945 by three former prime ministers, Papandhréou (1944), Kanellópoulos (1945) and Sophoklís Venizélos (for 12 days in 1944). Their opponents, supporting a monarchy, were the Populists (Laikó Kómma), led by the future prime minister Konstantínos Tsaldháris, and supported by some smaller groups. For the sake of clarity, even though at the risk of oversimplification, the two main groups are here collectively called republicans and royalists.

While the successive governments were immersed in these constitutional issues, they had little time or energy, or indeed the ability, to deal with the pressing problems of the country. Greece after liberation was in a terrible state. In the countryside over 2,000 villages had been destroyed, forcing the inhabitants into the towns, while cultivated acreage – olive groves, vineyards, tobacco fields – had been wrecked. Industry could not function because there were virtually no raw materials. Land communications were in complete chaos. Half the total road mileage and almost all major road bridges were unusable. At least two-thirds of cars, vans, trucks and buses were out of action. On the railways, the main line to the north and its rolling stock had been comprehensively wrecked by the Germans during their 1944 retreat, and in the Peloponnese 80 per cent of the rolling stock and all large bridges had been demolished. All ports had been damaged, especially Piraeus, which was full of sunken block ships.

It was UNRRA which saved Greece from starvation. As we have seen, after liberation relief supplies had been the responsibility of the mainly British body Military Liaison, in co-operation with UNRRA. UNRRA had to leave Greece during the battle for Athens, but returned on 1 April 1945. UNRRA then took over from Military Liaison the main task of providing relief, though Military Liaison continued to contribute, adding a further 250,000 to the 1.4 million tons of food supplied by UNRRA in its first year of full operations. Providing food was UNRRA's first priority, which accounted for well over half of its expenditure in Greece in the second half of 1945, with another fifth on the immediate needs of clothing and hygiene. By April 1946 the average calorie consumption for the population as a whole had been raised to 2,300 a day, a marked increase on the earlier Military Liaison achievement of 2,000 a day for Athens and Salonika alone. UNRRA had staved off immediate disaster, but there remained the wider problem of how to put the Greek economy on a sustainable footing, and for this the first step was a new attempt to stabilise the currency.

Waley's reforms of November 1944, apart from the introduction of the new drachma at one to 50,000,000,000 old ones, had achieved no lasting improvement. Even the new drachma steadily lost value against gold, and by May 1945 to buy a gold sovereign cost six times as much in new drachmas as it had in November 1944. Every other element in Waley's plan had failed. The government had not cut its pay bill, little had been done to collect more taxes, charging for relief supplies had been ineffective and the government was still printing money. As a result inflation continued, government expenditure massively exceeded its income, and the cost of living rose relentlessly as price increases outstripped wage increases.

The Plastíras government of January to April 1945 had no answer to these problems apart from demanding a British loan. Without this it claimed it could do nothing in the present war-ravaged condition of the country. The British view was that Greece should solve its own problems, or at least take steps towards doing so, and in any case Britain could not afford any substantial loan. Thus in effect the Greeks were asking the British to do the politically unpalatable and economically undesirable by providing money, while the British were asking the Greeks to do the proverbially impossible and haul themselves up by their own boot straps.

The Voulgáris government, composed mainly of non-politicians, took over from Plastíras in April 1945 and at last acted on the financial crisis. With British encouragement, if not pressure, Kiriakós Varvaréssos, the governor of Greece's central bank, was appointed on 3 June as minister of supply, in effect minister for the economy. He lost no time in announcing the start of his already well thought out reform programme. His aims were both economic and social. On the national economy he intended to end monetary instability, and this also had a social purpose. 'Monetary instability', he wrote later, 'is in my view the greatest enemy of the poorer classes.' To achieve a fairer society he planned heavy taxation of the rich, including industrialists, professionals and traders down to shopkeepers and taverna owners. These, he believed, were 'a new economic oligarchy devoid of principles'.[5] He wanted, he said, to end 'the feasts of Kolonaki', the conspicuous consumption of the Athens elite.[6]

Varvaréssos' first proposals appeared in the press on 6 June 1945 and more followed in the subsequent weeks. Wage rates were increased, and the prices charged for UNRRA relief supplies were halved. Price controls were imposed on domestically produced goods, starting with food and clothing and later extended to everything else. Varvaréssos announced his intention to reduce civil service over-manning by the long-deferred plan of sacking Metaxás and occupation appointees, though in the end he did not dare to do it.

On taxation, he instituted the so-called Special Contribution. All business premises, commercial, industrial or professional, were to be charged a multiple of their rent, or notional rent for freeholds. The rent was seen as a broad indication of profitability. The actual rent was obviously too low as rents had been frozen during the occupation, hence the multiples, which varied from 6 to 15 times. The tax was to be paid monthly for the next nine months. Even Varvaréssos agreed that this tax was hardly scientific. A further measure was a retrospective tax on war profits from contracts with the occupation forces, wartime investments and gold purchases. The rate varied from 30 per cent to 90 per cent, and this tax too was hardly scientific.

The Varvaréssos reforms achieved a short-lived success. Price controls temporarily cut inflation dramatically from its level in May 1945, but by September inflation had returned to its May level. The drachma initially strengthened against the gold sovereign, and the sovereign was 17 per cent cheaper in June than in May, though once again this effect lasted only a few months. But there was opposition to the reforms from all the groups affected. Traders withheld supplies, expecting prices to rise when price controls were eased or simply failed. This produced shortages of basic commodities – cheese, sugar, butter, soap, and most importantly olive oil – leading to higher prices on unofficial markets and in turn to higher inflation. Businesses resisted the rent-related Special Contribution, appealing against the assessments and delaying payment.

In one historian's opinion, the basic flaw in the Varvaréssos reforms was that 'success was to depend on the compliance of better-off taxpayers with measures designed to ruin them.'[7] The rich are always the most adept at minimising their taxes, and Varvaréssos' aim of using taxation to reduce the budget deficit was in the end frustrated. The deficit was in fact halved in July compared with June, but like the other economic indicators was back to its old level by August. Varvaréssos resigned as minister on 1 September, and a week later all price controls on food were lifted.

Varvaréssos deserves credit for introducing perhaps the most comprehensive and most socially progressive economic reforms yet attempted in Greece. They were modelled on the successful measures used in wartime Britain. But in Britain those measures were introduced by a widely respected government of all parties, the British had a tradition of paying taxes, especially as a contribution to the war effort, and Britain had a highly developed and efficient civil service. The misfortune of Varvaréssos was that not one of these British factors was present in Greece.

While the Greek government struggled to find a way forward, politically as well as financially, the Communist KKE was faced with its own set of decisions. Its basic dilemma was whether to seek power by democratic means or by resuming the armed struggle. The balance of power in the KKE shifted when Níkos Zachariádhis returned to Greece in 1945. A decade earlier in 1934 Zachariádhis had become secretary general of the KKE, in 1936 had been arrested and imprisoned under the Metaxás regime and in 1942 was transferred by the Germans to Dachau. Liberated by the Allies, he was flown back to Greece in an RAF transport plane on 30 May 1945 and resumed his position as KKE secretary general, displacing Siántos. The KKE and therefore ELAS was nominally controlled by a 35-member Central Committee drawn from the different regions, but in reality power lay with a small inner group, the Secretariat. Its four members were Zachariádhis, his predecessor Siántos and two others.

Some in ELAS denounced the Varkíza Agreement because its terms would rule out any future seizure of power by force. Chief among these was Áris Velouchiótis, one of the earliest and most striking resistance leaders. Áris was determined to continue the armed struggle and led his own band to the north-west, and into Albania, returning to Greece at the end of May. There he found that Zachariádhis, immediately on return from Germany, had denounced him: 'If anyone from within our ranks continues to resist, we will attack him openly and expel him.'[8] After roaming the hills a little longer, hounded by the authorities and betrayed by villagers, Áris shot himself on 16 June, and his severed head was displayed on a pole in Tríkala.

It seemed that Zachariádhis was rejecting the use of force. He had denounced Áris and had also asserted that a people's democracy could only be established through free and genuine elections. However, there were soon signs that this attitude was changing. On 18 April the KKE's four most moderate non-Communist supporters, including Svólos, formed their own political party with a mildly socialist label, undermining the KKE claim to be a broad coalition of progressives and denting its chance of any electoral success. It was now exclusively the KKE and principally its secretary general Zachariádhis who decided policy. Speaking in Salonika on 24 August 1945, Zachariádhis declared:

> If the situation is not soon and drastically turned towards a normal democratic development, we will reply to Monarcho-Fascism in the towns, the mountains, and the villages with the same means. And if the supreme interests of the People demand it, the glorious marching-song 'Empros ELAS gia tin Ellada' (Forward ELAS for Greece) will sound again in the ravines and on the mountain-tops.[9]

In February 1946, on the first anniversary of the Varkíza Agreement, a formal meeting of the 35-member Central Committee decided to go ahead with the organisation of the new armed struggle against the so-called monarcho-fascist orgy.

Another reason for the Communist adherents to move towards armed conflict was the reciprocal terror that had developed between left and right. There were many claims by the left of terror inflicted by the right. On 12 May 1945 the Communist press listed outrages by the right in the first ten days of May, including 19 murders, 645 assaults and 1,183 illegal arrests. A later Communist Party publication of 1948 gave figures for February 1945 to March 1946, the year following Varkíza. These included 1,219 murders, over 100,000 arrests, a fifth of them with violence, 31,632 victims of torture and 165 rapes and acts of violence against women. Woodhouse, though treating all these figures with caution, concludes: 'up to the end of 1945 at least, so far as political labels could be attached to the perpetrators, the blame for bloodshed lay primarily on right-wing forces, particularly Grivas's Khi.'[10]

There was, however, a mass of evidence of outrages by the left. After the battle for Athens mass graves of ELAS victims had been discovered and seen with horror by Matthews among others. Nine such sites had already been found by January 1945 containing 1,500 bodies, 250 of them women, and later in the year on 2 September 1945 the government announced that by then the bodies of 8,752 ELAS hostages had been found, many mutilated. ELAS also had its own security apparatus, formerly known as OPLA (Units for the Protection of the People's Struggle), now simply called Avtoámina or Self-Defence. This included three-man murder squads who were introduced to each other under assumed names and, mission accomplished, disappeared into anonymity, taking another false name and even changing their clothing and personal habits.

If the Communists were to resume the armed struggle they would need weapons. The Varkíza Agreement had been designed to disarm them, and the numbers of weapons to be surrendered had been precisely specified: 41,500 rifles, 2,015 automatic weapons, 163 mortars and 32 pieces of artillery. As we have seen, ELAS actually handed in more than the required numbers, but this was misleading as much of what was surrendered was outdated or useless, including old Italian carbines and artillery for which there was no ammunition. ELAS still had a formidable supply of arms, and in the months after Varkíza British troops discovered caches of weapons hidden in caves, hollow walls of houses, haystacks and even dunghills. George Kousoulas, later historian of Greek Communism but then a prisoner-interpreter of ELAS at Lamía, witnessed weapons being taken away to mountain hideouts. Clearly the Communists' military option was being kept open.

There was now agreement on the order of events – elections first, plebiscite second – and the date for the elections. This brought a new attempt by the Sophoúlis government and the British to stabilise the Greek economy, or at least to prevent it deteriorating. It was in the interests of both to do so. The republican Sophoúlis government needed to win popular approval to improve its chances against the royalists in the forthcoming elections. The British wanted the elections to go smoothly to enable British troops to begin withdrawal, and to counter any claims that the elections were invalid because the country was not sufficiently tranquil.

In December 1945 two of Sophoúlis' ministers arrived in London: the minister of finance and Tsoudherós, the former prime minister of the government in exile, as minister of co-ordination. They had come to discuss a new financial plan with the British authorities, who had already offered to send to Greece a full economic mission of experts attached to different ministries. Discussions were in danger of dragging on endlessly until on 22 January Bevin laid down a 24-hour deadline for their completion, and on 24 January 1946 the new plan was announced.

The plan, known as the London Plan, had three main elements. First, the British overcame their reluctance to provide more money and agreed to lend Greece £10 million, a loan buttressed by $25 million (some £6 million) from an American bank. At the same time Britain waived Greece's £46 million wartime debt. These moves were against the objections, both from Dalton, Britain's Chancellor of the Exchequer, and from the governor of the Bank of England, that Britain would be, in their words, throwing money down the drain.

Second, two new bodies were to be set up to supervise the Greek economy. One was the British Economic Mission (BEM), composed wholly of British experts and whose remit included supply and distribution, labour, transport, finance and industry. However, the BEM was only to advise, not to control. The second body was the Currency Committee, with Greek, British and American members, and this had teeth. Crucially, its unanimous approval was needed for any new issue of drachmas, so the British and American members of the committee could in principle prevent the Greek government from resorting to its old self-defeating practice of simply printing more money. However, in practice they found that they could only restrain the printing of money and not completely stop it.

A third element accompanying the London Plan, though it was not formally part of it, was the one with the most immediate effect. This was to flood the market with gold sovereigns, some from British reserves and some from Greek. With more sovereigns available, their price in drachmas fell and the drachma exchange rate soon stabilised. Also businesses were more willing to sell goods for drachmas which could now be converted into gold, so they released stocks, which lowered prices and reduced inflation.

The London Plan achieved its immediate aim for producing economic stability at the time of the election on 31 March 1946, though by the spring of 1947 the Greek economy had fallen back into its earlier precarious state. The primary success of the plan was in reducing inflation, which for the month of January 1946 stood at over 100 per cent but for the rest of the year was never more than 4 per cent a month and in some months negative. Greek hyperinflation, if defined as continuous price rises of over 50 per cent in a month, had lasted since the German invasion of 1941. It had not been cured by the measures of Neubacher in 1942, Waley in 1944 or Varvaréssos in 1945, but thanks to the London Plan the period of hyperinflation had, at least technically, come to an end in 1946.

With the date for elections now fixed as 31 March 1946 the Communists had to decide whether to participate, and dithered over the decision. In January their supporters were told to register to vote, but in early February to abstain. Then advice was apparently received from Moscow to participate, but by the end of February the Communists nevertheless confirmed the decision to abstain. Four years later Zachariádhis reconsidered the options. By abstaining, which he now saw as a tactical error, they had expected to prepare the people 'in the best possible way for the new armed conflict'. But he thought that if they had participated, and had unmasked 'the British and the Monarcho-Fascists', they could have had 'a more effective and a broader preparation for the new armed conflict'.[11] Thus the choice between abstaining and participating was explicitly, in the view of Zachariádhis, a choice of the better way to prepare for armed conflict.

On 31 March 1946 60 per cent of those registered cast their votes, and the result was a resounding victory for the royalists, who received nearly two-thirds of the votes, and 238 parliamentary seats against the 116 of their republican opponents. The leader of the royalists, Tsaldháris, became prime minister, but Dhamaskinós continued as regent until the plebiscite had decided on the monarchy. The AMFOGE report on the elections said that there had been some irregularities in the voter lists, but they were not significant. It also accepted that there had been some examples of intimidation. The worst of these was at the seaside town of Litóchoro near Mount Olympus, where on the night before the election some 60 members of ELAS bands attacked, burning down buildings and killing eight people, forcing the postponement of elections in the area for a week. Nevertheless AMFOGE believed that 'intimidation was not extensive enough to affect seriously the election.' AMFOGE's conclusion was 'that conditions were such as to warrant the holding of elections, that the election proceedings were on the whole free and fair and that the general outcome represents a true and valid verdict of the Greek people'.[12] The election was the first since 1936 to produce a government chosen by the people, and a first step had been taken towards the restoration of democracy in Greece.

There remained the issue of the plebiscite, for which the date had still not been fixed. Bevin at first favoured postponement till 1948 to avoid the plebiscite interrupting reconstruction, but King George of Greece persuaded Bevin that the opposite was the case and that delay would distract from reconstruction. A further argument was that it would be risky to withdraw British troops from Greece before the plebiscite, and Britain wanted them out as soon as possible, certainly before 1948. Finally Prime Minister Tsaldháris wanted an early plebiscite on the realistic grounds that as time went on his royalist government was bound to make mistakes and these would damage the King's cause. On 13 May Dhamaskinós announced to the first session of the newly elected parliament that the plebiscite would be held on 1 September 1946.

Within weeks of taking office the royalist Tsaldháris government cracked down on its opponents. On 3 May it authorised committees of public security throughout the country, with power to exile within Greece anyone even suspected of helping ELAS. On 9 June it introduced a further decree, labelled Extraordinary Measures, listing new crimes and their punishments. One of these crimes was activity aimed at detaching territory from the state, obviously aimed at the Communists' wavering policy of uniting Greek and Yugoslav Macedonia as an independent Macedonian state. The punishment for this was banishment, imprisonment or death. Attending banned assemblies would also mean imprisonment, and participation in armed bands would incur life imprisonment or execution.

The British protested strongly that these laws were illiberal in themselves, and in particular that they did nothing to counter right-wing terrorism. However, the new British ambassador to Greece, Clifford Norton, who had replaced Leeper in May 1946, had been instructed not to try to control Greek affairs in the same way as Leeper and was against interfering with the decrees. 'We must constantly bear in mind', he wrote to the Foreign Office, 'that Greece is not England.'[13]

The plebiscite was duly held on 1 September 1946, and all parties participated, including the Communists. The result was overwhelmingly in the King's favour, 65 per cent voting for the return of the monarchy. The most decisive support was in the Peloponnese (over 90 per cent), but with a majority even in most of the north of the country, where Communist influence was strongest. The AMFOGE monitors, now exclusively British and American as the French had withdrawn, gave the results their guarded approval. They pointed out that the government figure of 94 per cent participation was unreal, but concluded:

> There is no doubt in our minds that the party representing the government view exercised undue influence in securing votes in support of the return of the King, but without that influence we are satisfied that a majority of votes for the King's return could have been obtained.[14]

King George returned to Greece on 28 September 1946. Of his previous 24 years as monarch he had spent 11 years in exile (1924–35) and five years out of the country (1941–6). His last months, as king of the Hellenes actually based in Greece, was to prove the shortest such period of his much-interrupted reign.

23

The Truman Doctrine

The 12 months following the September 1946 plebiscite on the monarchy brought massive changes to the situation in Greece. In February 1947 Britain announced that it would withdraw its troops from Greece after 31 March, passing responsibility for Greece to America. On 12 March 1947 Truman took up this challenge and committed America much further than before by proclaiming the Truman Doctrine, a policy of actively assisting free peoples against armed minorities or outside pressure. Within weeks of the announcement of the Truman Doctrine King George died, to be succeeded by his younger brother Paul and his controversial queen, Frederica. In October 1946 the Communist armed forces were formally brought together as the Democratic Army of Greece, with a single commander and covering the whole country.

By the beginning of 1947 the time had come for the British to make a drastic reduction in their commitments to Greece. They had overseen the formation of a Greek government elected by popular vote, the first such government for ten years, and the settlement of the question of the monarchy. They had assisted UNRRA in providing food and other immediate necessities for the Greek people. The problems of the economy were still far from being solved, but the London Plan had at least brought an end to five years of hyperinflation. It was a reasonable view that Britain had by now discharged its obligations to its wartime ally.

This led to heated debate within the British government on two related questions. One was when British troops could be withdrawn from Greece. The other was whether Britain could continue building up the Greek armed forces which after a British withdrawal would be the only protection against Communist aggression, internal or external. The internal threat had been intensified by the consolidation in October 1946 of the Communist forces into the Democratic Army of Greece.

The background to this debate on Greece was Britain's general reduction of overseas commitments. Attlee had announced that Britain would hand over its responsibilities in India by June 1948, and withdrawal from Ceylon (Sri Lanka) and Burma followed. Britain's troublesome mandate in Palestine was also to end in 1948. These were commitments which Britain could not afford to maintain, even if the local independence movements could be resisted.

It is sometimes maintained that by this time Britain was simply broke, or bankrupt, but this is not wholly true. Britain was still among the richest nations of the world, surpassed only by Sweden and Switzerland in Europe, and elsewhere only by the United States and Canada.[1] Cotton and shipbuilding were in decline, but Britain had a promising lead in the growth industries of cars and chemicals, radio and television, aircraft and electronics. Nevertheless the war had left Britain with international debts reckoned at $14 billion, and by early 1947 there were two further threats to the British economy.

One was the devastatingly harsh winter of 1946–7, which began with a blanket of snow falling on 23 January 1947. Coal was frozen at the pits, and anyway there were no trains to shift it. Unemployment quadrupled, and £200 million worth of exports were lost. Games of rugby were impossible because the pitch was rock hard, to the delight of the more timorous schoolboys. Big Ben ceased to chime because it was frozen solid. When the thaw followed in March it brought record-breaking floods, especially in East Anglia, with disruption of agriculture, widespread loss of household drinking water, and food having to be supplied by emergency army field kitchens.

A further problem which weighed on the mind of Dalton, the Chancellor of the Exchequer, was the prospect of full sterling–dollar convertibility. This would mean that any country with reserves of pounds sterling could use those pounds to draw on Britain's dollar reserves. This dangerous convertibility had been promised for 15 July 1947 and was the price Britain had paid in November 1945 for an American loan and the cancellation of some of Britain's lend-lease debts. It was a sword of Damocles except that the victim knew exactly when it would fall, and it haunted Dalton's sleep.

> I lay awake at night doing mental arithmetic. We had so many dollars; last month we spent so many; if we spend the same next month, we shall only have so much left. But we mustn't let our dollar reserves fall below so much, or we shall be sunk.[2]

In the event the dollar drain was as bad as Dalton had feared, and within weeks convertibility had to be suspended.

Thus the argument about British aid to Greece was basically a clash between Bevin's view, as foreign secretary, of a coherent foreign policy and Dalton's view, as Chancellor of the Exchequer, of the economic constraints. At the end of May 1946 Bevin warned the Cabinet that Greece could not possibly support on its own an army large enough, of around 100,000 men, to deter aggression. To do so would consume the whole of the Greek government's revenue, leaving nothing for other essential needs, let alone reconstruction. Bevin got Cabinet agreement to provide £15 million a year for the Greek army, at least until conditions stabilised. To Dalton this looked like an open-ended commitment, and two months later in July 1946 he persuaded the Cabinet to set a time limit of 31 March 1947 for British support of the Greek army.

British troop numbers in Greece began to be reduced well before the total withdrawal which was scheduled for 31 March 1947. In September 1946 their numbers were more than halved from 31,000 to some 14,000. Norton, Britain's ambassador in Athens, was thoroughly alarmed at this progressive scaling-down of British troops in Greece, not least because Communist guerrilla activity was increasing and they now controlled a broad swathe of territory in the north from Mount Olympus to the Albanian border. Norton wrote that the only way of thwarting the wider Communist aims was to make it 'absolutely clear that we will come to Greece's assistance at once: and [...] the only way of making this absolutely clear to a group of Powers both tough and psychologically crude, is to retain a British force on the spot'.[3] The Foreign Office was equally anxious about the ending of the British presence:

> Can we in fact alone afford to keep the Northern neighbours out of Greece in the next year? Are we prepared to keep British troops in Greece? Are we prepared to pay the Greeks to keep up forces on their own adequate for the task? If not what is the alternative to a Communist Greece next year?[4]

If Britain pulled out of Greece, it could be seen as 'the beginnings of a new Munich.'[5]

However, many of the British authorities, from the prime minister downwards, were becoming fed up with Greece. In January 1947 the

Greek prime minister, Tsaldháris, resigned, no longer able to hold his government together, and was replaced by Dhimítrios Máximos, a politically neutral figure, but Tsaldháris remained the dominant figure, and the seven-month government of Máximos proved no more able than its predecessors to solve Greece's problems. Bevin confessed to 'a temporary revulsion against all things Greek',[6] and for others revulsion was more lasting. General Clark, head of the British Economic Mission to Athens, wanted to abandon the mission as a failure, citing the abysmal quality of the Greek civil service and the government's well-known propensity to do nothing, adding that 'in the Greek language the word for "lunatic asylum" and for "Greece" must be the same.'[7] In December 1946 Attlee was inclined to the view that Britain's Mediterranean interests could be defended from Cyprus, and Greece could be abandoned. Some of these comments echo the bitter conclusions of David Wallace in 1944 just before he was killed, that the Greek people were not capable of being saved from themselves, nor for themselves worth it. A more measured judgement was made by the Foreign Office minister Hector McNeil:

> With all our advice, with considerable economic assistance, with the presence of our troops, with the maintenance of a military and police mission, the position has continued to worsen until today the economic situation is almost as bad as it ever has been, the state of public order is much worse than at any time since immediately after the civil war [i.e. the battle for Athens], and the Communists are exerting apparently an increasing influence.[8]

While the British government debated what to do about Greece, the US administration had been aware that it might be called on to take up the load and had taken tentative steps to prepare for it. This potential load had two related parts: support for the Greek economy and support for the Greek army. A State Department study of Greece's economy in July 1946 concluded unsurprisingly that a massive overhaul of the whole system was essential. Nevertheless, as an interim measure the United States provided Greece in September 1946 with credits for the purchase of ships and other economic needs, totalling $35 million. In January 1947 an eight-member team of American economists, headed by Paul Porter, arrived in Athens to assess the Greek economy. Porter's report was damning. The country was stricken by black marketeering, profiteering and speculation. Virtually nothing had been done about reconstruction. Greek politicians were weak, stupid and venal, solely interested in power and with no interest in reforms. What was needed was a long-term US economic mission to Greece to provide aid which would be directly administered by Americans. These should not be limited to advice, a restriction which had been the downfall of British aid efforts. Porter was persuaded by US ambassador MacVeagh that the immediate priority for aid was the Greek army. But there was still no agreement on what aid the United States could offer, nor any US commitment to provide it.

The issue was resolved in the course of a dramatic week in February 1947. The British *Economic Survey for 1947* was about to be published, which *The Times* described as 'the most disturbing statement ever made by a British government'.[9] On 18 February Bevin finally yielded to Dalton's argument that Britain could not afford further aid to Greece, and they agreed on a formal note to the US government. The note said that after 31 March, only six weeks away, Britain could provide no further assistance whatsoever to Greece. The crucial date of 31 March had long been planned by the British but not yet formally announced, and the ultimatum was designed, as Bevin privately admitted, to bring matters to a head. The note was delivered on the afternoon of Friday 21 February to the State Department, which was shocked by the suddenness of this decision. George Marshall, the recently appointed secretary of state, was away for the weekend, and State Department officials worked throughout Saturday and Sunday preparing a draft proposal for Marshall on the Monday morning of 24 February. The draft covered both economic and military aid to Greece. Marshall approved it and passed it to Truman, who said, 'This is the right line.'[10]

The Truman Doctrine, announced by the President a fortnight later, went much further than aid to Greece. It was primarily based on an 8,000-word assessment of the Russian and Communist threat sent a year earlier, on 22 February 1946, by George Kennan, a senior official at the US Embassy in Moscow. This assessment became known as the Long Telegram.

Kennan began with an analysis of how Russian leaders saw the world. They had two basic ideas: that peaceful co-existence with the capitalist west was impossible, and that Russia was in danger of attack. Both premises, said Kennan, were simply not true, but derived from the long-standing Russian sense of insecurity, the country having been traditionally under threat from aggressive neighbours, and its rulers, from medieval tsars to Stalin, aware that their rule was archaic, fragile, and artificial. Marxist dogma provided

> justification for their instinctive fear of the outside world, for the dictatorship without which they did not know how to rule, for cruelties they did not dare not to inflict, for sacrifice they felt bound to demand. In the name of Marxism they sacrificed every single ethical value in their methods and tactics.[11]

Russia's solution to its difficulties, Kennan wrote, was expansion, overtly through treaties designed in their favour, and covertly by controlling local Communist parties, penetrating other organisations such as labour unions and fomenting social and industrial unrest. To Kennan the implications for US policy were clear. The Russian leadership was 'impervious to logic of reason, and [...] highly sensitive to logic of force. For this reason it can easily withdraw – and usually does when strong resistance is encountered at any point. Thus, if the adversary has sufficient force and makes clear his readiness to use it, he rarely has to do so.'[12] This was the US policy which Kennan later encapsulated in the single word 'containment'.

Kennan's Long Telegram did not mention Greece, but it did pinpoint Turkey and Iran as targets of Russian expansion. From Turkey Russia was demanding, as a price for renewal of the 1925 treaty of friendship between the two countries, joint Russian and Turkish control of the Bosphorus, Sea of Marmara and the Dardanelles, as well as border changes in eastern Turkey favourable to Russia. In January 1947 Truman had declared, 'There isn't a doubt in my mind that Russia intends an invasion of Turkey and the seizure of the Black Sea Straits.'[13] In Iran Soviet interference in the country triggered a formal complaint by Iran to the United Nations. The US State Department saw Greece, Turkey and Iran as a single issue in which Greece was the first Russian objective. If Greece fell to Communist control and Turkey and Iran came under Russian influence, the route to the Middle East and its oil would be blocked. Not only that, but Communists would be encouraged to take over in France and Italy and possibly in the whole of Western Europe.

What became known as the Truman Doctrine was announced by the President to a joint session of both Houses of Congress on 12 March 1947.[14] His opening words emphasised that the present grave situation involved the national security of the United States, a point which he expanded later in his speech. The main theme of his address was that the United States must provide economic aid, especially to Greece, and military aid received only a few passing mentions.

Though the subject of the speech was aid to both Greece and Turkey, Turkey received little more than a tenth of the space devoted to Greece. In Greece, the President said, a militant minority had created political chaos, and the Greek government had asked the United States both for financial aid and for US experts to improve its public administration. Military aid was passed over in a few lines: the Greek army was small and poorly equipped, and needed supplies if it was to establish the Greek government's authority.

Truman then turned to his broader theme of US national interest. 'Totalitarian regimes', he said, 'imposed on free peoples by direct or indirect aggression, undermine the foundations of international peace and hence the security of the United States.' Therefore, he added, in words that became known as the essence of the Truman Doctrine, 'I believe that it must be the policy of the United States to support free peoples who are resisting attempted subjugation by armed minorities or by outside pressures.' Finally Truman outlined the immediate action to be taken. He asked Congress to authorise $400 million in aid to Greece and Turkey in the period ending on 30 June the following year, an amount which was, he pointed out, only about a tenth of 1 per cent of what the United States had contributed to winning World War II. He further asked for authority to send both civilian and military personnel to both countries to help with reconstruction and to supervise the use of US aid. His concluding words stressed again the US national interest: 'If we falter in our leadership, we may endanger the peace of the world – and we shall surely endanger the welfare of our own Nation.'

For Truman's proposals to become law, approval was needed from Congress, and in both Senate and House of Representatives the Republicans now had a majority. In the next two months many questions critical of Truman's proposals were raised in State Department committees, by newspaper columnists – though the press was broadly favourable – and in hearings before Congressional committees, where the administration's main spokesman was Undersecretary of State Dean Acheson. Many of these questions were precursors of the doubts that have been raised ever since about international intervention.

Some questions were frankly cynical. Was it worth supporting the Greek government, which Porter had castigated and ambassador MacVeagh described as feeble, foolish and disgraceful? This had been answered by Truman in his original address, where he said that the Greek government was far from perfect but nevertheless represented 85 per cent of the Greek parliament's freely elected members. A second sceptical question was about the British. Was the United States simply pulling British chestnuts out of the fire? No, Acheson replied, freedom was at stake, not the British Empire.

Other questions were more considered. Should the problem be handed over to the United Nations? No, for several reasons: the UN lacked funds for economic aid, it did not have the necessary experts, and above all it could not act quickly. Could the problems in Greece be solved by economic aid alone, without any military support? Kennan now believed that they could, in spite of his earlier emphasis on the logic of force. The answer again was no. Only military aid could provide the security needed for economic stability. 'What good was economic reconstruction when the bandits simply blew up bridges and railroads as fast as Americans built them?'[15] Even those supporting military aid were concerned about what military aid would involve. Were combat troops to be sent? No, the US military would act only as observers and advisers, and their numbers would be limited, probably to no more than 100 for Greece. In the event this limit was soon breached and the numbers eventually ballooned.

Finally, were Truman's proposals in fact a plan promoted by US oil interests, to protect American oil supplies from the Arab states? No, replied Acheson, 'the policy would have been exactly the same if there had not been a single drop of oil in the Near East.'[16] This was probably true, but less than the whole truth. America's oil reserves were diminishing, and oil from the Near East, where it had a quarter of control (Britain had the rest) was becoming increasingly important. It was only realistic to accept that oil was as vital a commodity as food.

Truman's proposals became law on 22 May 1947 when Congress approved 'An Act to provide for assistance to Greece and Turkey.'[17] It authorised the full $400 million for which Truman had asked, but stipulated that there must be free access for US government officials to observe whether aid was being effectively used. It also approved the dispatch of a limited number of military personnel, though no limit was specified, and laid down that they were to act in an advisory capacity only. Thus Greece and Turkey had their aid and the

United States had its safeguards. The Truman Doctrine and the Act which followed it were a remarkable combination of idealism and self-interest between which, Acheson declared, there was no conflict. Truman's initiative ushered in a new phase of the struggle in Greece, and of relations between Greece and the United States.

Between the announcement of the Truman Doctrine and its passage into law there was another shift in Greece's fortunes. On 1 April 1947 King George II died unexpectedly of a heart attack at the age of 56. His was a sad and unfulfilled life. His sense of duty to his country was frustrated by long periods of exile, and when in Greece he had been beset by the manoeuvres of Greek politicians. He was blackened for his association with Metaxás as so-called dictator, but not redeemed when Metaxás became the national hero who said 'Ochi' to the Italians. If, as Macmillan thought, the King was the villain of the piece in the constitutional argument at liberation, Churchill's support was at the root of the villainy. King George had no settled home life, and those close to him believed that he planned to abdicate and live in London with his mistress Joyce Brittain-Jones, known as 'J', plans overtaken by his early death.

His successor was his younger brother Paul, whose wife Frederica quickly became a more prominent figure than her husband. She had been born Princess Frederica (plus nine other names) of Hanover, and in 1937 aged 20 had married Paul who was 16 years her senior. When the Germans invaded in 1941 she left with the rest of the Greek royal family, but before doing so she visited wounded soldiers in hospital almost daily. 'I could not just go into a ward with a cheerful greeting and visit a few beds. The only way was to go from bed to bed and talk to each patient.' She was already convinced of her own and her husband's importance: 'This country cannot live without us.'[18] She went first to Crete, where she and her small children were bombed, and then spent most of the war in South Africa. While there she raised funds to buy and equip 25 mobile clinics, which were sent to the Greek Red Cross at the end of 1944. She also became very close to General Jan Smuts, corresponding with him at least once a week until he died in 1950. She recorded two pieces of advice which Smuts gave her. The first was 'when you have something to say, either talking or writing, then say it,' advice which she said often got her into trouble. The second was 'when in doubt always choose to do the courageous thing.'[19]

After liberation, while Paul was still Crown Prince, she went with him on a tour of Macedonia to see at firsthand the ravages of war. Six months after his accession her profile was further enhanced because Paul fell ill with typhoid fever and in November 1947 she represented him at the London wedding of Princess Elizabeth and Prince Philip, only son of Prince Andrew of Greece. At a dinner party she nobbled Churchill and tried to justify to him the execution of captured guerrilla fighters, which she said was only after a fair trial. She also arranged a meeting with US Secretary of State Marshall and argued for mountain artillery to be sent to the Greek army. The pattern was set. She would not hesitate to involve herself with the immediate needs of the Greek people, but nor would she hesitate to put herself on a level with international statesmen. The first characteristic deserved acclaim, but all too often the self-importance that went with the second trait undermined that popularity.

24

1947 – Civil War and American Involvement

As we have seen, in February 1946 the Central Committee of the Communist KKE abandoned any idea of peaceful progress to power and 'decided to go ahead with the organisation of the new armed struggle against the Monarcho-Fascist orgy'.[1]

This decision raised a number of questions for the KKE. The first was how to organise its forces. Should they be used as a guerrilla army, limited to harassing the government as they had done since the battle of Athens? Or should they be formed into a conventional army, aiming not just to inflict short-term disruption but to make permanent gains? The second question was whether it should set up its own government which would direct a conventional army and, it was hoped, win international recognition and eventually become the government of Greece. Thirdly, how much help could the KKE get from sympathetic Communist countries on Greece's northern border – Yugoslavia, Bulgaria and Albania? And finally, what opposition could it expect from the Greek National Army and its American supporters?

Within Greece in early 1946 the KKE's military resources were a number of small bands of seven to ten men under their own leader, which might combine for a particular operation. They were, in Woodhouse's view, at about the same stage of development as ELAS had been in 1942 before Gorgopótamos. They had enough weapons left over from the war and not handed over under the Varkíza Agreement, though the weapons were of wildly assorted types. These bands were instructed to attack only Greek targets such as army garrisons and police posts, and to avoid any confrontation with British troops. There were probably no more than 10,000 active guerrilla forces at any time during 1946, mainly former members of ELAS.

These bands were capable only of small-scale guerrilla operations, of inflicting pinpricks rather than any decisive blow. Their tactics were to select a target, make a surprise attack at night, overwhelm the police station or garrison, collect food, and recruit villagers voluntarily or, increasingly, by force. By dawn they had returned to their hideouts in the mountains. These tactics were simple but effective.

Zachariádhis believed, at least in retrospect, that as well as its military resources the KKE had widespread popular support. He claimed that

> Communism was then dominant in the trade unions and agricultural co-operatives, in the commercial and professional classes, in the Army, among the young, the intellectuals, the athletic clubs; the British were unpopular, the Slavo-Macedonians were overwhelmingly favourable, and the foreign situation was encouraging.

Woodhouse comments drily that 'It would have been a very naive Communist who believed all these things,'[2] but they were not completely groundless. In 1947 Georgios Vláchos described the widespread support for leftism (*aristerismós*). It was seen, he said, as a cause that promised something which, though undefined, was new, easy to achieve and a bringer of hope. It permeated politics, writing and the arts as well as everyday life, and a man asked what his job was would reply, 'I'm a leftist.' The point of Vláchos' article was to show the dangers of these beliefs.[3]

The Communist bands initially had no overall commander, as Saráphis had returned to the Greek army after Varkíza and had not been replaced. His successor was appointed in August 1946 when Márkos Vaphiádhis was instructed to leave Salonika for the mountains and to co-ordinate the activities of the armed bands. Márkos, as he was generally known, had been an active Communist since 1927, and was leader of the ELAS division in Macedonia during the occupation. He shared much of Zachariádhis' background: both had been born in Turkey, and both were imprisoned under the Metaxás regime. The BBC correspondent Kenneth Matthews provided a glowing description of Márkos:

Once in effective control of the rebellion, he grew in stature; the halo of the guerrilla chieftain quickly settled round his head. He was shrewd, temperate; his moustache, drooping at the ends, gave him a sad, avuncular appearance. Among his men, he affected a brigandish looseness of dress rather than military uniform; he carried a walking-stick instead of a gun; and his message was suited to the times – all he wanted was freedom and democracy and the destruction of Fascism. The longer he held out the more his romantic image swelled; to the rebels of mankind he was King of the Mountains.[4]

A further step was taken in October 1946 when the guerrilla bands were formed into a united body as the Democratic Army of Greece (Dhimokratikós Stratós Elládhos), with Márkos in general command. Under him were seven regional commands, five in northern Greece, one in central Greece and one in the Peloponnese. The units in the field were now larger, of 70 to 100 men rather than seven to ten, each unit with not only a commander but also an officer to act as political commissar. But they were still to use hit-and-run tactics, and continued to be called guerrillas, rebels or insurgents.

Zachariádhis said later that promised support for the Democratic Army from 'Tito and his clique' – that is, Yugoslavia, Albania and Bulgaria – had 'played a decisive role' in the decision to resume the armed struggle.[5] This support was first discussed as early as December 1945 in a meeting at Petrich in Bulgaria between the KKE and representatives of Yugoslavia and Bulgaria. Both promised substantial assistance if the KKE launched an armed rebellion, but with as yet no details. These were provided at a second meeting in August 1947, at Bled in northern Yugoslavia, and now including Albanians. By this time the Democratic Army had been established and was actively pursuing more aggressive tactics. At the Bled meeting it was agreed that the Albanian, Yugoslav and Bulgarian armies would provide the Democratic Army with instructors, supplies, arms, trucks, radios and other equipment. They would also organise forces along their southern frontiers to protect the Democratic Army from cross-border pursuit by the Greek National Army.

A separate agreement at Bled, not published at the time, was less helpful to the KKE. Yugoslavia, Bulgaria and Albania were to form a Balkan federation which would include Greek Macedonia, and Bulgaria would absorb Greek Thrace, giving Bulgaria an outlet to the Aegean. As the KKE had long known, any suggestion that it favoured the surrender of Greek territory would have a disastrous effect on its popular support.

Training for the Democratic Army was mainly provided at the huge camp in Buljkes, 40 miles north-west of Belgrade and some 300 miles from the frontier with Greece. It had formerly been the home of German settlers, now long since departed, and consisted of about 600 buildings and 20,000 acres. In the summer of 1946 Buljkes was established as a camp for Greek refugees, but was then converted to a training camp, and by the end of 1947 it housed over 20,000 Greeks. Military training was part of its function, and groups as large as 1,500, trained and armed at Buljkes, went south to cross into Greece and join the Democratic Army. Buljkes also housed some 1,600 hostages, and a hospital treated over 1,000 patients, many with tuberculosis. The camp was also – and some believed primarily – an indoctrination centre, where under severely strict conditions Stalinist doctrine was taught to Greek fighters, and to the increasing number of the Democratic Army's political commissars.

Training camps such as Buljkes – there were 12 others in Yugoslavia alone – were only part of the assistance from Greece's Communist neighbours. All three provided military supplies, from rifles and mines to artillery and anti-aircraft guns. All three had hospitals for sick and wounded fighters. In Yugoslavia the Democratic Army was able to set up its own Radio Free Greece near Belgrade. There were civilian as well as state initiatives, and committees were formed among the civilian population to collect, voluntarily or otherwise, food, money, clothes and medical supplies for the Greek insurgents.

In December 1946 Tsaldháris, in his last weeks as prime minister before being replaced by Máximos, appealed to the United Nations to investigate the position on Greece's northern borders, and on 19 December the Security Council established a United Nations Commission of Investigation. It had 11 members, including from one side Britain and the United States, from the other Russia and Poland, and in June 1947 submitted a 767-page report. This concluded that, though the Greek government had been provocative, its three northern neighbours were indeed giving supplies and refuge to the insurgents, were allowing them to cross the borders and were firing from their own borders on the Greek National Army. To the disappointment of the Greeks, this report produced absolutely no action. Of the Commission's members France disagreed with parts of it and Russia and Poland rejected it altogether. Security Council resolutions based on it were vetoed, usually by Russia, and in September 1947 the Commission was disbanded. Although it produced no action, it did generate a successor, the United Nations Special Committee on the Balkans (UNSCOB), which was established in October 1947 and reported on the later stages of the civil war.

The limitations of the Communists' hit-and-run tactics of 1946 became apparent in 1947, when the Democratic Army tried to seize and hold towns. It met with a string of failures. On 28 May 1947 a force of 650 men, personally commanded by Márkos, tried to take Flórina, but the garrison of 500 forced them to withdraw after five hours of fighting. Three days later the attack was renewed, but was no more successful. On 13 July a larger force of 2,500, again under Márkos, moved against Kónitsa, but after three days of fighting had to pull back. Between May and July 1947 there were unsuccessful attacks on Grevená and the smaller towns of Kastanoússa, Kastoriá and Alexandhroúpoli, mostly commanded by Márkos, and all in the far northern parts of Greece where the Communists were strongest. It was clear that the Democratic Army in its present form, and using its present tactics, was not going to win the armed conflict.

This led to the KKE decision, discussed since mid-1947 and formally announced in September 1947, to abandon guerrilla tactics and to operate as a regular army fighting a conventional war. Conventional war meant controlling large areas of territory, seizing and holding important towns, and confronting the Greek government forces directly. The decision was effectively made by Zachariádhis, and was opposed by Márkos, who still believed in guerrilla tactics. Nevertheless Márkos complied.

The Communist forces were by now structured on conventional lines, with divisions, brigades, battalions and so on. Support services were provided by the self-defence organisation Avtoámina, which probably had about 50,000 members scattered throughout Greece. Its responsibilities included supply, intelligence gathering, raising and distributing funds, recruitment and on occasion assassination.

Three months later the KKE proclaimed that the PEEA was a rival government of Greece. Its control of territory, mainly in northern Greece, had up to now been informal, but now it would come under the authority of a government, at least in name. A further consequence was that this government needed a capital to make it more likely that the Provisional Government would be recognised by Russia and the Communist satellites. Kónitsa was selected, in spite of the failed attack on the town in the previous summer, and against the argument of Márkos that a capital outside Greece would be more secure. On Christmas Eve 1947 the formation of the Provisional Government was announced, with Márkos as prime minister and minister of war. The next day Márkos led the attack on Kónitsa with two brigades totalling 2,000–2,500 men.

Kónitsa had been chosen as the target because of its strategic position. It lay on the route north to the Albanian border and on the route south and east via Métsovo to central Greece. Also the holder of Kónitsa could threaten Ioánnina, the main town of Epirus and only 40 miles due south. Kónitsa is dominated on three sides by mountains, and the capture of four of these heights was crucial to the Democratic Army's success. One was quickly occupied, two were threatened though not taken, but the fourth and most important, Prophítis Ilías, was unaccountably left alone. After two days of fighting Márkos' troops were withdrawn on the night of 26/27 December from the two threatened heights to attempt to occupy the town. Only on 31 December was the crucial height of Prophítis Ilías attacked, but by evening the assault had been called off. On 4 January 1948 the Democratic Army withdrew at all points.

Its failure was in part its own doing. Initial targets had not been well chosen, and without sufficient wireless links communication between Márkos and different groups was highly uncertain. But the failure of the Democratic Army was also due to the resolute defence by the government's National Army, led by the energetic General Konstantínos Vendíris. Reinforcements were brought in from Métsovo, over mountain routes cleared of snow, bringing the defending numbers to around 2,000, and supplies were dropped into Kónitsa by Greek air force Dakotas. Battle losses were estimated at 650 dead and wounded for the Democratic Army and some 500 for the National Army.

Within days of the end of the battle, and while machine-gun fire could still be heard in the surrounding hills, Queen Frederica visited Kónitsa. King Paul was ill with typhoid fever, and despite not wanting to leave him and despite the danger to herself, she insisted that 'Greece comes first.'[6] With some difficulty and only by exercising royal prerogative, she persuaded the army chief of staff in Ioánnina to take her and a small group to Kónitsa. They travelled in two jeeps, and where bridges had been broken waded across rivers on foot. In Kónitsa a crowd surrounded her and shouted, 'Tell [the King] the communists shall never pass our lines.' She visited a children's home, where 'they looked at me first in utter silence and disbelief, then I heard a heart-breaking whisper "Vasilissa?" ["Is it the Queen?"]' Her account ends: 'I hated leaving. Somehow the heroism and endurance of these people had a purifying effect and I felt free and elated [...] Kónitsa has been one of the great incidents of my life.'[7]

Frederica's memoirs often, as here, show her as self-regarding, but there was another side to her. Michael Ward, formerly of SOE and now with UNSCOB, was in Kónitsa at the time, and he and a colleague went to Frederica's temporary lodgings to sign the visitors' book. As they did so Frederica walked in, her eyes bloodshot from fatigue, her face covered with mud slicks, and her shoes and stockings caked with mire. Instead of dismissing them after a few polite words, she asked her lady-in-waiting to fetch 'the bottle of Scotch vitamins' and insisted that her visitors stay for a long discussion of the civil war, fortified by the vitamins. Frederica was obviously quite ready to step down from her pedestal.[8]

The Greek National Army had developed only slowly into a force strong enough to defeat a Communist force intent on seizing Kónitsa. During the war years of 1941–5 it had virtually ceased to exist apart from a few units, principally the Mountain or Rimini Brigade formed from loyal troops after the 1944 army mutiny in Egypt. By the beginning of 1947 army numbers had reached 90,000, but this figure was deceptive. Only half the men were active infantry. For good reason recruits were mainly those opposed to Communism, but in the Greek forces the Communists had their own clandestine organisation to gather information and spread dissension. It was known as KOSSA (Communist Organisation of the Army and Security Corps). In September 1945 it was estimated that 15 per cent of the army belonged to KOSSA. Information from KOSSA and from Communist networks in towns and villages meant that the National Army's movements were known to the insurgents in advance.

Initially the responsibility for dealing with the Communist threat lay not with the army but with the National Guard, a militia formed at liberation to deal with internal security, assisted by the local gendarmerie and city police. Both the Greek government and the British were opposed to sending the army to deal with citizens who belonged to a still legal political party and were demonstrating, even if with sporadic violence, for political change. But by October 1946 it was clear that the National Guard could not cope with the insurgents, and the National Army took over the responsibility.

At first the army was no more successful than the National Guard had been. The National Army tactics had two elements: static defence and time-limited operations. Static defence meant that when one unit was attacked other units were not allowed to leave their assigned positions and rush to the rescue. This was partly to avoid the relieving force being ambushed en route, and partly because politicians in Athens were anxious that their own constituents should not be left undefended.

Time-limited operations meant that at the end of the prescribed time the National Army would pull back, whether or not it had been successful. The time limit, from a month down to as little as five or seven days, meant that the insurgents would withdraw under attack but return once the army left. This led to the failure of the National Army operations of late 1946 and 1947, grandly named as, for example, Hawk, Eagle, Terminus or Whirlwind. A further failing was that the operations were mainly from south to north, pushing the Democratic Army towards its northern strongholds and its sources of support across the northern frontiers. In October 1947 the British Military Mission, still present in Greece, reported on the National Army's recent failures, omitting only the time limit as a reason:

> There are a number of factors which now limit the success of any operation which is undertaken. These are: lack of sufficient troops for each operation, political interference in the allocating of regular Army units to static defence, and efficient guerrilla intelligence which thus far has pre-determined imminent areas of government operation and, finally a deterioration in morale due to the extended nature of campaigning in Greece.[9]

The National Army's victory at Kónitsa at the end of 1947 thus followed a string of failures elsewhere: why this success? First, the battle was the most important so far of the civil war. If the Democratic Army had taken and held Kónitsa, it could have become the capital of the new Communist Provisional Government, giving that government added credibility and possibly recognition by the Communist world. It was vital for the Greek national government to deny it this success. Also the Democratic Army was now aiming to seize and hold, not simply to attack, plunder and withdraw. It was attempting conventional war but its forces had still not been fully transformed from a guerrilla to a conventional army.

There were two further differences from the recent past. The National Army forces were, as we have seen, commanded by General Vendíris. He had previously been the army's chief of general staff, but had resigned in the previous October under political pressure after a series of military failures and demoted to army commander, a post for which he was much better suited. He was energetic and determined, and he ignored the static defence tactic, bringing in reinforcements to defend Kónitsa through the winter snows. The final factor was that thanks to US military aid the National Army was now much better supplied. Between August and December 1947 the United States had sent to Greece 74,000 tons of military materiel.

Providing military supplies was the most straightforward part of US assistance, and in the course of 1947 arguments raged among the American authorities about three main issues. Should the United States agree to an enlargement of the Greek National Army? Should US combat troops be sent to Greece? And should Americans give operational advice, in effect telling the Greek National Army how to fight its battles?

These issues, difficult enough in themselves, were further complicated because there were three separate sources of American authority in Greece. The first to reach Athens, in May 1947, was the United States Army Group Greece (USAGG), headed by General William Livesay. Livesay's responsibility was in theory limited to advising the Greeks on the use of military equipment, but he soon became involved in the wider issues. The second group was the American Mission for Aid to Greece (AMAG), which arrived in Greece in July 1947. AMAG was authorised by Congress to undertake a much broader role: to supervise all expenditure and administer both the civilian and military aid programmes. Head of AMAG was Dwight Griswold, the abrasive former Republican governor of Nebraska. The third US authority was the ambassador Lincoln MacVeagh, and ultimate decisions were supposed to be made by him. Not surprisingly, there were clashes between these three, especially between MacVeagh and Griswold.

The first issue needing resolution was the question of the size of the Greek National Army. At the beginning of 1947 its nominal strength was 90,000 men. In the previous November the British before their withdrawal had authorised an increase of 15,000, and in April 1947 the Americans soon after their arrival agreed to the Greek request for a further increase of 15,000, a total enlargement of 30,000. However, of the original 90,000 only half were active infantry and many of these only partly trained, and the extra 30,000 did not become effective until late 1947. In the summer of 1947 the Greek government appealed for yet another increase, and Livesay, head of USAGG, complained that the Greeks' 'continued cry is for more and more of everything'.[10]

In 1947 the fighting force of the Communists numbered about 24,000, including 11,000 active reserves, and there was a somewhat hypothetical argument over the necessary ratio of government troops to insurgents. The Greeks argued for five soldiers to one guerrilla, the British recommended two to one provided that the army was properly trained, and the Americans thought that generally three to one was enough, though it might have to rise to ten to one for particular operations. But numbers, of course, were only part of the picture, and leadership and morale were equally important. In February 1947 a Greek general in a secret report, soon published by the Communist paper *Rizospástis* to the embarrassment of the government, listed the reasons for the low morale of the National Army:

The lack of provision for soldiers' families, the exemptions from military service granted for political reasons to the rich and influential, the lack of adequate recognition of merit, the inadequacy of nationalist propaganda and the success of Communist propaganda.[11]

The Americans did not speak with one voice on this question of numbers. Livesay, head of USAGG, argued for an increase in numbers of a further 30,000, accepting that this would cost $20 million of American aid. Griswold, head of AMAG, thought present numbers were enough to defeat the insurgents, and that if there was a large-scale Communist invasion of Greece foreign troops, presumably American, would be needed anyway. The outcome was an increase of the National Army manpower from 90,000 at the beginning of 1947 to 132,000 at the end of the year. It was not the last increase before the civil war was ended.

The possibility of a large-scale Communist invasion also made the Americans very anxious that the remaining British forces should stay in Greece. These had not all been withdrawn, as Bevin had seemed to threaten. After 31 March 1947 Britain still had 5,000 soldiers in Greece apart from those training the Greeks in the use of British weapons, and of this 5,000 some 3,500 were fighting troops. The numbers were small, but their presence meant that any Communist aggression would be aimed at Britain as well as the United States.

In fact, though it was not known for certain at the time, there was no likelihood of a Russian invasion of Greece. Stalin had never shown much interest in Greece, and in February 1948 he made his view of the Greek struggle completely clear to a Yugoslav mission to Moscow:

> They have no prospect of success at all. What, do you think that Great Britain and the United States – the United States, the most powerful state in the world – will permit you to break their line of communication to the Mediterranean? Nonsense. And we have no navy. The uprising in Greece must be stopped, and as quickly as possible.[12]

Another question debated in the summer of 1947 was whether US combat troops should be sent to Greece. To do so, it was argued, would show the Kremlin and its satellites that the United States meant business, and encourage Soviet neighbours such as Turkey and Iran to resist Russian aggression. But there were powerful reasons for opposing the idea. The United States would be accused of international violations not only by Communist states but by much of public opinion at home and in Western Europe. It would amount to a 'private undeclared war between the US and Russia'.[13] Any large-scale Communist invasion was bound to succeed initially because of overwhelming superiority in numbers. For a Greek army to be overcome would be a disaster, but for US forces to be defeated would be a catastrophe. In any case, sending combat troops would need new authorisation from Congress, which had laid down explicitly that US military would act 'in an advisory capacity only'. The suggestion of combat troops was firmly rejected in September 1947 by the military in Washington. General Norstad, director of the army's Plans and Operations and later supreme allied commander of NATO, commented: 'It was usually the military people who had to hold back the sporadic and truculent impulses of political people and diplomats who [did] not realize the consequences of aggressive action.'[14] The idea was finally quashed in the following June.

Once combat troops had been ruled out, the question arose of whether the US military should give operational advice to the Greek National Army. Influential views were raised against the idea. The columnist Joseph Alsop warned that operational advice would constitute: 'open acknowledgement of an almost unlimited American strategic and political liability in Greece'.[15] Moreover, giving operational advice would take Americans up to the front line: what would be the repercussions if even one US soldier was killed or captured? On the other hand, there was little point in pouring supplies into an inadequate Greek army without making sure that these were used effectively, and those on the spot saw operational advice as essential. They disagreed on who should provide it. The British Military Mission thought USAGG should be responsible, while Griswold argued that his own group AMAG should be. It was eventually decided that for operational advice a new group should be established, though Griswold was adamantly opposed to this. On 31 December 1947, at the end of a tumultuous year, this new group was set up. It was called the Joint United States Military Advisory and Planning Group with the unwieldy acronym JUSMAPG. 'Joint' signalled that it would work jointly both with the Greek military and with the British. In February 1948 James Van Fleet was appointed as head of JUSMAPG and commander of US military forces in Greece. Griswold was abrasive, but Van Fleet was out and out aggressive.

The next bitter and divisive clash of the US authorities in Greece was between MacVeagh the US ambassador and Griswold the head of AMAG. Griswold, previously state governor of Nebraska, had no experience of foreign affairs and was simply intent on getting things done in Greece. MacVeagh, however, had years of experience of the complexities of Greek politics and was well aware that heavy-handed intervention would provoke violent criticism of the American mission both in Greece and at home. Griswold was a Republican, appointed in part to win support from Republican members of Congress, but MacVeagh had been appointed by one Democrat president, Roosevelt, and confirmed by another, Truman.

The antagonism between Griswold and MacVeagh came to a head over the question of the composition of the Greek government. On 23 August 1947 the short-lived government of Máximos fell, and King Paul called on Tsaldháris, as leader of the royalist majority in parliament, to form a government again. It seemed, to adapt Omar Khayyam, that Greek politicians evermore came in by the same door as out they went.[16] Griswold, MacVeagh and the US State Department were all agreed that a more broadly based Greek government was essential, but the divisive question was how to bring it about. Griswold, before leaving for Athens, had told senior officials that his first responsibility would be to change the Greek government. The State Department responded that it would be necessary to proceed discreetly, preferably so that the Greeks would feel that they themselves had made the changes, and that in all such matters Griswold must 'have the advice' of MacVeagh. Griswold's reply to this was that MacVeagh:

continues to use such words as 'gradually' and 'we of course must not intervene' to such an extent that I feel somewhat alarmed. In my judgment we do not need to be affected by a fear that we will be accused of 'interfering'. That accusation will be made even if we do nothing.[17]

A new more broadly based government was eventually formed on 4 September 1947 when the republican Sophoúlis, now aged 87, returned as prime minister, with the royalist Tsaldháris as deputy prime minister and foreign minister. But MacVeagh was now beset by personal problems. His wife died in Athens on 7 September, and five days later he was provided with a special plane to bring her body home for burial. He then fell ill himself, was granted sick leave at the end of October, and soon afterwards was in hospital for major surgery. Marshall was determined not to appoint another ambassador to be bullied by Griswold, and a chargé d'affaires temporarily took over the embassy.

On 23 October a directive was drafted, and approved by Truman, which made the ambassador's overriding authority absolutely clear: 'The Ambassador is and should be universally recognised as the American representative in Greece charged with dealing with the Greek Government on matters of high policy.'[18] Matters of high policy included changes in the Greek government or its policies, changes in the military high command and the troop numbers, and relations with the British and the United Nations. If the ambassador and the head of AMAG disagreed, the issue would be settled by the State Department. In the face of Griswold's violent objections this directive was suspended, but Griswold's days of power were numbered and he resigned from AMAG in the following August. Only then was Henry Grady appointed as the new ambassador to Greece.

In February 1948 MacVeagh's temporary withdrawal from Athens was made permanent, and he was appointed ambassador to Portugal. When told of this transfer he broke down in tears, and wrote, 'I am left to appear as if I had failed.'[19] He had indeed failed to control Griswold but, as Marshall had implied, no other ambassador would have done any better. It was MacVeagh's tragedy that the clear directive on the ambassador's powers, not drafted until October 1947 and then suspended, was not put firmly into effect at the beginning of his dealings with AMAG and Griswold.

25

Terror from Left and Right

I n the traumatic years of the 1940s nothing set Greek against Greek as violently as the issue of terror from left and right. As we have already seen, terror from the left, the red terror, included the mass killings by ELAS during the January 1945 battle for Athens and murders by its Avtoámina death squads, while terror from the right, the white terror, was seen in acts of violence by paramilitary groups, mainly the Chi band of Grívas, and by the government's own security forces. Widespread government arrests crammed the prisons and detention camps on some of the islands.

Each side used the excesses of the other as propaganda, and historians are still divided on the question of blame. Those broadly sympathetic to the left tend to see the activities of the Communist bands and the Democratic Army as the inevitable reaction to the oppressive measures of the government and its supporters against an idealistic movement, and to blame outsiders, the British and the Americans, for not curbing the government's disregard for civil liberties. Those on the other side point to the government's need to take all possible measures against the very real threat of a Communist take-over of Greece.

From northern Greece, where Communist forces were dominant, there are three personal accounts of the terror inflicted by the left and the right, both during the occupation and later. The first is from the Australian Joice Loch in her book *A Fringe of Blue*. She and her husband Sydney, both Quakers, had lived during the 1920s and 1930s in Ouranópoli, the last village before the monastic territory of Mount Athos. There they worked for the refugees from Turkey after the 1923 population exchange, especially by setting up a rug-making industry for them. In this remote spot, reached only by mule-track from the nearest road 50 miles to the north, they restored the 700-year-old Byzantine tower, the village's outstanding building, and they lived in the tower until the outbreak of war in 1939. After a war spent helping exiled Poles in Romania and Palestine, the Lochs returned in 1945 to their home in Ouranópoli. There they quickly learnt about the actions of the Communist resistance during and since the war.

Every account which Joice Loch heard put the blame for cruelty squarely on ELAS andártes. Even before she reached Ouranópoli she learnt that Sophia, who had looked after the tower in the Lochs' absence, had been murdered by andártes immediately after the Germans left, and so had Sophia's son. Joice Loch's journey back to Ouranópoli was a long one, by bus from Salonika to the Aegean coast and then by a succession of boats and a walk across the narrowest part of the Athos peninsula. At one point the bus had to lurch precariously over a Bailey bridge, built by the British after liberation and since badly damaged by andártes. She passed through a bullet-splattered village of young widows in their teens. Other villages were crowded with refugees from the mountains. She saw burnt forests and was told that they had been set alight by the andártes to hide the bodies of their victims.

Back in Ouranópoli Joice Loch heard about the 'black letters'. These were sent to village boys and girls telling them that unless they joined the andártes they and their families would be killed and their houses burnt. She also heard the story of Aspasia, a fierce termagant whose husband had been killed by the andártes. When they came to Ouranópoli to take away her daughter she flew at them, beating them with her stick and, joined by the other villagers, drove them off. Joice Loch says that 'This is the only occasion I have heard of women fighting back for their daughters.'[1]

Joice Loch did not personally witness any of these events: were all the accounts true? There was probably some embellishment in the prevailing atmosphere of hatred of the andártes, but Joice Loch was not some naive outsider. She knew the Greeks, and had seen the effects of war on other people in other countries. There can be little doubt that her picture of terror from the left in her part of Greece is substantially accurate.

The second account, from Nicholas Gage's life of his mother, *Eleni*, is of events during 1947–8 in the village of Liá, in the far north-west of Greece and only a few miles from the Albanian frontier. During the occupation the village had been dominated by the Communist resistance ELAS, which virtually all the villagers still supported (see Chapter 10). Liá had been untroubled since the liberation until on 27 November 1947 news came that Democratic Army forces were approaching. The gendarmes were ordered to leave with their weapons for a town a dozen miles to the south. Some villagers realised that they risked being conscripted, but others were sanguine, expecting the Communist forces to leave in a few days. Eleni was sent with a message to the Democratic Army camp and was astonished at what she saw:

> The last time she had seen the ELAS guerrillas in Lia they wore clean grey uniforms and carried new weapons taken from the Italians. Now they all were in rags, their beards matted, some barefoot, and others wearing shoes held together with twine. They sat like stones, watching the women with terrible eyes. None of them got up to greet her.[2]

Eleni was in a difficult position. Her husband Christos, a man from Liá, was in the United States, where he had first gone in 1920 at the age of 17 and where he had since prospered and could send her money. He made extended visits to Liá, on the first of which in 1926 he married Eleni. In spite of his long absences, not uncommon among mountain villagers, she now had five children: Olga 19, Kanta 15, two younger daughters Fotini and Glykeria, and her last-born, Nicholas, aged eight. When the guerrilla forces arrived in Liá she wanted to leave with her children, but her husband wrote from America forbidding it.

> You have no business going anywhere. You stay in your home with your children. After all, who are these andartes? They're Greeks, fellow villagers some of them, fighting for their rights. I have worked for my living all my life and never bothered anyone. Why should they bother my family?[3]

Eleni was desperately afraid that 19-year-old Olga, already engaged to be married, would be taken away as an andártissa. On a rare visit to Ioánnina Eleni had been shocked to see two National Army trucks carrying weeping and distressed girls who had escaped from the Democratic Army. Eleni's main fear was that Olga would find herself having sex with one of the andártes, in spite of the Democratic Army's strict ban on sexual relations. Apart from anything else, this would ruin forever Olga's chances of marriage.

Eleni eventually decided that the only way to save Olga was to mutilate her so that she was too disabled to be recruited. There follows a horrifying description of how this was done, which eight-year-old Nicholas witnessed. Eleni heated water and poured it boiling on Olga's right foot which was extended on a stool. This produced blisters but was not disabling enough, so Olga's grandmother made a poker red-hot in the fire and pressed it on the scald, from which it came away with strips of skin hanging from it.

Olga had been saved, but on 14 December 1947, shortly before the Kónitsa battle, 15-year-old Kanta was ordered to join the Democratic Army. Kanta was tough, and as she left told her mother to stop crying because she would be all right. The girls were given political lessons and army uniforms, including for the first time in their lives trousers, and on 27 December, as the battle for Kónitsa could be heard in the distance, they were moved 100 miles to the south for military training. A week later the girls were divided into two groups, those who would make andártissas and the rest to go home. Kanta was in the second group, apparently thanks to one of the andárte officers who, as an ELAS fighter on the run during the war, had been given shelter by Eleni. As for so many under oppressive regimes, personal ties could override political loyalties, and terrified uncertainty could be as hard to bear as the anticipated experience itself.

The third account is by Geoffrey Chandler in his book *The Divided Land*. Chandler arrived in Greece immediately after liberation in September 1944 aged 21 and was there until the end of 1946, mainly in northern Greece but spending three months in the Peloponnese. He acted variously as a member of the Allied Military Mission to Greece, as part of the Anglo-Greek Information Service and as representative of the British Embassy's Information Department, so he saw and knew much more than Joice Loch or Nicholas Gage. Their accounts laid the blame for terror squarely on the Communist left, but Chandler was firmly impartial, writing in his preface: 'The story as told in this book is an unpalatable one for those who seek single scapegoats.'[4]

Chandler therefore described the excesses of both left and right. He cites the mass graves of ELAS victims discovered after the battle for Athens. He saw documents from the left's murder squads which ordered executions, with an instruction to bury the bodies deep. Near Kozáni a grave was found of 20 to 30 men, with their hands bound and their feet bare and scored with deep cuts, undoubtedly the work of the left. In October 1945 a left-wing band attacked two villages near Véria, killing four men and a woman and proclaiming that the Communists' time had come. On a number of occasions gendarmes sent to arrest Communists were killed.

Terror from the right came partly from the Chi bands led by Grívas. These were now active both in the north, claiming 3,000 members in the Véria area, and in the Peloponnese. There was also terror from one section of the National Guard, 143 Battalion, which made arbitrary arrests, incited civilians to attack its opponents and sometimes gave them weapons to do so. In March 1946 the left-wing paper *Elevthería* listed incidents in the last six months of terror from the right – the government, its army, gendarmerie and paramilitaries: 40 executed, 579 assassinated, 1,644 tortured and 3,942 imprisoned. The figures were undoubtedly exaggerated but were a clear indication of how the left viewed the right.

Chandler's grim catalogue of violence was relieved by his often lyrical descriptions of Greece's natural beauty. In the Peloponnese 'Spring was advancing swiftly. Scarlet anemones splashed the roadside with colour; almond blossom illuminated every garden; plum, pear, peach, and apple flowered together. In the mountains thousands of sweet-scented jonquils were in bloom.'[5] Near Kozáni he saw fields full of purple crocus, laboriously picked by hand and sold for medicines and dyes. He watched the storks in Véria which were nesting everywhere, and at the mouth of the river Axiós saw spoonbills and pelicans. As a keen lepidopterist he was delighted to find his house near Salonika adorned with white jasmine which was beset by humming-bird hawk moths, a species which hovers above flowers with wings furiously beating while the moth sucks out the nectar through an extended tongue.

Chandler introduces his book by saying that it is an indictment of both right and left, which it clearly is, and of British policy. One reads on to discover in what way he believes Britain is culpable, but finds instead many instances where the British are praised. Chandler believed that Britain's role in the battle for Athens halted the otherwise inevitable extension of ELAS rule, and that the presence of British troops in the north of Greece prevented full ELAS control there. British troops broke up armed clashes between left and right and were appealed to as peace-keepers by both sides. British officers also secured the release of men imprisoned unjustly.

Chandler's criticism of the British is not for what they did but for what they did not do, for their failure to control the Greek government's actions against its opponents. The British, Chandler thought, did not intervene forcefully enough because they were too concerned with nice scruples, too laissez-faire, too gentlemanly, too naive. But active intervention in Greece's internal affairs was always resisted and resented, as the Americans too discovered, and was particularly contentious once Greece acquired in March 1946 a democratically elected and thus legitimised government. The grounds for Chandler's criticism of the British are not strong.

His sincerity is not in doubt, and it may be that his view stemmed from his idealism. He was committed to reconciliation between all Greeks after the civil war, and for the rest of his life did all he could to promote it. Reconciliation was impossible while each side blamed the other, so another culprit was needed. For Chandler that was the reputation of British policy, a sacrifice in a good cause.

In fact there was often no way to allocate blame between left and right because action by one side or the other provoked a vicious spiral of violence. An example is the series of incidents in January 1946 at Kalamáta in the southern Peloponnese. Leftists were alleged to have made earlier attacks on rightists and became targets for rightist revenge. In retaliation, leftists killed a rightist leader and his six-year-old daughter in Sparta some 20 miles to the east. Apparently in response to that, two leftists were shot dead in a taverna and within days of the Sparta killings about 1,000 rightists entered Kalamáta, killed six people, released rightist prisoners and withdrew with 76 hostages. The crisis was resolved by the arrival of 900 soldiers of the Greek army led by a colonel formerly of the Mountain Brigade, who replaced most of the Kalamáta gendarmes and secured the release of the hostages, except for six who had been executed.

Not all such acts of violence were ideologically driven. In the late 1940s Kevin Andrews, a young American classics student who was travelling round Greece, asked an elderly farmer in the southern Peloponnese for his view of the conflict: 'Which side, then, has committed more crimes here, the Right or the Left?' Andrews had not asked whether left or right had committed more crimes overall and so by implication was the more to blame, and the farmer's reply was simply from his own experience: 'I can only tell you the side that happens to have most power *in one district or another* [italics added] also has the most opportunity to commit them.' The farmer also said:

One act of violence doesn't produce just one other but ten or twenty more. In this country people take up arms against each other not because of politics, not because of ideology, but simply because one individual can't stand another individual to be as strong as he is. Here nobody takes sides for abstract reasons. And here the greatest dishonour is not to take revenge.[6]

Terror inflicted by rightist groups gradually declined from 1945 on. As we have seen, the main band was Chi, led by Grívas, though others with the same anti-Communist aims were loosely linked to it. Chi strongholds in Athens had been destroyed by ELAS in January 1945 during the battle for the city, but Chi was still recruiting in the following summer, though rallies in Salonika and Athens drew disappointing numbers. Wealthy donors to Chi switched their support to monarchist politicians, and other groups who had hoped for a share of these funds cut their links to Chi. In January 1946 the government closed the Chi offices and Chi was a spent force. From now on terror from the right, in the eyes of the left, stemmed from the actions of the government.

Government measures to control the left began with the Varkíza Agreement of February 1945 which ended the battle for Athens. The Varkíza Agreement had stated that there would be an amnesty for political crimes committed during the battle for Athens, but that 'from this amnesty shall be excluded common-law crimes against life and property which were not absolutely necessary to the achievement of the political crime concerned.'[7] Obviously the phrase 'not absolutely necessary' was open to interpretation and the government interpreted it widely, arresting for common-law crimes many who regarded their own acts as political. Also Varkíza did not cover ELAS members who refused to surrender their weapons, and significantly it did not cover political crimes, however defined, committed after Varkíza. By the end of 1945, from a combination of widespread arrests and creakingly slow court procedures, the prisons were crammed. Ministry of Justice figures showed that by then prison numbers had reached around 18,000, mainly, it seems, of the left, and that charges were pending against nearly 50,000 ELAS supporters.

To resolve the situation, and under determined pressure from Britain's ambassador Leeper, the government passed on 21 December 1945 Emergency Law 753. This provided that those only 'morally responsible' but not directly responsible for common-law crimes were now covered by the amnesty. This law also limited the period awaiting trial to 100 days. As a result, by April 1946 7,471 prisoners had been released.

Emergency Law 753 had loosened the screws, but in the period between Varkíza and the March 1946 elections the government tightened them by reviving two older pieces of legislation. One reintroduced a law of 1929 known as the *idhiónimo* or special crime law. This stated that 'whoever aims at the implementation of ideas whose manifest purpose is the overthrow of the established social order by violent means or the detachment of part from the whole of the country, or proselytizes in favour of these ideas' could be imprisoned or exiled.[8] Thus advocating an independent Macedonia, the KKE's Achilles heel, was drawn into the criminal net and, more importantly, not only acts but also the promotion of ideas became crimes.

The other piece of legislation reintroduced an even older law of 1871 against banditry, significant because it revived public security committees in every district. These consisted of the local governor, the head of the gendarmerie and the public prosecutor, and could banish for a year (later extended) anyone suspected of 'breaching the public order, peace and security of the country.'[9] Eventually there were four different bodies with powers to exile, detain or imprison. Two were the courts and the public security committees. In addition, there were special courts martial with power of the death sentence dealing with offences against the state as now defined, and finally the army, which could send soldiers suspected of Communism to camps for reindoctrination.

The Tsaldháris government, soon after its election in March 1946, extended further the *idhiónimo* law. By Resolution 3 of 15 June 1946 the *idhiónimo* law now also covered organising armed groups and coming to an understanding with foreigners. Further legislation followed. On 23 December 1947, three days after the formation of the rebel Provisional Democratic Government, the hitherto still legal KKE was banned. A fortnight later on 8 January 1948 loyalty certificates were introduced. Now anyone who held or applied for a job in the public sector had to complete a questionnaire, be examined by a loyalty board, and if approved sign a declaration of loyalty to the state and rejection of Communism.

Conditions in Greek prisons had always been bad, but were now made worse by over-crowding. Not only was the total prison population almost doubled but also 16 prisons had been ruined and 15 seriously damaged during and soon after the occupation. UNRRA reported on a number of prisons between 1945 and 1946. In Salonika the number of prisoners was not doubled but tripled. In Trípoli there was no doctor or sick bay, and lice were prevalent. In Tríkala there were no beds or lavatories, so prisoners slept on mattresses on the floor and used chamber pots. In Patras there was running water for only an hour a day and no soap, so scabies was widespread.

Remote island camps as well as prisons held detainees. The main ones were in the Cyclades group of islands 100 miles or so east of the Peloponnese, and the islands near the Turkish coast, where the Áyios Evstrátios camp was one of the largest. At the end of 1948 a camp was established on Makrónisos as the main holding centre to which those held on other islands were transferred. By September 1949, when the civil war had ended, Makrónisos housed 12,000 people, 80 per cent of all detainees.

Some of those detained on Makrónisos gave dreadful descriptions of life there. It began with arrival:

> From the hill twenty soldiers come around armed with batons. They attack us furiously. They strike us anywhere with the batons and their feet. They drag some men by their hair and throw them fully clothed into the sea. There is no way to protect yourself. Not far from me they had a comrade of mine, a sailor. They took his heavy clothes off him, they threw him into the sea and afterwards they beat him till he fell unconscious onto the paving stones.[10]

The guards clearly felt that they had to dominate from the start. They were outnumbered by the detainees, and they were a long way from help in case of trouble, even on Makrónisos, the camp closest to the mainland. Similar intimidation was used when the detainees were put to work:

> On 20 May 1948, one hundred and fifty detainees unload 3,000 sacks with cement during the night, whilst the guards beat them. The same day one hundred detainees carry sacks full of sand and lime to the pillbox on the highest hill. On the way up they are chased and beaten by the tormentors. They carry them for twenty kilometres without a break. At eleven o'clock in the morning when they return the guards force them to carry sacks full of cement for the whole day from

the beach to the generators buildings without food or water under ceaseless thrashing. They return late at night.[11]

The official purpose of the Makrónisos camp was reindoctrination, to be achieved by getting the detainee to sign a 'declaration of change of mind' (*dhilosí metánias*) which secured his release. A typical declaration said:

> I state that during the December rebellion I was misguided into the EAM organisation by deceptive words without knowing of its antinational activities and its treasonous and destructive actions against my Motherland. I renounce the organisation as the enemy of my Motherland, by whose side I stand. Moreover, I pledge the quick extermination of the bandits.[12]

It appears that torture was sometimes used to force a declaration, though it seems paradoxical that a man should be tortured into gaining his freedom. Dominance and sadism clearly played a part. Some would have resisted signing – committed Communists, or those who would return to a predominantly Communist home village. But many had been compelled into the Communist ranks, and Márkos Vaphiádhis later admitted that from mid-1947 90 per cent of recruits to the Democratic Army had been obtained by force. It is therefore not surprising that about 70 per cent of the 30,000 who passed through Maskrónisos eventually renounced Communism.

Two spectacular murders in the summer of 1948 gave a further twist to the violence between left and right. On 1 May Chrístos Ladhás, the minister of justice, was killed outside an Athens church. The location may have been chosen as a reminder of the death of Greece's first president Kapodhístrias, murdered in 1831 at the entrance of a Návplion church. The Greek rebel radio in Belgrade praised the action and called for other government ministers to be killed. Two months later six men were executed for implication in the death of Ladhás.

The second murder was that of the American George Polk, the correspondent for CBS, and responsibility was far less clear. On the morning of 16 May 1948 Polk's body, bound, gagged and shot through the head, was found floating in Salonika harbour. Polk's reports had been outspokenly critical of the Greek government, and at the time of his death he had reportedly been on his way to the journalistic coup of a secret meeting with Márkos. The murder caused an outcry in America, especially from Polk's fellow journalists. Theories about his death abounded. Had he been killed at the instigation of the government, or by some independent rightist group, to silence his criticisms? Or had he been killed by Communists to prevent him meeting Márkos and then revealing where Márkos was? Three Communists were accused of the murder and convicted in a trial seen as heavily slanted against them. The Polk murder was an example of the accusations made by both sides in a time of reciprocal terror.

It is impossible to make sense of this conflict between left and right by drawing clear-cut conclusions. Unless responsibility is specifically claimed, each argument accusing one party or another meets a counter-argument. Violence might be attributed primarily to the left or the right, but it was often a reaction to the violence of the other, and some of the violence was not ideological at all. Successive governments had offered no social policy, leaving the way open for the Communists, but the KKE social policy, however utopian in party propaganda, was seen by many as pernicious in practice. The government during the civil war trampled on civil liberties, but any government would be expected to take extraordinary measures when the country faced a serious threat from both within and without. The British and later the Americans could have intervened more strongly to curb government excesses, but to do so would bring charges of unwarranted interference and imperialism. One is left with the words of Georgios Seféris, Greece's Nobel Laureate poet. He had said of the disputed destruction of the town of Smyrna in 1922, 'The wrong has been committed. The important thing is: who will redeem it?'[13] His question applies to this later conflict too.

26

The Plight of the Greek Children

As the civil war gathered momentum, the number of refugees increased. In the course of 1947 it rose from under 20,000 to over 430,000, and by July 1949 when the war was at its climax there were almost 700,000, around 10 per cent of the total Greek population. The refugees moved mainly to the outskirts of the larger towns, where they lived in huts or tents in appalling conditions. About half of these refugees were children, and a report by the United Nations Educational Scientific and Cultural Organisation (UNESCO) of 1949 described them as living in 'an undesirable state of physical debility and moral distress', with extreme emaciation, pale faces and terror-stricken looks.[1]

Queen Frederica had seen this misery for herself, particularly on a 12-day tour with the King in January 1947 of the northern areas of Greece, from Kavála in the east to Kónitsa in the west. 'It became my job', she decided, 'to try and save the children of Greece.'[2] The Queen's Fund (Vasilikí Prónia) was initiated by Frederica's radio appeal on 5 July 1947, in which she described the children's misery and appealed for donations: 'I do not ask for what you can spare. I am asking you to deprive yourselves.'[3] More money was raised from businessmen, and from workers who contributed a day's pay. A distinguished committee was set up to guide the fund, with representatives of the Church, including Archbishop Dhamaskinós, and of academia, business, labour organisations and charities. The president of this committee was the redoubtable Aléxandhra Méla, and 72 well-to-do Athens women, who became known as the 'Queen's Ladies', volunteered their active help on arduous journeys through the troubled areas.

The Queen's Fund quickly established homes for the displaced children, known as *pedhópolis* or children's cities. The first, near Salonika, was founded the day after the Queen's appeal. There were eventually 54 *pedhópolis*, 23 in Athens, 11 in Salonika, and others in major towns and on the islands, caring for some 20,000 children. There were also subsidiary ventures: youth centres teaching agriculture, carpentry and masonry, and home industry centres producing fabrics, pottery and cheese for sale.

Every *pedhópolis* was visited by representatives of the International Red Cross, who always reported favourably. The regime was strict. There were lessons morning and evening, there were daily prayers, all the children wore the uniforms provided, they had few personal possessions, and there was corporal punishment for misbehaviour. The values of religion and patriotism were inculcated. The system might seem draconian by today's standards, but anyone who experienced an English boarding school in those years would find every aspect of the *pedhópolis* regime completely familiar.

Many of the children in the *pedhópolis* had been moved by the National Army because their homes were in a battle area. These children of course remained in Greece. But on 3 March 1948 the Democratic Army announced its own programme to move children out of Greece and across the northern frontier. A total of 4,784 children aged three to 13 were to be moved to Yugoslavia, Romania, Poland and Czechoslovakia, and it was claimed that this would be with their parents' consent.

Greeks were outraged. On 18 March 1948, a fortnight after the announcement of Communist removals, Georgios Vláchos published an impassioned article in his newspaper *Kathimeriní*. It was headed '*To Pedhomázoma*', recalling the historical removals of Greek children by the Turks, but, wrote Vláchos, even the Sultan took only one boy from each family, not all the children. Shame on the Democratic Army, he said, for arming and paying men to seize children. Vláchos called for action now, today, by starting a different *pedhomázoma*: 'Let them come here. Here is their great Mother, Greece. Let us gather them all in. Let us clothe them, wash them, nourish them, teach them and comfort them, until the storm has passed.'[4]

The Greek government made a formal and forceful complaint to the United Nations about the Communist removal of children, claiming that it was a crime against humanity and amounted to genocide. The issue was passed to the United Nations Special

Committee on the Balkans (UNSCOB). UNSCOB, successor to the original UN Commission of Investigation, had been established in the previous October, charged with investigating and trying to resolve cross-border incidents on Greece's northern frontier. The matter of Communist removal of children was now added to its remit.

The plight of these children who were to be taken out of Greece became an important element in appeals by the Queen's Fund. Frederica spoke in another radio broadcast of 'the tragedy of those whose children had been kidnapped and of those who lived in danger of having them kidnapped'. In her memoirs 20 years later she confusingly wrote that 'the main project, *at the beginning* [emphasis added]' was to save these children. If she meant 'at the very beginning' she was mistaken, if she meant 'near the beginning' she was correct.[5]

We have followed in Nicholas Gage's *Eleni* the fortunes of the village of Liá since the first appearance there of the Communists. Toward the end of the book there is an account of Eleni's last months in Liá and of the Communist *pedhomázoma* at its most destructive. In early April 1948 all mothers in Liá with children aged between three and 14 were summoned to the church beside the village square. At first there was only a call for volunteers to send their children away, then persuasion followed – 'If you truly love [your children] you will send them away.'[6] Finally incentives were tried: the children were given slices of luxury white bread with thick sweet jam, and the mothers were told that in the people's democracies the children would eat like this every day.

Nevertheless, by the end of April only a dozen children from Liá had been volunteered, and it became clear that the Communists would not leave it at that. For Eleni this belief was reinforced by a conversation between guerrilla leaders about more forceful methods which was overheard by nine-year-old Nicholas and reported to his mother. Eleni decided that, in spite of her husband's instructions to stay, she and her five children must try to escape. They would have to move south, creeping through the guerrilla outposts and the minefields, to where the Greek National Army was encamped some miles away.

Eleni brought her friend and cousin Soula into the plan. Soula's husband, a somewhat unreliable man who was a tinker by trade, would be the leader. The first attempt involved Eleni and Soula, each with five children, and other relatives. But as they approached the guerrilla outposts Soula's baby started crying and could not be silenced. The escape had to be abandoned. When they assembled for a second attempt, a thick mist descended and this too had to be given up.

The third attempt in the summer of 1948 was planned for Sunday 20 June, but was disrupted even before it began by guerrilla demands for one woman from Eleni's family to go and work on the harvest in fields some 10 miles north of the village. Fourteen-year-old Glykeria volunteered to go, boldly saying that she was too young to be an andártissa and too old for the *pedhomázoma*, and that she could escape from there alone. On the day before the planned flight there was a demand for a second woman from Eleni's household, and this time Eleni went, to join Glykeria at the harvest.

On the Sunday night the escapers assembled again, without Eleni and Glykeria but joined by another family, making a group of 20. They walked for two days and nights, coming close to guerrilla forces who were pursuing them after finding their village houses empty. After many other hazards, they were close to the Greek National Army lines on the Wednesday morning, and the women used their underclothes to make improvised white flags of surrender. Against the odds they had finally escaped.

Eleni's children, with others of the escape party, were taken first to Philiátes in army trucks, then by bus to Igoumenítsa, and finally by sea to Athens. At the end of February 1949 they sailed for America, and three weeks later landed at New York harbour for a meeting, not altogether easy, with the father who had spent most of the years since 1936 in America, whom the girls hardly knew and Nicholas had never met.

Meanwhile Glykeria had returned from the harvest fields to Liá and when the village was evacuated as government forces approached she was taken to Albania. There she was drafted as an andártissa and sent back to the front line in Greece, from which she managed to escape and surrender to the Greek National Army. On 10 February 1950, nearly a year after the rest of her family, she joined them in New York.

On the Tuesday two days after the escape Eleni and two other women of the escapers' families were taken away from the harvest and brought back to Liá. There they were imprisoned and interrogated, at this stage suffering no worse than slaps as they maintained their ignorance of the escape. After a week the three women were released but kept under close watch, their captors hoping that their meetings would betray anyone else who was planning to leave. This revealed nothing, but other villagers were brought in for questioning.

There was no lack of women willing to give testimony against the Amerikana. They resented seeing Eleni walking about the village alive and well after the whole family had succeeded in slipping through the guerillas' fingers. She had always had privileges and an easy life, the village muttered, and it was time she was toppled from her high horse.[7]

At the beginning of August Eleni and her two companions were taken back to prison. Interrogation, now using villagers' testimony, became brutal – beatings with rods, and shoulders forced back against the interrogator's knee on the spine. After several days Eleni broke and admitted planning the escape, though still denying that she had tried to persuade anyone else to join it. There was now enough evidence for a public trial of Eleni and other suspect villagers, a group of four women and three men.

The trial was held in the village square on 19 August in front of virtually the whole population of Liá. It was presided over by a man known only as Katis, nominally as one of three judges but effectively as prosecutor. The charges were scatter-gun: that the accused had organised escapes, had passed information to the enemy, had slandered guerrilla fighters, and had hoarded food and valuables which should have been handed to the Democratic Army. It was also held against Eleni that her husband was American, a country now supporting the monarcho-fascist Greek government. Much of the villagers' testimony told against the accused, but five braved the hostile atmosphere and spoke in their favour. When Katis pronounced judgement on the seven defendants, two of the women were found not guilty but the other five, including Eleni, were condemned to death.

The sentences were confirmed and, on Gage's evidence already predetermined, by Kostas Kaliyanis, political commissar for the region, who years later became head of the Greek Communist Party. On 28 August, after further torture to make the accused confess to every charge brought against them, Eleni and the other condemned were taken to an isolated spot north of the village, and on the edge of prepared graves shot by an execution squad.

Nicholas Gage's book is more than a personal memoir. For details of conversations, he said he followed the example of Thucydides, who wrote: 'I put into the mouth of each speaker the sentiments proper to the occasion, expressed as I thought he would be likely to express them.'[8] Only in this sense is Gage's account fictional. He interviewed scores of people – Liá villagers, Communist and National Army officers, and even Katis who had passed the death sentence on Eleni. He used his professional skills as an investigative journalist to test all the evidence. But Gage's account is of course the story of only one village.

A more comprehensive examination of the experiences of all the Greek children can be found in other books, and one of the most recent (2012) is *Children of the Greek Civil War*, by Danforth and Van Boeschoten – the Danforth book for short.

The central section of the book gives the personal accounts of seven children, boys and girls, who were removed during the civil war: four who went to Communist countries and three to *pedhópolis*. They describe their removal, their education including the element of indoctrination, and their later careers either in Greece or abroad.

For both groups of children the inducements to their mothers to let them go were on a spectrum of coercion, from invitation to persuasion and then compulsion and finally, as seen at Liá, death for those who arranged their children's escape. It seems from these accounts that most of the Communist evacuees left because their families saw no other option. The grandfather of one girl said to her mother,

> This is the worst of the storm. I would advise you just to take your children and go because otherwise you'll be taken by the Greek Army and sent somewhere to the islands or to prison because your husband is with the partisans. Or else you're going to be taken into the partisans yourself. You have no other choice. This way at least you'll go with the children.

The mother did leave on the first part of the exodus but once in Yugoslavia was forcibly separated from her eight-year-old daughter.[9]

Of the children removed to the *pedhópolis*, one said, 'The fact is, we were taken by force,' but another just as explicitly said, 'No one took us by force; we wanted to go. That's important; I want to emphasise that.' Mothers often accompanied their children to the *pedhópolis*, where they were visited by other relatives.[10]

Some of the children in each group speak well of the education they received, leading to a trade or professional qualification. Many mention the values that were instilled. In Bulgaria one Communist evacuee was taught that the Greek government and its National Army were the bad guys. 'In Greece *we* had been the bad guys. Now our teachers were telling us that *we* were the *good* guys and *they* were the *bad* guys.' But this propaganda did not always work. Another Communist evacuee in Hungary said, 'They started talking to us about politics. We weren't interested. [They] lectured us about the Communist Party. It was really boring.'[11]

Things were different in the *pedhópolis*. One boy said, 'I want to stress this. It's a lie that they filled our heads with propaganda. There was no propaganda.' On the other hand a Macedonian boy felt he was being imbued with Greek patriotism against his Macedonian heritage. Some disliked the strict regime of the *pedhópolis* and their offshoots, especially at the technical school on Léros. But there was genuine affection for Queen Frederica and gratitude for what she had done. One boy wrote, 'She was the queen, our second mother,' and a girl said, 'To tell you the truth, I felt like the queen was my mother. I respected her; I still do. I'm grateful to her as our benefactor.'[12]

After the civil war *pedhópolis* children usually went back to their families, but many found the return to village life difficult, with relentless work in the fields and, for girls, an arranged marriage. Sometimes children returning from a *pedhópolis* were resented because 'they looked down at their own people and thought of themselves as more cultured, more educated.' Of the Communist evacuees many stayed in Eastern Europe and made a good life for themselves, or emigrated. One who went to Canada was fearful of going to a capitalist country, but once there said, 'Capitalism, poverty, exploitation! I was always looking to find it. But my fears were unfounded.' A boy who had been sent to Hungary returned to Greece in 1958 and tried life in his village. After 18 days 'I couldn't stand it. They were all strangers.' He managed to get into the technical school on Léros, worked as a builder and eventually set up his own construction business. He concluded:

> I realised that I was better off here in Greece. You have to work hard here, but you can accomplish a lot more. In Eastern Europe you didn't have the same opportunities. Everything belonged to the state. Here you could become a rich man.[13]

These seven individual accounts are valuable testimony, and are fairly selected to give a range of reactions, but obviously cannot tell the whole story. UNSCOB tried to produce a general assessment of the Communist removals of children, in particular the degree of coercion used. UNSCOB's first report, in June 1948, only three months after the removals began, came to no firm conclusions. In some cases children were taken with their parents' consent and many parents were happy to see their children go. In other situations the parents were unhappy but dared not complain, or the children were parted from their parents by compulsion. The solution proposed was that the Greek government should ask the Communist countries to which children had been taken to return them. The Greek government immediately did so, but all their requests were either ignored or rejected.

The view of US Secretary of State George Marshall in 1948 was that there were varying degrees of Communist coercion, as UNSCOB reported, that the Communist removals were primarily to save the guerrilla forces from having to look after these children and to demonstrate that they got better care in Communist countries than in Greece. It was not genocide as the Greek government maintained. But he concluded that these motives did not make the removals any the less reprehensible. The American administration was unwilling to intervene actively on the basis of inconclusive evidence, in spite of pressure from public opinion. To antagonise the Communist countries to the north of Greece risked intensifying and prolonging the Greek civil war which the United States was committed to ending.

The basic thesis of the Danforth book is summarised in two sections, one comparing the education received by the children in the two groups, and the other a comparison of the actual evacuation programmes. On the subject of education it says: 'In Eastern Europe, most refugee children received a good education and were able to earn a decent living as skilled labourers or professionals' whereas in the *pedhópolis* the children learnt only trades and crafts.[14] However, most of the *pedhópolis* children came from villages and would go back to them, and it was sensible to provide them with skills that would be useful on their return.

In their comparison of the two evacuation programmes the Danforth book claims striking similarities. Each side, it says, had genuinely humanitarian motives, but it does not add that Communist coercion could be at the darkest end of the spectrum – death for recusants. The drafting of children into the guerrilla forces is presented as equivalent to call-up to the National Army, but it was not. Conscription at 18 into your country's armed forces is not the same as conscription at a much younger age into forces attacking your country. The degree of indoctrination is said to be similar in Eastern Europe and in the *pedhópolis*, but the accounts of the seven children do not support this, and learning Communist ideology is not equivalent to learning respect for Queen Frederica. Finally the authors point to one major difference: that Communist evacuees spent far longer away from their parents than *pedhópolis* children. However, they do not add that the reason for this was that the Communist evacuees were not free to leave but the *pedhópolis* children could return to their families at any time.

Nicholas Gage was furious with the Danforth book's thesis, maintaining that the Communists had not evacuated the children as refugees but had kidnapped them, and that the book's authors had presented a perverse and dishonest revision of history. He asked, 'Why would my mother have sacrificed her life to prevent us from being saved from harm?'[15] The authors in turn belittled Gage's account, claiming in the book that Gage had provided a politically motivated narrative and that he 'obviously supports a right-wing agenda.' This is not obvious at all, and Nicholas Gage's account should be accepted as just as valid, and deserving just as much respect, as those of any of the other participants in these traumatic events.

The United Nations' involvement in the question of the Greek children was given added impetus by UNSCOB reports that children as young as 14 were being sent back to Greece to fight for the Democratic Army. Gage's 14-year-old sister Glykeria was an example. UNSCOB condemned this as a 'violation of fundamental human principles.'[16] The UN General Assembly passed a series of resolutions demanding the return of the children, to be supervised by the International Red Cross, but returned to where? The first resolution of November 1948 demanded return to Greece, but some children had nowhere in Greece to go because of the widespread destruction of the civil war. A second resolution a year later called for return to their homes, whether these were in Greece or not. A final resolution of December 1950 specified that children should be returned to their parents.

The repatriations to Greece were slow. Between 1950 and 1965, in round figures, 12,000 refugees, adults as well as children, were repatriated, in the next decade 9,000 more, and 17,000 in 1981–3, leaving in the twenty-first century 12,000 who had emigrated or were still living in what were now post-Communist countries. Broadly speaking, the effects of the Communist evacuations had been undone. However, as the conflict between Nicholas Gage and the Danforth book shows, the battle over the interpretation of these events is still being fiercely fought.

27

The Marshall Plan

Two weeks after US Congress approved the Truman Doctrine there was another and even wider American initiative on Europe as a whole. On 5 June 1947 Secretary of State George Marshall, in a speech accepting an honorary degree at Harvard, spoke of the help that the United States might give to a programme for recovery in Europe. The objective, he said, was 'the revival of a working economy in the world so as to permit the emergence of political and social conditions in which free institutions can exist.' The policy, he went on, was 'directed not against any country or doctrine but against hunger, poverty, desperation and chaos.' Finally he stressed that it was not for America to draw up such a programme: 'The initiative, I think, must come from Europe.'[1]

Marshall's Harvard speech aroused virtually no interest in the US or UK press. Bevin only heard about the speech on a small radio by his bedside in a report from the BBC's American correspondent. It was, Bevin said later, 'like a lifeline to sinking men. It seemed to bring hope where there was none. The generosity of it was beyond our belief. We grabbed the lifeline with both hands.'[2] It was only after a year of complex negotiations that Truman signed on 3 April 1948 the Economic Cooperation Act giving legislative force to the Marshall Plan, and the plan began operations in July, bringing massive help to Greece as well as to other countries in shattered Europe.

The Truman Doctrine had presented US national security as dependent on the security of other free nations; similarly the Marshall Plan presented European prosperity as vital to US trade. Generosity played a part, but in both cases the offer of help was not purely altruistic. US national interest was not only an inescapable fact, but had to be stressed to win the backing of public opinion and, crucially, the support of Congress in authorising money.

The first issue to be determined was whether Russia and its Eastern Europe satellites should be included in the plan. From the US point of view to exclude them would be to make the Marshall Plan seem an imperialist American attempt to create a power bloc to rival Russia's. On the other hand to include them, though it might lead to the detachment of the satellites from the Soviet bloc, would jeopardise any chance of approval by a Congress now dominated by Republicans. It would also risk constant disruption by Russia and the possible failure of the whole enterprise. From the Russian point of view their participation would be an admission that a Communist economy needed help from a capitalist one.

The American decision was to invite Russia to join and take the risks that might follow Russian acceptance. The first meeting of European foreign ministers to discuss this plan was opened in Paris in late June 1947, and Molotov attended for Russia. At the end of the conference, during which Molotov launched vituperative attacks on the Marshall Plan, he rejected participation by Russia apparently on direct instructions from Stalin, and a few days later instructed Russia's satellites to follow suit. Molotov then walked out, according to Bevin, 'uttering threats'.[3]

The list of countries which would be covered by the Marshall Plan was now clear. There were 16 of them: Austria, Belgium, Britain, Denmark, France, Greece, Holland, Iceland, Ireland, Italy, Luxembourg, Norway, Portugal, Sweden, Switzerland and Turkey. Only Greece, and, to a lesser extent Turkey, were already receiving aid as a result of the Truman Doctrine. Germany, split into zones of occupation by Allied powers or Russia, was a separate issue.

The 16 countries were a widely divergent group. Some were large and some small, some had supported the Allies and some the Axis, some were near economic collapse while others were doing much better. Some welcomed and others feared two possible future developments: either greater European integration or the revival of Germany. The representatives of the 16 assembled on 12 July 1947, again in Paris, for a conference to work out how the Marshall Plan could be put into effect.

The conference was chaired by British Foreign Secretary Ernest Bevin and set a deadline of 1 September, less than two months away, to complete its work. A steering committee, the Committee for European Economic Co-operation (CEEC) was set up, headed by the British diplomat Oliver Franks. Under the CEEC four technical committees were established for food and agriculture, iron and steel, fuel and power, and transport. All 16 countries completed questionnaires on their economy and resources. The figures in their answers were not always reliable. The Greek delegate did not send the questionnaire to Athens, saying, 'You don't think anybody in Athens will know anything about this. I will just invent the figures myself.'[4]

By August the differing national interests of the 16 countries were coming to the surface. Britain was extremely suspicious of moves towards European economic integration, a wariness that was to characterise British policy towards Europe for decades to come. France was deeply concerned about a resurgence of Germany, with which it had been at war three times in the last century, in the Franco-Prussian War of 1870–1 and in two world wars.

The original US estimate of the cost of Marshall Aid was $16 billion. When in late August the 16 shopping lists were combined the total required was nearly double that at $28 billion, an amount far above anything Congress would approve. It was time for American views to be clearly expressed, and the task fell to Will Clayton, the US undersecretary of state for economic affairs. Clayton laid down some essential guidelines to the Europeans. The money asked for must be reduced to something more realistic. Plans should be based on the European economies becoming self-sustaining in four years, and on the assumption that aid would reduce in each successive year. Finally there must be a continuing organisation to promote European co-operation.

George Kennan summarised this new more forceful approach: 'We would listen to all that the Europeans had to say, but in the end we would not ask them, we would just tell them what they would get.' Many of the European representatives accepted this: 'We will squawk over every cut. Never mind that. Most of your cuts will be justified, and we will squawk anyway.'[5]

The 690-page report of the conference was ready for signature on 22 September 1947, only three weeks later than the original deadline. The original demand for $28 billion had been reduced to $19 billion. The following months saw an energetic campaign by Truman, Marshall and other members of the administration to swing public support behind the aid plan, and stormy arguments in both Houses of Congress. On 14 March 1948 the Senate authorised expenditure of $5.3 billion for year one and the House of Representatives did the same two weeks later, both by remarkable 80 per cent majorities. On 3 April

1948 Truman signed the aid bill into law, and Marshall Aid, officially known as the European Recovery Programme or ERP, was launched.

The next step was to set up an organisation to administer the aid, the European Co-operation Administration (ECA). One of the key features of the ECA operation was the ingenious system called counterpart funds. If, say, a European farmer wanted to buy a tractor manufactured in the United States he arranged its purchase through a local European dealer. The US government then paid the American tractor manufacturer in dollars from Marshall Aid funds, and the European farmer would pass the equivalent in local currency, the counterpart, to his government to be spent on the country's recovery. The ECA exercised tight control over the exchange rates involved, and the use which the government made of the counterpart funds.

The counterpart system had a number of advantages. First, it operated through normal market processes: the farmer had to pay for his tractor, and was not just given it. Second, it meant that European countries could buy from the United States without having to use their precarious, or perhaps almost non-existent, dollar reserves. Finally, for America it provided a boost to the export trade, and control over the use of counterpart funds.

The Marshall Plan came to an end on 31 December 1951 following the outbreak of the Korean War, six months before the completion of the plan's scheduled four-year life from June 1948 to June 1952. By then the plan and the efforts of the Europeans had produced impressive overall results. All the following factors in Europe were improved: industrial production, agricultural output, intra-European trade and European exports outside Europe. Transport systems and harbours had been rebuilt, and unemployment and inflation were generally low. Moreover, rising prosperity had much reduced the internal Communist threats of disruption by strikes and agitation, and the possibility of Communist parties coming to power through elections. In Greece, however, the operation of the Marshall Plan was far from straightforward.

A detailed account of Marshall Aid in Greece, and of its successes and failures, is given by C.A. Munkman. He was the chief of audits and surveys of the United States Economic Mission to Greece, which was the Greek section of the wider European Co-operation Administration. However, Munkman's interest in Greece was much wider than that of simply a public accountant. He knew the modern history of Greece and was constantly reminded of Ancient Greece: of

Homer's descriptions of landscapes, of Jason's departure from Vólos in search of the Golden Fleece, of St Paul preaching at Phílippi. He travelled widely, in three and a half years covering some 150,000 miles, often on poor roads. Some of his travels were hazardous: 'No other spot in my travels has given me more anxieties than Vermion. In the mist, which may come any time with low-lying cloud, one's sunlight memories of a twenty-foot road and five thousand feet of sheer drop become sharpest.'[6] Other journeys were delightful, as when he followed the annual spring trek of Vlach shepherds and their flocks from wintering on the plains to their summer pasture in the mountains.

Munkman was a 'third nation' national (he does not say from which nation), so he was able to listen impartially to Greek and American complaints about each other, and he believed that more third nation nationals, especially from Europe, should be used in Greece. 'A top expert', he wrote, 'is not essential, a good teacher in the best sense is. Even more important is a sympathetic mind, which can grasp the virtues of the world and the great glories of the Creator in the diversity of man.'[7]

The first topic described in detail by Munkman was agriculture. This was obviously of crucial importance: the majority of Greeks lived and worked on the land, and outside Athens–Piraeus and Salonika the overwhelming majority did so. With limited acreage available for agriculture, farms were consequently small. More than half were of 12 acres or less and the average size was 6 acres. It was essential to increase productivity, and in Greece this had to be done not by developing huge agricultural areas like those of the American Midwest but through the individual farmer, and Munkman estimated that well over a million had to be taught how to improve their land.

Marshall Aid funds supported the distribution of fertilisers and pesticides and the development of improved or new crop strains. The first priority was to improve the production of wheat, traditionally largely imported and so draining the country's foreign exchange reserves. The results were impressive. By 1953, thanks to improved crops and increased arable acreage, wheat production was almost double its pre-war level, and there were significant increases in other crops: barley and maize, fruit and vegetables and cotton. However, Munkman was candid about some of the fiascos in other agricultural projects: the refrigerators supplied for newly trained vets which worked on AC when the town's supply was DC, and expensive cheese-making equipment left for years in its original crates. He also records the disastrous project of importing horses to service donkeys and produce more working mules. The horses turned out to be elderly retired racehorses no longer interested in procreation. But he concludes with a tribute to the Greek farmer: 'Perhaps most deserving of credit is the simple Greek farmer who, working on his seven acre unit, with little or no capital and without scientific training, has been able to absorb and apply so many new ideas so quickly.'[8]

The problem of small farms at subsistence level could obviously be mitigated if more land was made productive, and this was the object of three major marsh-drainage schemes. One was in Macedonia, on the plains near Salonika and near Dhráma, a second in Thessaly, and a third south of Árta. Both the Macedonia and Thessaly schemes suffered from similar problems. The responsibility was divided between two ministries, one for river control and one for making the drained land productive, a split that too often led to no decision being made and which was never corrected in spite of Munkman's constant appeals to the Greek government. Also the farmers who settled on the reclaimed lands were supposed to pay the reclamation costs into the counterpart account, to provide a continuing fund for further work, but no steps were taken to collect this payment. Farmers in Macedonia told Munkman that they would willingly pay if the money went to help Macedonia, but not if it went to Athens where it would simply disappear. The Árta project was much more successful, and in three years local production was quintupled. Munkman believed that this was because here there was a single irrigation authority whose executive was elected by the farmers themselves.

Another way of increasing agricultural output, other than the reclamation of marshes for farmland, was to provide water for existing farms. 'With summer water I can quadruple my income,' said one farmer.[9] It was known that in summer, while surface rivers were dry, water continued to flow 500 feet or more underground, and in 1918 the British army in Salonika had tapped this water at about 1,000 feet down. Marshall Aid funds of $10 million were now allocated to provide Greece with 50 drilling rigs, plus the essential pipes, pumps and engines without which the drilling rigs produced only a hole in the ground. The rigs were of two types. Percussion rigs simply bashed down from the surface, were slow and could not go very deep, while rotary rigs of the type used in oil drilling were much faster and could go much deeper.

These rigs were capable of drilling 3,000 wells a year, but in the first two years only 700 were dug. Credit restriction was a barrier. Farmers would have to pay some $2,500 to have a well dug, and many were very willing to do so but could not get a loan. Too often the well was dug but none of the auxiliary equipment was provided and neither was instruction on its use. As one villager said, 'The drilling crew came. They made a well. They went away. We know nothing else.'[10] Munkman concluded, in sorrow and anger:

> This is a tragedy of good intentions. The virtually complete sterility of this investment is serious but the human tragedy of the farmers is far more serious. This summer these regions should be blossoming with new crops. This year family incomes should have risen from two hundred dollars a year to one thousand dollars. That they have failed to do so is due to bad administration on the part of the American Mission and the Greek government.[11]

Other schemes to develop agriculture were largely the responsibility of the Greek government's Mechanical Cultivation Services (MCS). Munkman had high praise for the MCS, describing it as a formidable organisation and the spearhead of the Greek drive for increased productivity. The MCS was responsible for the use of tractors and bulldozers and the tools needed to maintain them, financed by $17 million of Marshall Aid, and for the building by 1955 of 6,000 miles of roads to bring the farmers' produce to market. However, the MCS was bedevilled by the practical problems of machines that broke down, when an enterprising Greek mechanic would make a substitute for a broken part which could lead to the wreckage of a $10,000 machine. The MCS was also hampered by the tightening squeeze on credit. Expansion of credit, it was maintained, would lead to inflation. Munkman thought this argument ridiculous, because the credit would be used to produce more goods and this would have the opposite effect of bringing prices down.

The problems of Greek industry were even more intractable than those of agriculture. Industry employed only 300,000 people, less than 5 per cent of the population, and consisted of small units, usually owned and managed by the proprietor and his family, and employing on average two and a half people. The industries with the largest total workforce were textiles, food and drinks, and clothes and footwear.

Electrical power was essential to industry, and this was uncoordinated. The Athens–Piraeus Electric Company had a capacity of 130,000 kilowatts, while outside Athens there were many small independent plants, some AC and some DC, with a combined capacity of 80,000 kilowatts. Austria, for example, had at this time over ten times as much electricity per head of the population as Greece. Virtually all Greek power generation depended on imported fuel.

Marshall Aid funds of some $120 million were used to establish generating plant supplying most of Greece. Hydroelectricity was generated by new stations at Édhessa in Macedonia, near Árta in western Greece, and near Olympia in the Peloponnese, and local lignite powered a plant on Évvia. Their total capacity was 180,000 kilowatts, almost doubling Greece's previous electrical supply, and none required the problematic import of foreign fuel.

Industry also needed transport by road or rail to take goods to internal markets or to ports. Roads, and especially bridges, had been extensively wrecked during the war by occupation and resistance forces, and further damage was done by the Communists during the civil war. Marshall Aid provided $44 million for road reconstruction, with impressive results. By 1951 the total length of Greek roads was almost double what it had been before the war, with minor local roads showing the most spectacular increase.

The development of rail is a less happy story, though $105 million of Marshall Aid was invested, over double the amount for roads. Wartime destruction of railways was even worse than on roads, and in 1948, compared with pre-war, only two-thirds of track was operating with a fifth of the rolling stock. To add to the difficulties, the Greek railway system was run by six different organisations, five of them state owned and one, the short Athens–Piraeus link, in private hands. Track was of different gauges, and all but one of these lines ran at a loss.

The rail programme had its successes. Bridges, tunnels and embankments were repaired and track replaced with a gauge compatible with other lines. Diesel engines replaced steam engines, one of which with its tall funnel reminded Munkman of Stephenson's *Rocket*. However, two of the main problems remained – costs and over-manning. Co-operative groups of workers, effectively local labour unions, had a legal right to charge what they liked for loading and unloading rail freight, and resisted any attempt to reduce the workforce. As a result, by the mid-1950s the Greek railway system was losing $20 million a year. The improvements had led to a marked increase in passenger traffic, but freight carried by rail, which now had to compete with a better road system, was still below the pre-war figure.

The question remains of whether help to industry, in particular better power supply and better transport, actually increased industrial production. The answer is mixed. By 1950 total industrial production was no greater than in 1939. Some sectors were up, notably cigarettes and electrical goods, and some were down, especially clothing and footwear. Five years later the picture was brighter, with the total figure up by 50 per cent compared with 1939, and a big increase in production of building materials reflecting the housing demand of the growing population. However, these successes did little to increase job opportunities because improved practices meant that production could be increased with the same number of workers. They also did little to help Greece's balance of trade since, in manufactured goods, the value of imports remained ten times that of exports.

Munkman was sometimes gloomy about what had been achieved. He estimated that only 5 to 10 per cent of the aid had been used effectively and wrote that 'the four years have been a period of unrelieved depression to interested American Mission personnel and to Greek government officials.'[12] He had many suggestions for improving aid administration. For any new installation, plans and funds for instruction on use and for maintenance must be included, as otherwise the new construction would be misused, deteriorate or simply lie idle. There should be publicity to show that the aid came from a friendly nation and not from the government, which among Greeks was widely distrusted. However, publicity was not an easy matter in Greece: a village might have only one radio, promotional films could only be seen in towns and anyway were not produced until 1950, and Greek television was still a decade away.

Munkman's most passionately argued proposal was that aid funds should be committed not for a year at a time but for at least three years. Under the existing system Congress voted the funds for aid in July, the amounts for each country were not known until September, several months of detailed planning inevitably followed, and there was a rush to spend the year's allocation before the end of May, when it would lapse. There was also the continuing uncertainty over whether Congress would vote any funds at all and the threat that aid might simply cease.

Proffering some aid this year, perhaps some next year, but threatening all the time a definite cut-off, is the height of stupidity [...] To hold a cup of water to the lips of a thirsting man, and to snatch it away after one sip, is torture, not help.[13]

Munkman accepted that no nation could be expected to sign a blank cheque to benefit another, but he believed that international aid programmes were just as essential as national welfare. There would be failures: there was no training scheme for aid administrators so they had to learn from experience, and experience inevitably involved mistakes. In a final judgement he wrote:

I would like to close this book with what I think to be the fairest view of the Aid Program. Since 1945, the American people have faced a responsibility and carried a burden which has been exceedingly heavy. The fact that the burden and responsibility have been faced to the utmost of their ability is itself a great achievement.[14]

It is probably safe to say that the Marshall Plan is generally regarded as an act of generosity, and as playing an important if not vital role in reviving the economies of Europe. However, it is equally safe to say that there are as many views on the wisdom, altruism and effectiveness of this US aid as there are historians who have written about it.

Greg Behrman acknowledges the ways in which the Marshall Plan served America's interests, but for him it was primarily, as his book's title says, 'The most noble adventure'. Alan Bullock's judgement is similar: 'As bold and imaginative idea as any in European history'.[15] However, Alan Milward, who excludes Greece from consideration, maintains that US aid to Western Europe was largely unnecessary, as those countries would have recovered economically without it.

For Lawrence Wittner, who concentrates on Greece, US aid to that country was not only a failure, but it 'helped fasten upon Greece right-wing governments and policies which met badly the needs of an underdeveloped society' and 'accomplished little beyond fortifying the privileged position of the Greek upper class'. It was also in his view wholly self-interested: 'The US government treated Greece much as the Soviet Union treated its Eastern European satellites – as a piece of Cold War real estate.'[16] Jon Kofas, who also focuses on Greece, takes the comparison with Soviet satellites further. He maintains that it would have been better for Greece to have followed a recovery programme like that of Eastern Europe's Communist countries, which entailed 'sweeping land reforms, nationalisation of industry and the financial apparatus, and the monopoly of foreign trade by the State'.[17] However, anyone who has seen abandoned and dilapidated factories in Bulgaria, or in Albania functioning factories with appalling safety standards and shops with virtually nothing to sell but 'Partisani' cigarettes, is unlikely to be enthusiastic about this alternative vision for Greece.

28

The Ending of
the Civil War

At the beginning of 1948 it was far from clear how the civil war would develop and what its eventual outcome would be. The government forces, the Greek National Army, had achieved only minor successes in 1947. In spite of superiority in numbers and substantial American military aid, they were hampered by low morale, over-cautious tactics and, in the view of many, inadequate leadership. The rebel forces, now the Greek Democratic Army, had also had limited success in spite of support from Albania, Yugoslavia and Bulgaria. When they had attacked towns they had held them for only a few days before being forced out again. Their major effort, the attack on Kónitsa on Christmas Day 1947, had ended in failure after a week. It remained to be seen whether their decision to choose conventional warfare over guerrilla operations would help them or not.

In the course of 1948 the Greek National Army launched its attacks on the Communist forces in four phases. The first was Operation Dawn, from April to May, to push the insurgents out of central Greece. The second and third were against their strongholds in the mountains in the far north-west of Greece: Operation Crown, from June to August, against the Grámmos range on the Albanian border and Operation Vítsi, from August to October, against the Vítsi mountains some 50 miles north-east of Grámmos and on the Yugoslav frontier. The last phase was Operation Pigeon, from December 1948 until March 1949, to clear the Peloponnese. If these operations had all been successful the civil war would have ended in 1948 or soon after, as many hoped and some confidently predicted.

Operation Dawn in central Greece began on 15 April 1948, and the National Army had learnt from the previous year's failures.

Time limits for operations and restrictions on troop movements had both been abandoned, and so had the strategy of a sweep from south to north which simply pushed the rebels into their northern strongholds. Now the aim was to concentrate the rebels and then crush them in central Greece, with attacks from all four quarters of the compass and sweeping pursuit to prevent them returning. A further difference was that the commander of one army corps involved was General Tsakalótos, who was to figure prominently in the later stages of the war. The operation ended on 15 May 1948, and though some rebels had escaped to the north it was generally reckoned a success.

The second phase was Operation Crown to take the insurgent strongholds in the Mount Grámmos area, and it began on 20 June 1948. The peak of Mount Grámmos itself is only a few hundred yards from the Albanian border and the mountain's lower slopes are thickly forested while the upper parts are open pasture or rocky ground. The 12,000 or so troops of Márkos, facing 50,000 or more government forces, formed an outer and inner line of defence.

In Operation Crown the government forces were for the first time heavily supported by the Greek air force, which flew nearly 3,500 sorties in the two months of the offensive. One of its weapons was napalm, the incendiary substance whose very name is now shocking after the images of its use in Vietnam. Napalm was effective in driving out the enemy from shelter in the forests into the open, but the Greek government feared forest fires and retaliation in kind, and pilots were afraid of setting fire to themselves in low-altitude attacks. In the face of these objections the use of napalm was limited in 1948 and was temporarily suspended, but was resumed on a large scale in the final battles of 1949.

It was only after seven weeks of fighting that the insurgents' outer line was taken on 7 August, leaving Márkos and his remaining 9,000 troops cornered. It was a situation Márkos had always feared – being forced to defend a position as in a conventional war. But on the night of 20/21 August Márkos broke through the encirclement, allowing some of his troops to slip over the border into Albania with all their artillery and some 3,000 wounded, while the bulk of them moved north to the Vítsi range. 'This was a masterly break-through and withdrawal,' writes one historian, 'and much credit must go to General Markos for organising and conducting it. Markos, the guerrilla fighter, had been successful again.'[1]

Only a week after the end of Operation Crown against Grámmos the government forces on 21 August launched Operation Vítsi against the neighbouring mountain range, where the insurgent numbers had been swelled by those of Márkos from Grámmos. Attack and counter-attack led to no clear-cut success for either side, and in mid-September the operation was ended on the orders of Van Fleet. He declared that the Greek army was 'incapable, due to a thousand and one reasons but mainly one of command' and maintained that 'the overall picture has worsened rather than improved since the Grámmos victory.'[2]

By contrast the last government offensive of 1948, Operation Pigeon in the Peloponnese, was a complete success. It began on 19 December and was led by Tsakalótos, with 11,000 men against 4,000 combatants of the Democratic Army. Tsakalótos' first move was against Avtoámina, responsible for the insurgents' information and supply network as well as security, and on the night of 28/29 December Tsakalótos, on his own initiative, arrested some 4,000 suspected Avtoámina members; it seems that there was one supporter for every combatant. On 3 January aggressive clearing operations began, and by 25 March the Democratic Army in the Peloponnese was virtually eliminated. The victorious Tsakalótos was then transferred to the north.

By the beginning of 1949 the situation of the Greek National Army had greatly improved. The number of men in the armed forces had reached 168,500. Military aid from the United States by now totalled $260 million, over twice as much as for economic aid, and the United States had supplied massive amounts of equipment: 140 aircraft, 3,890 artillery and mortars, 97,000 rifles and 10,000 motor vehicles. The Greek government was receiving $1 million a day from the Truman Doctrine and Marshall Aid combined.

As well as this direct US aid, Van Fleet was making his energetic presence increasingly felt. In April 1948 at his instigation all but one of the army's lieutenant-generals were sacked as incompetent. Also in his view US military advice should not be restricted to divisional level, and advisers must have firsthand experience of the problems confronting soldiers in the field. He therefore went to the front line himself, and during a lull in the fighting on Grámmos in the summer of 1948 he publicly berated the Greek commanders and demanded that they resume the attack. But Van Fleet's belligerence made him unpopular, especially with the new US ambassador Henry Grady, and Truman in response to Grady's complaints wondered whether 'we ought probably to send somebody there [...] who gets along better with the other American officials and who does not just run a one-man show.'[3] Perhaps fortunately Truman did not act on this, and Van Fleet remained in his post.

The National Army was also strengthened by the appointment at the beginning of 1949 of Papágos as commander-in-chief of the armed forces. Papágos, now 59, had been the hero of the campaign against the Italians in 1940–1, had later been captured and had spent two years in a German prison camp. Since his return to Greece he had been close to the royal family but had stayed out of politics.

His appointment was on the initiative of the Greek government of Sophoúlis, supported by Van Fleet and the British military. It had been discussed several times during 1948, but Papágos demanded tough conditions for accepting: complete control of planning, order of battle, appointments and operations over all branches of the services, and no interference by the US and British missions. The Greek government and the allied missions eventually accepted these terms, and Papágos was appointed on 19 January 1949.

While the Greek National Army was being strengthened the Greek Democratic Army was meeting increasing difficulties. It had always been heavily outnumbered and in January 1949 had some 23,000 troops against government forces of 168,500. Recruitment to replace losses was increasingly difficult and was now achieved almost entirely by force.

Also from the beginning of the civil war the insurgents had been heavily dependent upon help from the three northern neighbours, Albania, Yugoslavia and Bulgaria, which provided training, hospitals and a base for the Democratic Army's radio station. Even more important was their supply of military equipment. There is no precise tally of the total, but the scale of it is shown by how much was captured from the Democratic Army. In one engagement in the summer of 1949 the National Army seized artillery (14 pieces), anti-aircraft guns (19), anti-tank guns (7) mortars (192) and machine guns (637). It was also estimated that in the course of the civil war the Democratic Army had been supplied with over 51,000 mines to be planted under roads, causing 3,640 explosions. As early as June 1948 the first UNSCOB report confirmed, if cautiously, that the Democratic Army was being supplied from abroad:

No definite conclusions can be drawn as to the origin of armament from the evidence. The quantity of mortar bombs and mines being used by the guerrillas in this remote mountain zone, however, leads to a strong presumption that the source of origin lies outside Greece.[4]

The three northern neighbours were providing sanctuary as well as armament. In October 1947 UNSCOB had been set up both to investigate cross-border incidents and to try to resolve them. All three countries to the north banned UNSCOB from entering their territories, so UNSCOB was limited to observing from the Greek side of the frontiers. What UNSCOB was actually able to record was described by one of its members, Michael Ward, who spent time on all three of the northern frontiers.

Ward reported that from a village on the Albanian border and not far from the coast 17 rebels had abducted seven men as forced recruits and taken them into Albania. The rest of the inhabitants fled to the nearby port hoping to get to Corfu, where Ward saw them: 'A pitiful sight; throngs of villagers, mostly women and children, surrounded by their chattels, chickens and goats, jostling for a place on the waiting caiques.'[5]

Ward also saw many instances of rifle and machine-gun fire across the Yugoslav border, which the government forces were barred from returning. This was clearly with the connivance of the Yugoslavs. Rebels were seen openly crossing the line and being cordially greeted at the Yugoslav guard post. Ward was particularly appalled by rebels' indiscriminate use of foreign-supplied mines and witnessed what happened to one peasant cart:

> With a frightening detonation the cart was splintered to matchwood, the two peasant women were killed instantaneously and the two animals thrown apart with their hind quarters blown away. Not one of us had a pistol to put the poor beasts out of their misery.[6]

Ward's evidence and that of other UNSCOB observers left no doubt of rebel support from Greece's northern neighbours.

The second part of UNSCOB's remit was to try to resolve border incidents, but these attempts proved farcical. Contact could be made only by an interpreter shouting across the frontier. On Ward's first attempt the Yugoslav sentry 20 yards away said, 'Go away. I'm not allowed to talk to you,' and an officer later appeared to confirm the message. On the Bulgarian frontier the UNSCOB group was told that the nearest officer was miles away and they must wait for three hours. After four hours they were told that the awaited officer was away on leave and nobody else was competent to engage in parleys. Ward had always believed that 'the policy of mediation was naive, unworkable and unrealistic', and so it had proved.[7]

The vital support for the Democratic Army from its Communist neighbours began to crumble with the establishment in September 1947 of the Cominform. This was the successor to the Comintern, which had been dissolved four years earlier. The Cominform, despite its innocuous label as simply an information bureau, was designed like its predecessor to co-ordinate the activities of Communists internationally under Russian direction. There were nine members: Russia, the six Soviet satellites including Yugoslavia, plus France and Italy, but significantly excluding Greece. Its first location was in Belgrade.

However, Yugoslavia's Prime Minister Tito became increasingly resistant to subordinating Yugoslav national interests to Russian international policy, declaring in April 1948 'No matter how much each of us loves the land of Socialism, the USSR, he can in no case love his country less.'[8] In June 1948 a Cominform conference which Tito refused to attend expelled Yugoslavia, and Tito saw no Yugoslav national interest in continued support for the Greek Communists. Yugoslav aid to the Greek Communists did not stop immediately, but by May 1949 UNSCOB reported that it was significantly reduced, and by July as the civil war reached its climax the Yugoslav border was closed to the Democratic Army.

Divisions were also emerging in the leadership of the Greek Communists. In November 1948 Márkos argued for a return to 'intensive, guerrilla-type activity [...] to cause the Americans and the Monarcho-Fascists a continuous military and economic haemorrhage [and] a deepening political instability.'[9] This was furiously resisted by Zachariádhis, and the Communist Party passed a vote of no confidence in Márkos. Also there is evidence that after Tito split from the Cominform Márkos supported Yugoslavia and Zachariádhis the Cominform members Bulgaria and Albania. In January 1949 Márkos was removed, ostensibly on health grounds, from all his posts – as commander-in-chief, prime minister and war minister in the Provisional Democratic Government, and as member of the Politburo. The commander-in-chief role went to a figurehead, but Zachariádhis was now effectively in control of the Democratic Army.

The Tito–Cominform split also led to a shift in Greek Communist policy which was ultimately damaging to the Democratic Army. Bulgarian backing was now vital to the Democratic Army, and Bulgaria demanded an independent Macedonian state. At the end of January 1949 the Greek Communists re-adopted the policy of support for an autonomous Macedonia, involving a cession of Greek territory, which had always been anathema to almost all Greeks.

Thus by early 1949 the Greek Communist forces seemed to be in total disarray. The operations of 1948 had gone against them, and they had been eliminated from the Peloponnese. Support from Yugoslavia had virtually ceased. Their leaders were divided over strategy, and Márkos, commander-in-chief since 1946, had been removed. Popular support was further eroded by their return to championing an independent Macedonia. Against increasingly effective government forces it looked as if the Communists were almost finished.

However, the appearance was deceptive. Between November 1948 and February 1949 the Democratic Army attacked major towns and held them, usually for only a few days but sometimes for several weeks. Most of these towns were in the far north-west of Greece where the Communists were strongest – Grevená, Kastoriá, Édhessa and Náoussa. But two were further south in central Greece, an area from which Operation Dawn of the previous spring had been meant to clear them. One attack was on Kardhítsa, due west of Vólos, and the town was held for three days. The second was on Karpenísi, a further 40 miles south and was held for three weeks from 19 January to 9 February 1949, one of the longest town seizures of the whole civil war.

The Communist forces at both Kardhítsa and Karpenísi were led by Kóstas Karayeóryis, who had experience in the resistance during the occupation and since 1944 had been editor of the Communist paper *Rizospástis*. He proved himself an effective military commander, eventually losing Karpenísi only to government forces under Tsakalótos. There is an account of life at this time in the Democratic Army by one of its field officers, Mítsos Katsís. He had served in ELAS during the occupation, and in July 1946, after a spell of imprisonment, he joined the Communist forces that were to become the Democratic Army.

Katsís provides an insight into how the insurgents' morale was maintained. There were encouraging addresses from their immediate officers before they attacked a town: 'Beloved fellow fighters! We know the serious task that has been given us for this evening. I promise you that the town will burn, and that with the soldiers of this platoon I will open a breach in its defences.' Sometimes, however, Katsís would resist an unrealistic order to advance with his squad: 'I was furious, I became a wild beast, and my hair stood up like the quills of a porcupine.' Katsís eventually went forward after a friend appealed to his sense of honour, his *philótimo*. Another way of keeping up morale was to exaggerate minor achievements. Náoussa for example was seized in January 1949 and held for five weeks before the insurgents were driven out, a limited success but hardly the great victory claimed by Katsís.[10]

Shortly before the attack on Náoussa, Katsis was wounded, shot by a machine-gun bullet which entered at one of his shoulder blades and lodged above the other. He was treated at a field hospital, for which he had high praise, and then taken with other wounded to the Yugoslav border. There they were refused entry, and reacted furiously: 'Tito has joined the imperialist camp. Yugoslavia's policy is treachery.'[11] They were eventually let in, and taken to hospital in Skopje where Katsis' bullet was removed, but they were not allowed to return to Greece. It was a taste of the realities of the Democratic Army's crumbling position.

In spite of limited successes by the Communist forces and their continuing commitment to the struggle, they were clearly weakening. They recognised this by making peace offers, one in January 1949 and a second in August. Both were firmly rejected by the Greek government, which was well aware, after the failure of the Varkíza peace agreement of 1945, that a truce would simply allow the Communists to resume the war when it suited them. There had to be total victory, and the government planned this for 1949.

The plan was in four phases. The first was Operation Rocket, to complete the clearance of central Greece, and this was to be followed by Operation Torch A, B and C. Torch A was a diversionary attack in the Mount Grámmos area to draw attention away from the Mount Vítsi area which was the objective of Torch B. Torch C was the final assault on Grámmos.

Operation Rocket, to drive the insurgents out of central Greece, began on 25 April 1949 and was successfully completed by the end of July. Torch A, the divisionary attack on Grámmos under the command of Tsakalótos, began on 5 August and lasted a week. It succeeded in capturing some of the heights in the Grámmos area, cutting the insurgents' link on Greek territory between Grámmos and Vítsi, though the more difficult route through Albania remained open.

Torch B, the assault on Vítsi, began with an air and artillery bombardment at 5 a.m. on 10 August. Four days later the insurgents were beginning a retreat into Albania, and at least 2,000 were able to return from Albania to Grámmos. About 1,000 crossed into Yugoslavia where, as Katsís had found, they were no longer welcome but were disarmed and interned. The Democratic Army had suffered heavy casualties in Torch B: well over 1,000 had been killed and over 600 captured, as well as a mass of equipment lost.

Torch C, the final assault on Mount Grámmos, began on the night of 24/25 August. Confident of success, both Van Fleet and King Paul came to the front line. Some 7,000–8,000 insurgents were outnumbered at least ten to one by government forces commanded by Vendíris, the victor at Kónitsa 18 months earlier. By 30 August all Democratic Army positions on and around Mount Grámmos had been captured. Their remaining troops fled into Albania, but by now they were not welcome there either and were disarmed and detained. The government victory was complete. On 16 October the Greek Communists announced their decision 'to discontinue the armed struggle for the time being', but defiant to the end warned that 'the monarcho-fascists would be mistaken if they think that the struggle has ended.'[12]

Defiance could not disguise the fact of failure and there were many obvious reasons for the Democratic Army's defeat. It was massively outnumbered, its opponent was much better and more consistently supplied, it lost support and sanctuary from its northern neighbours, and its leadership was divided. Perhaps the most damaging effect of that division was the decision to move to conventional warfare, successfully championed by Zachariádhis against Márkos' arguments for continuing guerrilla warfare. Theorists of insurgency identify three essential stages if it is to succeed: first guerrilla raiding, second more substantial action to establish territory and resources, and finally a full-scale military offensive. In effect Zachariádhis was arguing for an immediate move from the first stage to the last, while Márkos held that they were not ready to move out of the first guerrilla stage. Márkos was right, as events proved, but Zachariádhis was also in a sense correct in recognising that the move to the third stage was essential for victory.

A more difficult question to answer is how, in the face of the odds against them, the Democratic Army troops held out for so long. In part this was due to the ruthlessness of their officers, described by

Ward as 'a small fanatical nucleus driving a mass of press-ganged villagers to do its bidding under conditions of rigid discipline and internal terrorism'.[13] There was also fear of what would happen to them if they fell into government hands. Some continued to believe in the Communist cause, which was the only political programme which held out the promise of social change and improvement of the lot of ordinary citizens. Perhaps the underlying reason for defiance to the end was the Greek characteristic of *philótimo*, that combination of honour, pride and self-belief which meant that, whatever the circumstances and whatever the rights and wrongs, no Greek would ever allow himself to be bested by another Greek.

Epilogue

The costs of the civil war between 1945 and 1949 were appalling. In the Communist Democratic Army over 24,000 had lost their lives, and over 16,000 in the government forces, as well as over 5,000 civilians executed by Communist troops or killed by mines. Thousands more were wounded or missing.

The grim catalogue continues. Some 62,000 homes and farm buildings had been ruined, rail and road bridges had been destroyed, and civilian and military vehicles wrecked. The combined effect of the civil war and the earlier occupation was to leave a quarter of all buildings damaged, a quarter of all cultivated land put out of production and a third of the population surviving on public assistance. From these figures one might get a picture of Greece as a country totally war-ravaged and desolate, but what was equally remarkable was how much had survived

A number of books had been published by the early 1940s describing Greece and the Greeks before the war. Lawrence Durrell in *Prospero's Cell* had written a delightful account of his life in 1930s Corfu. Dilys Powell, in *The Traveller's Journey is Done*, described her years in the 1930s with her archaeologist husband Humfry Payne at an ancient site on the Gulf of Corinth. Payne died tragically young at 34, and the book was a tribute to the Greeks as well as to him. An altogether different work was Henry Miller's *The Colossus of Maroussi*. This was mainly a portrait of the rumbustious man of letters Georgios Katsímbalis, the Colossus of the title, spiced with Miller's own self-promotion and rants against harmless people who offended him. Each of these books in its own way presented a glowing picture of pre-war Greece. This tradition was followed by Patrick Leigh Fermor, who cast his own golden glow over postwar Greece, and perhaps best showed how much of the past Elysium had remained.

Leigh Fermor was born in London in February 1915 and was educated in England, twice being expelled from school. He did not like England and found English life 'slightly provincial and a crashing bore', and 'everything attractive or exciting seemed to be foreign'.[1]

His wartime exploits in Crete, especially the kidnapping of General Kreipe, became legendary. At the end of the war he met Joan Monsell and though five years later she was ready to marry, he was not. They were eventually married in 1969. To friends who asked 'Why suddenly now?' he replied that he disapproved of long engagements.

His postwar years were spent on a long intermittent odyssey to different parts of the world which inspired books or articles. He returned many times to Crete and other parts of Greece, to Cyprus, and to the Caribbean, France, Italy and the Himalayas. He was an adventurer sexually as well as geographically, sometimes in brothels but more often with happily willing partners.

In 1964 he and Joan bought a plot of land on a hill-top above the village of Kardhamíli, on the west coast of the central prong of the southern Peloponnese. They built a house there which was their home for the rest of their lives, and it was there that he wrote his later books. For the reader his books have the easy flow of genial spontaneity, but for the writer the process was laborious and painstaking, and his manuscripts, written on a variety of sheets of paper, sometimes on both sides, are a tangle of erasions, corrections, and insertions circled and arrowed. The writing consequently went very slowly, to the exasperation of his publisher John Murray, as deadlines for text delivery came and went. Both his first book on Greece, *Mani*, and his second, *Roumeli*, took years to write. His friend the poet Georgios Seféris accused him of 'doing a Penelope' and determinedly never finishing the tapestry on which he was working.

His Greek friends also included Georgios Katsímbalis, but there were many others from his time in Crete, notably the Cretan runner George Psichoundhákis whose book Leigh Fermor translated and helped to get published. His English friends included many fellow writers, among them Henry Miller, Lawrence Durrell and Xan Fielding, and ranged from the raffish, like Dylan Thomas in postwar London, to the distinguished, such as Lady Diana Cooper and Debbo, Duchess of Devonshire. It seems that all his friends delighted in his company, and even Freya Stark, a stern critic of male chauvinism, said 'I do like him. He is the genuine buccaneer.'[2]

Leigh Fermor's first book on Greece, *Mani* is an account of a 1951 journey to the Mani region in the far south of the Peloponnese, and it was published seven years later. He travelled partly by caique and partly on foot, with Joan and a group of friends, but mainly describes his experiences as those of a solitary traveller.

His descriptions of the scenery are lyrical.

The Taygetus mountains shot into the sky in a palisade which looked as sheer and unscalable as the Himalayas. Up the flank of this great barrier a road climbed, scaling it in mile-long sweeps and acute angles like a collapsible ruler; up, up, until it vanished among peaks whose paler rocks gave a half-convincing illusion of eternal snow.

Dawn brought a special magic to the mountains:

Laying soft shadows along their flanks, dawn turns the ashen slag to champagne-colour and apricot and lilac and unfolds the dark branching torrent beds and pins them espalierwise across the ranges until they shrink and vanish under the climbing sun, waiting for dusk once more to expand and subdue them.

The evening light too had its own effect:

Sunbeams streamed obliquely through the mountain rifts, filling with green and gold and gentle shades the swellings and the subsidences of hollow Lacedaemon. The sauntering loops of the Eurotas had shrunk now to a thread whose track was marked by oleanders opening cool green sheaves of spiked leaves and pretty flowers of white and pink paper over little more than the memory of water.[3]

He described the new and the old with equal interest. One of the caiques was new, or at least newly decorated:

Everything was as bright as a pin. There was silver paint on the cleats and along the bows, touches of grass green, ox-blood and gilding in the swirl of carved wooden foliage from which the bowsprit sprang. The mast was painted in the blue and white Greek colours in a bold barber's pole spiral for a third of its height.[4]

Some of the small churches were pristine, others abandoned and derelict. A striking feature of the Mani was the conglomeration of huge towers, shown in one of Joan's photographs, which were built for safety in the days when the vendetta was an ever-present threat.

Each village was a long solid sheaf of towers. There were scores of them climbing into the sky in a rustic metropolis, each tower seeming to vie with the others in attaining a more preposterous height: a vision as bewildering as the distant skyline of Manhattan. A hundred sombre towers, each cluster thrust aloft on a coil of terraces, sailed up into the morning to break the parallel slanting rays of the sun, every campanile shedding a long blade of shadow along the sun's advance.[5]

Leigh Fermor sometimes met the villagers en masse, at celebrations of a wedding, a baptism or a name-day, and there are also vivid portraits of individual Greeks. There was the girl 'carrying a lamb slung over her shoulders and round her nape, fore and hind feet held in either hand in the manner of many archaic statues.' A man was making a fish trap, feeding the string between his big toe and its neighbour 'as the airy sphere turned and shifted in his skilful brown fingers with a dazzling interplay of symmetrical parabolas'. And under a sign reading 'Death to all Traitors', a relic of the war years, two old women sat croaking together: 'There was something baleful about these two black-coiffed figures under the snarl of the slogan: they looked implacable and fate-spinning crones.'[6]

Leigh Fermor saw two sides to the Greek character, a distinction which he elaborated in his later book *Roumeli*. One was the Romios, the Greek of the centuries of Turkish rule, and was portrayed in the traditional puppet and shadow plays called *Karagiósis*. These were something like Punch and Judy shows, and there were over 100 of them. The eponymous anti-hero, Leigh Fermor wrote, is

> the epitome of the poverty-stricken and downtrodden subject of the Turks. He is ragged, barefoot, illiterate, nimble and versatile, bold and timid by turns, soon dashed but swift to recover. He is deeply likeable, a comic David surrounded by Goliaths. A small man pitched against intolerable odds.[7]

The Romios was one aspect of the Greek character and the other was the nobler Hellene element deriving from Ancient Greece. Leigh Fermor believed that all Greeks were an amalgam of both. In hospitality the Hellene was the same as in Homer's *Odyssey*.

> There is still the same unquestioning acceptance, the attention to the stranger's needs before even finding out his name: the solicitous plying of wine and food, the exchange of identities and autobiographies; the entreaties to stay as long as the stranger wishes, and finally, at his

departure the bestowal of gifts, even if these are only a pocketful of walnuts or apples, a carnation or a bunch of basil; and the care with which he is directed on his way, accompanied some distance, and wished godspeed [...] This is based on a genuine and deep-seated kindness, the feeling of pity and charity toward a stranger who is far from his home.[8]

His own response was equally warm: 'This country, even after years of familiarity, often calls forth these sudden feelings of naive and Marvellian gratitude: What wondrous life is this I lead?'[9]

Over all were the Greek sky and the special light it shed.

The sky is higher and lighter and surrounds one closer and stretches further into space than anywhere else in the world. It is neither daunting nor belittling but hospitable and welcoming to man and as much his element as the earth. The light also performs several simultaneous and contradictory acts, it chisels and sharpens everything so that the most fluid curve can be broken up at once, by a shift of focus, into an infinity of angles; it acts like an X-ray, giving mineral and tree and masonry an air of transparence; and it sprinkles the smoothest and most vitreous surface with a thin layer of pollen like the damask on a moth's wing.[10]

Who, reading these words, could fail to feel an urgent longing to visit such an enchanted land?

The main theme of the present book has been the story of Greece and the Greeks during ten years of war, but a subsidiary theme has been the relations between the Greeks and the British. These were often warmly appreciative and affectionate on both sides. The Greeks and especially the Cretans gave unstinting help and protection to British escapers and SOE agents. In return, one of the British who served in Crete said that they all considered Crete as their second country and Cretans as their brothers. Churchill's loyalty and commitment to Greece as an ally, though maybe sometimes ill-judged, was undoubtedly warm-hearted and generous. But there were tensions too. Myers was constantly frustrated in his efforts to bring the resistance groups together. After liberation the British protested against the Greek government's illiberal laws and became fed up with constant Greek demands for money. Even David Wallace, who spent so much of his short adult life serving the Greeks, said in the end that the Greek people were not capable of being saved from themselves nor for themselves worth it. Ernest Bevin was said at one point to be overcome by a revulsion against all things Greek, though it is significant that the revulsion was only temporary.

In spite of these rifts the bond between British and Greeks remained strong, a bond going back to Byron and to Admiral Codrington the victor of Navarino, reinforced by many wartime experiences and given fresh life by twentieth-century writers. Perhaps Geoffrey Chandler summed up the relationship best. He too could be irritated by Greek demands from the British: 'Many people looked to us with the attitude of a man clinging to a raft and disappointed that it was not a luxury liner.' But he concluded:

It was as though to be wedded to a wife of infinite beauty and charm who would drive you to despair and thoughts of divorce and at the last moment win you back each time by some display of her innate qualities.[11]

Chronology

1936   *August*, Metaxás prime minister, until 1941
1939   *7 April*, Italy invades Albania
        22 May, Pact of Steel between Italy and Germany
1940   *28 October*, Metaxás' 'Ochi' to Italy, followed by Italian invasion of
           Greece
        22 November, Greeks take Koritsa in Albania
1941   *6 April*, German invasion of Yugoslavia and Greece
        24–9 April, Allied forces leave Greek mainland
        20 May, German invasion of Crete
        30 May, two Greeks remove swastika from Akropolis
        1 June, last Allied forces leave Crete
        9 October, first SOE agents to Crete
        Winter 1941/42, starvation in Athens
1942   *20 January*, Wannsee Conference adopts 'final solution' of Jewish
           question
        October, Neubacher's attempt to stabilise Greek currency
        25 November, demolition of Gorgopótamos railway bridge
1943   *March*, deportation of Salonika Jews begins
        March, first mutiny of Greek troops in Egypt; King George moves to
           Cairo
        14 March, 'First Military Agreement' between resistance groups
        29 June, Security Battalions established
        14 July, David Wallace to Greece as Eden's envoy
        25 July, Mussolini deposed
        9 August to 16 September, Cairo Conference of resistance groups
        9 September, Italian armistice
        16 September, Italian General Carta smuggled out of Crete
        9 October, ELAS attacks on EDES begin
1944   *29 February*, Pláka Agreement between ELAS and EDES
        26 March, Communist PEEA provisional government formed
        April, second mutiny of Greek troops in Egypt
        25 April, General Kreipe kidnapped and removed from Crete
        26 April, Papandhréou appointed prime minister of Greek
           government in Cairo
        20 May, Lebanon Charter plans post-liberation Greece

26 September, Caserta Conference puts all resistance groups under
  control of Greek government and British
9 October, Percentages Agreement between Churchill and Stalin
18 October, Greek government returns to Athens
November, Waley attempts to reform Greek currency
3 December, demonstration in Síntagma Square
4 December, battle for Athens, until 15 January 1945
25 December, Churchill to Athens

1945 Year of five successive Greek prime ministers
3 January, Dhamaskinós appointed regent
12 February, Varkíza Agreement on demobilisation of ELAS
23 May, last Germans on Crete surrender
30 May, Zachariádhis returns to Greece to lead Communists
June, Varvaréssos attempts to reform Greek economy

1946 *24 January,* London Plan ends Greek hyperinflation
22 February, Kennan sends Long Telegram from Moscow
31 March, first Greek elections for ten years, won by royalists
1 September, plebiscite votes for return of King George
26 October, Communist Democratic Army formed as conventional
  army under Márkos Vaphiádhis

1947 *12 March,* announcement of Truman Doctrine
1 April, King George of Greece dies, succeeded by his brother Paul
5 June, Marshall proposes aid to Europe
5 July, Queen Frederica announces establishment of *pedhópolis*
September, KKE decision to fight conventional, not guerrilla, war
24 December, PEEA proclaimed as rival government of Greece
25 December–4 January 1948, Communist Democratic Army fails to
  take Kónitsa
31 December, JUSMAPG established in Greece

1948 *February,* Van Fleet to Greece as head of JUSMAPG
3 April, Marshall Aid established
June, Tito expelled from Cominform

1949 *January,* Papágos appointed commander of Greek National Army
January, Márkos Vaphiádhis dismissed as commander of
  Democratic Army
24–5 August, final attack on Democratic Army in Mount Grámmos
  area
16 October, Communists announce that struggle is discontinued

Notes

Prologue (pp. 1–2)

Of the many sources for this period, two that provide illuminating details are Winston Churchill, *The Second World War*, vol. 1 ; and Denis Mack Smith, *Mussolini's Roman Empire*.

1 Churchill, vol. 1, p. 169.
2 Ibid., p. 225.
3 Ibid., p. 261.
4 Ibid., p. 264.
5 Mack Smith, p. 59.

Chapter 1: The Albanian Gateway to Greece (pp. 3–9)

The main sources for this chapter are Denis Mack Smith, *Mussolini's Roman Empire*; Jason Tomes, *King Zog*; and Mario Cervi, *The Hollow Legions*.

1 Tomes, p. 101.
2 Ibid., p. 214.
3 Ibid., p. 219.
4 Ibid., p. 230.
5 Mack Smith, p. 153.
6 Ibid., p. 154.
7 Cervi, pp. 4–5.
8 Ibid., p. xii.
9 Ibid., pp. 311–20.
10 Ibid., p. 315. The Koritsa attack is dramatised in Louis de Bernières, *Captain Corelli's Mandolin*, ch. 10.
11 Cervi, p. 116.
12 P.J. Vatikiotis, *Popular Autocracy in Greece 1936–41*, p. 177.
13 G. Vláchos, *Politiká Árthra (Political Articles)*, p. 91.

Chapter 2: Mussolini's War on Greece (pp. 10–20)

The main source is Mario Cervi, *The Hollow Legions*. Cervi served in the Italian army during the Greek–Italian war. When Italy changed sides in 1943 and he was on the run from the Germans, he was sheltered by a Greek couple and met their daughter. Reader, he married her. His detailed account of 1940–1 sympathises with the sufferings of both sides. Other sources are Churchill, *The Second World War*, vols 2 and 3; C. Hadjipateras and M. Fafalios (eds), *Greece 1940–41 Eyewitnessed*; J.L. Hondros, *Occupation and Resistance*; and G. Vláchos, *Politiká Árthra (Political Articles)*.

1   Cervi, p. 25.
2   Ibid., pp. 29–33.
3   Ibid., p. 110.
4   Ibid., p. 139.
5   Vláchos, p. 94.
6   Hadjipateras and Fafalios (eds), *Greece 1940–41 Eyewitnessed*, p. 108.
7   Cervi, p. 125.
8   Ibid., p. 186.
9   Ibid., p. 245.
10 Hadjipateras and Fafalios (eds), *Greece 1940–41 Eyewitnessed*, p. 122.
11 Cervi, p. 180.
12 Ibid., p. 194.
13 Hadjipateras and Fafalios (eds), *Greece 1940–41 Eyewitnessed*, pp. 99–100, 121.
14 Cervi, p. 187.
15 Ibid., pp. 199–200, 208.
16 Ibid., p. 233.
17 Ibid., p. 235.
18 Ibid., p. 236.
19 Churchill, vol. 2, p. 423.
20 Ibid., p. 427.
21 Ibid., vol. 3, p. 133.
22 Vláchos, pp. 104–9.

Chapter 3: The German Invasion (pp. 21–32)

Churchill, *The Second World War*, vol. 3, is essential, but see David Reynolds, *In Command of History* for Churchill passages to be read with caution. Christopher Buckley, *Greece and Crete 1941* gives a detailed account of the campaign. See also Hadjipateras and Fafalios (eds), *Greece 1940–41 Eyewitnessed*, and John Keegan, *The Second World War*. Judgements on whether British intervention was justified are in B. Liddell Hart, *History of the Second World War*; Cyril Falls, *The Second World War*; Matthew Willingham, *Perilous Commitments*; and Anthony Beevor, *Crete*.

1   Churchill, vol. 3, p. 146.
2   Keegan, *The Second World War*, p. 123.
3   Beevor, *Crete*, p. 31.
4   Churchill, vol. 2, p. 431.

5 Buckley, p. 42.
6 Hadjipateras and Fafalios (eds), *Greece 1940–41 Eyewitnessed*, pp. 224–6.
7 Ibid., p. 178.
8 Buckley, p. 62.
9 Churchill, vol. 3, p. 186.
10 Buckley, pp. 63, 73, 55.
11 Ibid., p. 104.
12 Falls, p. 91.
13 Different but reasonably consistent figures for estimated losses are in Buckley, pp. 152–3; Churchill, vol. 3, pp. 188–9 (both writing in the late 1940s); and Willingham, p. 96 (2005). Among the captured British was Clive Dunn, later the much-loved actor in *Dad's Army*.
14 Reynolds, pp. 234, 235.
15 Liddell Hart, pp. 131–4, and see Beevor, *Crete*, p. 55 for other views.
16 Reynolds, p. 245.
17 Falls, p. 78.
18 Churchill, vol. 3, p. 190.

Chapter 4: The Battle for Crete (pp. 33–46)

The main sources are Churchill, Buckley, Beevor, *Crete*, and Willingham as for chapter 3, plus Alan Clark, *The Fall of Crete* and John Keegan, *Intelligence in War*. Revealing biographies are Paul Freyberg's biography of his father, *Bernard Freyberg, VC*, and Ronald Lewin, *The Chief, Field Marshal Lord Wavell*.

1 Churchill, vol. 3, pp. 67, 184.
2 Lewin, p. 131.
3 Queen Frederica, *A Measure of Understanding*, p. 44.
4 Buckley, p. 172.
5 Clark, p. 46.
6 Churchill, vol. 3, p. 217.
7 Freyberg, p. 271.
8 Buckley, pp. 170–1, and compare Beevor, *Crete*, p. 346.
9 Beevor, *Crete*, pp. 351–2.
10 Freyberg, p. 285.
11 Clark, p. 31.
12 Ibid., p. 54.
13 Hadjipateras and Fafalios (eds), *Crete 1941 Eyewitnessed*, pp. 75–6.
14 Clark, p. 65.
15 Freyberg, p. 301.
16 Buckley, pp. 236–7.
17 Ibid., p. 240.
18 Ibid., p. 265.
19 Clark, p. 123.

20   Ibid., p. 169.
21   Buckley, p. 297.
22   Ibid., p. 295.
23   Freyberg, p. 332.
24   Buckley, pp. 326–7
25   Keegan, *Intelligence in War*, pp. 207–8.
26   Lewin p. 127.
27   Freyberg, pp. 266–7.

Chapter 5: The Occupation Begins (pp. 47–52)

Many examples of Greek experience of the occupation are in the two volumes of C. Hadjipateras and M. Fafalios (eds), *Martiríes*. For a factual account see J.L. Hondros, *Occupation and Resistance*. For Crete see Clark, Beevor and Willingham as for chapters 3 and 4, and Nikos Kokonas, *The Cretan Resistance 1941–1945*.

1   Tsolákoglou, *Memoirs* (Athens, 1959), quoted in newspaper *Rizospástis*, 8 April 2001.
2   T. Couloumbis (ed.), *Greece in the Twentieth Century*, p. 141.
3   Hondros, p. 61.
4   Cervi, *The Hollow Legions*, p. 306.
5   Hadjipateras and Fafalios (eds), *Martiríes*, vol. 1, p. 22.
6   Ibid., p. 118.
7   Conversation with author and psychiatrist Níkos Kokántzis.
8   Hadjipateras and Fafalios (eds), *Martiríes* , vol. 1, p. 98.
9   Clark, p. 60.
10   Beevor, *Crete*, p. 236.
11   Clark, p. 198.
12   Kokonas, p. 140.

Chapter 6: Hyperinflation and Starvation (pp. 53–63)

Important sources are Michael Palairet, *The Four Ends of the Greek Hyperinflation of 1941–1946*, and Violetta Hionidou, *Famine and Death in Occupied Greece, 1941–1944*. See also R. Clogg (ed.), *Bearing Gifts to Greeks*; J. Iatrides (ed.), *Greece in the 1940s*, pp. 61–80; Hadjipateras and Fafalios (eds), *Martiríes* , vol 1, as for chapter 5; and Mark Mazower, *Inside Hitler's Greece*.

1   Hionidou, p. 92, n. 62.
2   Palairet, p. 32.
3   Ibid., pp. 128–32.
4   Ibid., p. 33.
5   Hionidou, p. 81.

6 Hadjipateras and Fafalios (eds), *Martiríes* , vol. 1, p. 218.
7 Ibid., p. 160.
8 Mazower, *Inside Hitler's Greece,* p. 40.
9 Hadjipateras and Fafalios (eds), *Martiríes* , vol. 1, pp. 182–3.
10 Churchill speech, 20 August 1940, available at www.churchill-society-london.org.uk (accessed 7 November 2015).
11 Clogg (ed.), *Bearing Gifts to Greeks,* p. 45.
12 Ibid., p. 101.
13 Hionidou, p. 142.

Chapter 7: The Emergence of the Communists (pp. 64–72)

The main sources are D.G. Kousoulas, *Revolution and Defeat: The Story of the Greek Communist Party;* and C.M. Woodhouse, *The Struggle for Greece 1941–1949.* Both are well supported by evidence. Neither is sympathetic to the Communists.

1 Kousoulas, p. 4.
2 Ibid., p. 14.
3 Ibid., p. 74.
4 Ibid., p. 7.
5 Ibid., p. 80.
6 Ibid., p. 81.
7 Ibid., pp. 116–7.
8 T. Gallant, *Modern Greece,* p. 157.
9 Kousoulas, p. 126.
10 Ibid., p. 130.
11 Ibid., p. 131.
12 Ibid., pp. 138–9.
13 Ibid., pp. 141–2.
14 Ibid., p. 60.
15 Woodhouse, in Foreword to Kousoulas, p. vi.
16 D. Close, *The Origins of the Greek Civil War,* p. 52.
17 J. Hart, *New Voices in the Nation,* p. 166.
18 R. Clogg (ed.), *Greece 1940–1949: A Documentary History,* p. 86.
19 Woodhouse, *The Struggle for Greece,* p. 20.

Chapter 8: Early Resistance (pp. 73–7)

The accounts of urban resistance are mainly from Hadjipateras and Fafalios (eds), *Martiríes,* vol. 2. See also Hondros, *Occupation and Resistance;* Mazower, *Inside Hitler's Greece;* and Woodhouse, *The Struggle for Greece.*

1 Hadjipateras and Fafalios (eds), *Martiríes,* vol. 2, p. 39.

2 Woodhouse, *The Struggle for Greece*, p. 5.
3 Hondros, p. 106.

Chapter 9: The SOE, the Andártes and Gorgopótamos (pp. 78–84)

The main sources are E. Myers, *Greek Entanglement* and C.M. Woodhouse's autobiography *Something Ventured*. See also A. Ogden, *Sons of Odysseus*.

1 Woodhouse, *Something Ventured*, p. 32.
2 Myers, p. 30.
3 Woodhouse, *Something Ventured*, p. 36.
4 Ibid., p. 41.
5 Myers, p. 69.
6 P. Papastratis, *British Policy Towards Greece During the Second World War*, p. 240, n. 18.
7 Myers, pp. 71–2.
8 Ibid., p. 81.
9 Woodhouse, *Something Ventured*, p. 52.

Chapter 10: Village and City (pp. 85–91)

For the events in the village of Liá, see Nicholas Gage, *Eleni*. See also Nigel Clive, *A Greek Experience 1943–1948*; Nicholas Hammond, *Venture into Greece*; and Mazower, *Inside Hitler's Greece*. C.M. Woodhouse's *Apple of Discord* was published in 1948 when, as he says, many of the facts which later emerged were unknown to him. It gives a young man's personal views, in contrast to his later and more comprehensive *The Struggle for Greece* (1976). For Athens see Hadjipateras and Fafalios (eds), *Martiríes*, vol. 2, and Mary Henderson, *Xenia – A Memoir*.

1 Hondros, in Iatrides (ed.), *Greece in the 1940s*, p. 42.
2 Clive, p. 83.
3 Ibid.
4 Clogg (ed.), *Greece 1940–1949*, p. 118.
5 Woodhouse, *Apple of Discord*, p. 147.
6 Woodhouse, *The Struggle for Greece*, pp. 62–3.
7 Gage, p. 123.
8 Hadjipateras and Fafalios (eds), *Martiríes*, vol. 2, p. 151.
9 Details, if required, are in Hadjipateras and Fafalios (eds), *Martiríes*, vol. 2, pp. 103–5.
10 Ibid., p. 95.
11 Ibid., pp. 139–40.
12 Ibid., pp. 69–70.

Chapter 11: The Destruction of the Jews (pp. 92–105)

Among the many memoirs of the Jewish experience in Greece Erika Kounio Amariglio, *From Thessaloniki to Auschwitz and Back* is outstanding. Elia Aelion's story is told in Rebecca Fromer's *The House by the Sea*, from her conversations with him (not interviews, she stresses) some 50 years later. See also K.E. Fleming, *Greece, a Jewish History*; Michael Molho (ed.), *In Memoriam*; and Níkos Kokántzis, *Gioconda*. For Athens see Hadjipateras and Fafalios (eds), *Martiríes*, vol. 2. A central section of Richard Evans, *The Third Reich at War* describes 'The Final Solution' in Europe as a whole.

1   Preamble to Law for the Protection of German Blood and German Honour, available at www.ushmm.org/wlc/en/article.php?Moduleld =10007903 (accessed 7 November 2015).
2   Preamble to minutes of Wannsee Conference, available at http://writing.upenn.edu/~afilreis/Holocaust/wansee-transcript.html (accessed 7 November 2015).
3   Minutes of Wannsee Conference, section III, at ibid.
4   Molho (ed.), vol. 1, p. 34.
5   Kounio Amariglio, p. 28.
6   Ibid., p. 31.
7   Molho (ed.), vol. 1, pp. 123–6.
8   Ibid., vol. 2, p. 9.
9   Kounio Amariglio, p. 45.
10 Ibid., p. 57.
11 Clogg (ed.), *Greece 1940–1949*, pp. 104–6, and Hadjipateras and Fafalios (eds), *Martiríes*, vol. 2, pp. 205–6 for Greek text.
12 Hadjipateras and Fafalios (eds), *Martiríes*, vol. 2, p. 207.
13 Clogg (ed.), *Greece 1940–1949*, p. 107.
14 Fromer, p. 77.
15 Ibid., p. 82.
16 Ibid., p. 86.
17 Ibid., p. 106.
18 Kounio Amariglio, p. 105.
19 Fromer, p. 126.
20 Ibid., p. 131.
21 Ibid., p. 138.
22 Kounio Amariglio, pp. 46–7.
23 Erríkos Sevíllias, *Athína-Auschwitz*, quoted in Hadjipateras and Fafalios (eds), *Martiríes*, vol. 2, p. 218.

Chapter 12: The Fractured Resistance (pp. 106–14)

The main sources are Myers, *Greek Entanglement* and Woodhouse's autobiography *Something Ventured,* as for chapter 9. See also W. Mackenzie, *The Secret History of SOE*; R. Clogg in Iatrides (ed.), *Greece in the 1940s*; P. Auty and R. Clogg (eds), *British Policy Towards Wartime Resistance in Yugoslavia and Greece*; and M.R.D. Foot, *Resistance* and *SOE, the Special Operations Executive 1940–46.*

1 Myers, p. 95.
2 Foot, *SOE,* p. 19.
3 M. Gilbert, *Churchill,* pp. 668–9.
4 Foot, *SOE,* p. 20.
5 R. Clogg, in Iatrides (ed.), *Greece in the 1940s,* p. 107.
6 Woodhouse, *Something Ventured,* pp. 8, 29, 46.
7 Woodhouse, *Apple of Discord,* p. 47.
8 Myers, p. 106.
9 Woodhouse, *The Strugle for Greece,* p. 20 and in Auty and Clogg (eds), p. 131.
10 Woodhouse, *Something Ventured,* p. 60.
11 M and B, standing for May & Baker, was an early antibiotic available only since 1936. Churchill was treated with it for pneumonia in 1943, and the present author in 1941.
12 Myers, p. 130.

Chapter 13: The Question of the King (pp. 115–23)

The main sources are Stelio Hourmouzios, *No Ordinary Crown*; Procopis Papastratis, *British Policy Towards Greece During the Second World War*; Woodhouse in *Apple of Discord, The Struggle for Greece,* and in Iatrides (ed.), *Greece in the 1940s*; and Reginald Leeper, *When Greek Meets Greek.* See also Thomas Gallant, *Modern Greece* for the history of the monarchy, and Michael Llewellyn Smith, *Ionian Vision: Greece in Asia Minor 1919–1922,* for the Asia Minor catastrophe.

1 Hourmouzios, pp. 71–2.
2 Leeper, in Clogg (ed.), *Greece 1940–1949,* p. 159.
3 Leeper, *When Greek Meets Greek,* p. 7.
4 Churchill, *The Second World War,* vol. 5, p. 415.
5 Papastratis, p. 23.
6 Ibid.
7 Woodhouse, *The Struggle for Greece,* p. 36.
8 Myers, *Greek Entanglement,* p. 213.

Chapter 14: The Cairo Conference, August 1943 (pp. 124–34)

The main sources are Myers and Clogg in Auty and Clogg (eds), *British Policy Towards Wartime Resistance in Yugoslavia and Greece*; Myers, *Greek Entanglement*; Wallace in Clogg (ed.), *Greece 1940–1949*; and Papastratis, *British Policy Towards Greece During the Second World War*. See also Mackenzie, *The Secret History of SOE*; and, for Wallace, Frances Osborne (Wallace's granddaughter), *The Bolter*; and Clive, *A Greek Experience*.

1　Myers, p. 216.
2　Ibid., p. 187.
3　Ibid., p. 201.
4　Osborne, p. 219.
5　Wallace, in Clogg (ed.), *Greece 1940–1949*, p. 121.
6　Wallace, in ibid., p. 136.
7　Wallace, in ibid., p. 144.
8　Codrington Papers, quoted in D. Brewer, *The Greek War of Independence* (London, 2001), p. 322. Original title *The Flame of Freedom*.
9　Wallace, in Clogg (ed.), *Greece 1940–1949*, pp. 151–2.
10　Myers, p. 245.
11　Hourmouzios, *No Ordinary Crown*, p. 152.
12　Myers, in Auty and Clogg (eds), p. 152.
13　Clogg, in ibid., pp. 180, 191, 173.
14　Clogg, in ibid., p. 185.
15　Mackenzie, p. 508.
16　Clogg, in Auty and Clogg (eds), p. 180.
17　Myers, p. 265.
18　Clive, p. 125.
19　Ibid., p. 128.
20　Osborne, p. 252.
21　Rudyard Kipling, 'Arithmetic on the Frontier' in *Departmental Ditties* (London, 1886).

Chapter 15: The Italian Armistice and the First Communist Offensive (pp. 135–42)

For Italy see F.W. Deakin, *The Last Days of Mussolini*; Christopher Hibbert, *Benito Mussolini*; and Richard Lamb, *War in Italy 1943–1945*. For Greece see Woodhouse, *Apple of Discord*, and *The Struggle for Greece*; Hondros, *Occupation and Resistance*; Mazower, *Inside Hitler's Greece*; and Kousoulas, *Revolution and Defeat*. For divergent views see Marion Sarafis (ed.), *Greece: From Resistance to Civil War*, the record of a conference held in London in 1978.

1　Hibbert, p. 202.
2　Lamb, pp. 13, 127, 129, 2.

3 Ibid., pp. 129–33. Louis de Bernières, acknowledging Lamb's book, dramatically describes the event in *Captain Corelli's Mandolin*, chs. 56–7.
4 Woodhouse, *Apple of Discord*, p. 301.
5 Woodhouse, *The Struggle for Greece*, p. 57.
6 Iatrides (ed.), *Greece in the 1940s*, p. 57.
7 Woodhouse, *Apple of Discord*, p. 302, and pp. 96–8 for Woodhouse's views on this denunciation.
8 Alexander in M. Sarafis (ed.), p. 45.
9 Thanasis Hajis, in M. Sarafis (ed.), p. 75.

Chapter 16: The Resistance in Crete (pp. 143–59)

The story as a whole is covered in Antony Beevor, *Crete*, and Nikos Kokonas, *The Cretan Resistance*. For Leigh Fermor see his *Words of Mercury*, pp. 85–96; Leigh Fermor's introduction to G. Psychoundakis (his published name), *The Cretan Runner*; and Artemis Cooper, *Patrick Leigh Fermor*. Xan Fielding described his wartime experiences in *Hide and Seek*. For Kiwi Perkins see Murray Elliott, *Vasili, the Lion of Crete*. Moss wrote an account of the Kreipe abduction in *Ill Met by Moonlight*.

1 Beevor, *Crete*, p. 26.
2 Kokonas, p. 154.
3 Fielding, p. 51.
4 Ibid., p. 4.
5 Ibid., p. 20.
6 P. Leigh Fermor, in Psychoundakis, *The Cretan Runner*, p. 5.
7 P. Leigh Fermor, in ibid., p. 2.
8 Kokonas, p. 15.
9 Beevor, *Crete*, p. 259.
10 Fielding, p. 33.
11 Ibid., p. 85.
12 Ibid., p. 142.
13 Ibid., p. 108.
14 Cooper, *Patrick Leigh Fermor*, pp. 175–6.
15 Leigh Fermor, *Words of Mercury*, p. 96. Leigh Fermor translated these opening lines as 'See Soracte's mighty peak stands deep in virgin snow.' The ode begins with winter but ends with spring and a secret lovers' tryst, a theme which no doubt appealed to the young translator.
16 B. Sweet-Escott, *Baker Street Irregular*, pp. 197–8.

Chapter 17: Upheaval in the Greek Government (pp. 160–8)

The main sources are Papastratis, *British Policy Towards Greece*; Woodhouse, *Apple of Discord*; Hondros, *Occupation and Resistance*; Leeper, *When Greek Meets Greek*; and L. Baerentzen, *The Liberation of Greece, 1944*. For the Soviet mission to ELAS, see Hammond, *Venture into Greece*, chapter 9.

1 Papastratis, p. 165.
2 Woodhouse, *Apple of Discord*, p. 41.
3 Ibid., p. 42.
4 Papastratis, p. 167.
5 Ibid., p. 175.
6 Alexander, in M. Sarafis (ed.), *Greece: From Resistance to Civil War*, p. 44.
7 Papastratis, p. 170.
8 Leeper, p. 47.
9 Ibid., p. 47.
10 Ibid., pp. 51–2.
11 Woodhouse, *Apple of Discord*, p. 305.
12 Papastratis, p. 195.
13 Baerentzen, *The Liberation of Greece*, p. 9.

Chapter 18: Liberation (pp. 169–79)

For this period as a whole see Woodhouse, *Apple of Discord* and *The Struggle for Greece*; Baerentzen *The Liberation of Greece*; Iatrides (ed.), *Greece in the 1940s*; and Papastratis, *British Policy Towards Greece*. For diplomacy see Harold Macmillan, *The Blast of War, 1939–1945*; Leeper, *When Greek Meets Greek*; and J. Iatrides (ed.), *Ambassador MacVeagh Reports*. For Athens see Hadjipateras and Fafalios (eds), *Martiríes*, vol. 2; and Henderson, *Xenia*. See also Clive, *A Greek Experience*; and Mazower, *Inside Hitler's Greece*.

1 Baerentzen, in Iatrides (ed.), *Greece in the 1940s*, p. 134.
2 Baerentzen, in ibid., p. 136.
3 In the Greek euro crisis which began in 2009 there was a widespread Greek view that Germany still owed money to Greece as repayment of a forced wartime loan.
4 Mackenzie, *The Secret History of SOE*, p. 478; and Woodhouse, *Apple of Discord*, p. 204.
5 Mackenzie, p. 479.
6 Papastratis, p. 206.
7 Macmillan, p. 586; and W. Byford-Jones, *The Greek Trilogy*, p. 117.
8 Ward, *Greek Assignments*, p. 188.
9 R. Capell, *Simiomata*, pp. 40–1.
10 Macmillan, p. 566.
11 Ibid., p. 563.

12 For text of the Caserta Agreement, see Woodhouse, *Apple of Discord*, pp. 306–7.
13 Iatrides (ed.), *Ambassador MacVeagh Reports*, pp. 605, 615, 624, 606; and J. Iatrides, *Revolt in Athens*, p. 198.
14 Clogg (ed.), *Greece 1940–1949*, pp. 176–86.
15 Hadjipateras and Fafalios (eds), *Martiríes*, vol. 2, p. 303.
16 Henderson, p. 67.
17 Ibid., p. 72.
18 Macmillan, p. 585.
19 Hadjipateras and Fafalios (eds), *Martiríes*, vol. 2, p. 398.
20 Ibid., p. 398.
21 Ibid., p. 400.
22 Iatrides (ed.), *Ambassador MacVeagh Reports*, p. 635.
23 Macmillan, p. 562.

Chapter 19: Towards Sunday 3 December 1944 (pp. 180–8)

For the episode and its context see Macmillan, *The Blast of War*; Leeper, *When Greek Meets Greek*; Byford-Jones, *The Greek Trilogy*; Woodhouse, *Apple of Discord* and *The Struggle for Greece*; Iatrides, *Revolt in Athens*; and McNeill, *The Greek Dilemma*. For relief operations, see Clogg (ed.), *Bearing Gifts to Greeks*; for the economy, Palairet, *The Four Ends of Greek Hyperinflation*; and for the events of 3 December, Baerentzen, *The Liberation of Greece* and *The Demonstration in Syntagma Square*.

1 Clogg (ed.), *Bearing Gifts*, p. 198.
2 Palairet, p. 54.
3 Macmillan, pp. 593–4.
4 Anthony Trollope, *Barchester Towers*, ch. 1.
5 Palairet, p. 75.
6 Woodhouse, *Apple of Discord*, p. 305.
7 Woodhouse, *The Struggle for Greece*, p. 119.
8 Baerentzen, *The Liberation of Greece*, p. 30.
9 Woodhouse, *The Struggle for Greece*, p. 123.
10 Baerentzen, *The Demonstration in Syntagma Square*, p. 14.
11 W. McNeill, *The Greek Dilemma*, p. 140.
12 Iatrides, *Revolt in Athens*, p. 191, n. 86.
13 Byford-Jones, pp. 139, 140.
14 Iatrides, *Revolt in Athens*, p. 135, n. 2.
15 Macmillan, p. 588.
16 Mazower, *Inside Hitler's Greece*, p. 370.

Chapter 20: The Battle for Athens (pp. 189–96)

Accounts by contemporaries are in Churchill, *The Second World War*, vol. 6; Macmillan, *The Blast of War*; Leeper, *When Greek Meets Greek*; Byford-Jones, *The Greek Trilogy*; and Woodhouse, *The Struggle for Greece.* See also Baerentzen, *The Liberation of Greece,* and Iatrides, *Revolt in Athens.*

1   Churchill, vol. 6, p. 252.
2   Ibid., p. 254.
3   Macmillan, pp. 607–8.
4   Leeper, p. 114.
5   Baerentzen, *The Liberation of Greece*, p. 52, n. 66.
6   Ibid., p. 52, n. 67.
7   Churchill, vol. 6, pp. 256–8.
8   Macmillan, p. 601.
9   Clive, *A Greek Experience*, p. 160.
10 Byford-Jones, pp. 173, 181.
11 Iatrides, *Revolt in Athens*, p. 210.
12 Ibid., pp. 218–9.
13 Macmillan, p. 611.
14 Byford-Jones, p. 172.
15 Ibid., p. 189.

Chapter 21: Dhamaskinós, Churchill and the Varkíza Agreement (pp. 197–204)

The main accounts are as for Chapter 20, above.

1   Churchill, vol. 6, p. 269.
2   Iatrides, *Revolt in Athens,* p. 50.
3   Macmillan, p. 612.
4   Ibid., p. 625.
5   Ibid., p. 624.
6   Churchill, vol. 6, pp. 272–3.
7   Ibid., p. 274.
8   Byford-Jones, p. 192.
9   London gossip, 1950s.
10 Churchill, vol. 6, p. 279.
11 Hourmouzios, *No Ordinary Crown*, p. 169.
12 Churchill, vol. 6, pp. 279–80.
13 Macmillan, p. 620.
14 Neni Panourgia, *Dangerous Citizens*, p. 70.
15 Byford-Jones, p. 246.
16 Ibid., p. 255.
17 Macmillan, p. 642.

18 Ibid., p. 655.
19 K. Matthews, *Memories of a Mountain War*, pp. 92–5.
20 The full text of the Varkíza Agreement is in Woodhouse, *Apple of Discord*, pp. 308–10.

Chapter 22: The Government, the Communists and the Elections (pp. 205–17)

The main sources are Woodhouse, *Apple of Discord* and *The Struggle for Greece*; Leeper, *When Greek Meets Greek*; G. Alexander, *The Prelude to the Truman Doctrine*; and Kousoulas, *Revolution and Defeat*. For the economy, see A. Lykogiannis, *Britain and the Greek Economic Crisis 1944–1947*; and Palairet, *The Four Ends of the Greek Hyperinflation*.

1 Alexander, pp. 106–7.
2 Ibid., p. 147.
3 Leeper, p. 194.
4 Woodhouse, *Apple of Discord*, p. 311.
5 Palairet, p. 78.
6 Lykogiannis, p. 118.
7 Palairet, p. 84.
8 Woodhouse, *The Struggle for Greece*, p. 140.
9 Kousoulas, p. 226.
10 Woodhouse, *The Struggle for Greece*, p. 163.
11 Kousoulas, p. 234.
12 Woodhouse, *Apple of Discord*, p. 264.
13 Alexander, p. 201.
14 Iatrides (ed.), *Ambassador MacVeagh Reports*, p. 700.

Chapter 23: The Truman Doctrine (pp. 218–27)

For the United States see Howard Jones, *A New Kind of War*; and George Kennan, 'The Long Telegram'. For Britain see Alan Bullock, *Ernest Bevin*, vol. 3; B. Pimlott (ed.), *The Political Diary of Hugh Dalton*; and P. Hennessy, *Never Again, Britain 1945–1951*. For Greece see Alexander, *The Prelude to the Truman Doctrine*. For King Paul and Queen Frederica see Queen Frederica, *A Measure of Understanding*; and Hourmouzios, *No Ordinary Crown*.

1 Sidney Pollard, *The Wasting of the British Economy* (London, 1984) p. 2, quoted in Hennessy, p. 99.
2 Hennessy, p. 302, quoting Dalton, *High Tide and After*, p. 254.
3 Alexander, p. 215.
4 Ibid., p. 215.
5 Ibid., p. 235.

6   Ibid., p. 224.
7   Ibid., p. 221.
8   Ibid., p. 225.
9   Woodhouse, *The Struggle for Greece*, p. 199.
10 Jones, p. 34.
11 Kennan, Part 2.
12 Ibid., Part 5.
13 Bullock, p. 218.
14 Jones, pp. 237–42 for full text.
15 Ibid., p. 47.
16 Ibid., p. 57.
17 Ibid., pp. 243–6 for full text.
18 Queen Frederica, pp. 28, 41.
19 Ibid., p. 67.

Chapter 24: 1947: Civil War and American Involvement (pp. 228–40)

The main sources for the civil war are Kousoulas, *Revolution and Defeat*; Woodhouse, *The Struggle for Greece*; and E. O'Ballance, *The Greek Civil War 1944–1949*. For American involvement see Jones, *A New Kind of War*; C. Shrader, *The Withered Vine*; Lawrence Wittner, *American Intervention in Greece, 1943–1949*; and Iatrides (ed.), *Ambassador MacVeagh Reports*.

1   Kousoulas, p. 231.
2   Woodhouse, *The Struggle for Greece*, p. 194.
3   Vláchos, *Politiká Árthra*, pp. 144–7.
4   Matthews, *Memories of a Mountain War*, pp. 134–5.
5   Kousoulas, p. 231.
6   Queen Frederica, *A Measure of Understanding*, p. 108.
7   Ibid., pp. 111–12.
8   Ward, *Greek Assignments*, pp. 269–70.
9   Shrader, p. 223.
10 Jones, p. 116.
11 Woodhouse, *The Struggle for Greece*, p. 205.
12 M. Djilas, *Conversations with Stalin*, p. 141.
13 Wittner, p. 236.
14 Jones, p. 94.
15 Ibid., p. 100.
16 *Rubaiyat of Omar Khayyam*, stanza XXVII: 'Myself when young did eagerly frequent/Doctor and saint and heard great argument/About it and about; but evermore/Came out by the same door as in I went.'
17 Iatrides (ed.), *Ambassador MacVeagh Reports*, pp. 718, 721.
18 Ibid., p. 728.
19 Ibid., p. 733.

Chapter 25: Terror from Left and Right (pp. 241–51)

The personal accounts are Joice Loch, *A Fringe of Blue*; Gage, *Eleni*; and Geoffrey Chandler, *The Divided Land*. See also Kevin Andrews, *The Flight of Ikaros*. Experiences of detainees and government actions are in Polymeris Voglis, *Becoming a Subject*. Government actions are also covered in Woodhouse, *The Struggle for Greece*; and David Close, *The Origins of the Greek Civil War*. For details of the Polk murder and trial, see Jones, *A New Kind of War* and Matthews, *Memories of a Mountain War*.

1   Loch, p. 237.
2   Gage, p. 263.
3   Ibid., p. 248.
4   Chandler, p. xix.
5   Ibid., p. 56.
6   Andrews, p. 185.
7   Woodhouse, *Apple of Discord*, p. 308.
8   Voglis, p. 35.
9   Ibid., p. 33.
10 Ibid., p. 104.
11 Ibid., p. 110.
12 Ibid., p. 74.
13 Quoted in Philip Sherrard, *The Wound of Greece* (London, 1978), p. 112.

Chapter 26: The Plight of the Greek Children (pp. 252–60)

The main sources are Loring Danforth and Riki Van Boeschoten, *Children of the Greek Civil War*; and Gage, *Eleni*. In the text the names from *Eleni* are generally as Gage gives them. See also Queen Frederica, *A Measure of Understanding*; and Lilika Papanicolaou (one of the 'Queen's Ladies'), *Frederica Queen of the Hellenes*.

1   Danforth and Van Boeschoten, pp. 88–9.
2   Queen Frederica, p. 133.
3   Hourmouzios, *No Ordinary Crown*, p. 197.
4   Vláchos, *Politiká Árthra*, pp. 158–60.
5   Queen Frederica, p. 134.
6   Gage, p. 389.
7   Ibid., p. 502.
8   Ibid., p. 697.
9   Danforth and Boeschoten, pp. 148, 149.
10 Ibid., pp. 169, 178, 160, 161.
11 Ibid., pp. 120, 139.
12 Ibid., pp. 179, 181, 162.
13 Ibid., pp. 173, 154, 143, 146.

14 Ibid., p. 244.
15 Ibid., pp. 2–3.
16 Ibid., p. 63.

Chapter 27: The Marshall Plan (pp. 261–71)

The main source for the Marshall Plan is Greg Behrman, *The Most Noble Adventure*. For other views see Alan Milward, *The Reconstruction of Western Europe 1945–51*; Lawrence Wittner, *American Intervention in Greece, 1943–1949*; and Jon Kofas, *Intervention and Underdevelopment*. For Marshall Aid in Greece see C.A. Munkman, *American Aid to Greece*.

1 Behrman, p. 69.
2 Bullock, *Ernest Bevin*, vol. 3, p. 405.
3 Behrman, p. 88.
4 Ibid., p. 98.
5 Ibid., pp. 110–11.
6 Munkman. p. 191.
7 Ibid., p. 248.
8 Ibid., p. 97.
9 Ibid., p. 164.
10 Ibid., p. 162.
11 Ibid., p. 171.
12 Ibid., p. 79.
13 Ibid., pp. 109, 294.
14 Ibid., p. 306.
15 Bullock, quoted in David Ellwood, *Rebuilding Europe* (London, 1992) p. 171.
16 Wittner, pp. 190, 312.
17 Kofas, p. 128.

Chapter 28: The Ending of the Civil War (pp. 272–81)

The main sources are Jones, *A New Kind of War*; Woodhouse, *The Struggle for Greece*; Kousoulas, *Revolution and Defeat*; and Shrader, *The Withered Vine*. For personal accounts see Ward, *Greek Assignments*; and D. Katsís, *To Imerolóyio Énos Andárti tou DSE 1946–1949* (*The Journal of a Fighter in the Greek Democratic Army 1946–1949*), vol. 4.

1 O'Ballance, *The Greek Civil War*, p. 173.
2 Jones, pp. 186, 183.
3 Ibid., p. 189.
4 Ibid., p. 173.
5 Ward, pp. 275–6.

6 Ibid., p. 302.
7 Ibid., p. 296.
8 Woodhouse, *The Struggle for Greece*, p. 251.
9 Kousoulas, p. 253.
10 Katsís, pp. 22–3, 34–5, 64.
11 Ibid., p. 50.
12 Woodhouse, *The Struggle for Greece*, p. 285.
13 Ward, p. 326.

Epilogue (pp. 282–7)

For Leigh Fermor's life see Artemis Cooper, *Patrick Leigh Fermor*. Most Greek words in this chapter are in the anglicised forms used by Leigh Fermor.

1 Cooper, p. 31.
2 Ibid., p. 242.
3 Leigh Fermor, *Mani*, pp. 3, 128, 6.
4 Ibid., p. 264.
5 Ibid., pp. 82, 128.
6 Ibid., pp. 137, 32, 84.
7 Leigh Fermor, *Roumeli*, pp. 101–2, 106–15.
8 Leigh Fermor, *Mani*, pp. 140, 204.
9 Ibid., p. 285. The reference is probably to Andrew Marvell's poem 'The Garden' in which the mind withdraws into its happiness, 'Annihilating all that's made/To a green thought in a green shade.'
10 Leigh Fermor, *Mani*, pp. 129, 287.
11 Chandler, *The Divided Land*, pp. 88, 94–5.

Select Bibliography

Alexander, G., *The Prelude to the Truman Doctrine* (Oxford, 1982).

Andrews, K., *The Flight of Ikaros* (London, 1959).

Auty, P. and R. Clogg (eds), *British Policy Towards Wartime Resistance in Yugoslavia and Greece* (London, 1975).

Baerentzen, L., *The Demonstration in Syntagma Square* (Copenhagen, n.d.).

—— *The Liberation of Greece, 1944* (Gainesville, 1953).

Beevor, A., *Crete, The Battle and the Resistance* (London, 1991).

—— *The Second World War* (London, 2012).

Behrman, G., *The Most Noble Adventure* (New York, 2007).

Bernières, L. de, *Captain Corelli's Mandolin* (London, 1994).

Buckley, C., *Greece and Crete 1941*, 2nd edn (Athens, 1993).

Bullock, A., *Ernest Bevin*, vol. 3 (London, 1983).

Byford-Jones, W., *The Greek Trilogy* (London, 1945).

Capell, R., *Simiomata, 1944–1945* (London, 1946).

Cervi, M., *The Hollow Legions* (London, 1972).

Chandler, G., *The Divided Land* (London, 1959).

Churchill. W., *The Second World War*, 6 vols (London, 1948–54).

Clark, A., *The Fall of Crete* (London, 1962).

Clive. N., *A Greek Experience 1943–1948* (London, 1985).

Clogg, R. (ed.), *Greece 1940–1949: A Documentary History* (London, 2002).

—— (ed.), *Bearing Gifts to Greece* (London, 2008).

Close, D., *The Origins of the Greek Civil War* (London, 1995).

—— *Greece Since 1945* (London, 2002).

Cooper, A., *Cairo in the War 1939–1945* (London, 1989).

—— *Patrick Leigh Fermor* (London, 2012).

Couloumbis, T. (ed.), *Greece in the Twentieth Century* (London, 2003).

Danforth L. and Van Boeschoten, R., *Children of the Greek Civil War* (Chicago, 2012).

Deakin, F., *The Last Days of Mussolini* (London, 1962).

Djilas, M., *Conversations with Stalin* (London, 1962).

Elliott, M., *Vasili, The Lion of Crete* (Auckland, 1987) (biography of Dudley Perkins).

Eudes, D., *The Kapetanios* (London, 1972).

Evans, R., *The Third Reich at War* (London, 2008).

Falls, C., *The Second World War* (London, 1948).

Fielding, X., *Hide and Seek* (London, 1954).

Fleming, K., *Greece, a Jewish History* (Princeton, 2008).

Foot, M., *Resistance* (London, 1976).

—— *SOE, the Special Operations Executive 1940–46* (London, 1984).

Fourtouni, E., *Greek Women in Resistance* (New Haven, n.d.).

Freyberg, P., *Bernard Freyberg, VC* (London, 1991).

Fromer, R., *The House by the Sea* (San Francisco, 1998).

Gage, N., *Eleni* (London, 1983).

Gallant, T., *Modern Greece* (London, 2001).

Gilbert, M., *Churchill* (London, 1991).

Hadjipateras, C. and M. Fafalios (eds), *Martiríes*, 2 vols (in Greek): Vol. 1, *Martiríes 40–41* (*Testimonies 40–41*) (Athens, 1982); Vol. 2, *Martiríes, I Athína tís Katochís 40–44* (*Testimonies, Athens Under Occupation 40–44*) (Athens, 1988).

—— *Greece 1940–41 Eyewitnessed* (Athens, 1995) (parts of the above in English).

—— *Crete 1941 Eyewitnessed* (Athens, 1993).

Hammond, N., *Venture into Greece* (London, 1983).

Hart, J., *New Voices in the Nation* (Ithaca, NY, 1996).

Henderson, M., *Xenia – A Memoir* (London, 1998).

Hennessy, P., *Never Again, Britain 1945–1951* (London, 1992).

Hibbert, C., *Benito Mussolini* (London, 1962).

Hionidou, V., *Famine and Death in Occupied Greece, 1941–1944* (Cambridge, 2006).

Hondros, J., *Occupation and Resistance* (New York, 1983).

Hourmouzios, S., *No Ordinary Crown* (London, 1972).

Iatrides, J., *Revolt in Athens* (Princeton, 1972).

Iatrides, J. (ed.), *Ambassador MacVeagh Reports* (Princeton, 1980).

—— *Greece in the 1940s* (Lebanon, NH, 1981).

Jones, H., *A New Kind of War* (Oxford, 1989).

Katsís, D., *To Imerolóyio Enós Andárti tou DSE 1946–1949* (*The Journal of a Fighter in the Democratic Army 1946–1949*), Vol. 4 (Athens, 1997) (in Greek).

Keegan, J., *The Second World War* (London, 1989).

—— *Intelligence in War* (London, 2003).

Kennan, G., 'The Long Telegram', available at www2.gwu.edu/~nsarchiv/coldwar/documents/episode-1/kennan.htm (accessed 7 November 2015).

Kofas, J., *Intervention and Underdevelopment* (University Park, 1989).

Kokántzis, N., *Tziokónta* (*Gioconda*) (Athens, 1975) (in Greek; English translation Athens, 1997).

Kokonas, N., *The Cretan Resistance 1941–1945* (Rethymnon, n.d.).

Kounio Amariglio, E., *From Thessaloniki to Auschwitz and Back* (London, 2000).

Kousoulas, G., *Revolution and Defeat: The Story of the Greek Communist Party* (Oxford, 1965).

Lamb, R., *War in Italy 1943–1945* (London, 1993).

Leeper, R., *When Greek Meets Greek* (London, 1950).

Leigh Fermor, P., *Mani* (London, 1958).

—— *Roumeli* (London, 1966).

—— *Words of Mercury* (London, 2003).

Lewin, R., *The Chief, Field Marshal Lord Wavell* (London, 1980).

Liddell Hart, B., *History of the Second World War* (London, 1970).

Llewellyn Smith, M., *Ionian Vision: Greece in Asia Minor 1919–1922* (London, 1973).

Loch, J., *A Fringe of Blue* (London, 1968).

Lykogiannis, A., *Britain and the Greek Economic Crisis 1944–1947* (Columbia, 2002).

Mack Smith, D., *Mussolini's Roman Empire* (New York, 1976).

Mackenzie, W., *The Secret History of SOE* (London, 2000).

Macmillan, H., *The Blast of War, 1939–1945* (London, 1967).

McNeill, W., *The Greek Dilemma* (London, 1947).

—— *The Metamorphosis of Greece Since World War II* (Chicago, 1978).

Matthews, K., *Memories of a Mountain War* (London, 1972).

Mazower, M., *Inside Hitler's Greece* (New Haven, 1993).

Mazower, M. (ed.), *After the War Was Over* (Princeton, 2000).

Milward, A., *The Reconstruction of Western Europe 1945–51* (London, 1984).

Molho, M. (ed.), *In Memoriam*, 2 vols: vol. 1 (Salonika, 1948); vol. 2 (Salonika, 1949).

Moss, W., *Ill Met by Moonlight* (London, 1950).

Munkman, C., *American Aid to Greece* (New York, 1958).

Myers, E., *Greek Entanglement* (London, 1955).

O'Ballance, E., *The Greek Civil War 1944–1949* (London, 1966).

Ogden, A., *Sons of Odysseus* (London, 2012).

Osborne, F., *The Bolter* (London, 2008).

Palairet, M., *The Four Ends of the Greek Hyperinflation of 1941–1946* (Copenhagen, 2000).

Panourgia, N., *Dangerous Citizens* (New York, 2009).

Papaioannou, V., *Images of Despair and Hope, Greece 1940–1960* (Athens, 1995).

Papanicolaou, L., *Frederica Queen of the Hellenes* (London, 1994).

Papastratis, P., *British Policy Towards Greece During the Second World War* (Cambridge, 1984).

Pimlott, B. (ed.), *The Political Diary of Hugh Dalton* (London, 1986).

Psychoundakis, G., *The Cretan Runner* (London, 1955).

Queen Frederica, *A Measure of Understanding* (London, 1971).

Reynolds, D., *In Command of History* (London, 2004).

Sarafis, M. (ed.), *Greece: From Resistance to Civil War* (Nottingham, 1980).

Sarafis, S., *ELAS: Greek Resistance Army* (London, 1980; 1st edn Athens, 1946).

Shrader, C., *The Withered Vine* (New Haven, 1999).

Skouras, P., *I Psicholoyía tis Pínas, tou Phóvou kai tou Ánchous (The Psychology of Hunger, Fear and Anguish)* (Athens, 1991) (in Greek).

Smothers, F., W. McNeill and E. McNeill, *Report on the Greeks* (New York, 1948).

Sweet-Escott, B., *Greece: A Political and Economic Survey, 1939–1953* (London, 1954).

—— *Baker Street Irregular* (London, 1965).

Tomes, J., *King Zog* (London, 2007).

Vatikiotis, P., *Popular Autocracy in Greece 1936–41* (London, 1998) (biography of Ioánnis Metaxás).

Vláchos, G., *Politiká Árthra (Political Articles)* (Athens, 1961) (in Greek).

Voglis, P., *Becoming a Subject* (New York, 2002).

Ward, M., *Greek Assignments* (Athens, 1992).

Willingham, M., *Perilous Commitments* (Staplehurst, 2005).

Wittner, L., *American Intervention in Greece, 1943–1949* (New York, 1982).

Woodhouse, C., *Apple of Discord* (London, 1948).

—— *The Struggle for Greece 1941–1949* (London, 1976).

—— *Something Ventured* (London, 1982).

Index